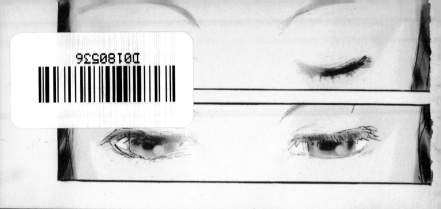

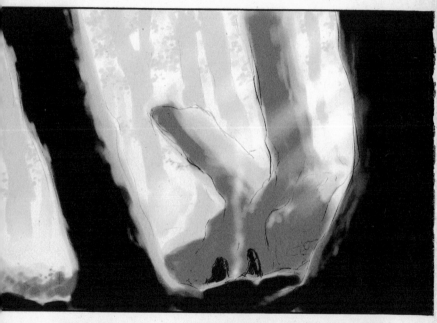

NASH...DO YOU REALLY THINK WE'LL FIND INFORMATION IN THE KUPUT FOREST THAT WILL LEAD TO MY FATHER?
MAYBE. BUT FIRST, WE'VE GOT TO FIND ALMA-KINAN...

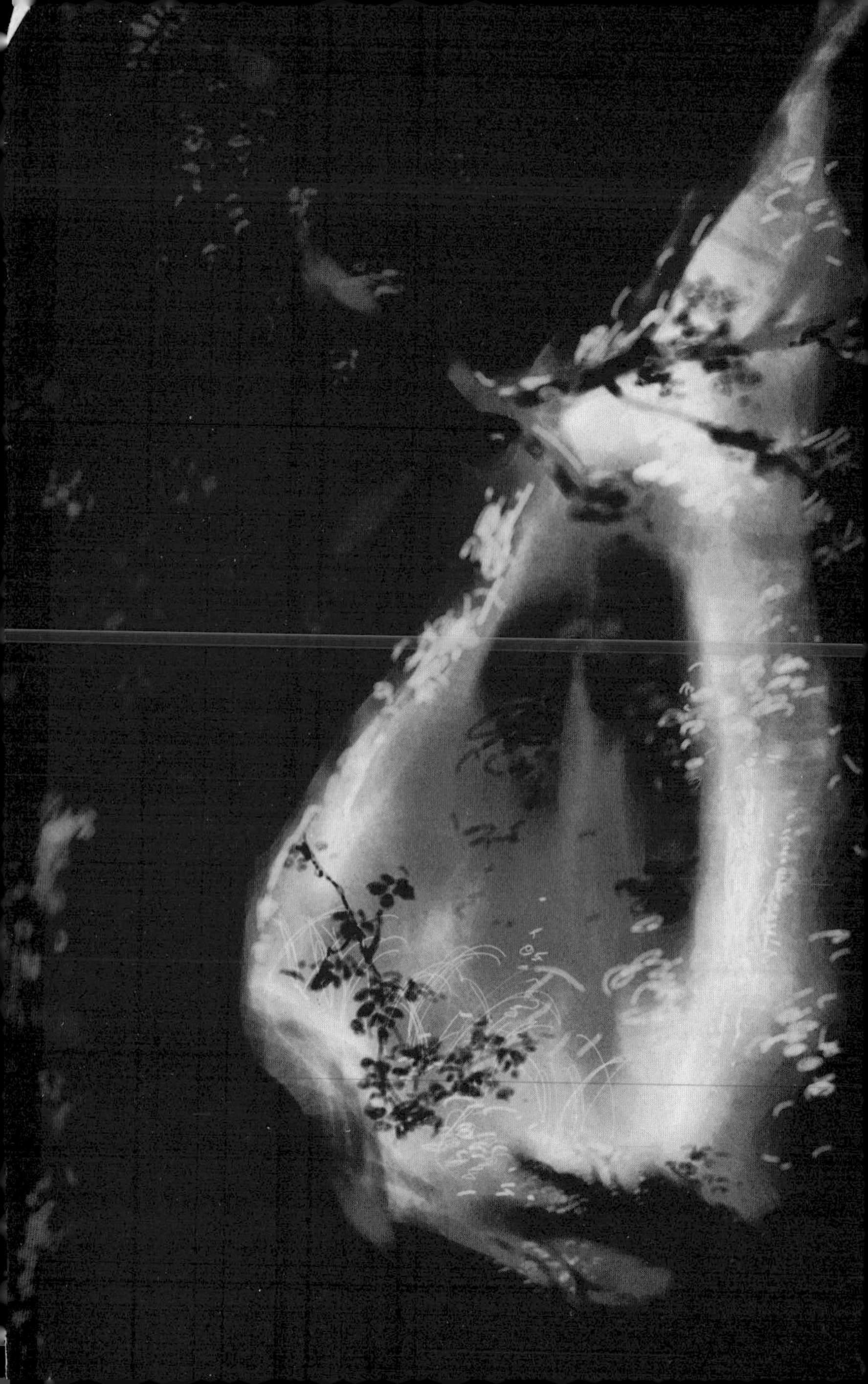

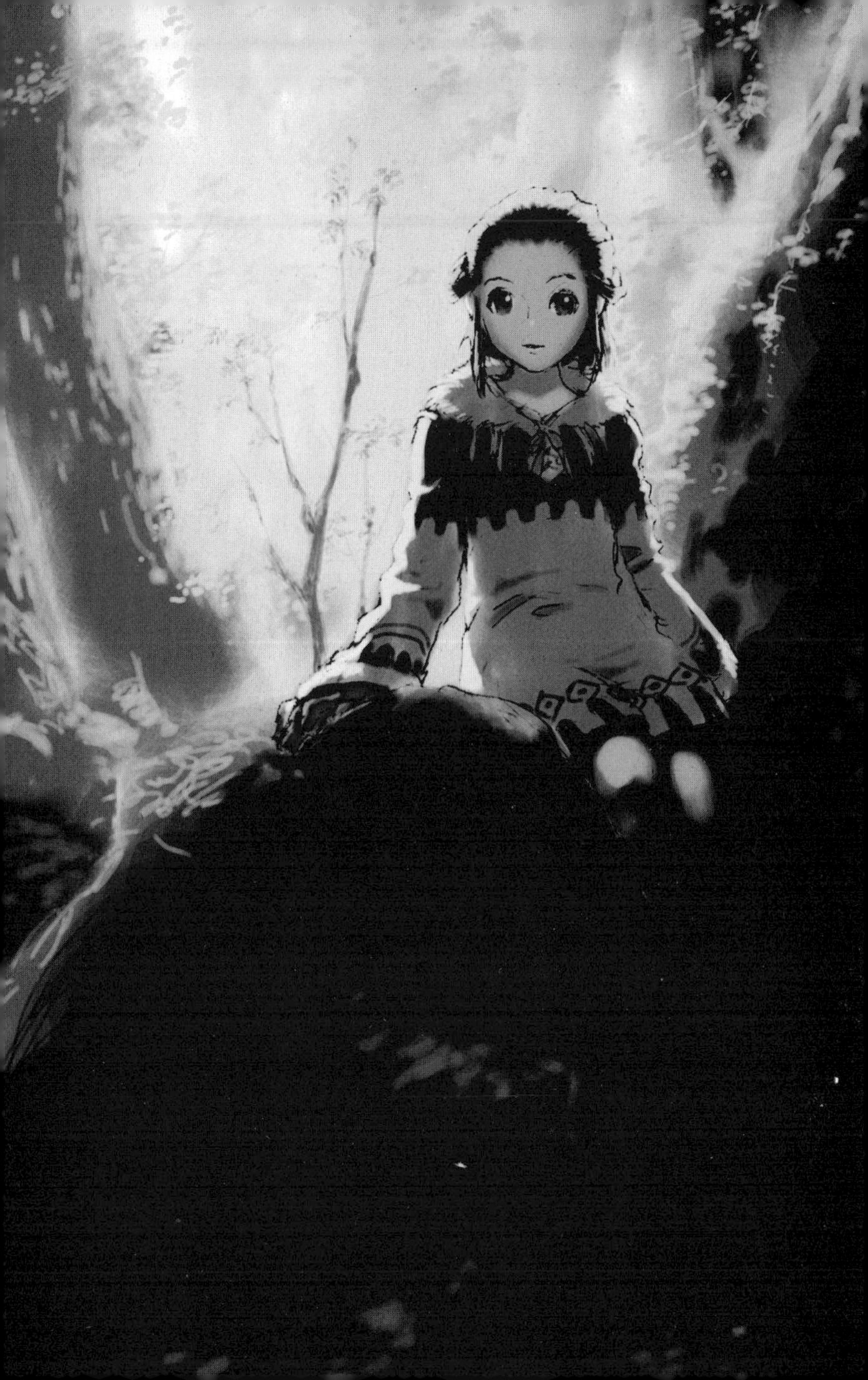

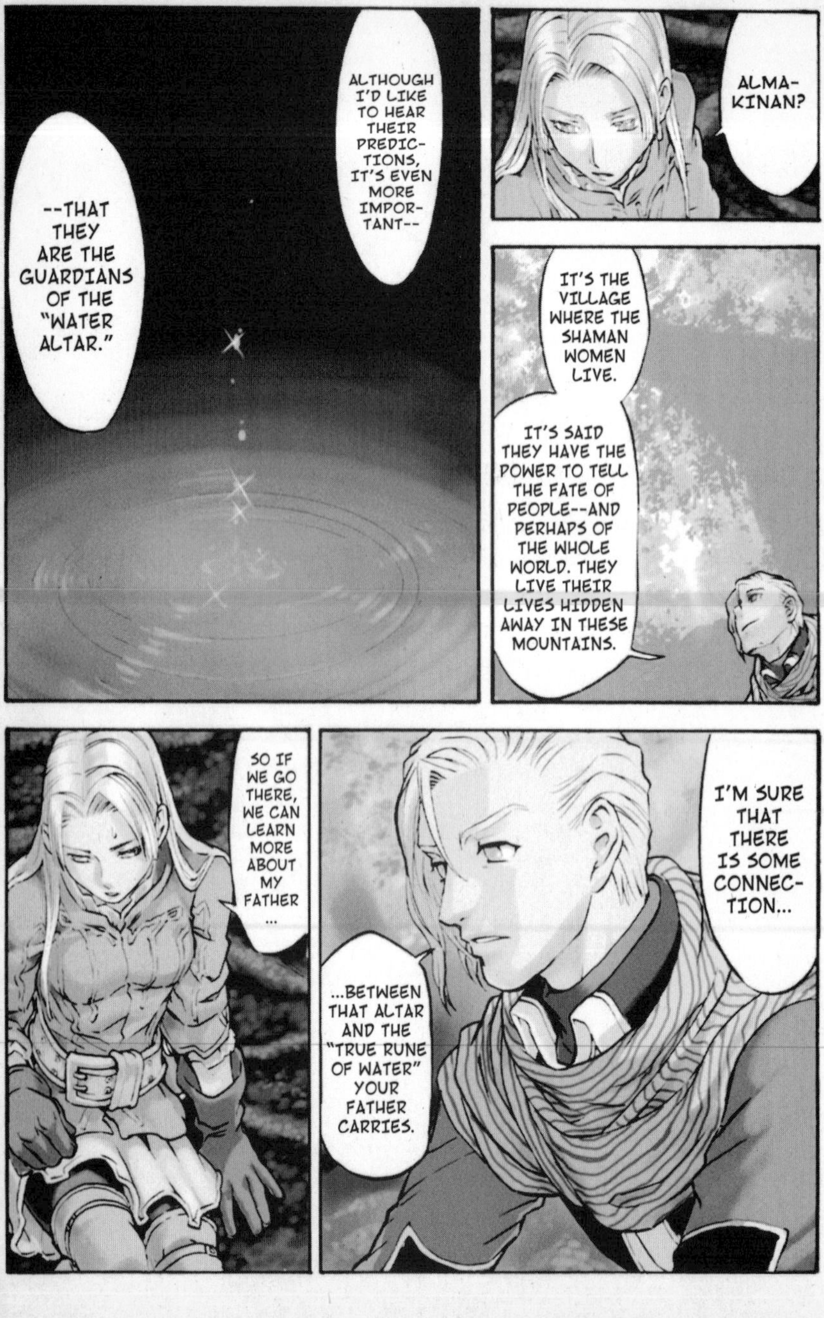
ALMA-KINAN?
IT'S THE VILLAGE WHERE THE SHAMAN WOMEN LIVE.
IT'S SAID THEY HAVE THE POWER TO TELL THE FATE OF PEOPLE--AND PERHAPS OF THE WHOLE WORLD. THEY LIVE THEIR LIVES HIDDEN AWAY IN THESE MOUNTAINS.
ALTHOUGH I'D LIKE TO HEAR THEIR PREDICTIONS, IT'S EVEN MORE IMPORTANT--
--THAT THEY ARE THE GUARDIANS OF THE "WATER ALTAR."
I'M SURE THAT THERE IS SOME CONNECTION...
...BETWEEN THAT ALTAR AND THE "TRUE RUNE OF WATER" YOUR FATHER CARRIES.
SO IF WE GO THERE, WE CAN LEARN MORE ABOUT MY FATHER ...

Suikoden III

幻想水滸伝

Suikoden III Vol. 4
created by Aki Shimizu

Translation - Patrick Coffman
English Adaptation - Alan Swayze
Copy Editor - Suzanne Waldman
Retouch and Lettering - Haruko Furukawa
Production Artist - Yoohae Yang
Cover Artist - Gary Shum

Editor - Rob Tokar
Digital Imaging Manager - Chris Buford
Pre-Press Manager - Antonio DePietro
Production Managers - Jennifer Miller and Mutsumi Miyazaki
Art Director - Matt Alford
Managing Editor - Jill Freshney
VP of Production - Ron Klamert
President and C.O.O. - John Parker
Publisher and C.E.O. - Stuart Levy

A  Manga

TOKYOPOP Inc.
5900 Wilshire Blvd. Suite 2000
Los Angeles, CA 90036

E-mail: info@TOKYOPOP.com
Come visit us online at www.TOKYOPOP.com

Editor's Note: Special thanks to Udi Hoh of Suikosource.com for her invaluable assistance in fact-checking this book.

ISBN: 1-59182-768-X

First TOKYOPOP printing: November 2004
10 9 8 7 6 5 4 3 2
Printed in the USA

Suikoden III
幻想水滸伝

...............successor of fate...

Vol.4
by Aki Shimizu

TOKYOPOP®

HAMBURG // LONDON // LOS ANGELES // TOKYO

Zexen

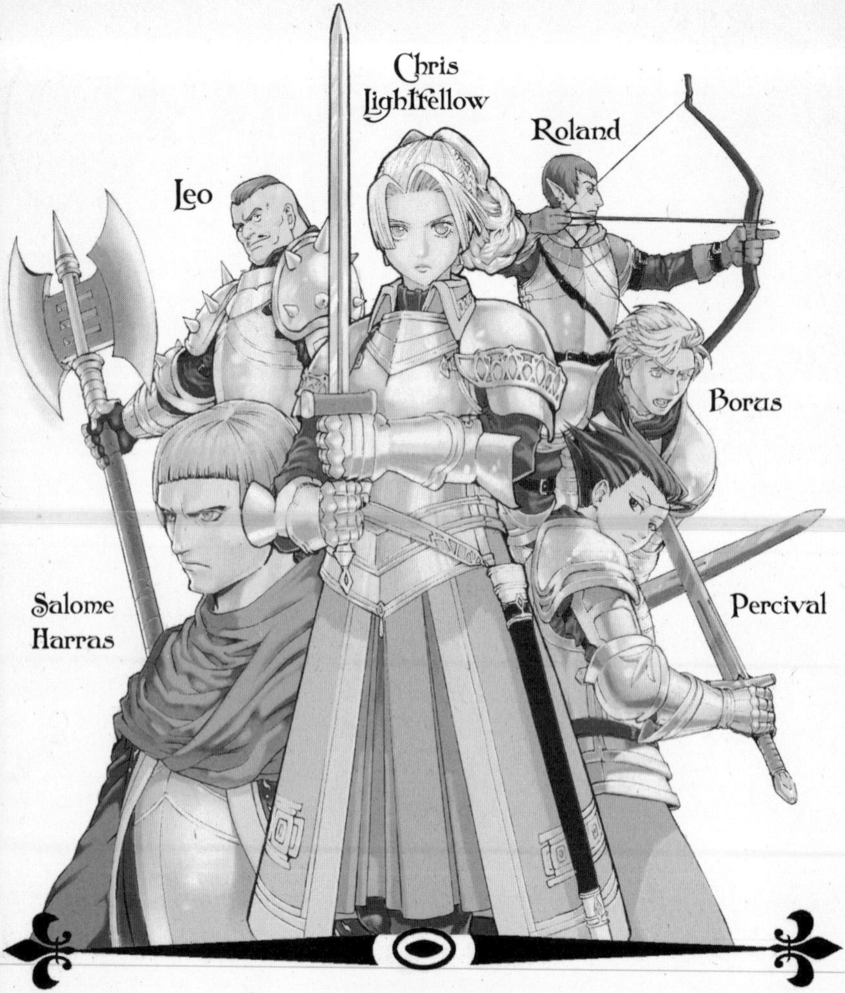
Chris Lightfellow
Roland
Leo
Borus
Salome Harras
Percival

Suikoden III
幻想水滸伝
Characters

Grasslands

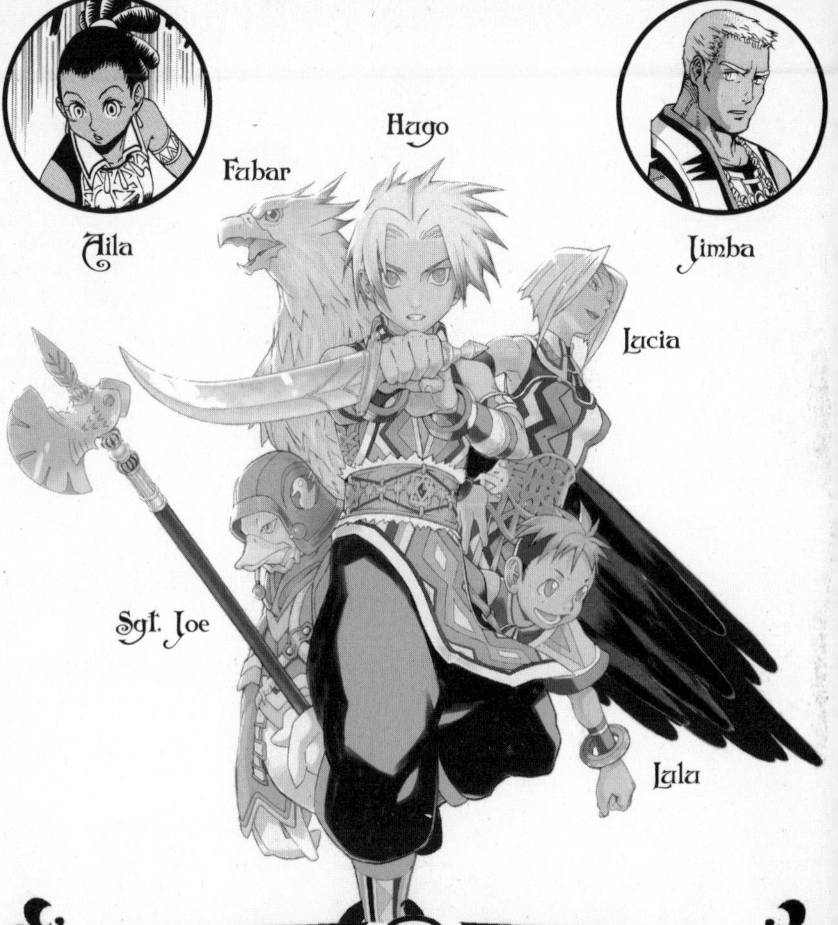
Hugo
Fubar
Aila
Jimba
Lucia
Sgt. Joe
Lulu

Suikoden III
幻想水滸伝
Characters

Nash
Clovis

Geddoe

Ace

Queen

Joker

Jacques

Suikoden III
幻想水滸伝
Characters

Story Thus Far...

The war between the Six Clans of the Grasslands and the Zexen Commonwealth dragged on far longer than either side expected. Tired of the seemingly pointless conflict, both parties sought a truce.

Lucia, chief of the Karaya Clan, sent her son Hugo to Vinay Del Zexay, while the Zexens sent Knight Captain Chris Lightfellow (a.k.a. the Silver Maiden) to the Grasslands. Almost immediately after the truce declarations, both sides appeared to be betrayed by their former enemies. The Lizard Clan reported that their leader had been secretly murdered by the Zexens, while Chris Lightfellow heard reports of the Grasslanders ambushing her forces.

Reluctantly, the Silver Maiden agreed to let her forces set fire to the Karaya village in order to create an escape route for her troops. While the Karaya village burned out of control, Hugo, his best friend Lulu, and the Duck Clan warrior Sgt. Joe returned and discovered Lady Chris in the midst of the chaos.

Enraged, young Lulu attacked Chris and--without thinking--the Knight Captain killed Lulu on the spot. Realizing their vulnerability, Sgt. Joe prevented Hugo from attacking Lady Chris and, in return, Chris spared both of their lives.

Hugo and Sgt. Joe eventually found the surviving members of the Karaya Clan taking refuge in the caves of the Lizard Clan. Shortly after Hugo bravely faced the awful task of telling Lulu's mother about her son's murder, he snuck away to seek his vengeance.

Aila and Jimba are two more Karayan warriors who are currently separated from their people. At the time of the attack, Aila was with Geddoe's visiting group of Harmonian mercenaries (who were looking for Jimba), but they were too far from the village and too few in number to be of any help. Rather than regroup with her people, Aila decided to accompany Geddoe in order to somehow avenge the destruction of her home.

Though physically unharmed by the battle, Lady Chris found herself mentally exhausted and plagued by guilty dreams of the recent massacre. An orphan, Chris lost her father to the flames of war at a young age, and she became a knight to honor his memory. Unfortunately, Chris realized that warfare was forcing her to ruin families the same way her own was wrecked...that the blood of all those she'd slain had tarnished the hands of the Silver Maiden...and that she could no longer remember her father's face.

Attempting to regain her composure, Chris joined the knight Percival for a festival in his hometown of Iksay, but the town soon came under attack by the Grasslanders. Surrounded by Grasslanders, Chris held her own in a one-on-one battle against Lucia. Before the battle could turn against her, Nash Clovis (a mysterious man who warned Chris of the impending attack) saved her by pitching both of them off a cliff and into a river.

Chris' confrontations with Grasslanders were far from over, as she and Nash ended up at Budehuc castle, which is owned by Sir Thomas...who was playing host to Hugo! Though Hugo attacked from behind, Chris quickly got the upper hand. Chris avoided killing Hugo, but her young opponent would not stop attacking her until Sir Thomas broke up the fight.

After the battle, Chris left her fellow knights to accompany Nash Clovis on a quest to find her father. According to Nash, Wyatt Lightfellow is not only alive, he's also a Fire Bringer--a person in possession of a True Rune that grants him incredible powers and longevity. Nash contends that Chris' father is one of the two men who were always at the side of the Flame Champion, the legendary hero who used the power of the True Fire Rune to end the war between the Grasslands and Holy Harmonia.

Soon after Lady Chris departed, a private army from a nearby council appeared at Budehuc castle to take Hugo into custody. With the help of Sir Thomas and his staff, Hugo made a clean getaway, only to discover that Harmonia had invaded the Grasslands and conquered the village of Safir. Hugo made his way to the village of the Duck Clan, where he met Hallec and Mua, two knights from the Grasslands territory of Kamaro. To save their home, the two men are on a quest to locate the Flame Champion, whom they've heard is currently in Chisha. Realizing the compatibility of their missions, Hugo, Hallec and Mua agreed to travel together.

Seemingly unbeknownst to any of the Zexens or Grasslanders, Chris' father Wyatt Lightfellow and Karayan warrior Jimba are one and the same person...and he's a friend of Geddoe, who wields the True Lightning Rune. Geddoe's secret possession of the True Lightning Rune was revealed to his allies and enemies alike when he recently used it in battle against an agent of the mysterious Masked Bishop of Holy Harmonia. Despite the revelation, Geddoe's group decided to stay together, though the consequences of the Masked Bishop's knowledge of Geddoe's secret are yet to be known.

Now, with the expiration of the 50-year treaty that maintained the truce between Holy Harmonia and the Grasslands, forces from many sides are converging on the Grasslands village known as Chisha. The big question is: who will survive the collision?

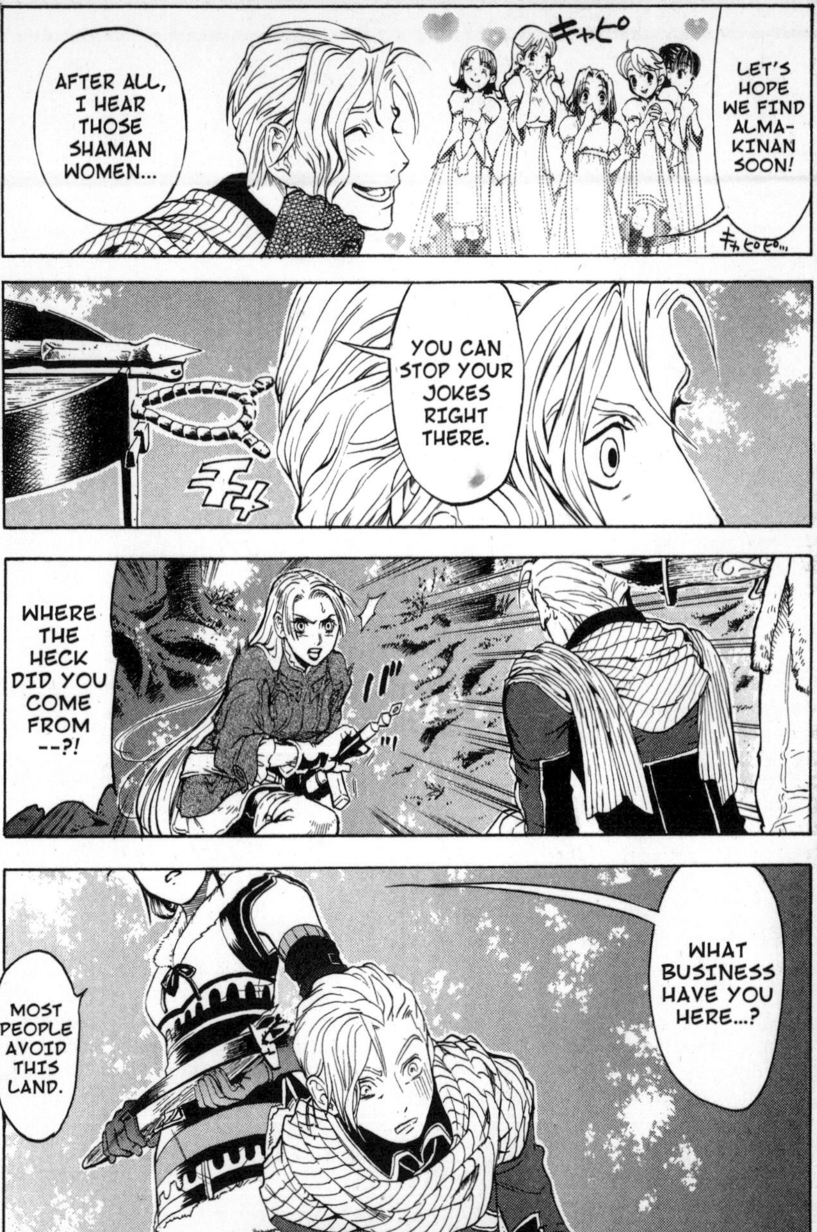
LET'S HOPE WE FIND ALMA-KINAN SOON!
キャピ
AFTER ALL, I HEAR THOSE SHAMAN WOMEN...
YOU CAN STOP YOUR JOKES RIGHT THERE.
WHERE THE HECK DID YOU COME FROM --?!
WHAT BUSINESS HAVE YOU HERE...?
MOST PEOPLE AVOID THIS LAND.

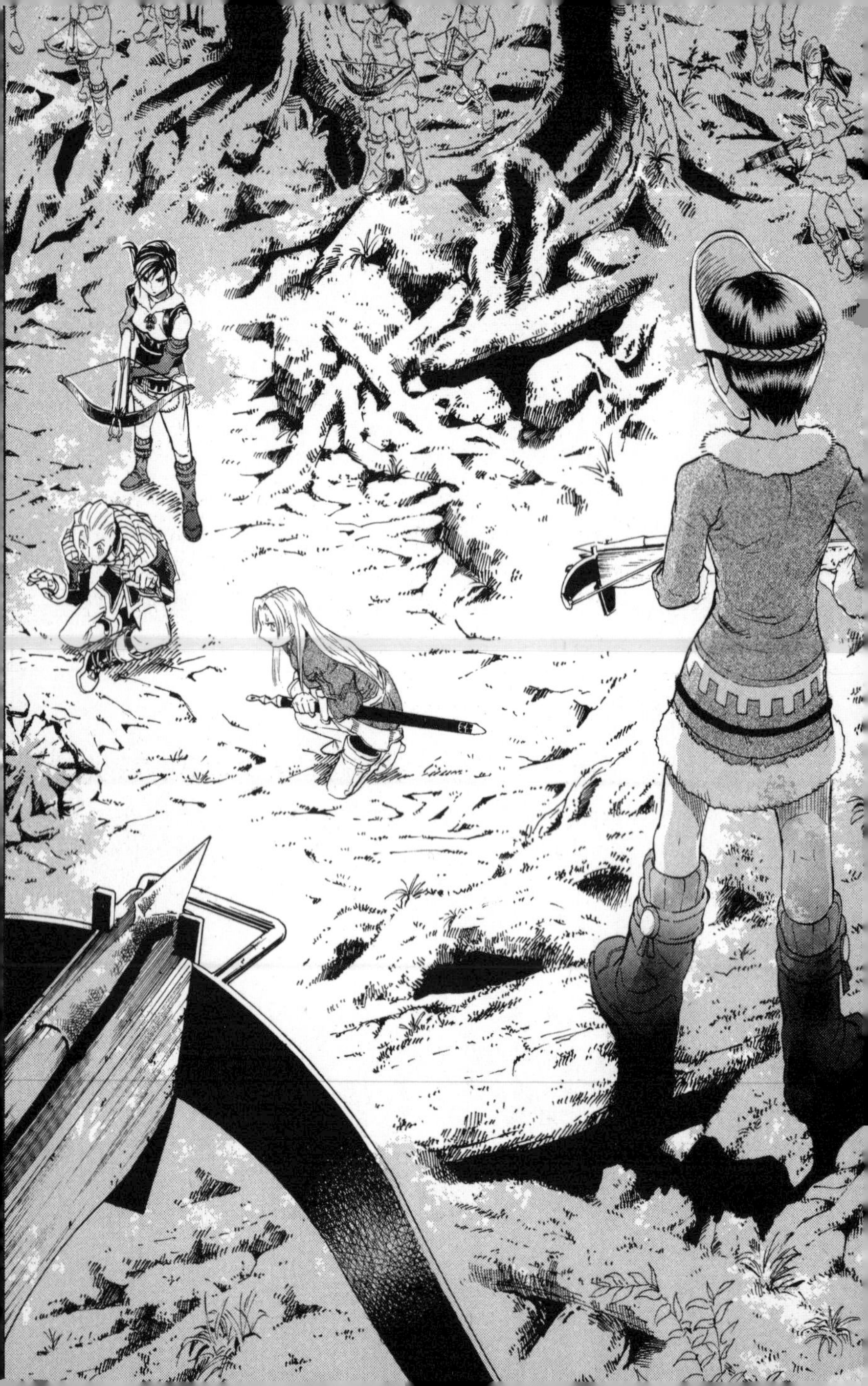

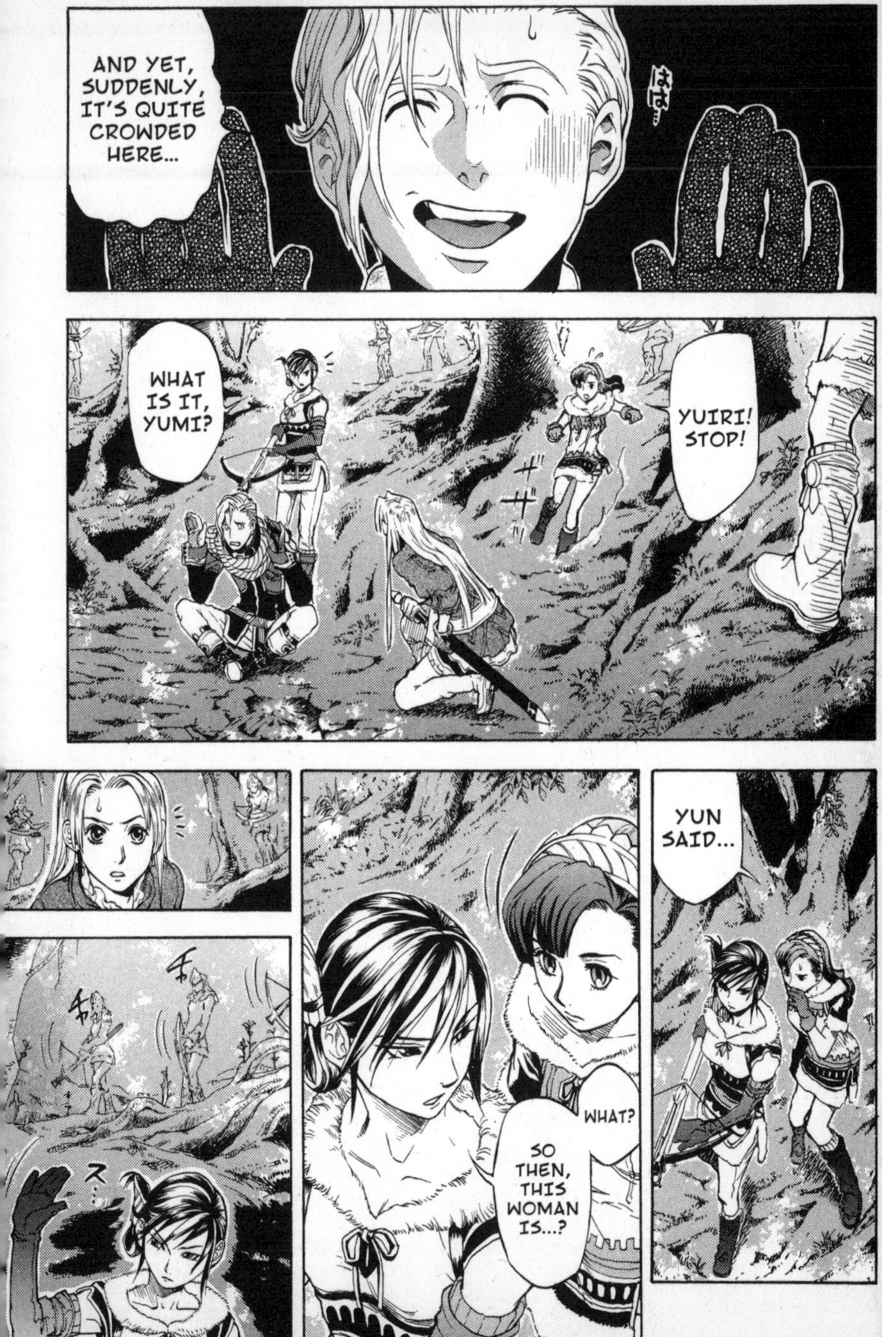
AND YET, SUDDENLY, IT'S QUITE CROWDED HERE...
はは…
YUIRI! STOP!
ザザッ
WHAT IS IT, YUMI?
YUN SAID...
WHAT?
SO THEN, THIS WOMAN IS...?
チャ
チャ
ス…

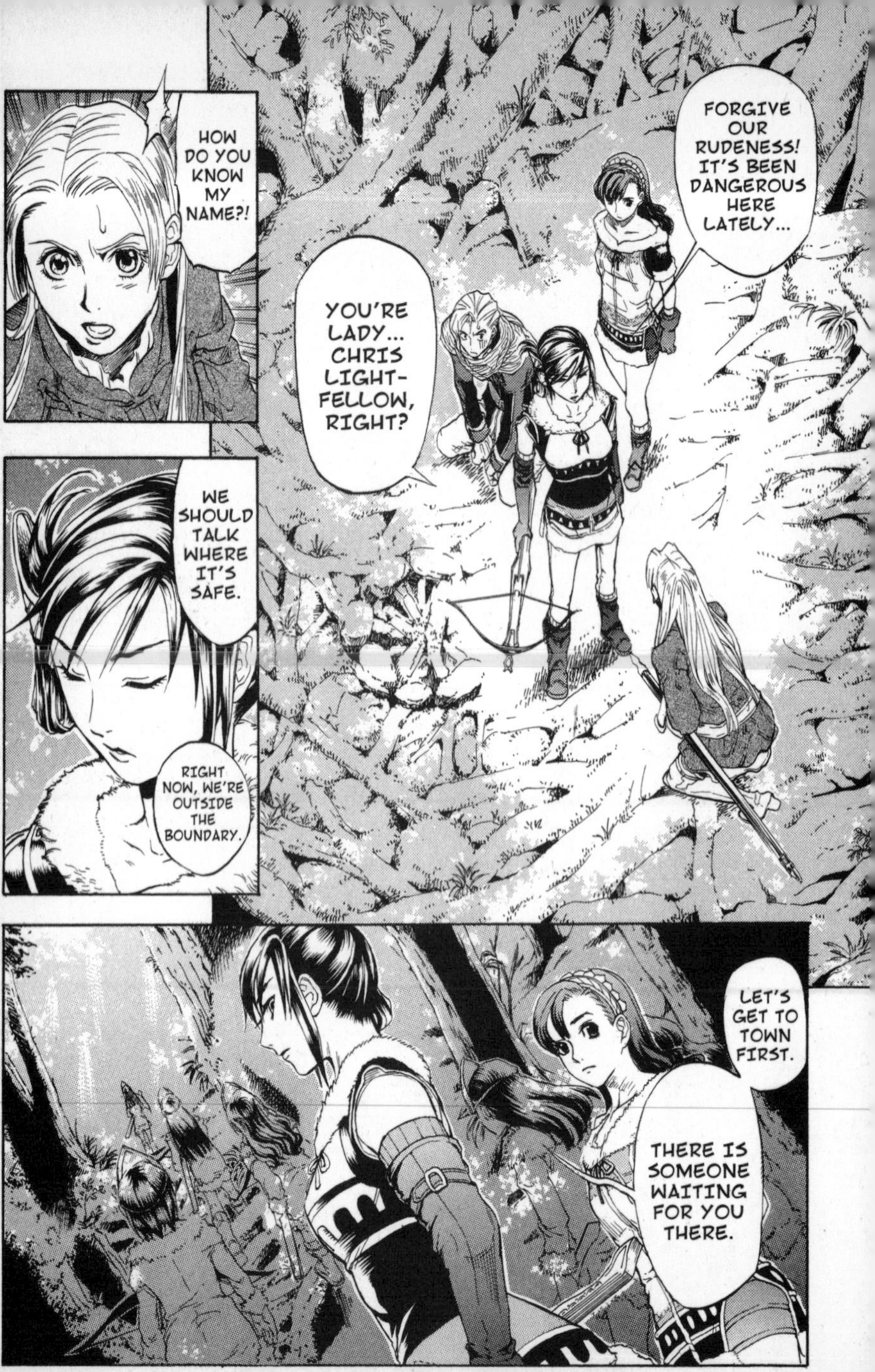
FORGIVE OUR RUDENESS! IT'S BEEN DANGEROUS HERE LATELY...
YOU'RE LADY... CHRIS LIGHT-FELLOW, RIGHT?
HOW DO YOU KNOW MY NAME?!
WE SHOULD TALK WHERE IT'S SAFE.
RIGHT NOW, WE'RE OUTSIDE THE BOUNDARY.
LET'S GET TO TOWN FIRST.
THERE IS SOMEONE WAITING FOR YOU THERE.

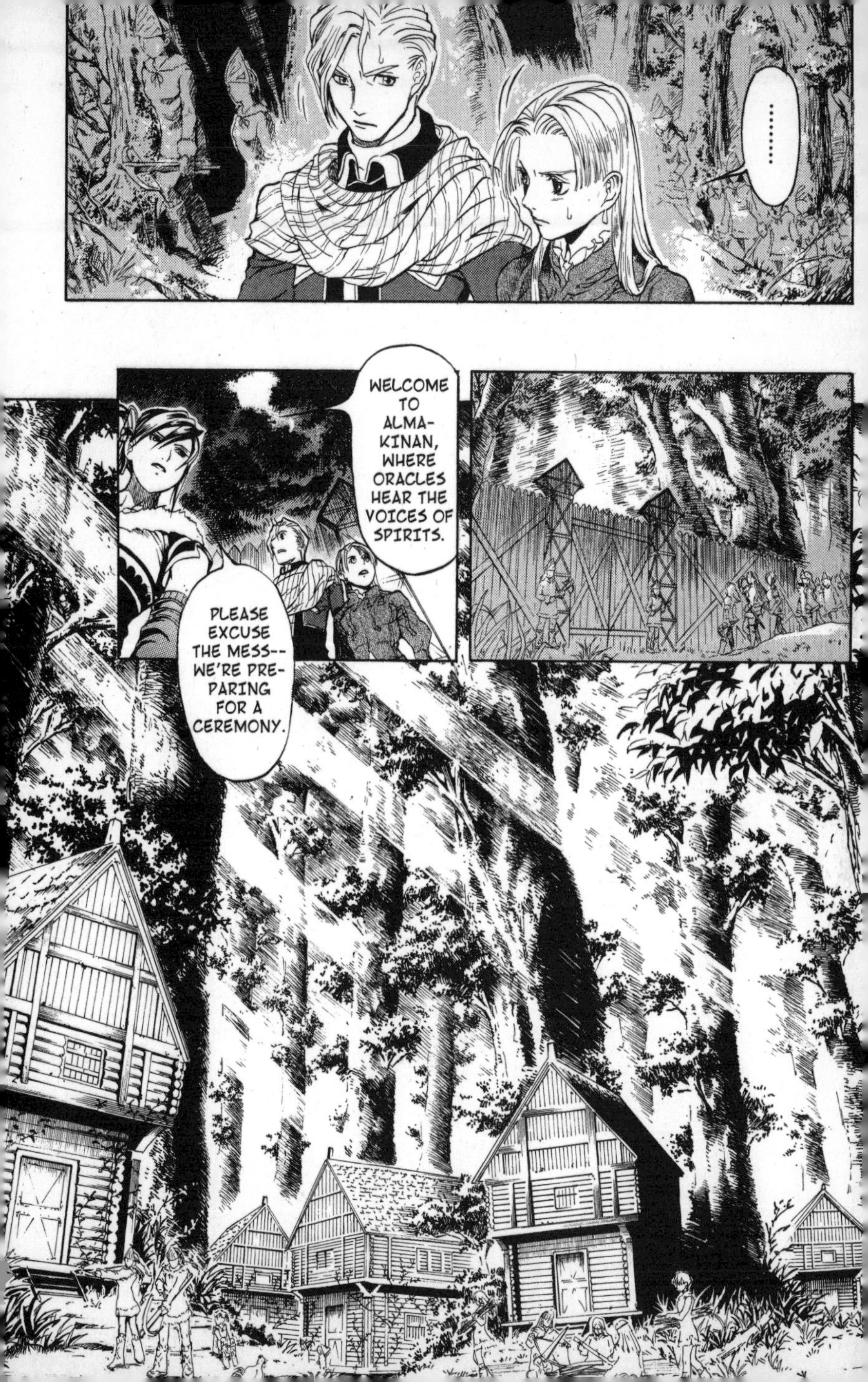
......
WELCOME TO ALMA-KINAN, WHERE ORACLES HEAR THE VOICES OF SPIRITS.
PLEASE EXCUSE THE MESS--WE'RE PRE-PARING FOR A CEREMONY.

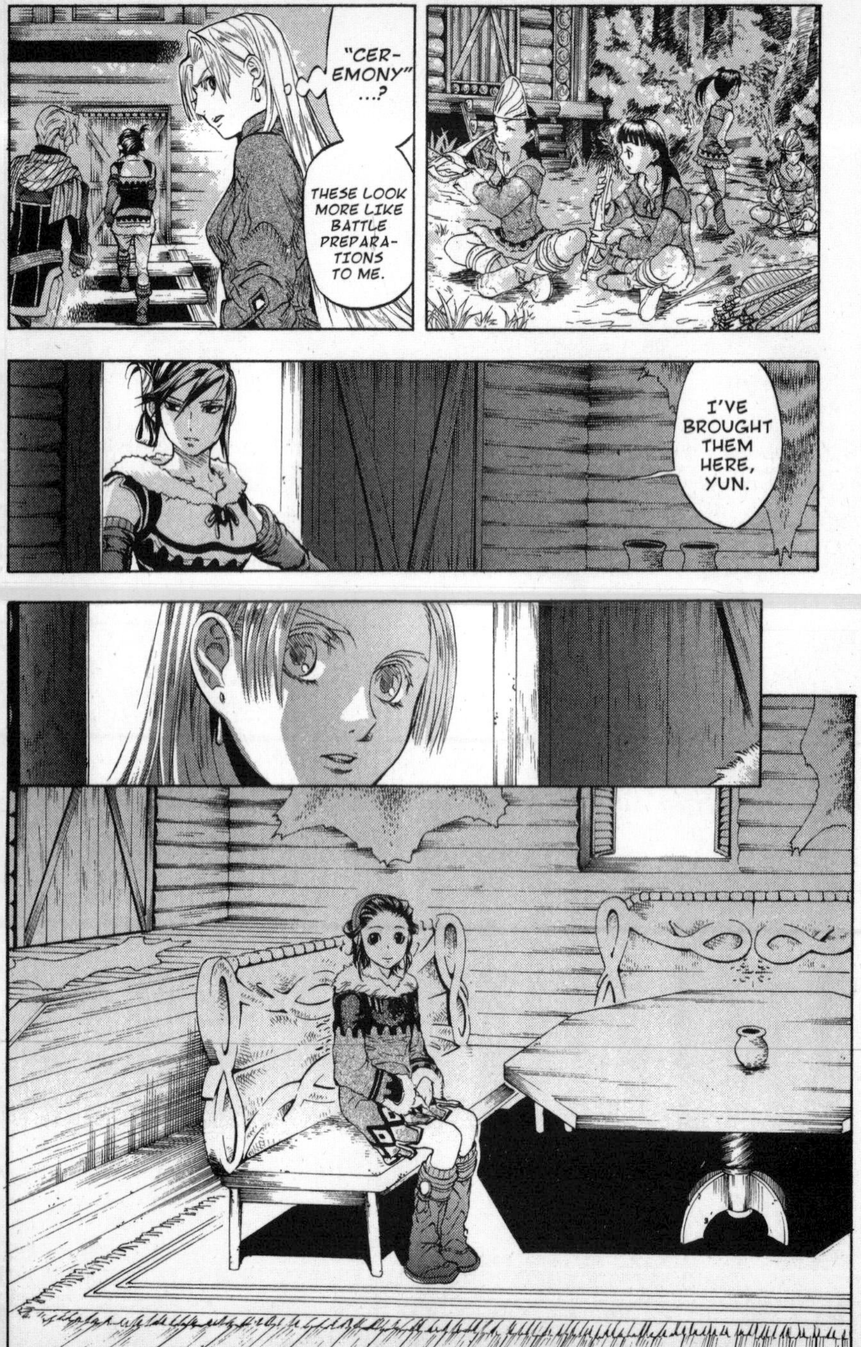
"CER-EMONY"...?
THESE LOOK MORE LIKE BATTLE PREPARATIONS TO ME.
I'VE BROUGHT THEM HERE, YUN.

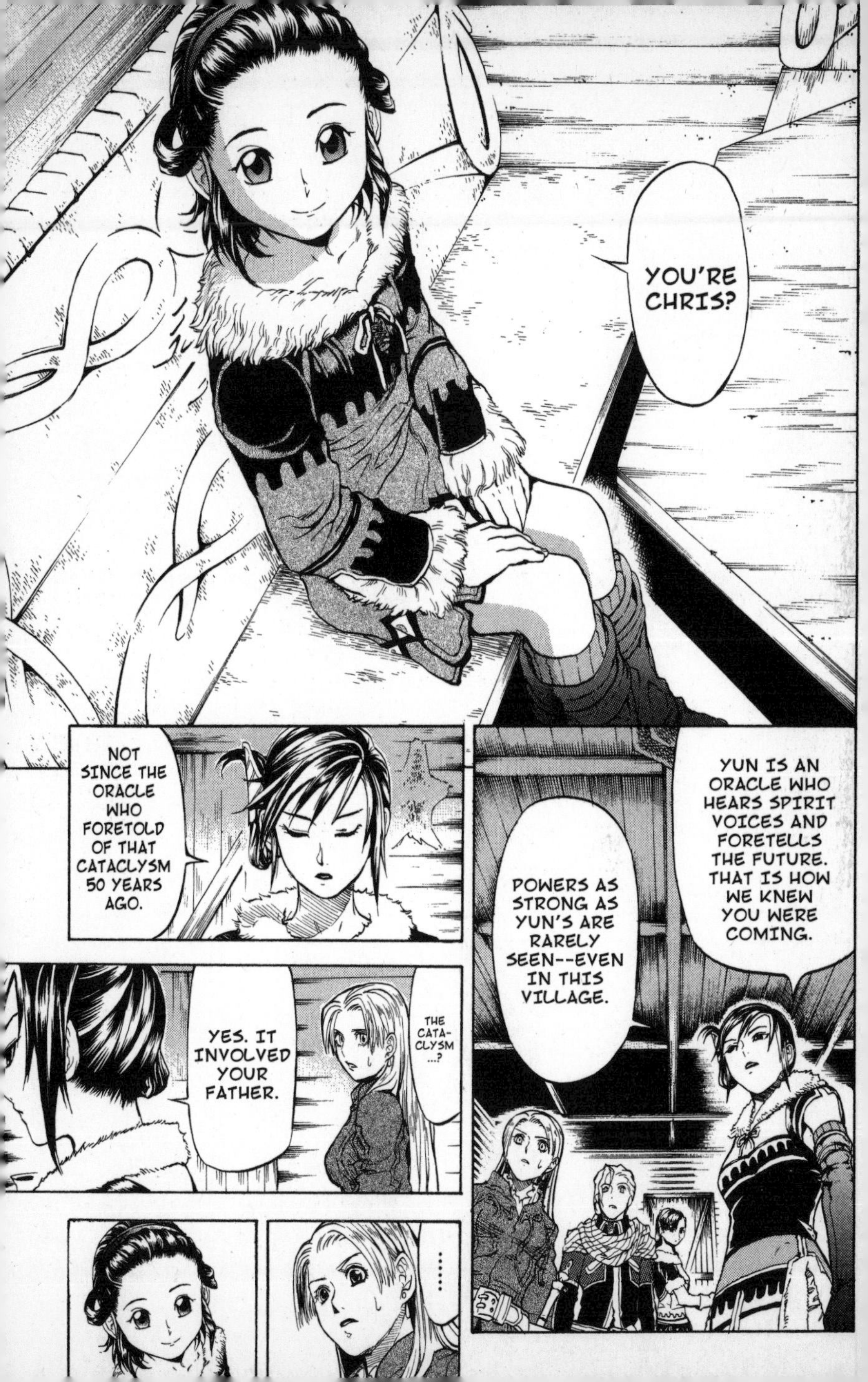
YOU'RE CHRIS?
YUN IS AN ORACLE WHO HEARS SPIRIT VOICES AND FORETELLS THE FUTURE. THAT IS HOW WE KNEW YOU WERE COMING.
POWERS AS STRONG AS YUN'S ARE RARELY SEEN--EVEN IN THIS VILLAGE.
NOT SINCE THE ORACLE WHO FORETOLD OF THAT CATACLYSM 50 YEARS AGO.
THE CATA-CLYSM ...?
YES. IT INVOLVED YOUR FATHER.
......

"50 YEARS AGO, AN ORACLE MADE THIS PREDICTION...

"THE WIND WILL BLOW MORE WILDLY ACROSS THE GRASSLANDS THAN THE WINDS FROM THE EAST, AND THE TINIEST FLAME WILL GROW TO BECOME AN ALL-CONSUMING INFERNO."

"FOR 10 DAYS, THE FIRE WILL BLAZE-- SO BRIGHTLY IT WILL BE LIKE A NEW STAR BEING BORN."

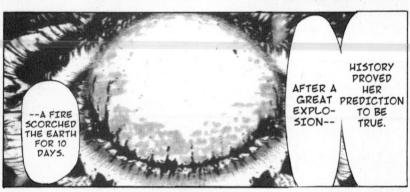

HISTORY PROVED HER PREDICTION TO BE TRUE.

AFTER A GREAT EXPLO-SION--

--A FIRE SCORCHED THE EARTH FOR 10 DAYS.

BY FATE, A SPECIAL GROUP UNDER THE COMMAND OF THE FLAME CHAMPION FOUGHT TO PROTECT THE GRASSLANDS FROM THE INVADING HARMONIAN ARMY.

THEY WERE THE "FIRE BRINGERS." WYATT WAS ONE OF THEM.

BY "FATE," WHAT... DO YOU MEAN?

....

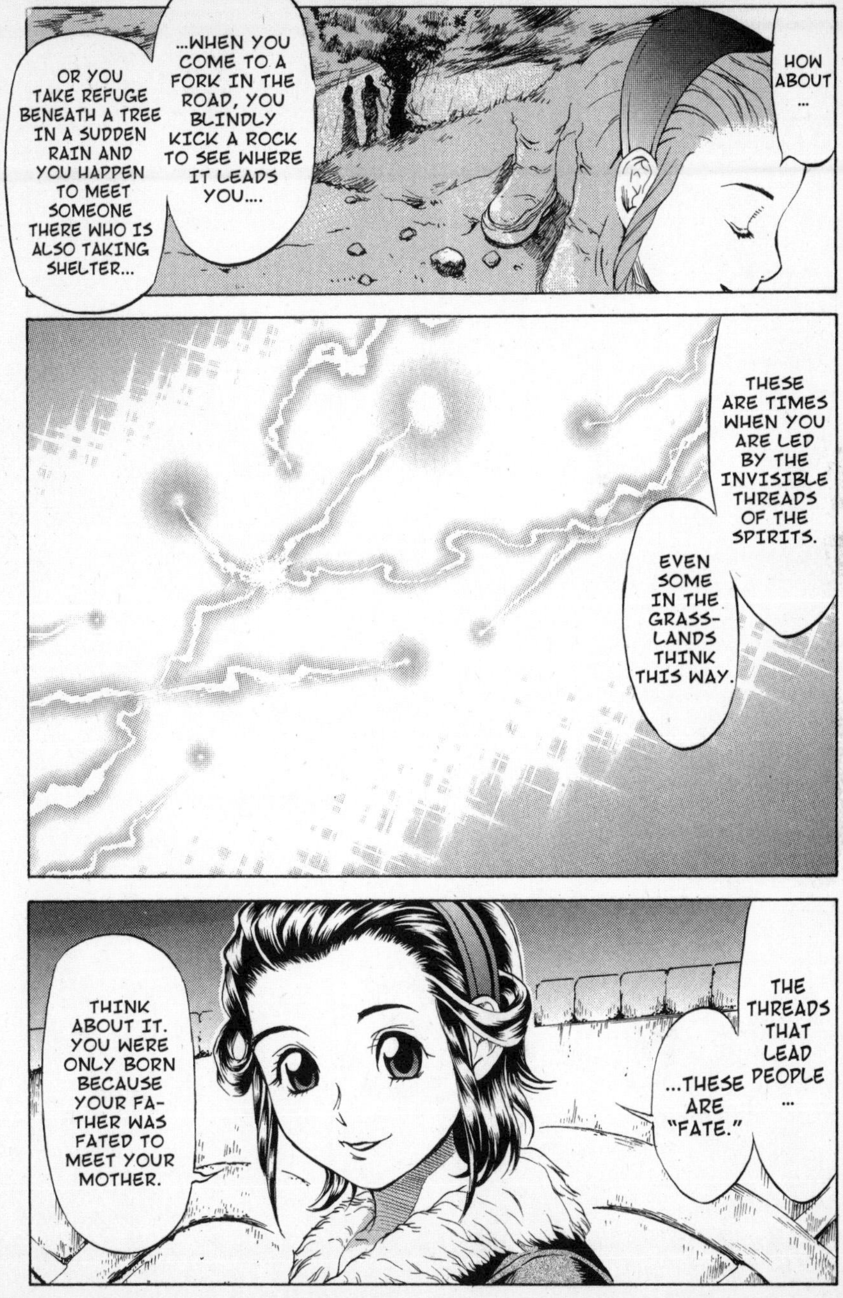
HOW ABOUT...
...WHEN YOU COME TO A FORK IN THE ROAD, YOU BLINDLY KICK A ROCK TO SEE WHERE IT LEADS YOU....
OR YOU TAKE REFUGE BENEATH A TREE IN A SUDDEN RAIN AND YOU HAPPEN TO MEET SOMEONE THERE WHO IS ALSO TAKING SHELTER...
THESE ARE TIMES WHEN YOU ARE LED BY THE INVISIBLE THREADS OF THE SPIRITS.
EVEN SOME IN THE GRASS-LANDS THINK THIS WAY.
THE THREADS THAT LEAD PEOPLE...
...THESE ARE "FATE."
THINK ABOUT IT. YOU WERE ONLY BORN BECAUSE YOUR FA-THER WAS FATED TO MEET YOUR MOTHER.

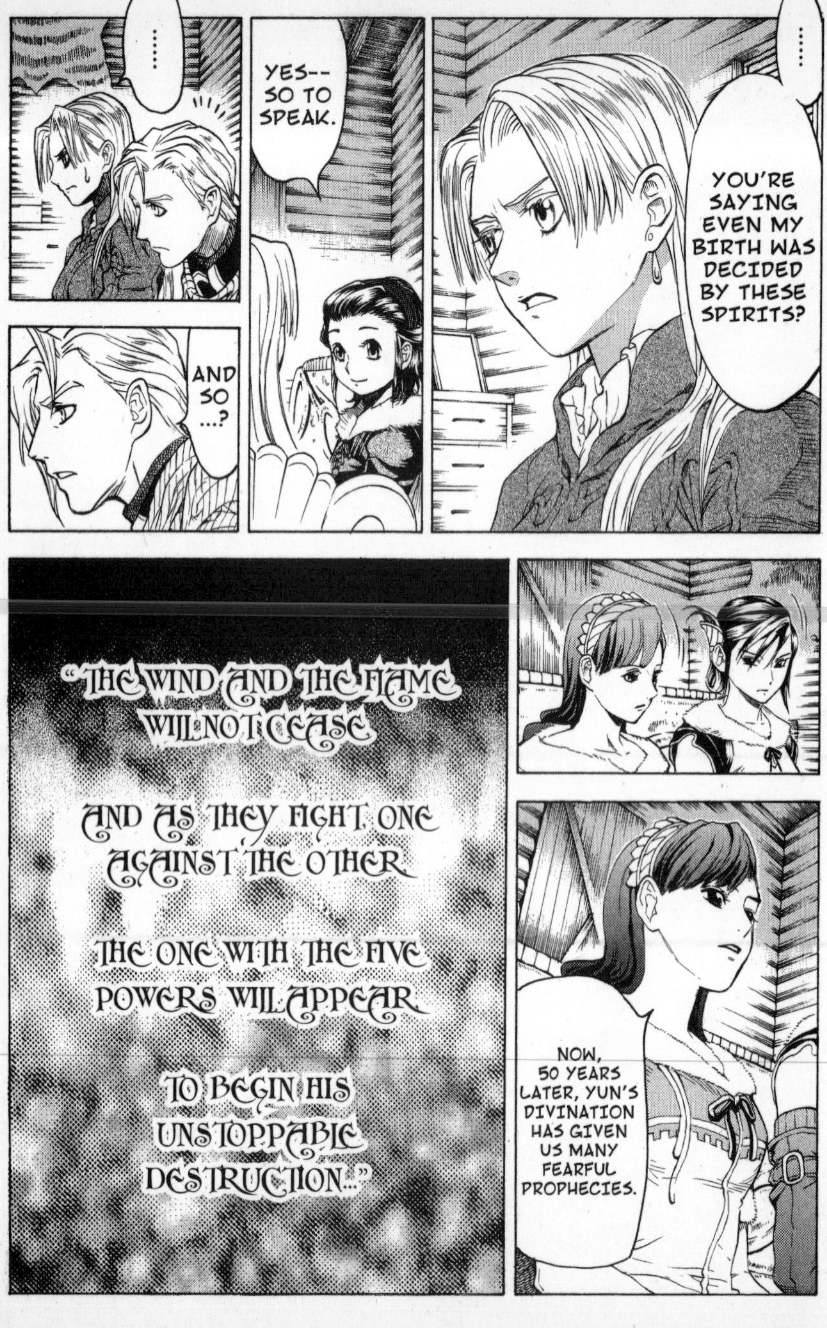
......
YOU'RE SAYING EVEN MY BIRTH WAS DECIDED BY THESE SPIRITS?
YES-- SO TO SPEAK.
......
AND SO ...?
NOW, 50 YEARS LATER, YUN'S DIVINATION HAS GIVEN US MANY FEARFUL PROPHECIES.
"THE WIND AND THE FLAME WILL NOT CEASE
AND AS THEY FIGHT ONE AGAINST THE OTHER,
THE ONE WITH THE FIVE POWERS WILL APPEAR,
TO BEGIN HIS UNSTOPPABLE DESTRUCTION..."

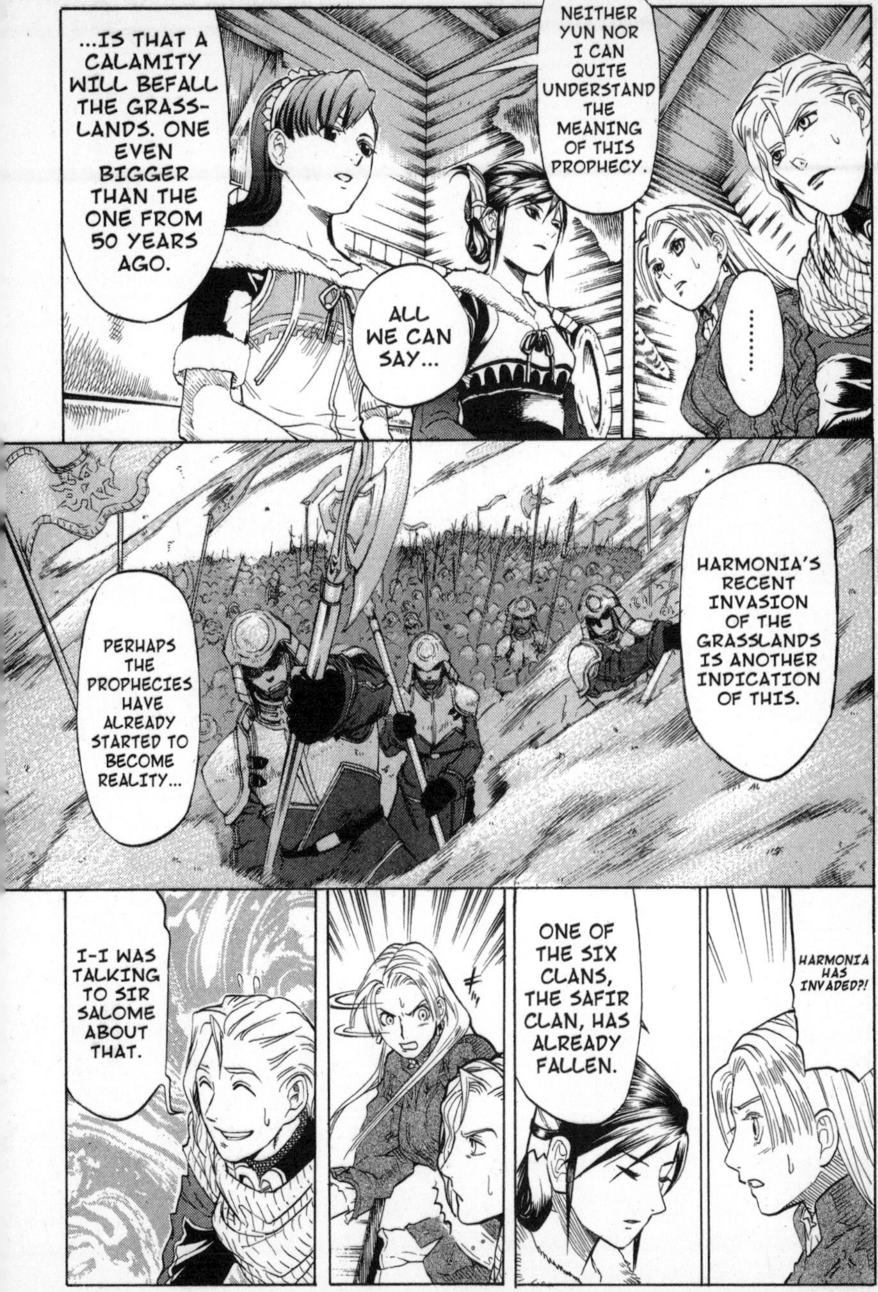
......
NEITHER YUN NOR I CAN QUITE UNDERSTAND THE MEANING OF THIS PROPHECY.
ALL WE CAN SAY...
...IS THAT A CALAMITY WILL BEFALL THE GRASS-LANDS. ONE EVEN BIGGER THAN THE ONE FROM 50 YEARS AGO.
HARMONIA'S RECENT INVASION OF THE GRASSLANDS IS ANOTHER INDICATION OF THIS.
PERHAPS THE PROPHECIES HAVE ALREADY STARTED TO BECOME REALITY...
HARMONIA HAS INVADED?!
ONE OF THE SIX CLANS, THE SAFIR CLAN, HAS ALREADY FALLEN.
I-I WAS TALKING TO SIR SALOME ABOUT THAT.

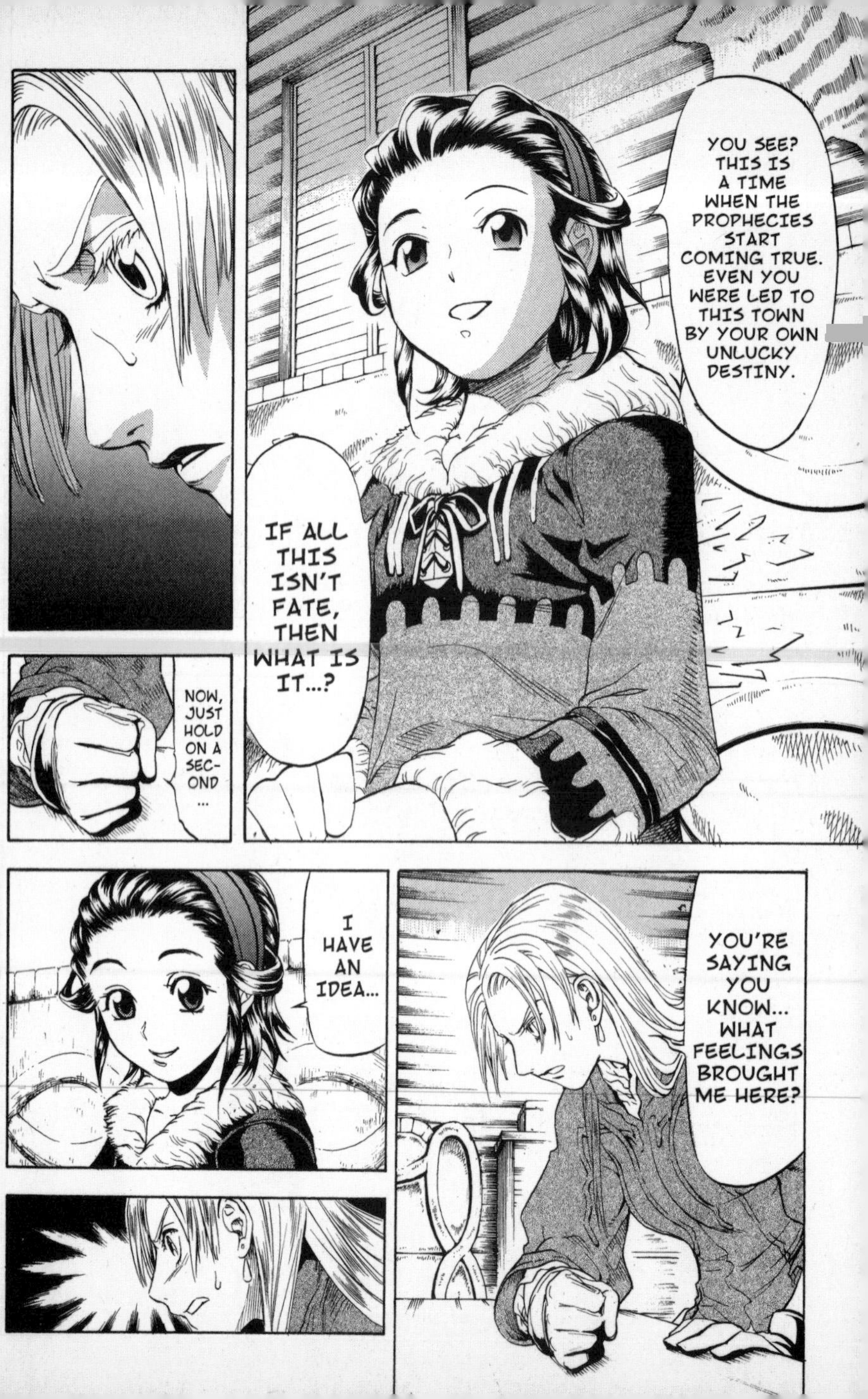
YOU SEE? THIS IS A TIME WHEN THE PROPHECIES START COMING TRUE. EVEN YOU WERE LED TO THIS TOWN BY YOUR OWN UNLUCKY DESTINY.
IF ALL THIS ISN'T FATE, THEN WHAT IS IT...?
NOW, JUST HOLD ON A SEC-OND...
YOU'RE SAYING YOU KNOW... WHAT FEELINGS BROUGHT ME HERE?
I HAVE AN IDEA...

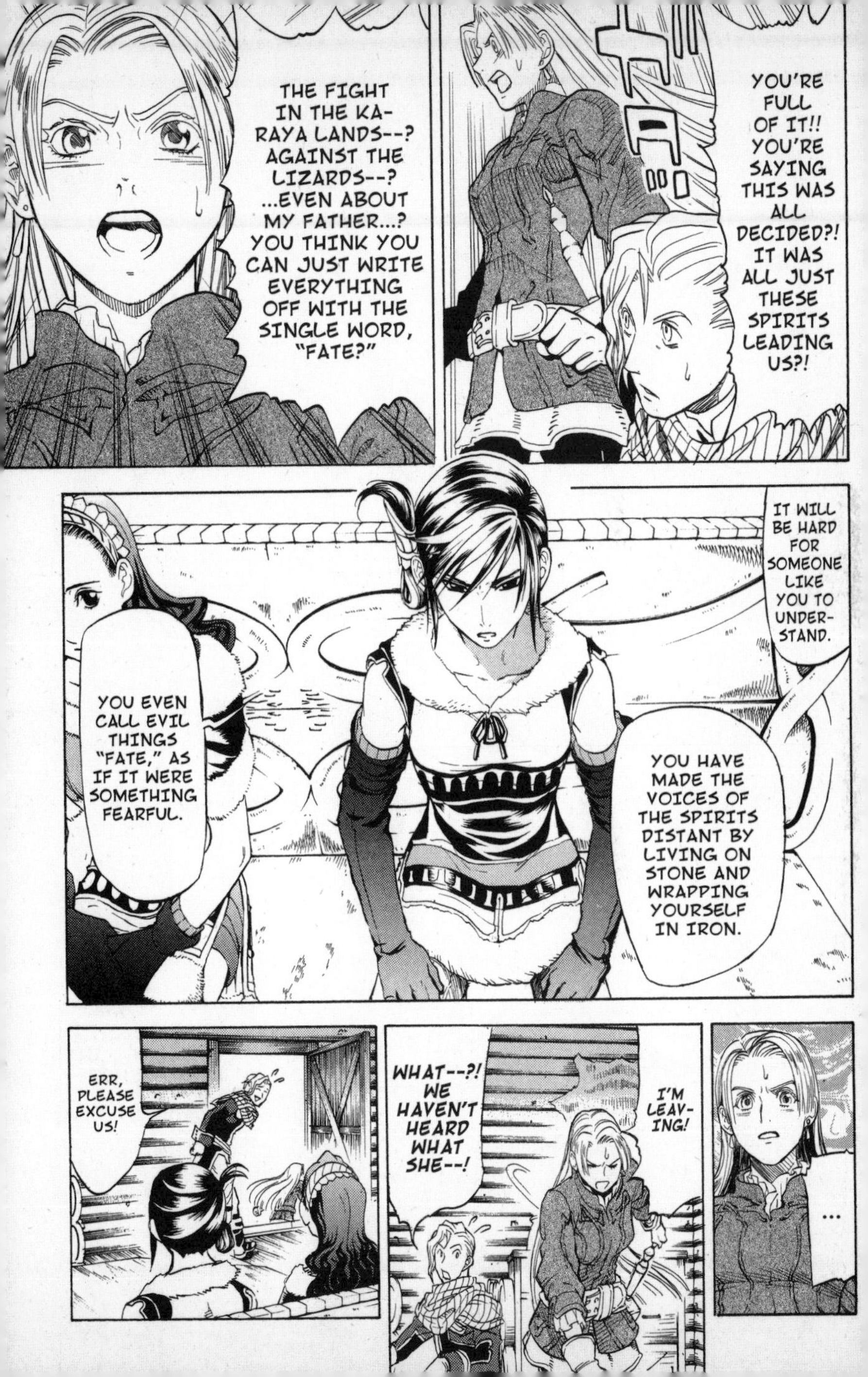
YOU'RE FULL OF IT!! YOU'RE SAYING THIS WAS ALL DECIDED?! IT WAS ALL JUST THESE SPIRITS LEADING US?!
THE FIGHT IN THE KA-RAYA LANDS--? AGAINST THE LIZARDS--? ...EVEN ABOUT MY FATHER...? YOU THINK YOU CAN JUST WRITE EVERYTHING OFF WITH THE SINGLE WORD, "FATE?"
IT WILL BE HARD FOR SOMEONE LIKE YOU TO UNDER-STAND.
YOU EVEN CALL EVIL THINGS "FATE," AS IF IT WERE SOMETHING FEARFUL.
YOU HAVE MADE THE VOICES OF THE SPIRITS DISTANT BY LIVING ON STONE AND WRAPPING YOURSELF IN IRON.
...
I'M LEAV-ING!
WHAT--?! WE HAVEN'T HEARD WHAT SHE--!
ERR, PLEASE EXCUSE US!

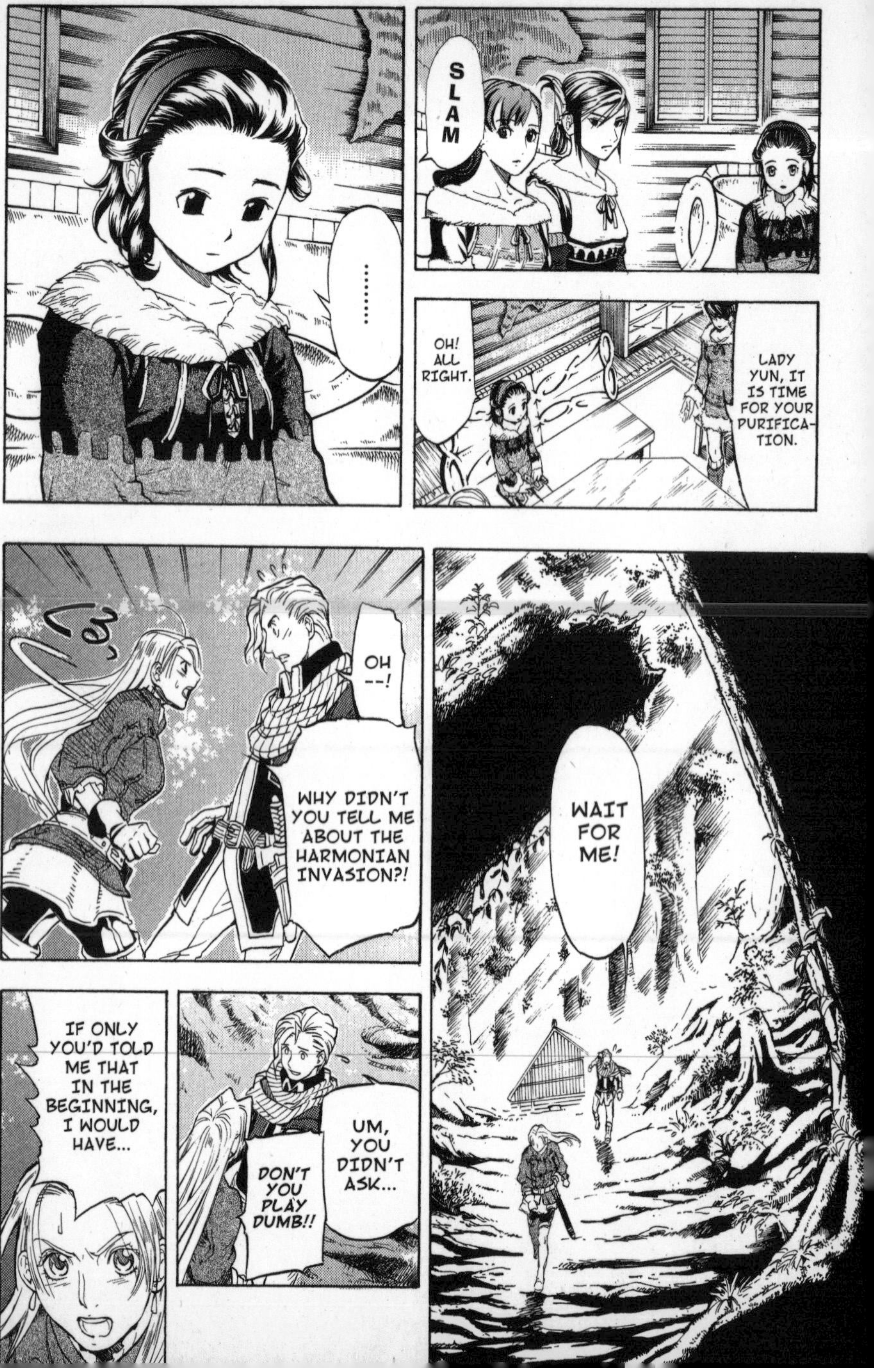

SLAM
LADY YUN, IT IS TIME FOR YOUR PURIFICA-TION.
OH! ALL RIGHT.
......
WAIT FOR ME!
くるっ
OH --!
WHY DIDN'T YOU TELL ME ABOUT THE HARMONIAN INVASION?!
UM, YOU DIDN'T ASK...
DON'T YOU PLAY DUMB!!
IF ONLY YOU'D TOLD ME THAT IN THE BEGINNING, I WOULD HAVE...

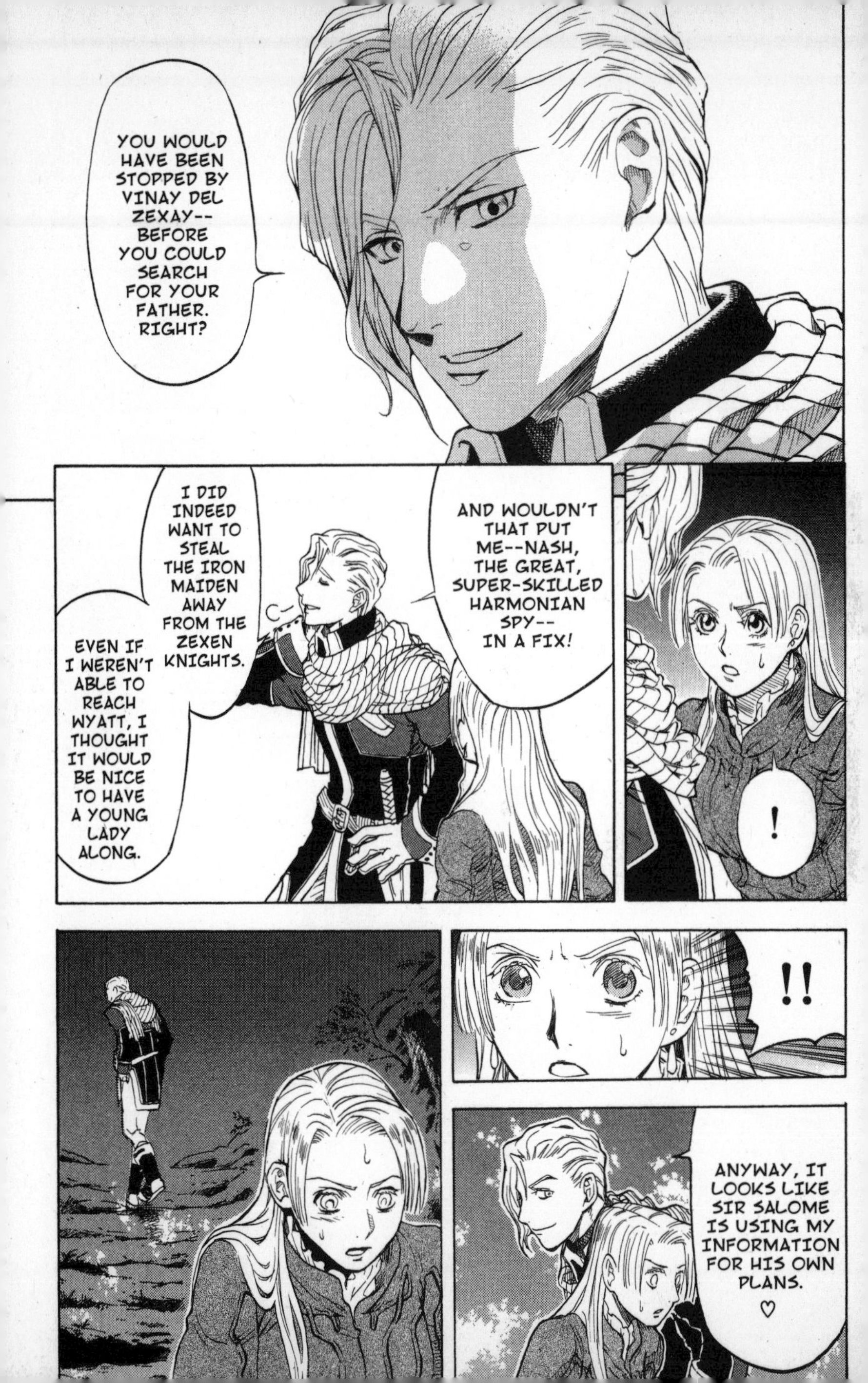
YOU WOULD HAVE BEEN STOPPED BY VINAY DEL ZEXAY-- BEFORE YOU COULD SEARCH FOR YOUR FATHER. RIGHT?
!
AND WOULDN'T THAT PUT ME--NASH, THE GREAT, SUPER-SKILLED HARMONIAN SPY-- IN A FIX!
I DID INDEED WANT TO STEAL THE IRON MAIDEN AWAY FROM THE ZEXEN KNIGHTS.
EVEN IF I WEREN'T ABLE TO REACH WYATT, I THOUGHT IT WOULD BE NICE TO HAVE A YOUNG LADY ALONG.
!!
ANYWAY, IT LOOKS LIKE SIR SALOME IS USING MY INFORMATION FOR HIS OWN PLANS. ♡

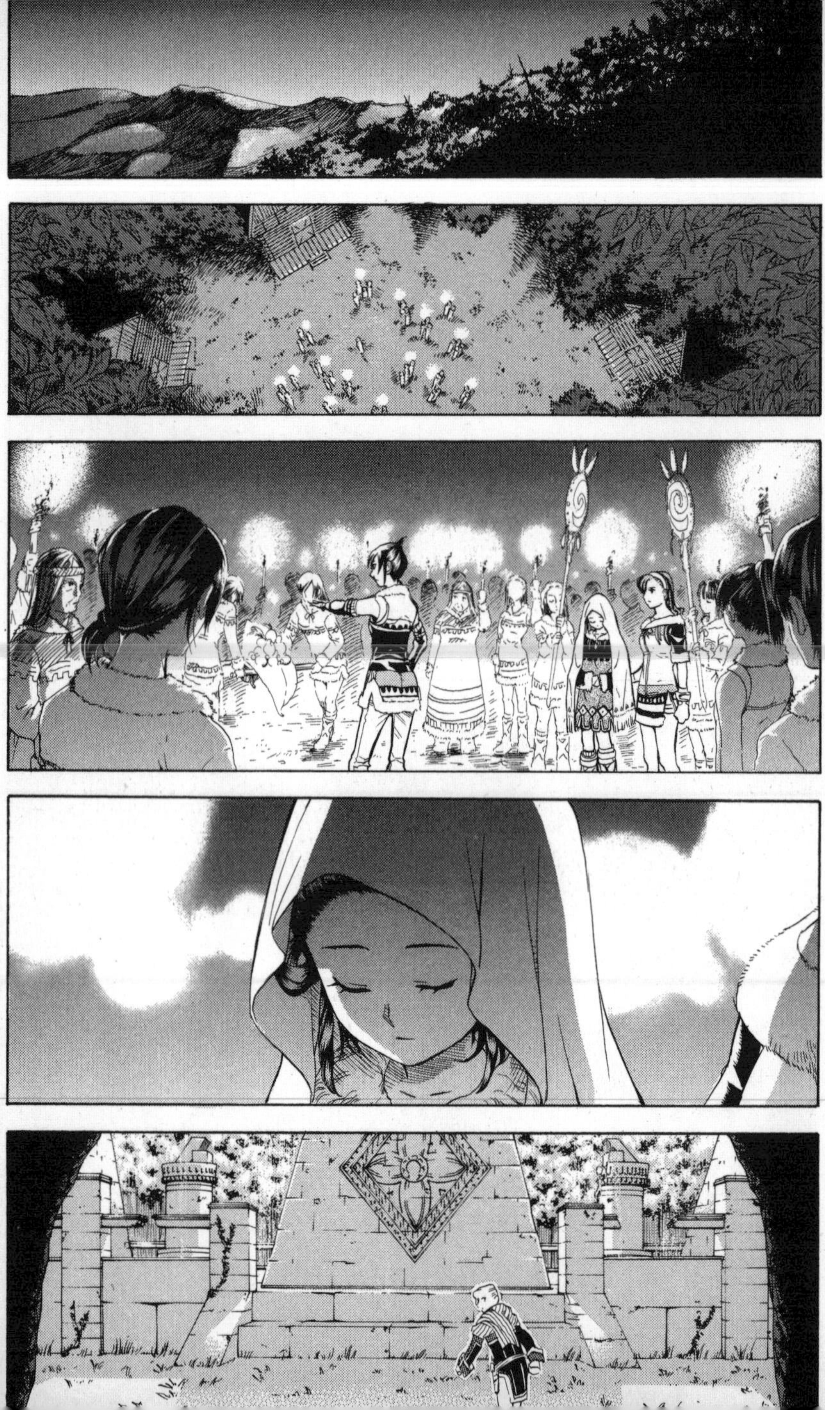

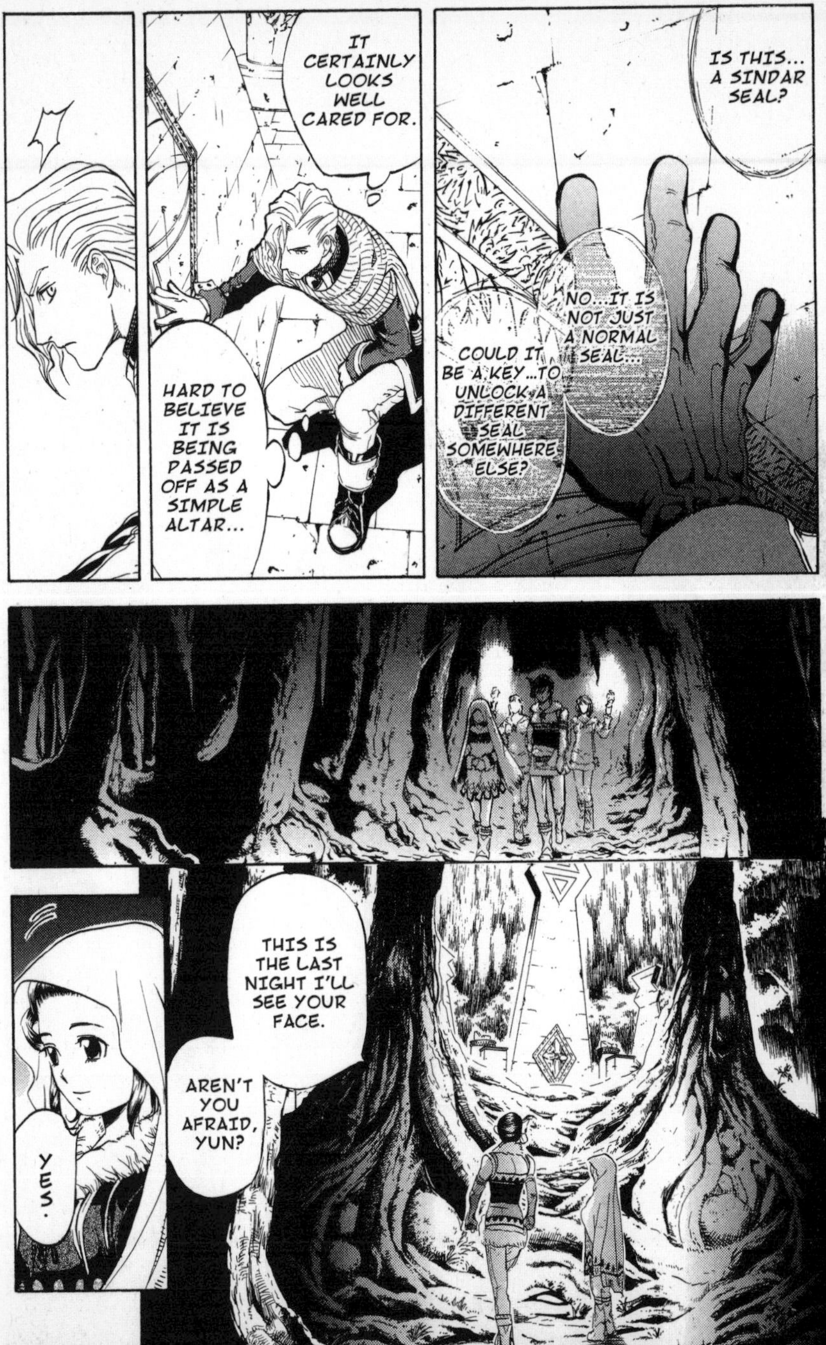
IS THIS... A SINDAR SEAL?
NO...IT IS NOT JUST A NORMAL SEAL...
COULD IT BE A KEY...TO UNLOCK A DIFFERENT SEAL SOMEWHERE ELSE?
IT CERTAINLY LOOKS WELL CARED FOR.
HARD TO BELIEVE IT IS BEING PASSED OFF AS A SIMPLE ALTAR...
THIS IS THE LAST NIGHT I'LL SEE YOUR FACE.
AREN'T YOU AFRAID, YUN?
YES.

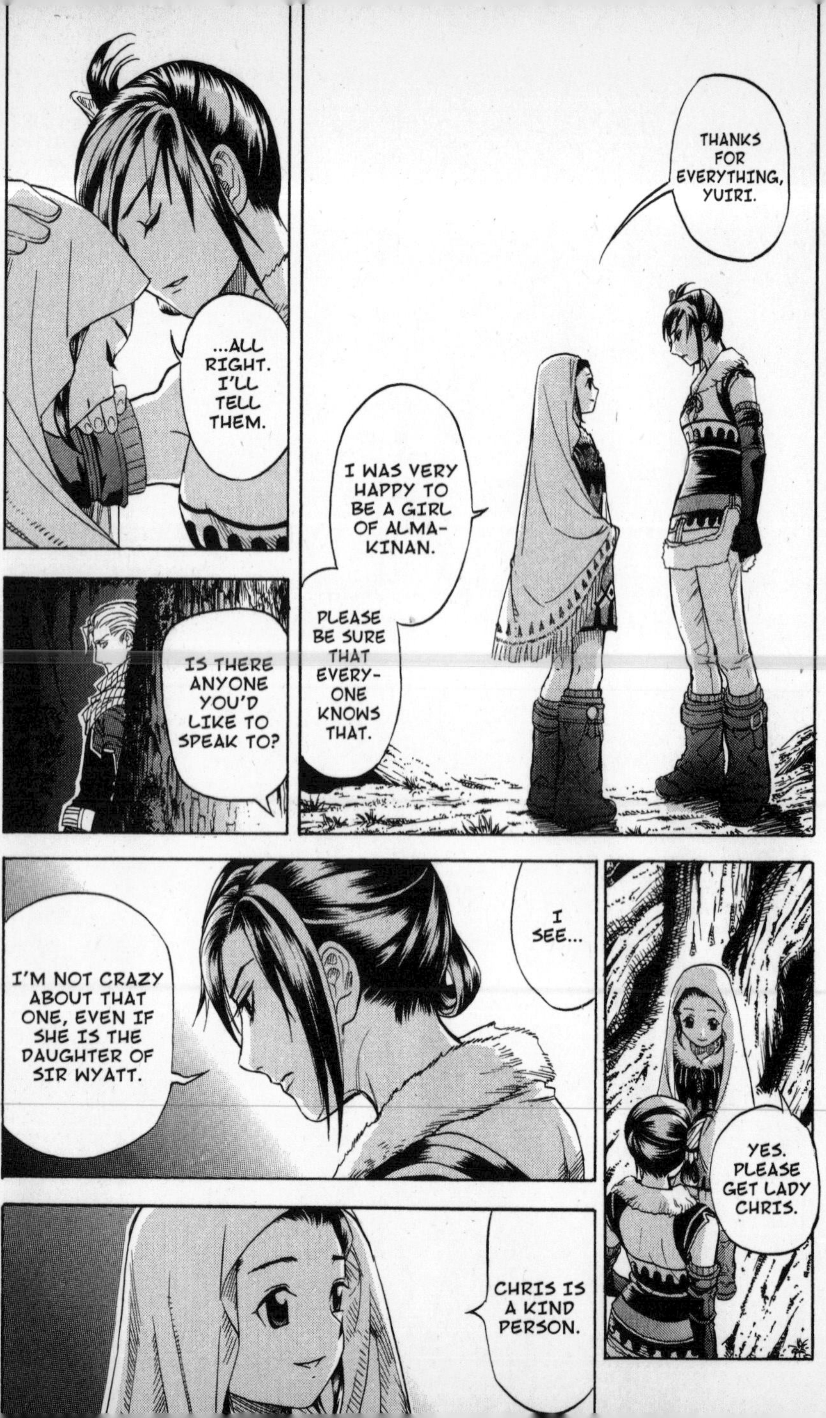
THANKS FOR EVERYTHING, YUIRI.
I WAS VERY HAPPY TO BE A GIRL OF ALMA-KINAN.
PLEASE BE SURE THAT EVERY-ONE KNOWS THAT.
...ALL RIGHT. I'LL TELL THEM.
IS THERE ANYONE YOU'D LIKE TO SPEAK TO?
YES. PLEASE GET LADY CHRIS.
I SEE...
I'M NOT CRAZY ABOUT THAT ONE, EVEN IF SHE IS THE DAUGHTER OF SIR WYATT.
CHRIS IS A KIND PERSON.

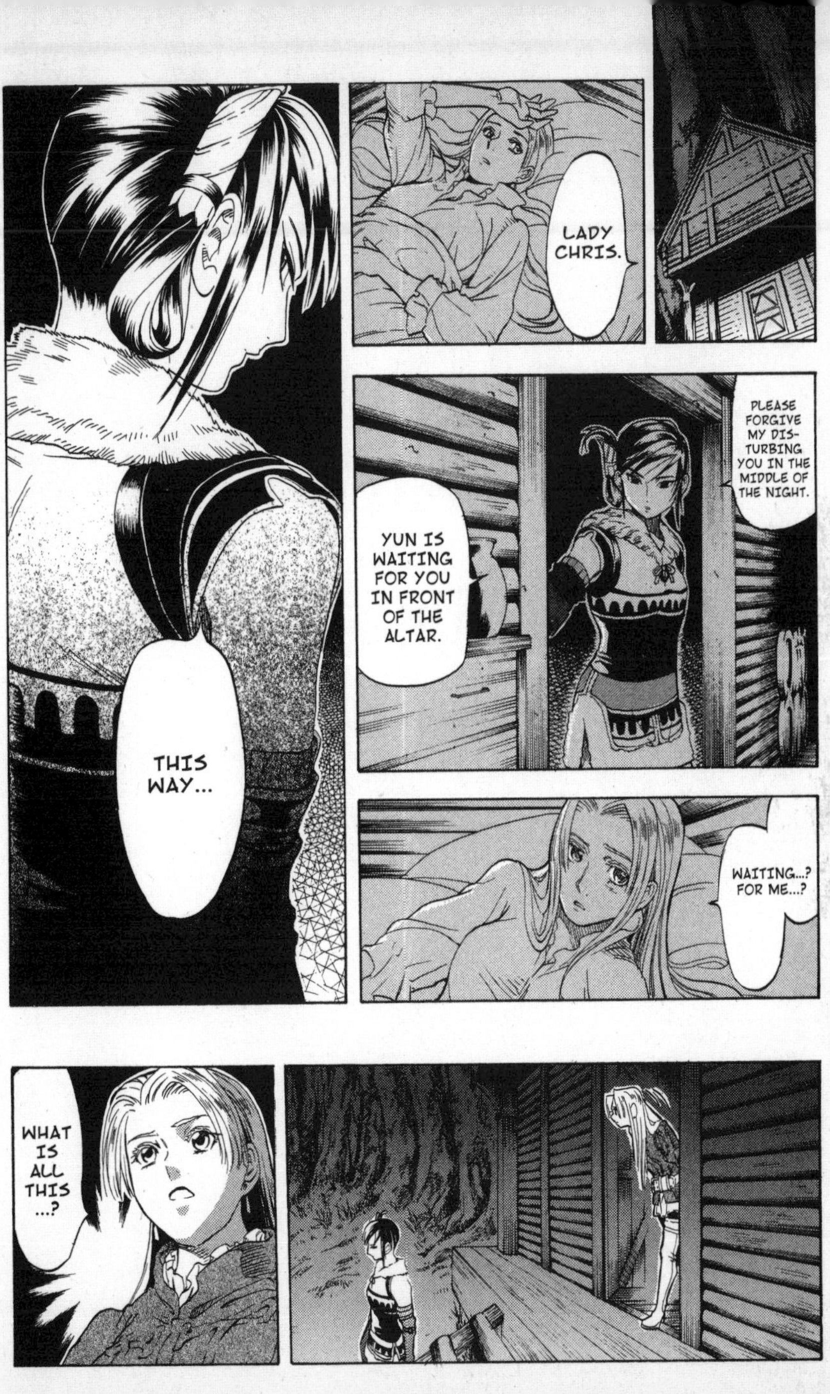
LADY CHRIS.
PLEASE FORGIVE MY DISTURBING YOU IN THE MIDDLE OF THE NIGHT.
YUN IS WAITING FOR YOU IN FRONT OF THE ALTAR.
WAITING...? FOR ME...?
THIS WAY...
WHAT IS ALL THIS ...?

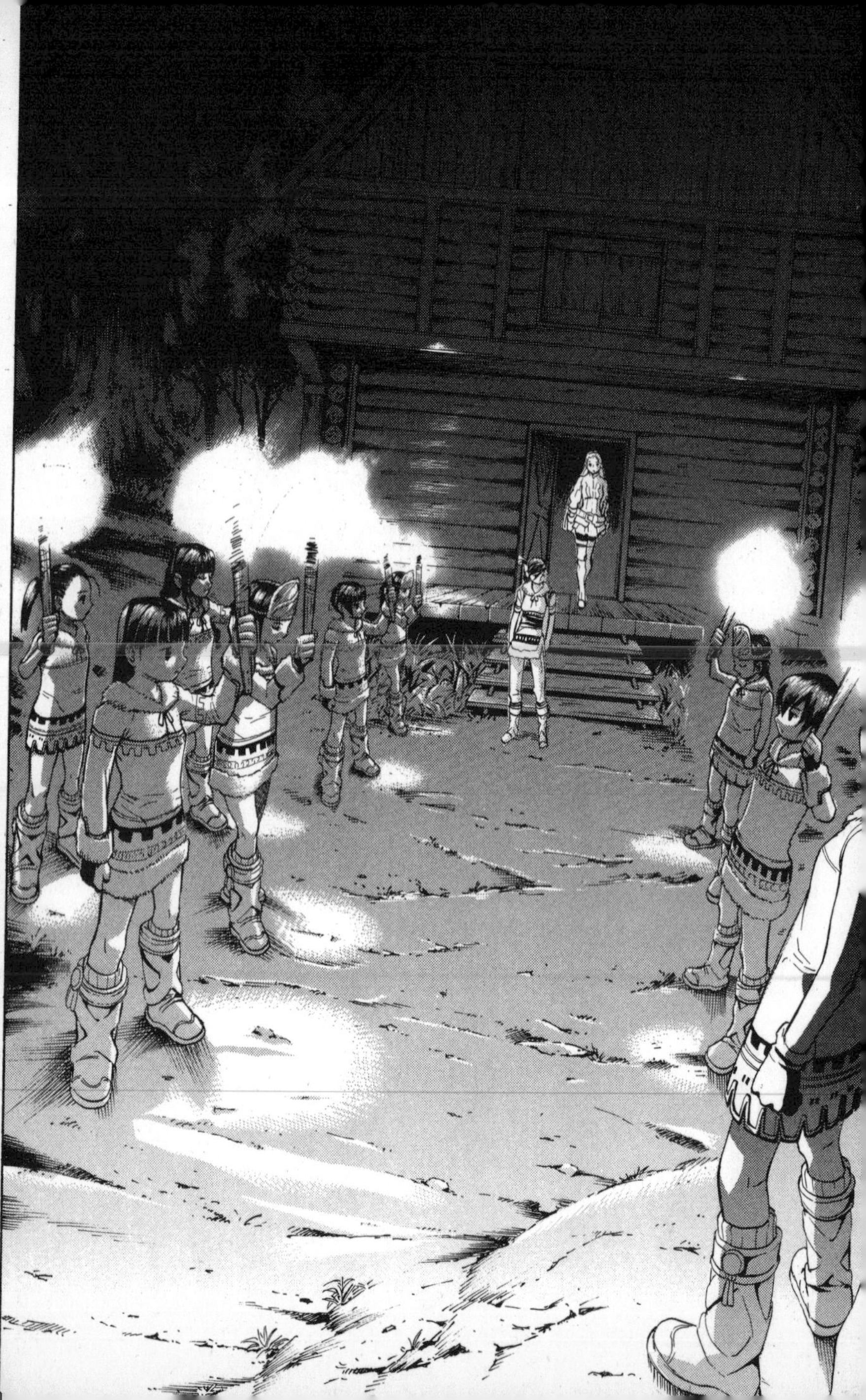

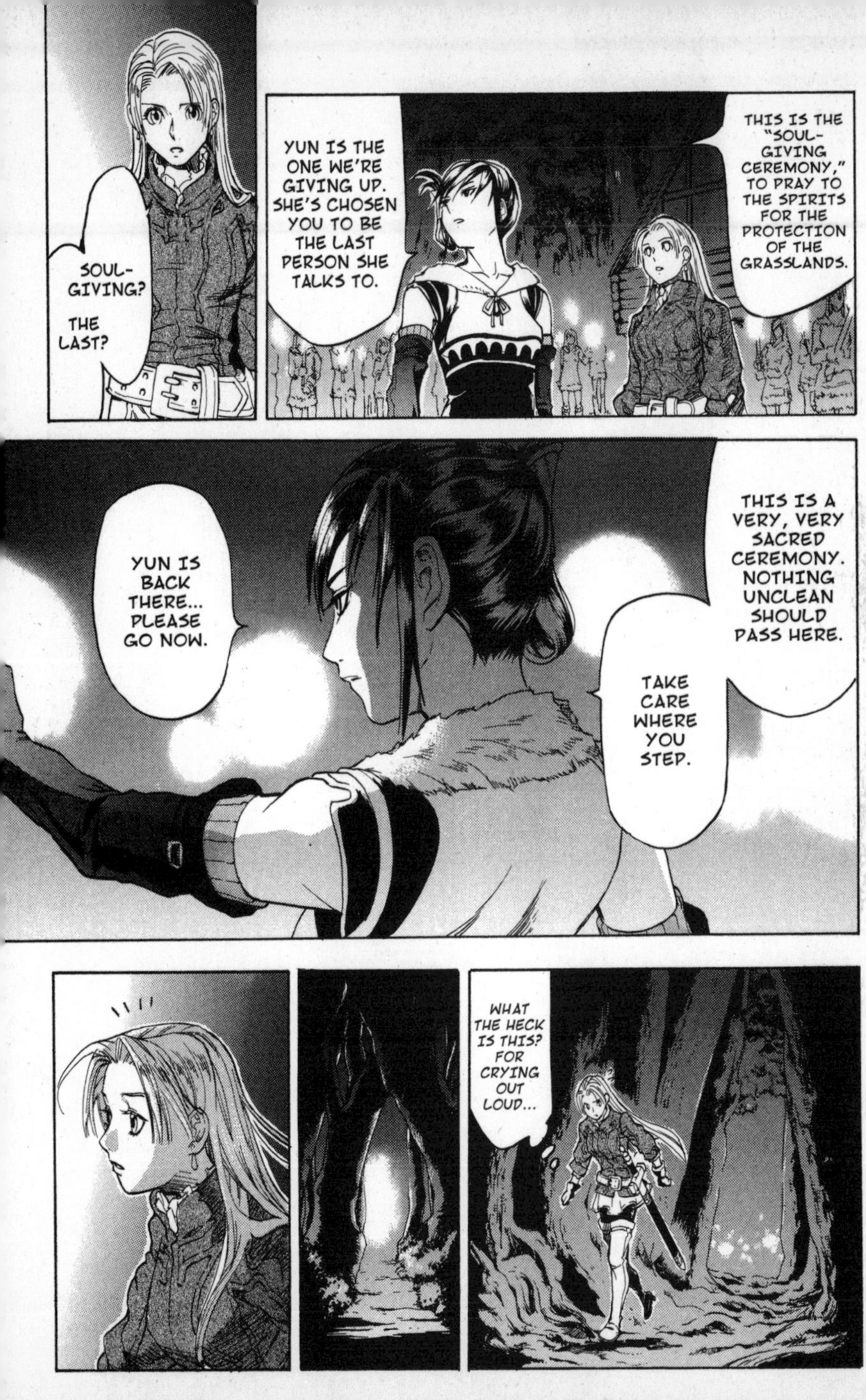
THIS IS THE "SOUL-GIVING CEREMONY," TO PRAY TO THE SPIRITS FOR THE PROTECTION OF THE GRASSLANDS.
YUN IS THE ONE WE'RE GIVING UP. SHE'S CHOSEN YOU TO BE THE LAST PERSON SHE TALKS TO.
SOUL-GIVING?
THE LAST?
THIS IS A VERY, VERY SACRED CEREMONY. NOTHING UNCLEAN SHOULD PASS HERE.
TAKE CARE WHERE YOU STEP.
YUN IS BACK THERE... PLEASE GO NOW.
WHAT THE HECK IS THIS? FOR CRYING OUT LOUD...

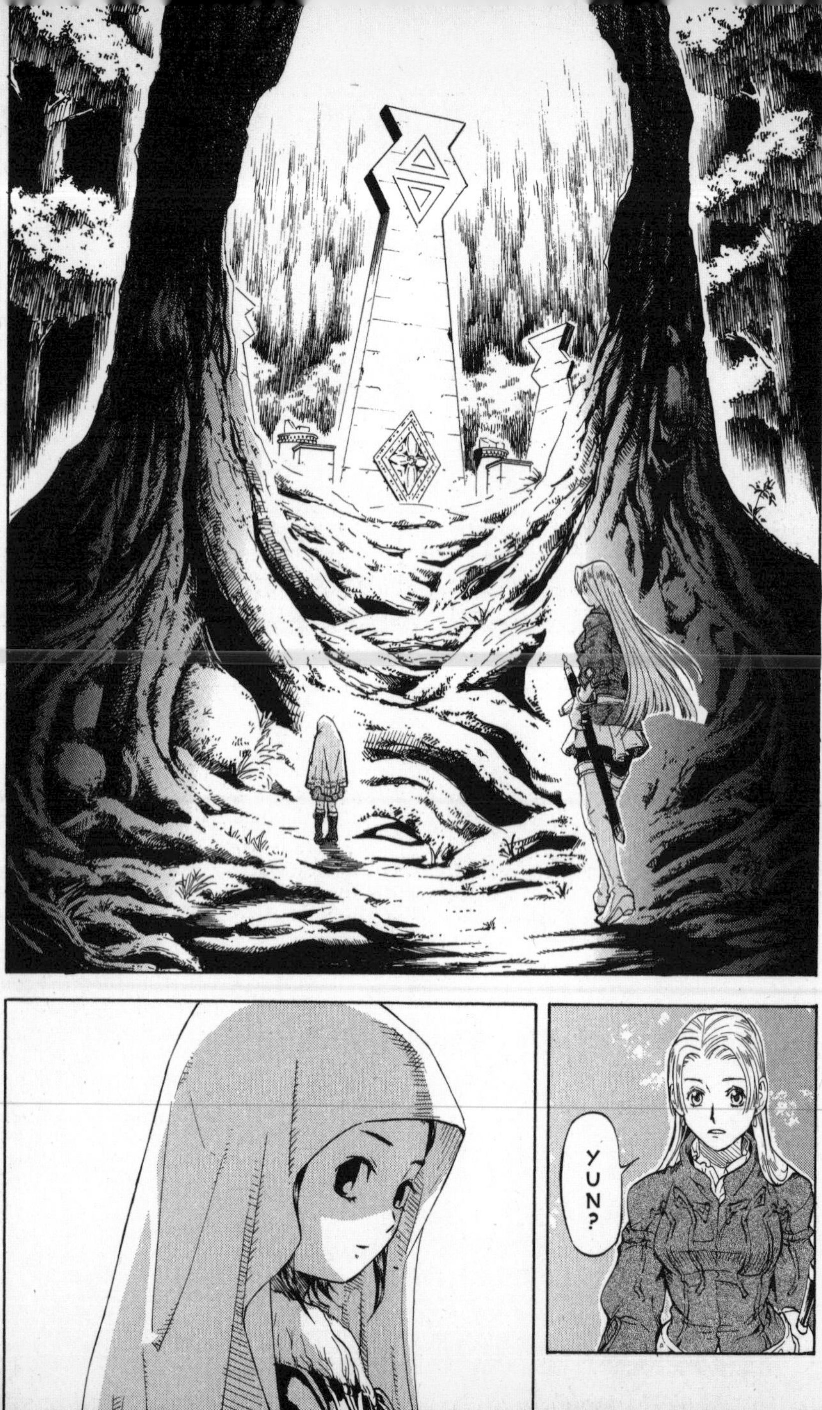
YUN?

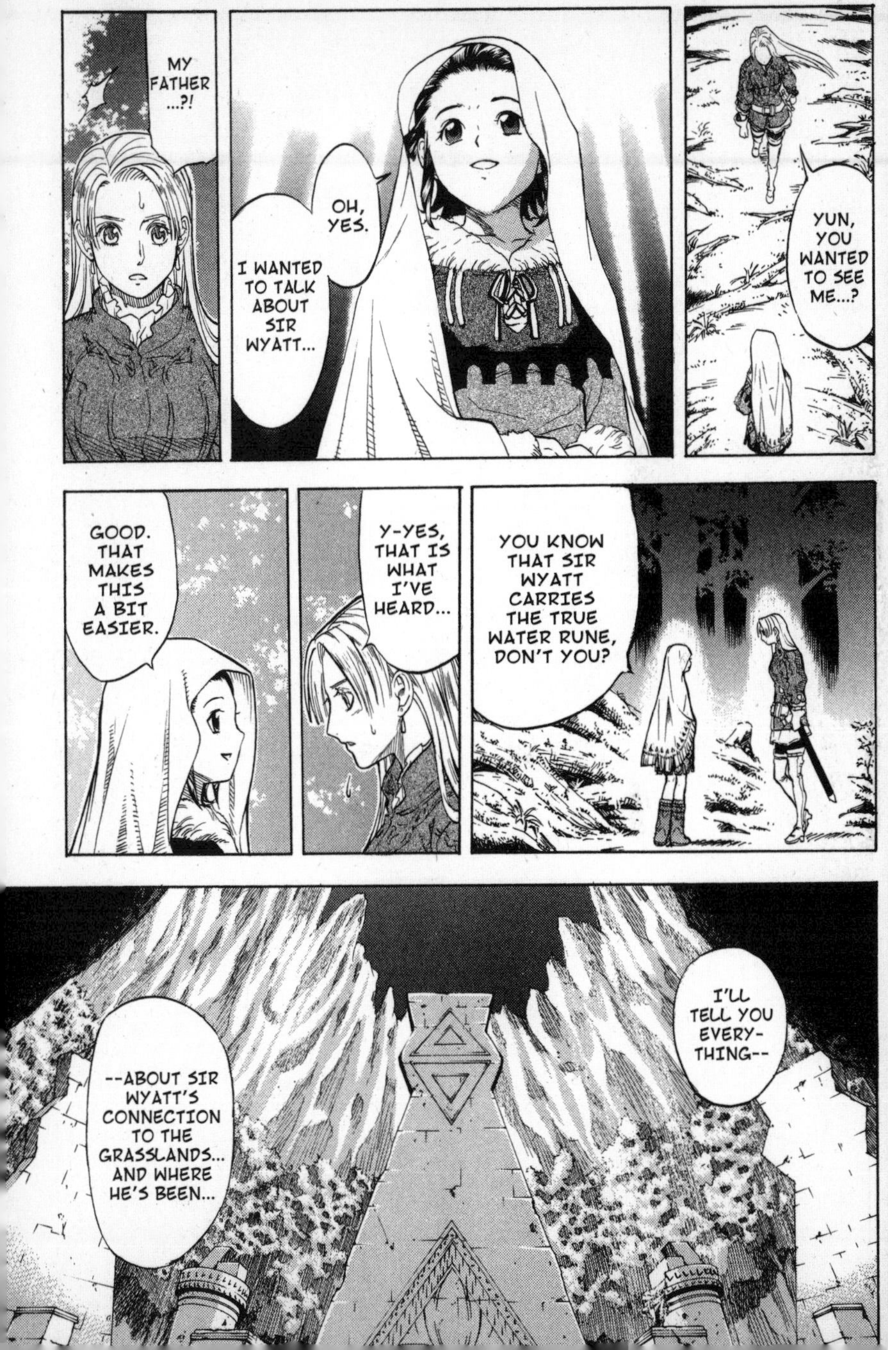
YUN, YOU WANTED TO SEE ME...?
OH, YES.
I WANTED TO TALK ABOUT SIR WYATT...
MY FATHER ...?!
YOU KNOW THAT SIR WYATT CARRIES THE TRUE WATER RUNE, DON'T YOU?
Y-YES, THAT IS WHAT I'VE HEARD...
GOOD. THAT MAKES THIS A BIT EASIER.
I'LL TELL YOU EVERY-THING--
--ABOUT SIR WYATT'S CONNECTION TO THE GRASSLANDS... AND WHERE HE'S BEEN...

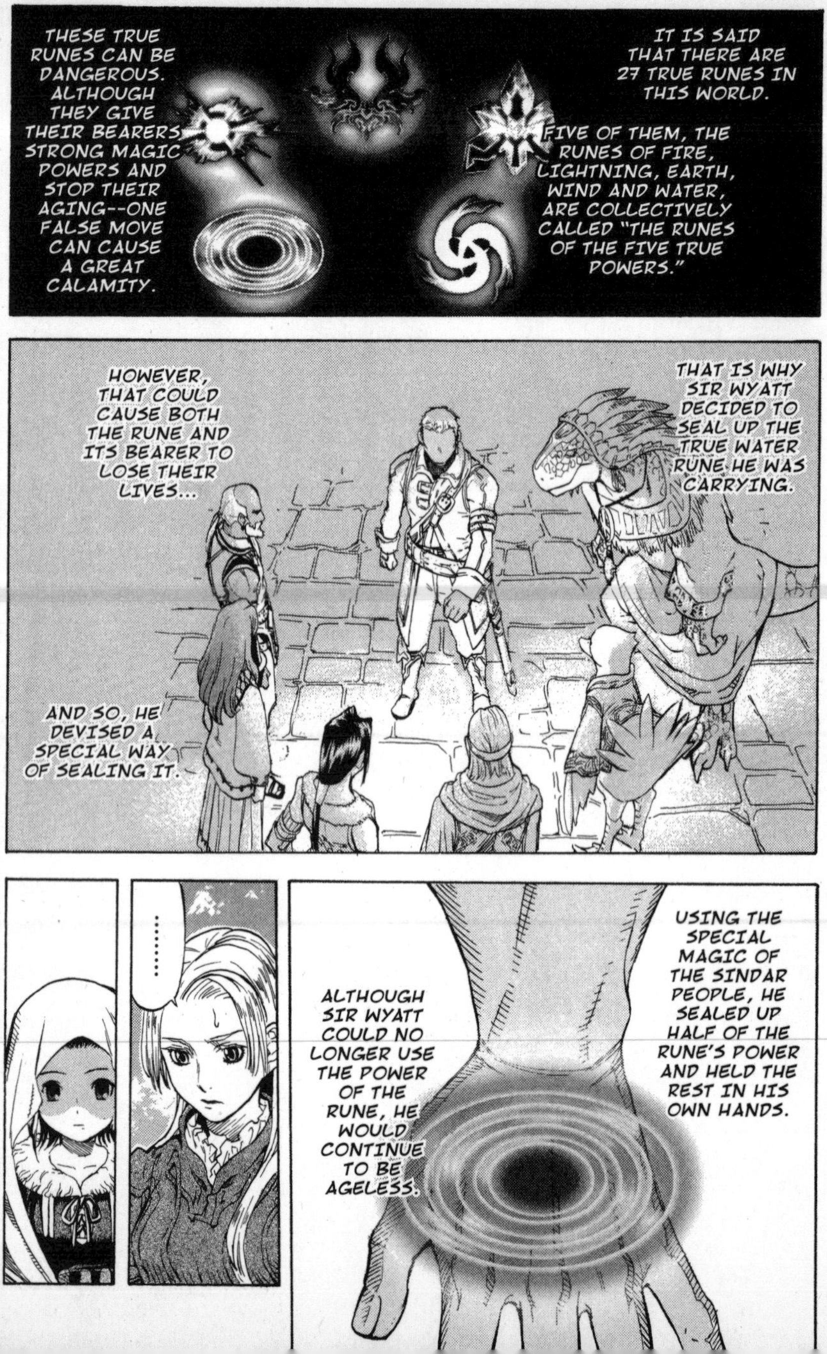
IT IS SAID THAT THERE ARE 27 TRUE RUNES IN THIS WORLD.
FIVE OF THEM, THE RUNES OF FIRE, LIGHTNING, EARTH, WIND AND WATER, ARE COLLECTIVELY CALLED "THE RUNES OF THE FIVE TRUE POWERS."
THESE TRUE RUNES CAN BE DANGEROUS. ALTHOUGH THEY GIVE THEIR BEARERS STRONG MAGIC POWERS AND STOP THEIR AGING--ONE FALSE MOVE CAN CAUSE A GREAT CALAMITY.
THAT IS WHY SIR WYATT DECIDED TO SEAL UP THE TRUE WATER RUNE HE WAS CARRYING.
HOWEVER, THAT COULD CAUSE BOTH THE RUNE AND ITS BEARER TO LOSE THEIR LIVES...
AND SO, HE DEVISED A SPECIAL WAY OF SEALING IT.
USING THE SPECIAL MAGIC OF THE SINDAR PEOPLE, HE SEALED UP HALF OF THE RUNE'S POWER AND HELD THE REST IN HIS OWN HANDS.
ALTHOUGH SIR WYATT COULD NO LONGER USE THE POWER OF THE RUNE, HE WOULD CONTINUE TO BE AGELESS.
......

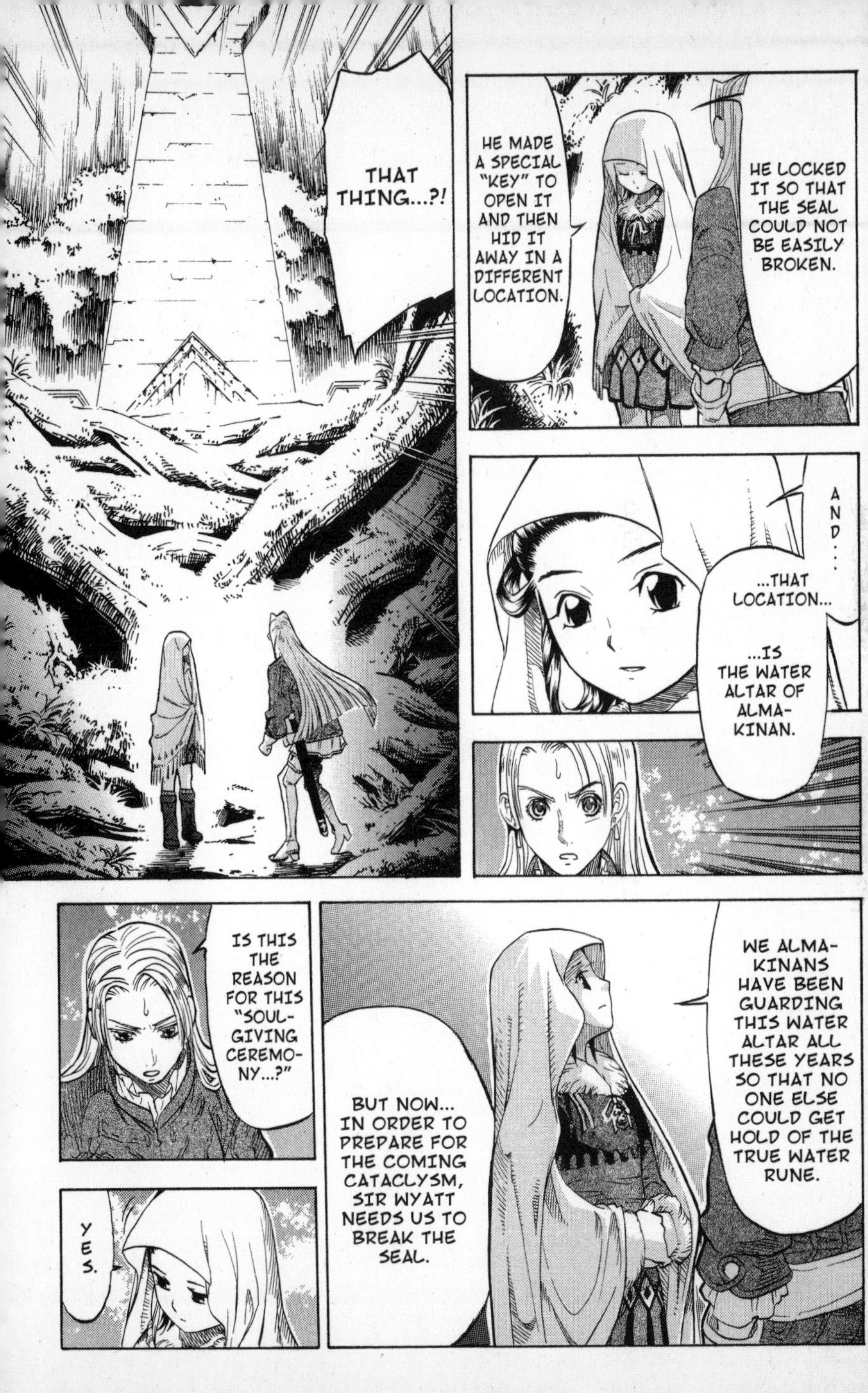
HE LOCKED IT SO THAT THE SEAL COULD NOT BE EASILY BROKEN.
HE MADE A SPECIAL "KEY" TO OPEN IT AND THEN HID IT AWAY IN A DIFFERENT LOCATION.
AND...
...THAT LOCATION...
...IS THE WATER ALTAR OF ALMA-KINAN.
THAT THING...?!
WE ALMA-KINANS HAVE BEEN GUARDING THIS WATER ALTAR ALL THESE YEARS SO THAT NO ONE ELSE COULD GET HOLD OF THE TRUE WATER RUNE.
BUT NOW... IN ORDER TO PREPARE FOR THE COMING CATACLYSM, SIR WYATT NEEDS US TO BREAK THE SEAL.
IS THIS THE REASON FOR THIS "SOUL-GIVING CEREMONY...?"
YES.

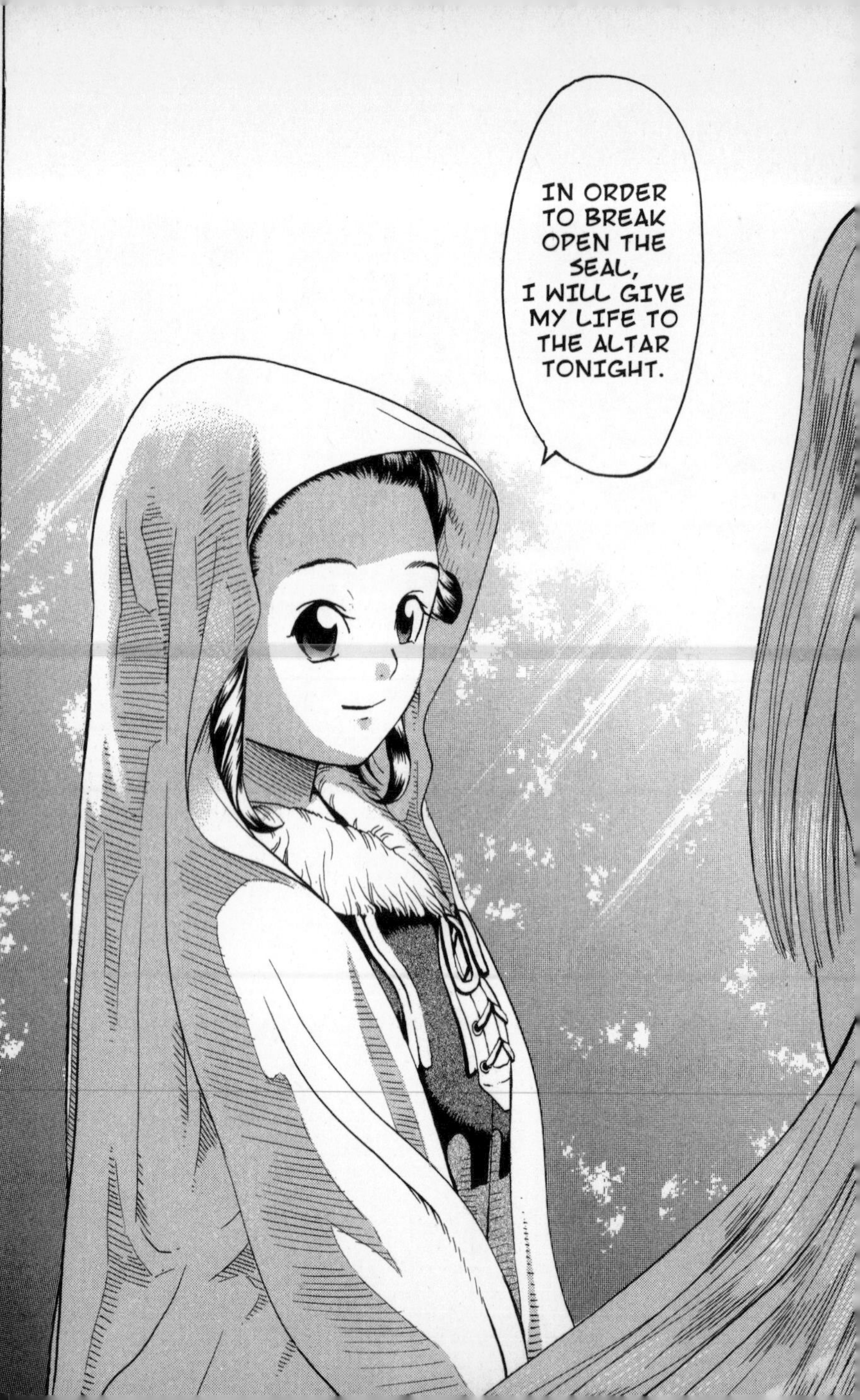
IN ORDER TO BREAK OPEN THE SEAL, I WILL GIVE MY LIFE TO THE ALTAR TONIGHT.

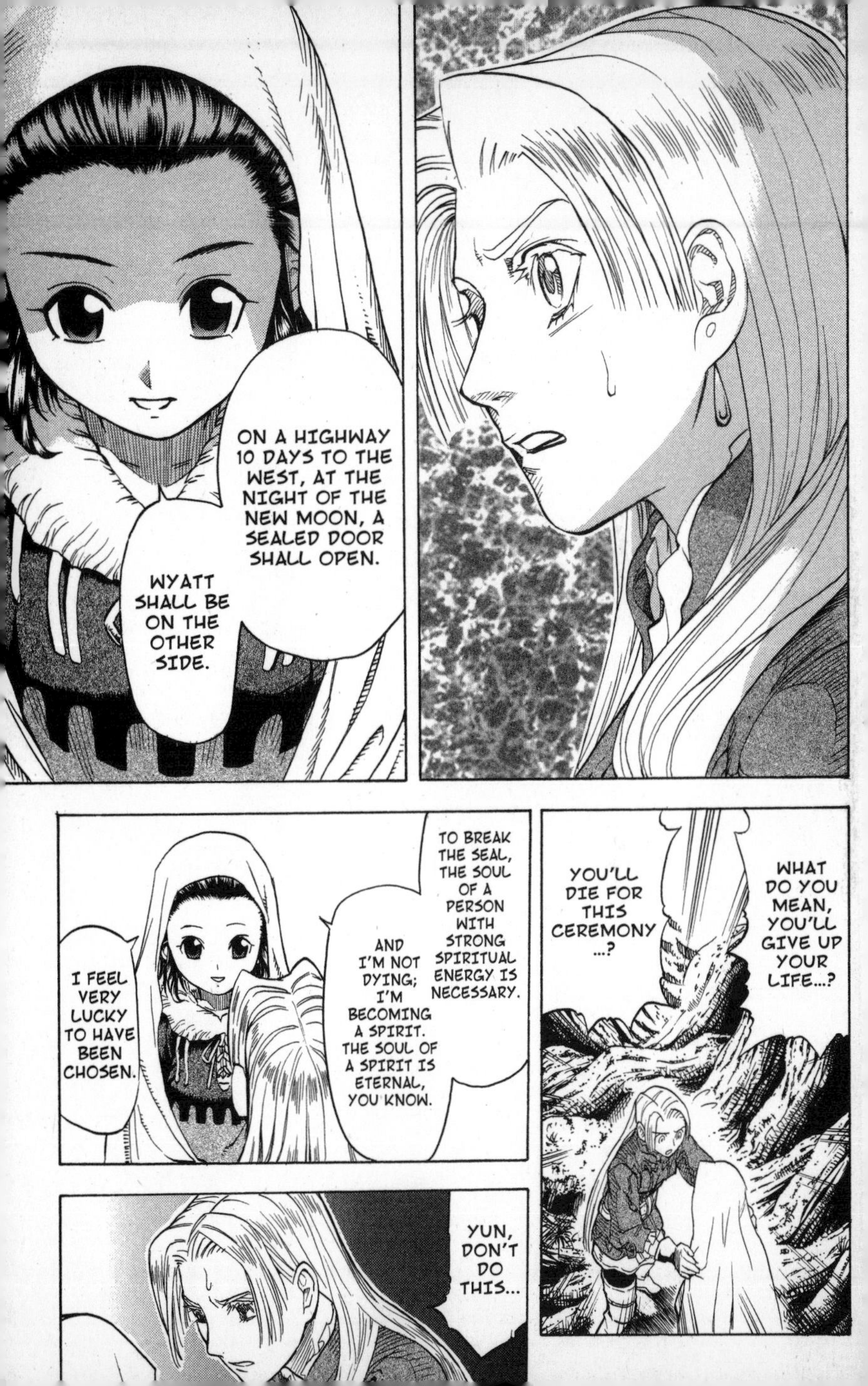
ON A HIGHWAY 10 DAYS TO THE WEST, AT THE NIGHT OF THE NEW MOON, A SEALED DOOR SHALL OPEN.
WYATT SHALL BE ON THE OTHER SIDE.
WHAT DO YOU MEAN, YOU'LL GIVE UP YOUR LIFE...?
YOU'LL DIE FOR THIS CEREMONY...?
TO BREAK THE SEAL, THE SOUL OF A PERSON WITH STRONG SPIRITUAL ENERGY IS NECESSARY.
AND I'M NOT DYING; I'M BECOMING A SPIRIT. THE SOUL OF A SPIRIT IS ETERNAL, YOU KNOW.
I FEEL VERY LUCKY TO HAVE BEEN CHOSEN.
YUN, DON'T DO THIS...

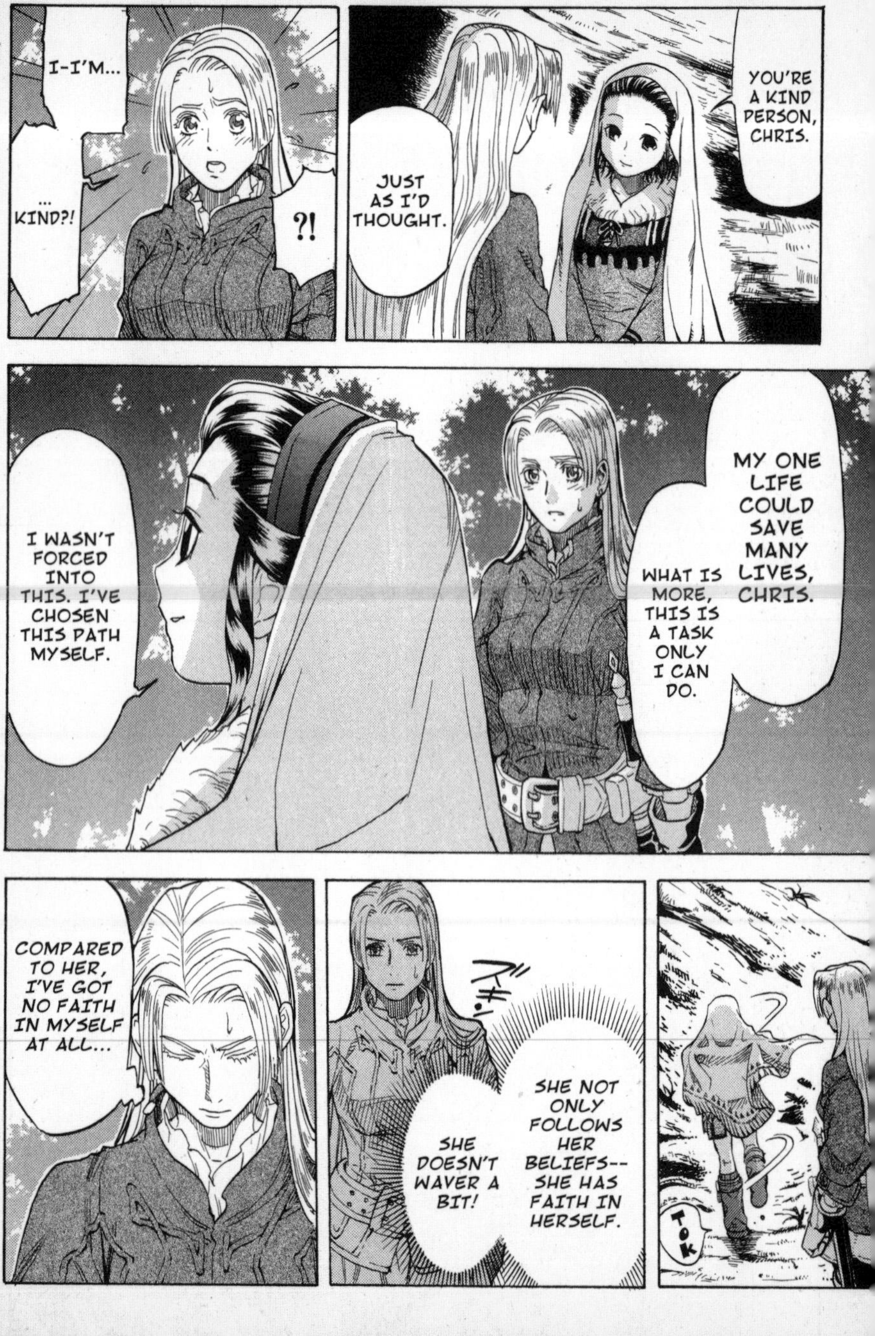

YOU'RE A KIND PERSON, CHRIS.
JUST AS I'D THOUGHT.
I-I'M...
...KIND?!
?!
MY ONE LIFE COULD SAVE MANY LIVES, CHRIS.
WHAT IS MORE, THIS IS A TASK ONLY I CAN DO.
I WASN'T FORCED INTO THIS. I'VE CHOSEN THIS PATH MYSELF.
TOK
SHE NOT ONLY FOLLOWS HER BELIEFS--SHE HAS FAITH IN HERSELF.
SHE DOESN'T WAVER A BIT!
COMPARED TO HER, I'VE GOT NO FAITH IN MYSELF AT ALL...

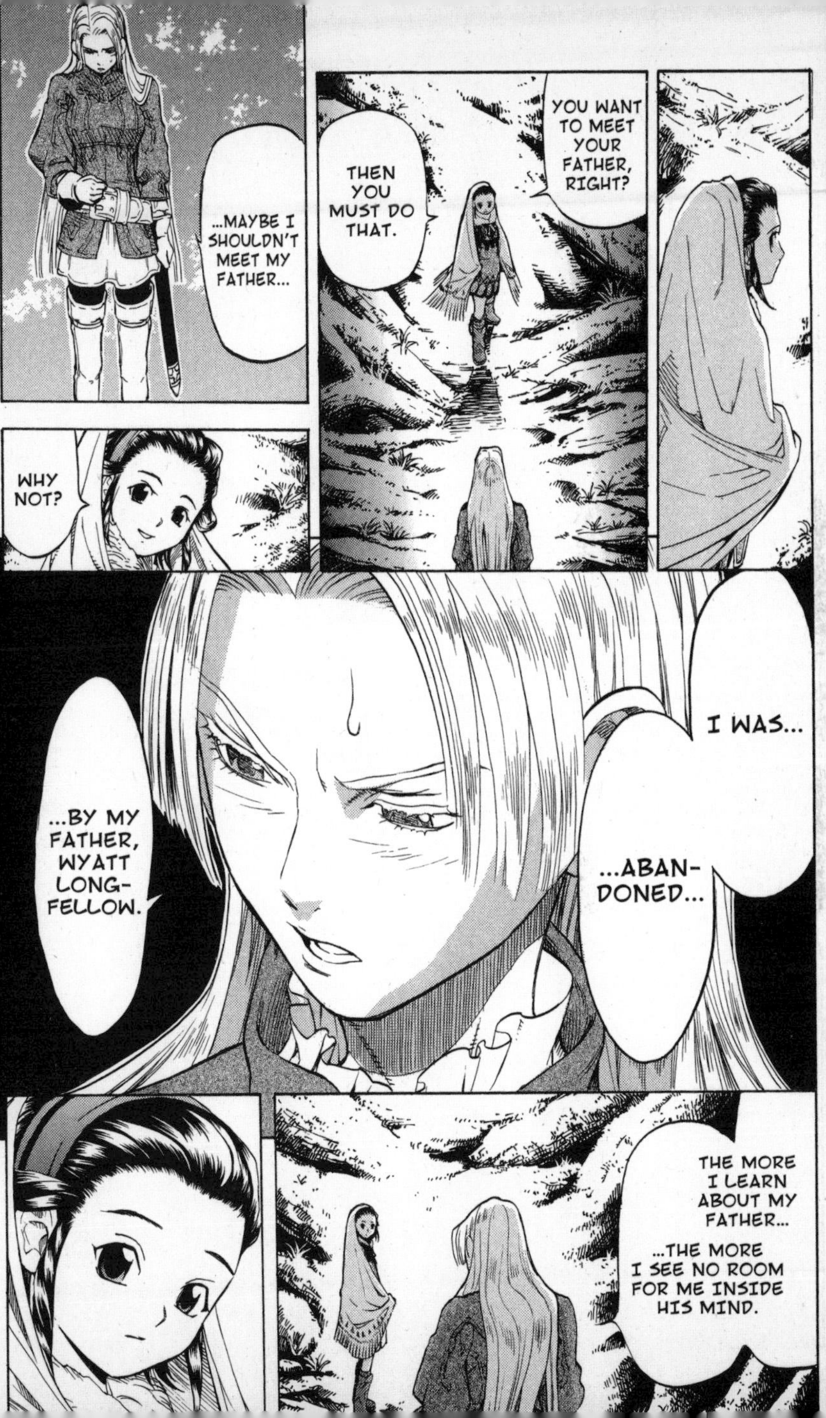
YOU WANT TO MEET YOUR FATHER, RIGHT?
THEN YOU MUST DO THAT.
...MAYBE I SHOULDN'T MEET MY FATHER...
WHY NOT?
I WAS...
...ABAN-DONED...
...BY MY FATHER, WYATT LONG-FELLOW.
THE MORE I LEARN ABOUT MY FATHER...
...THE MORE I SEE NO ROOM FOR ME INSIDE HIS MIND.

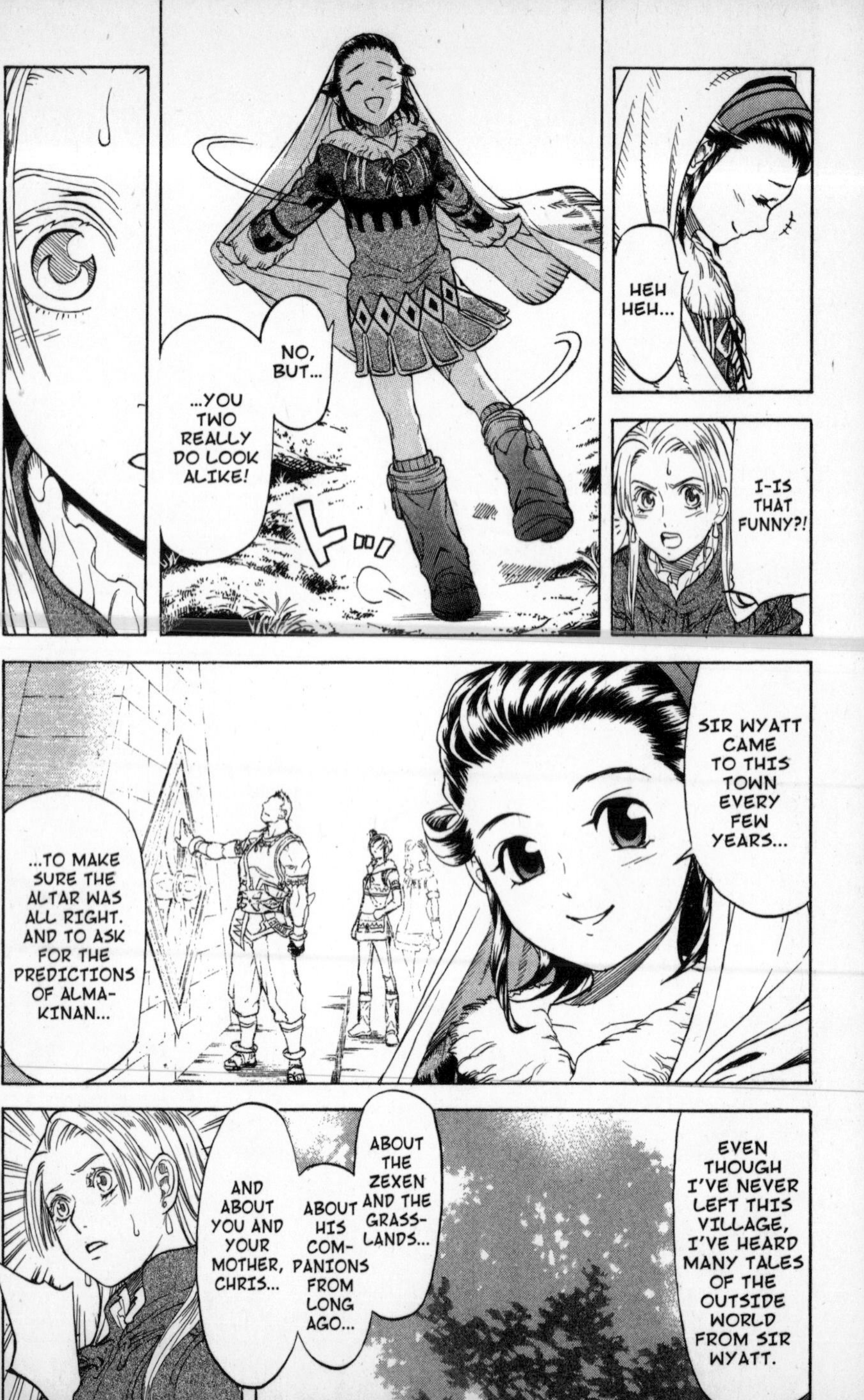
HEH HEH...
I-IS THAT FUNNY?!
NO, BUT...
...YOU TWO REALLY DO LOOK ALIKE!
トッ
SIR WYATT CAME TO THIS TOWN EVERY FEW YEARS...
...TO MAKE SURE THE ALTAR WAS ALL RIGHT. AND TO ASK FOR THE PREDICTIONS OF ALMA-KINAN...
EVEN THOUGH I'VE NEVER LEFT THIS VILLAGE, I'VE HEARD MANY TALES OF THE OUTSIDE WORLD FROM SIR WYATT.
ABOUT THE ZEXEN AND THE GRASS-LANDS...
ABOUT HIS COM-PANIONS FROM LONG AGO...
AND ABOUT YOU AND YOUR MOTHER, CHRIS...

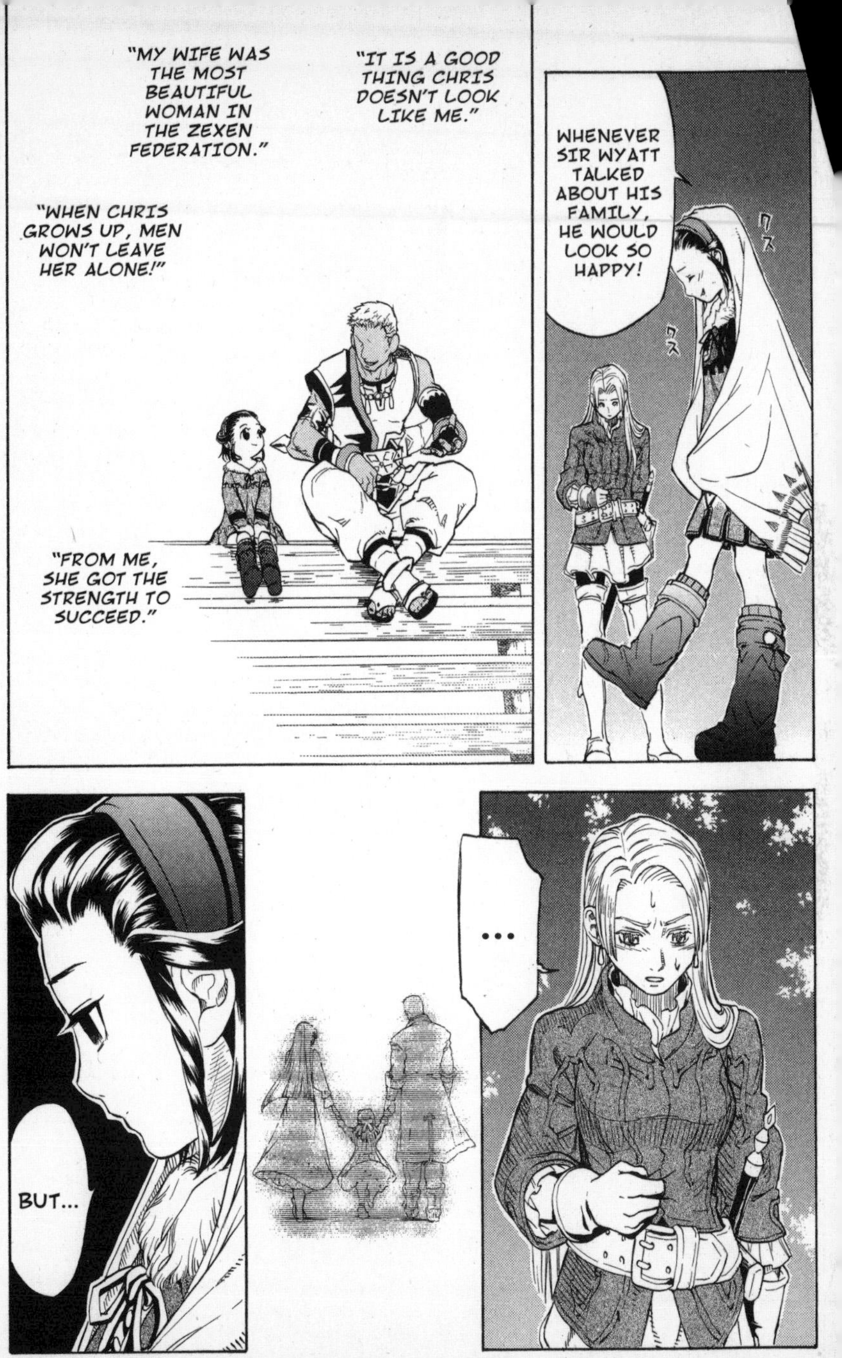
WHENEVER SIR WYATT TALKED ABOUT HIS FAMILY, HE WOULD LOOK SO HAPPY!
クス
クス
"IT IS A GOOD THING CHRIS DOESN'T LOOK LIKE ME."
"MY WIFE WAS THE MOST BEAUTIFUL WOMAN IN THE ZEXEN FEDERATION."
"WHEN CHRIS GROWS UP, MEN WON'T LEAVE HER ALONE!"
"FROM ME, SHE GOT THE STRENGTH TO SUCCEED."
...
BUT...

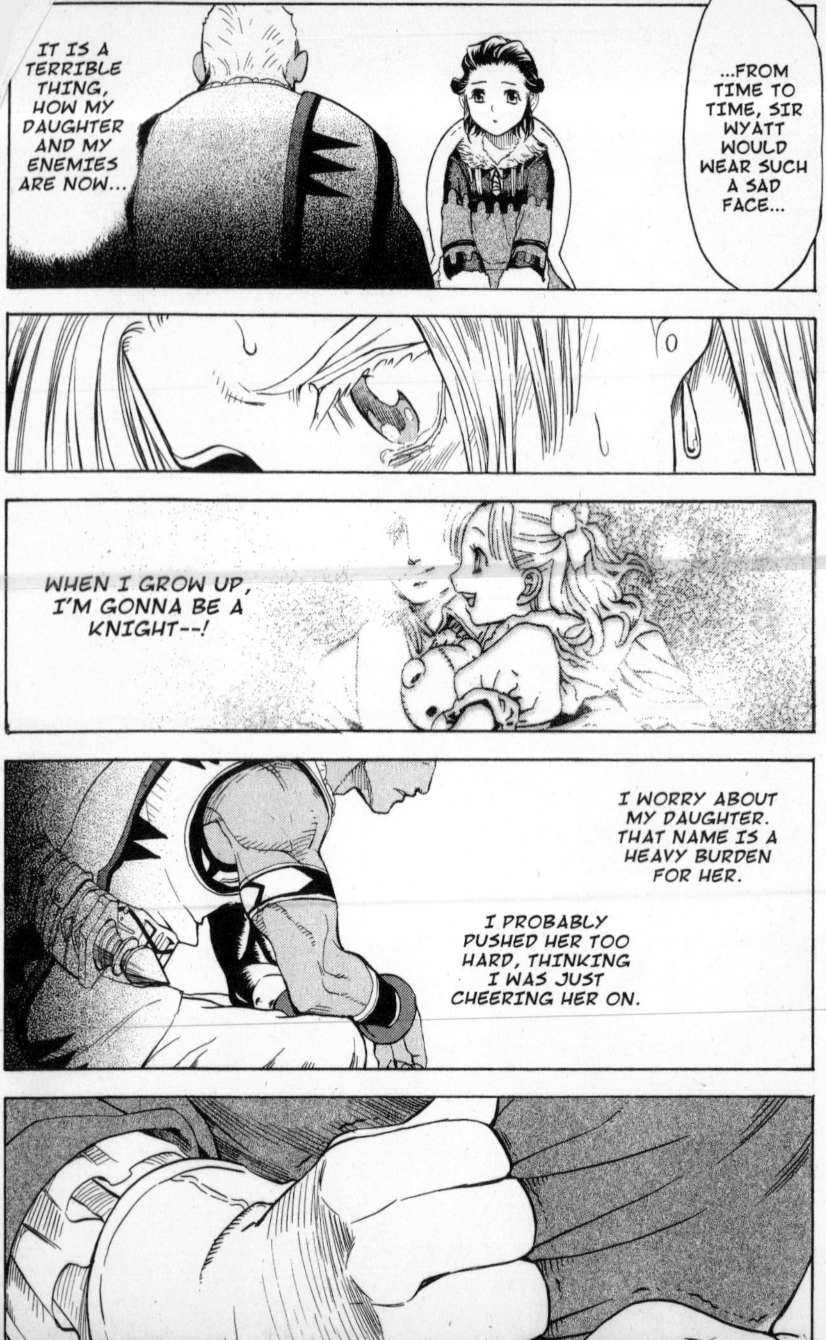
...FROM TIME TO TIME, SIR WYATT WOULD WEAR SUCH A SAD FACE...
IT IS A TERRIBLE THING, HOW MY DAUGHTER AND MY ENEMIES ARE NOW...
WHEN I GROW UP, I'M GONNA BE A KNIGHT--!
I WORRY ABOUT MY DAUGHTER. THAT NAME IS A HEAVY BURDEN FOR HER.
I PROBABLY PUSHED HER TOO HARD, THINKING I WAS JUST CHEERING HER ON.

IF ONLY I COULD HAVE BEEN THERE FOR MY WIFE'S FINAL MOMENTS...

I MUST STOP... IT IS NOT LIKE ME TO WORRY LIKE THIS...

NOT SINCE I ABANDONED MY FAMILY WHEN I WAS ESCAPING...

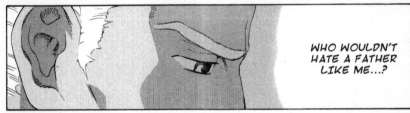

WHO WOULDN'T HATE A FATHER LIKE ME...?

--AND ONCE I'M A KNIGHT, I'LL STAY AT FATHER'S SIDE--

CHRIS...

SIR WYATT...

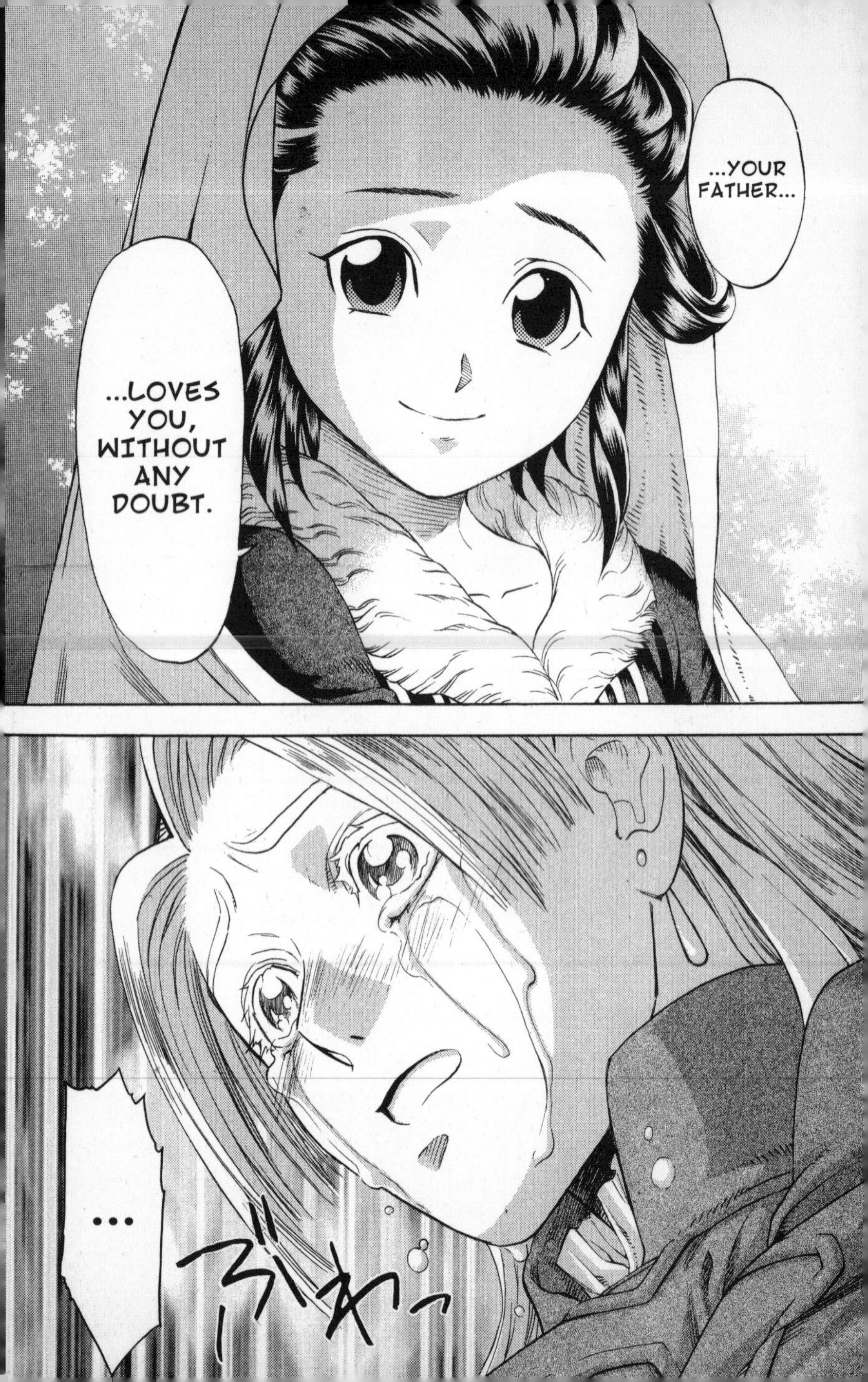
...YOUR FATHER...
...LOVES YOU, WITHOUT ANY DOUBT.
...
ぶわっ

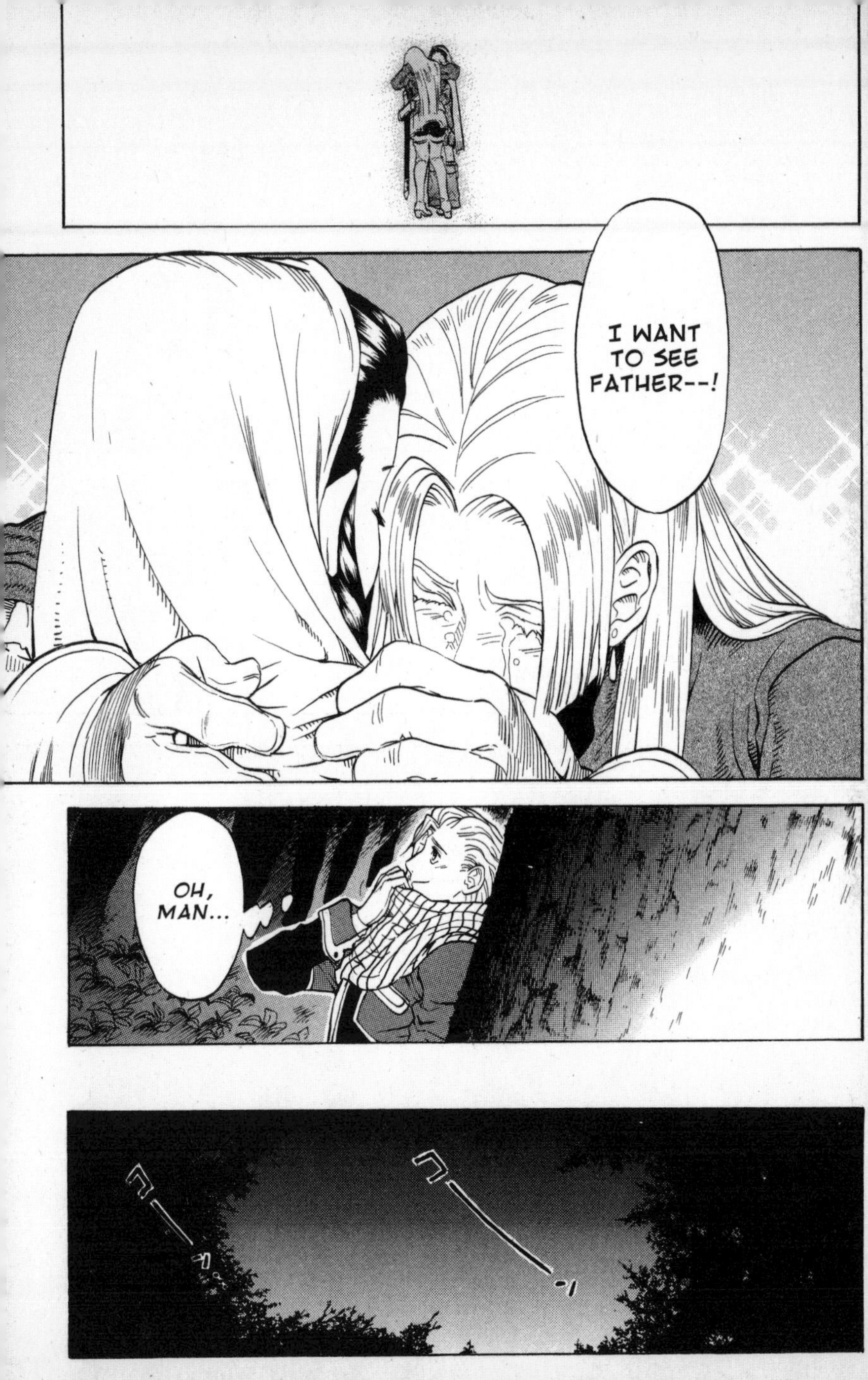
I WANT TO SEE FATHER--!
OH, MAN...

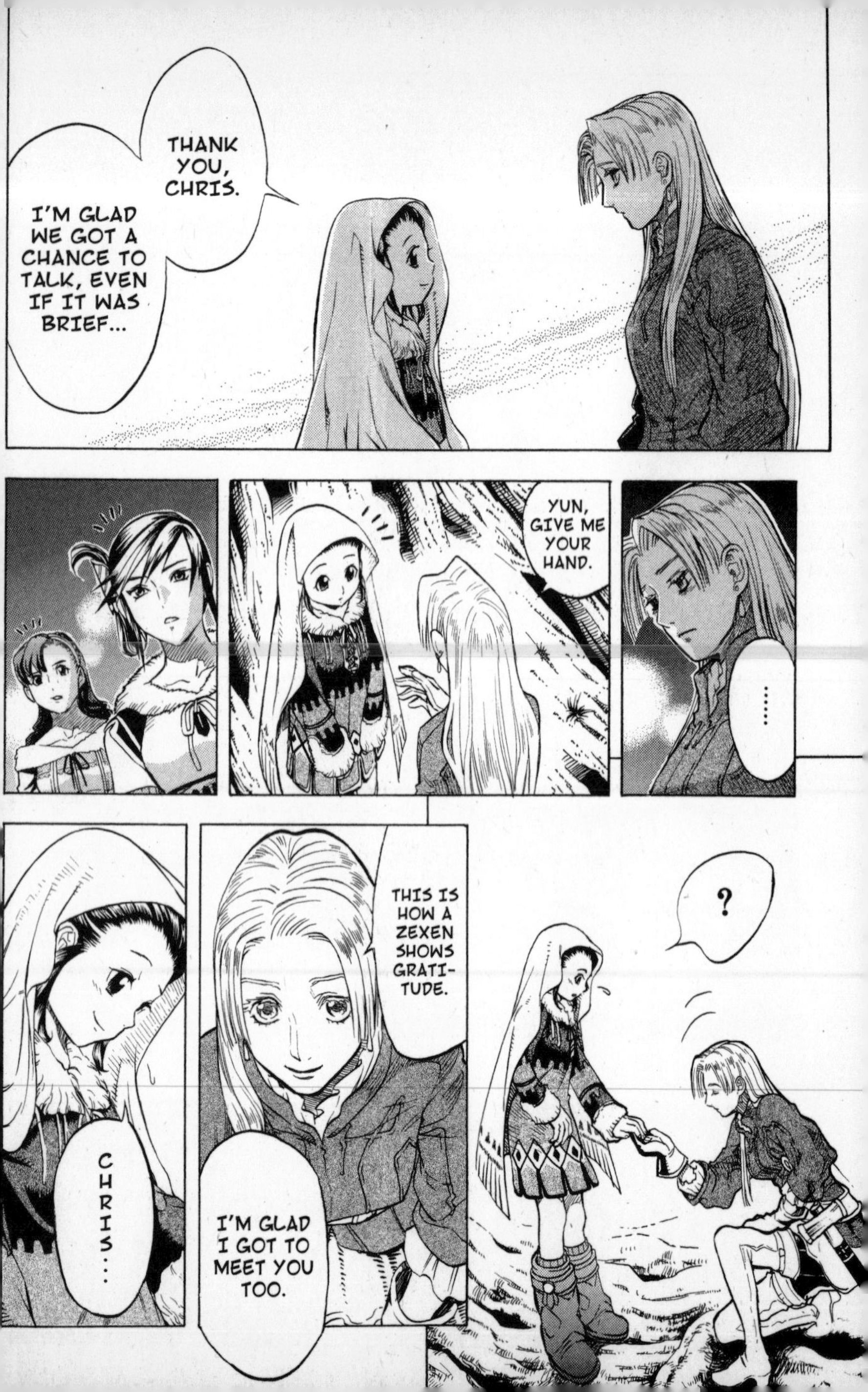
THANK YOU, CHRIS.
I'M GLAD WE GOT A CHANCE TO TALK, EVEN IF IT WAS BRIEF...
......
YUN, GIVE ME YOUR HAND.
?
THIS IS HOW A ZEXEN SHOWS GRATITUDE.
I'M GLAD I GOT TO MEET YOU TOO.
CHRIS...

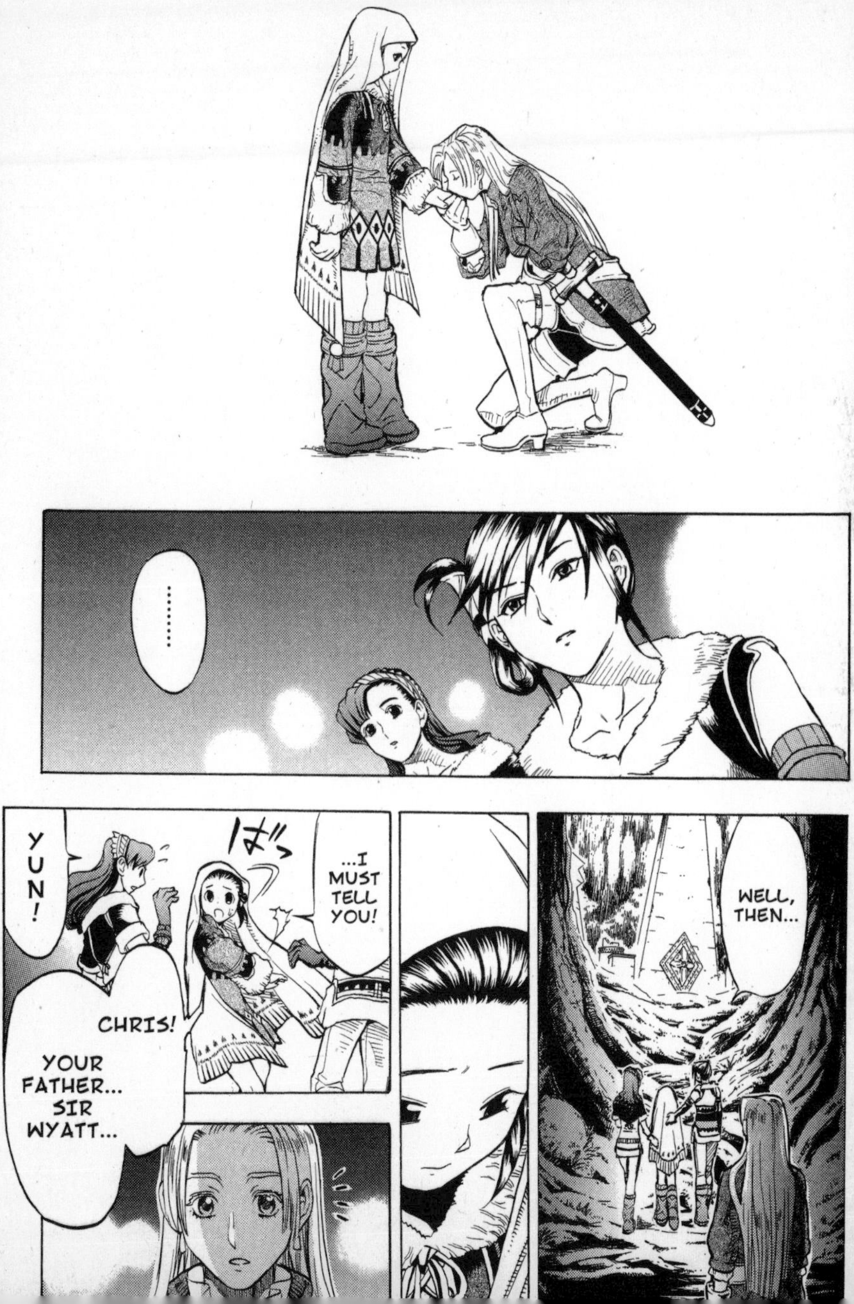
......
WELL, THEN...
...I MUST TELL YOU!
ばっ
YUN!
CHRIS! YOUR FATHER... SIR WYATT...

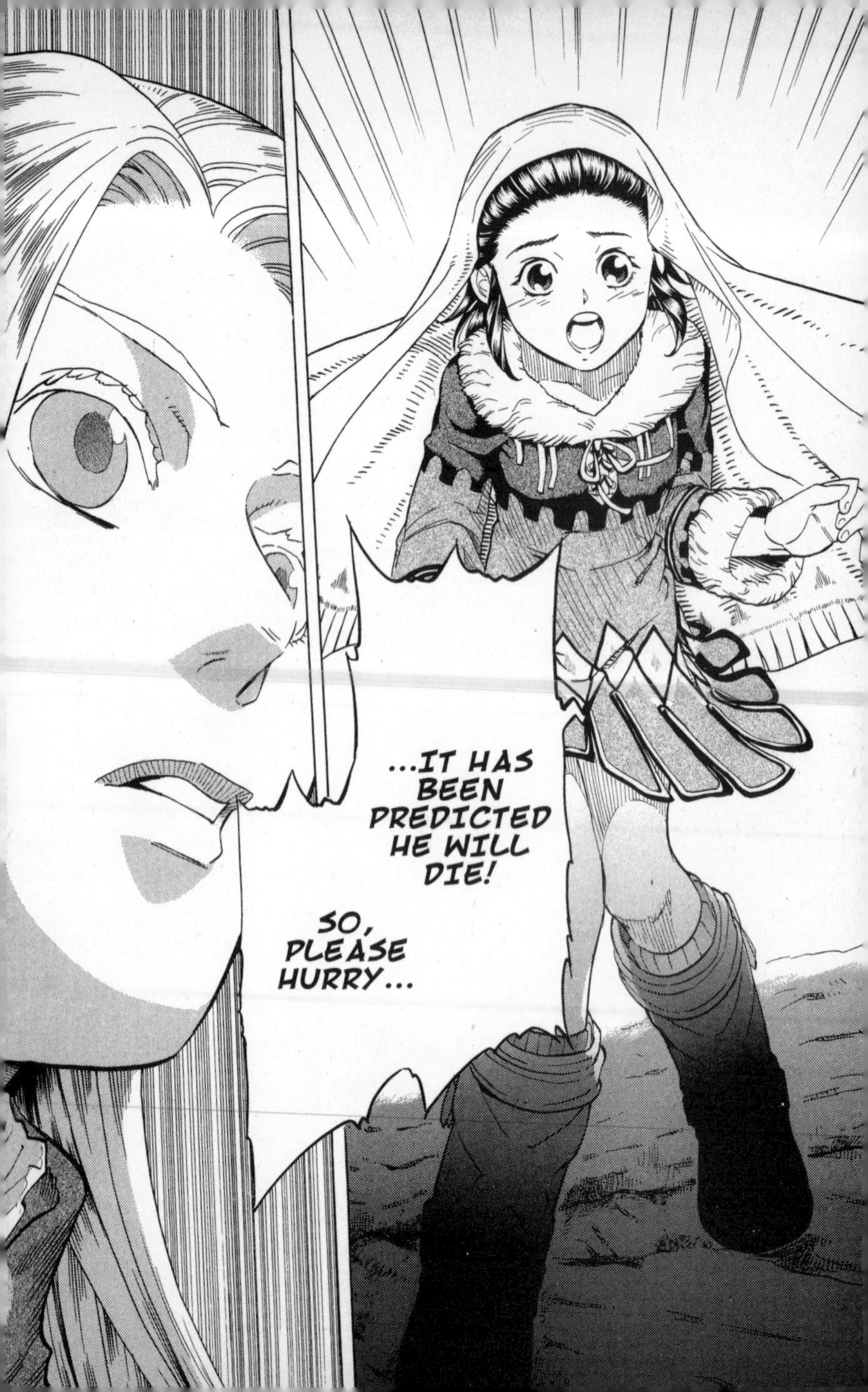
...IT HAS BEEN PREDICTED HE WILL DIE!
SO, PLEASE HURRY...

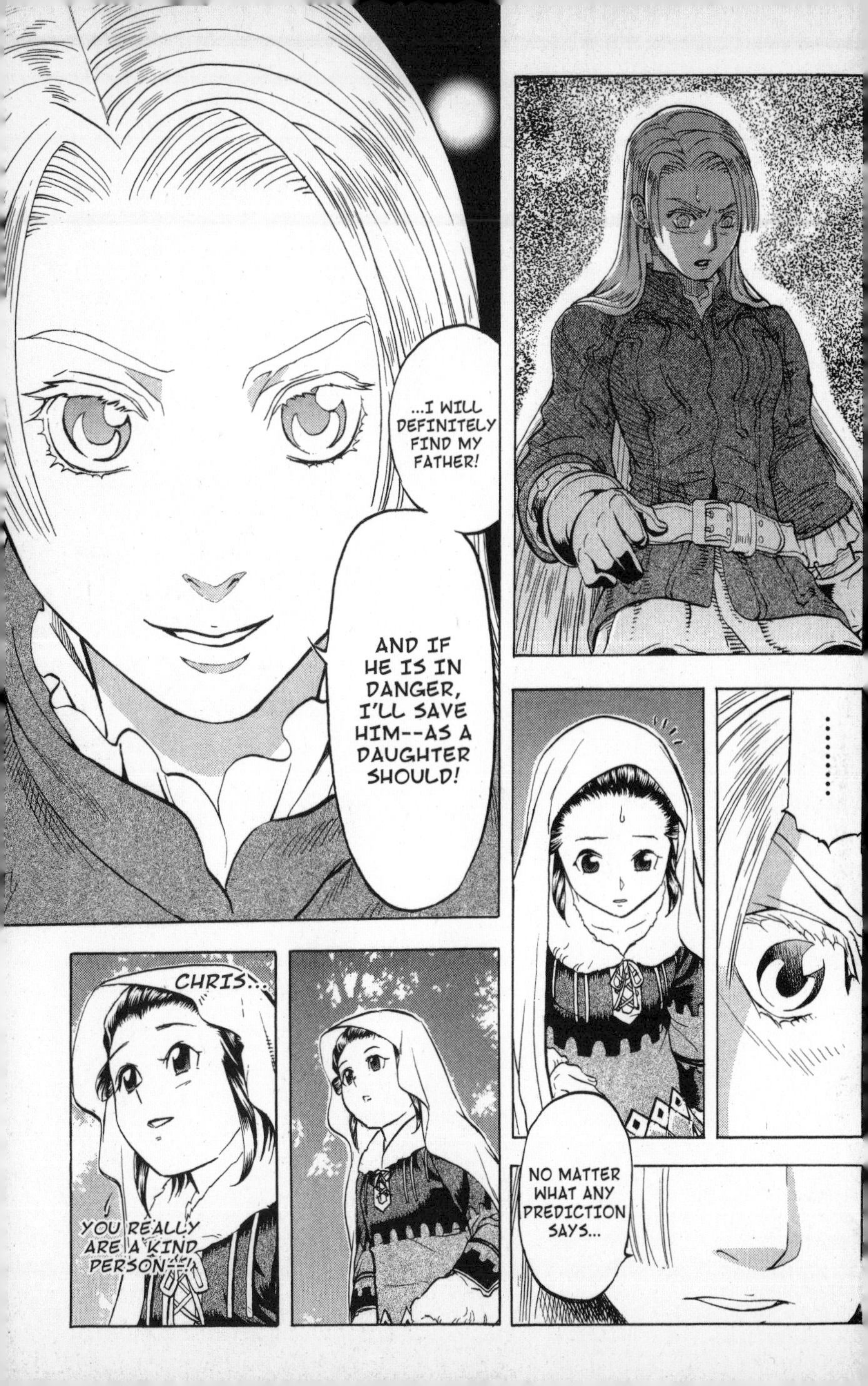

......
...I WILL DEFINITELY FIND MY FATHER!
AND IF HE IS IN DANGER, I'LL SAVE HIM--AS A DAUGHTER SHOULD!
NO MATTER WHAT ANY PREDICTION SAYS...
CHRIS...
YOU REALLY ARE A KIND PERSON--!

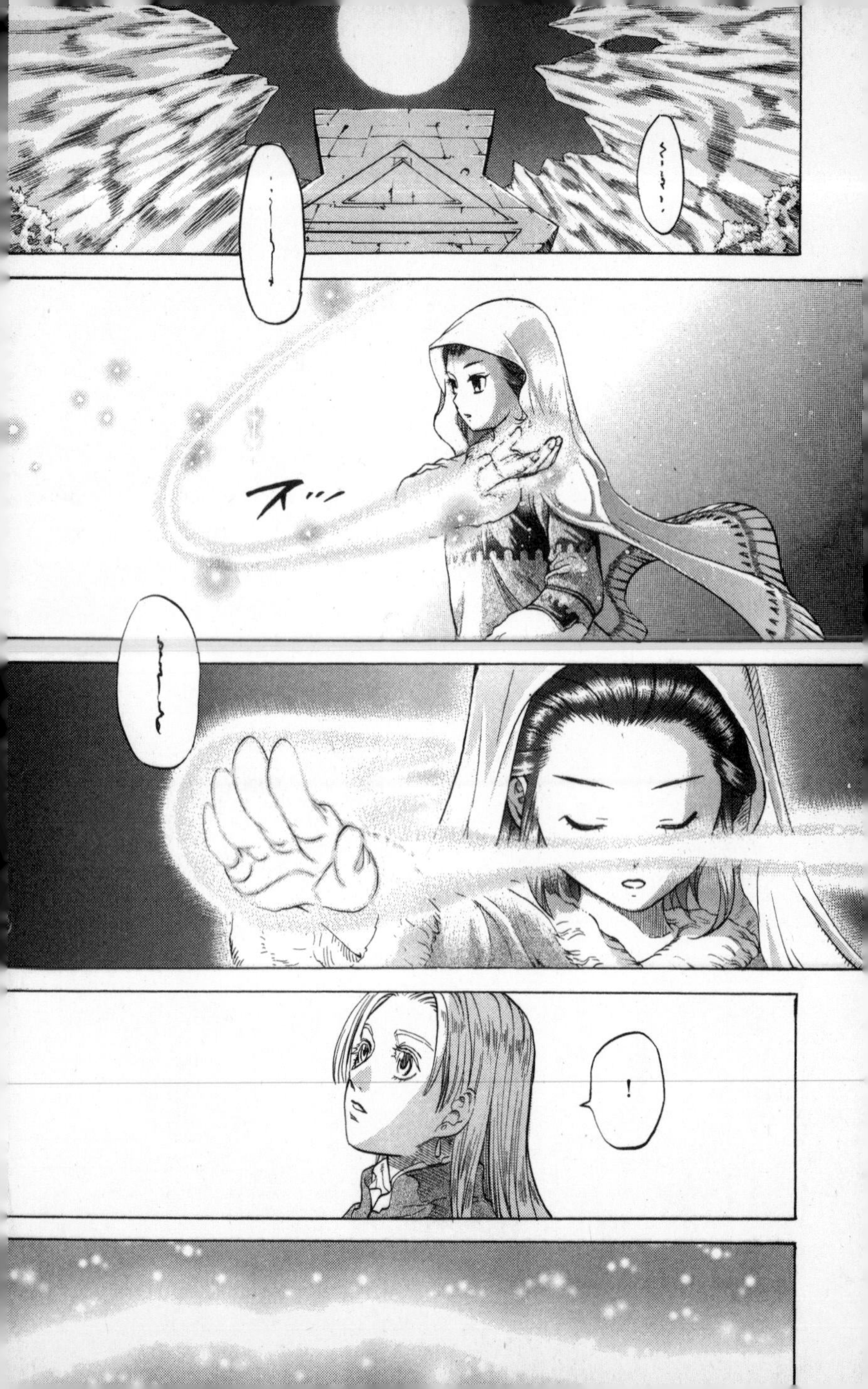
ズッ
!

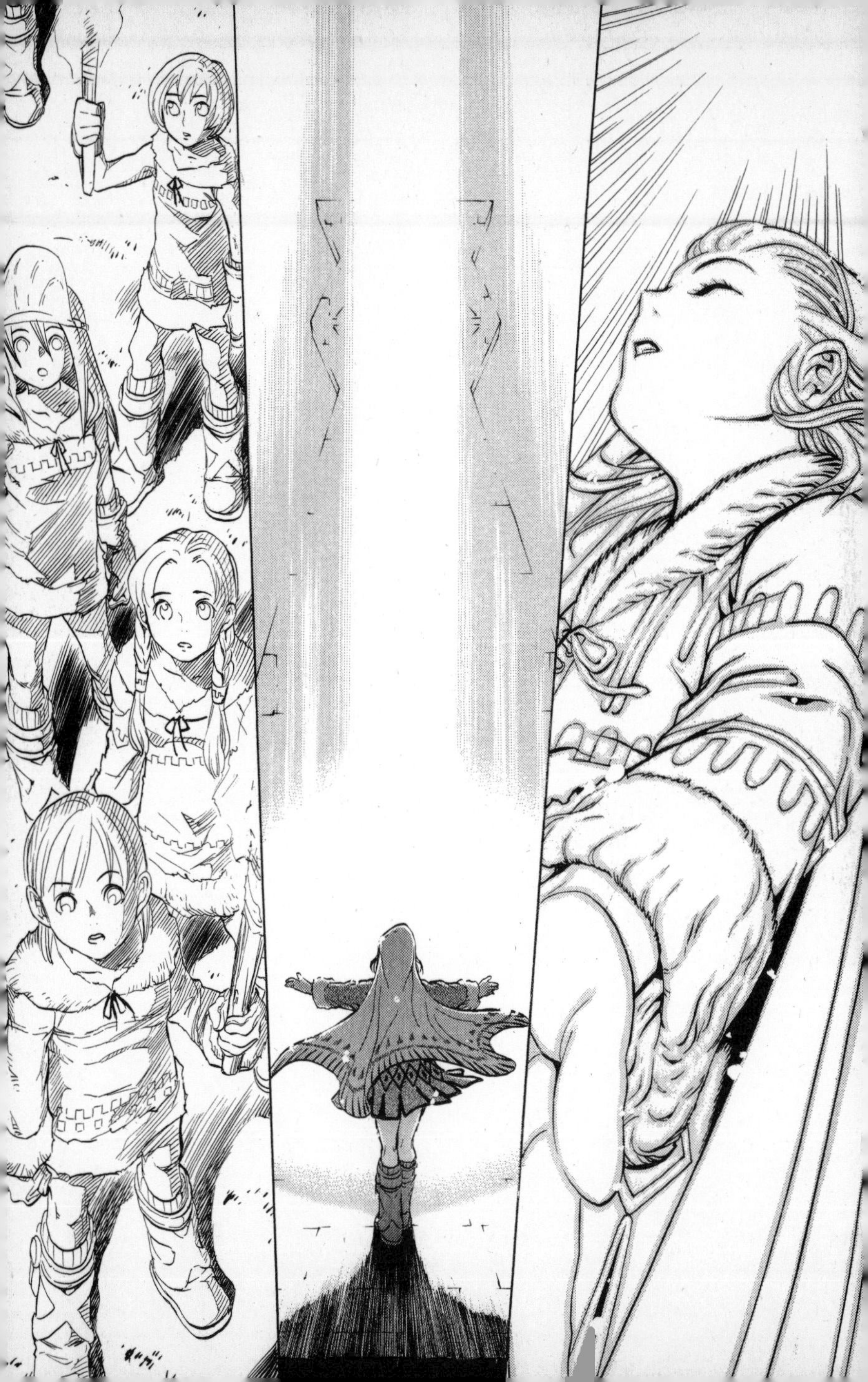

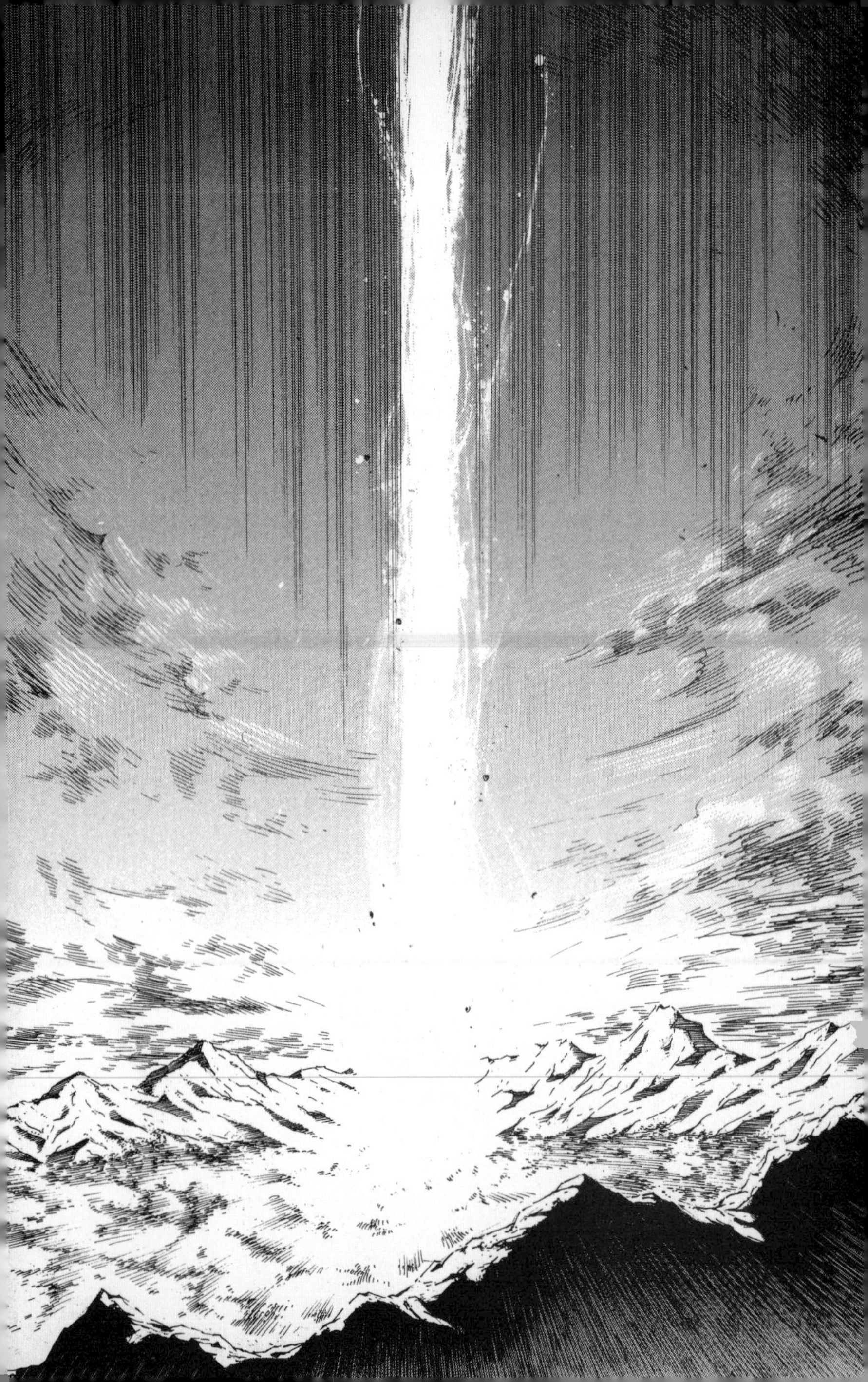

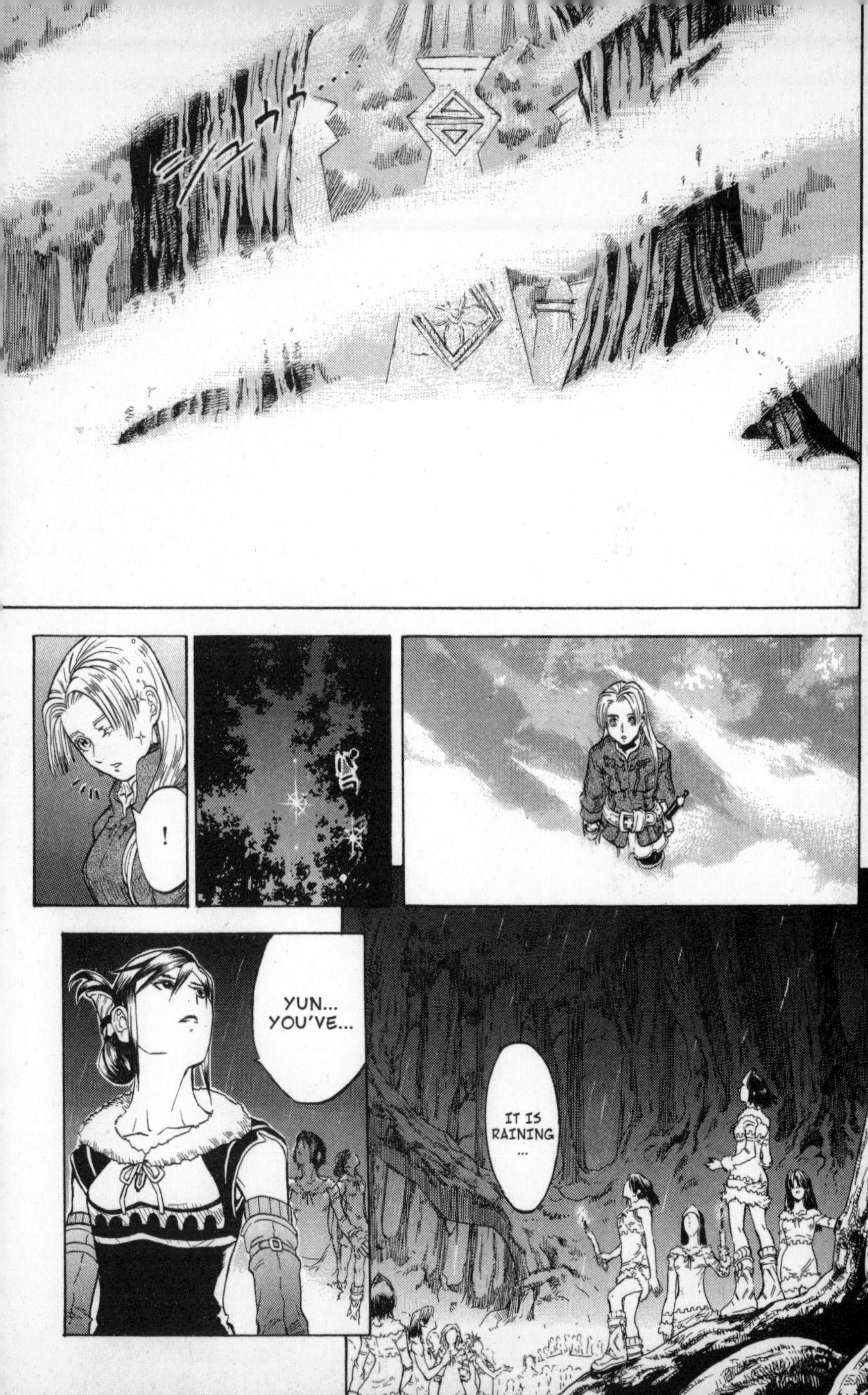
シュウウ…
!
IT IS RAINING ...
YUN... YOU'VE...

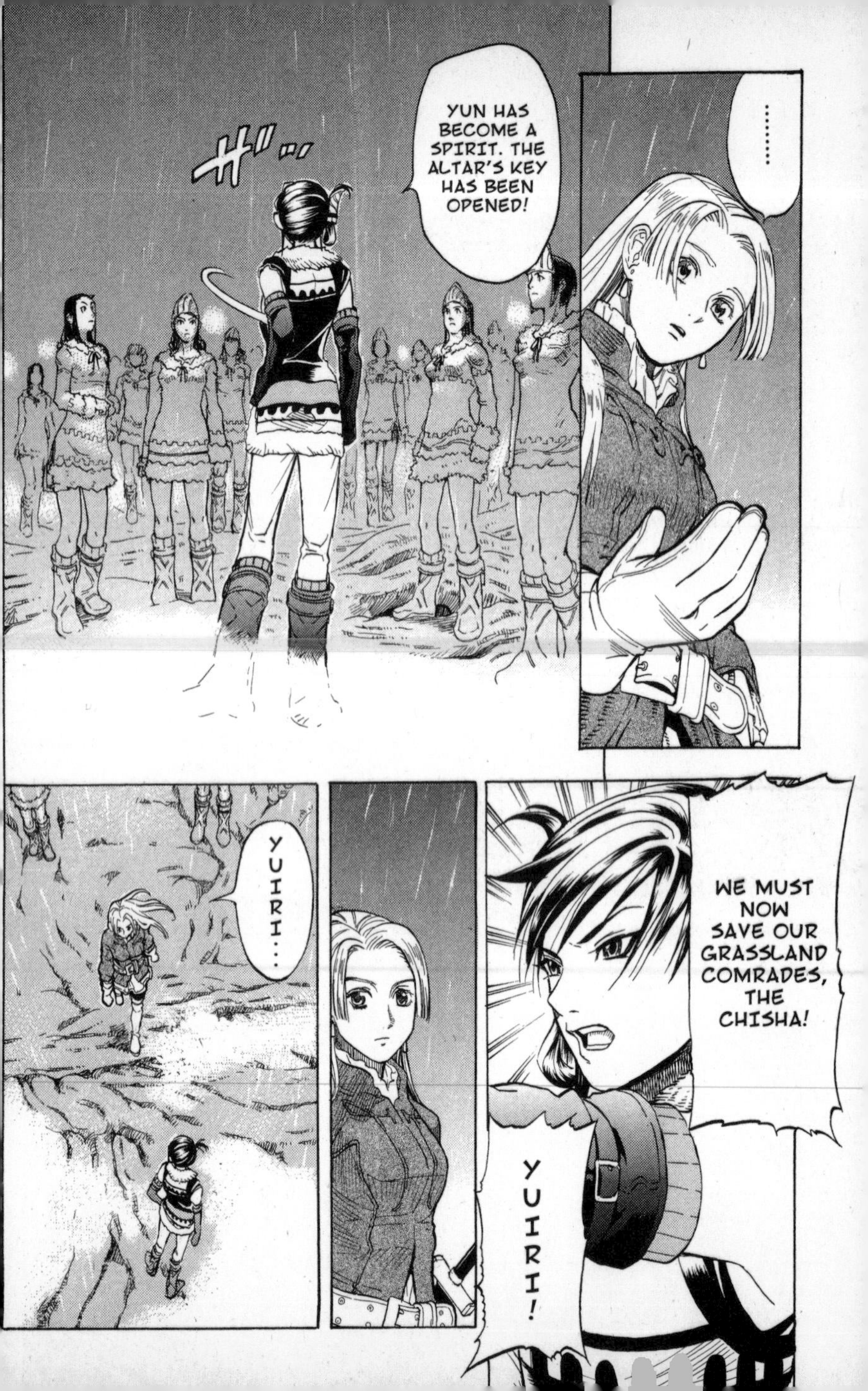

……
ザッ
YUN HAS BECOME A SPIRIT. THE ALTAR'S KEY HAS BEEN OPENED!
WE MUST NOW SAVE OUR GRASSLAND COMRADES, THE CHISHA!
YUIRI!
YUIRI…

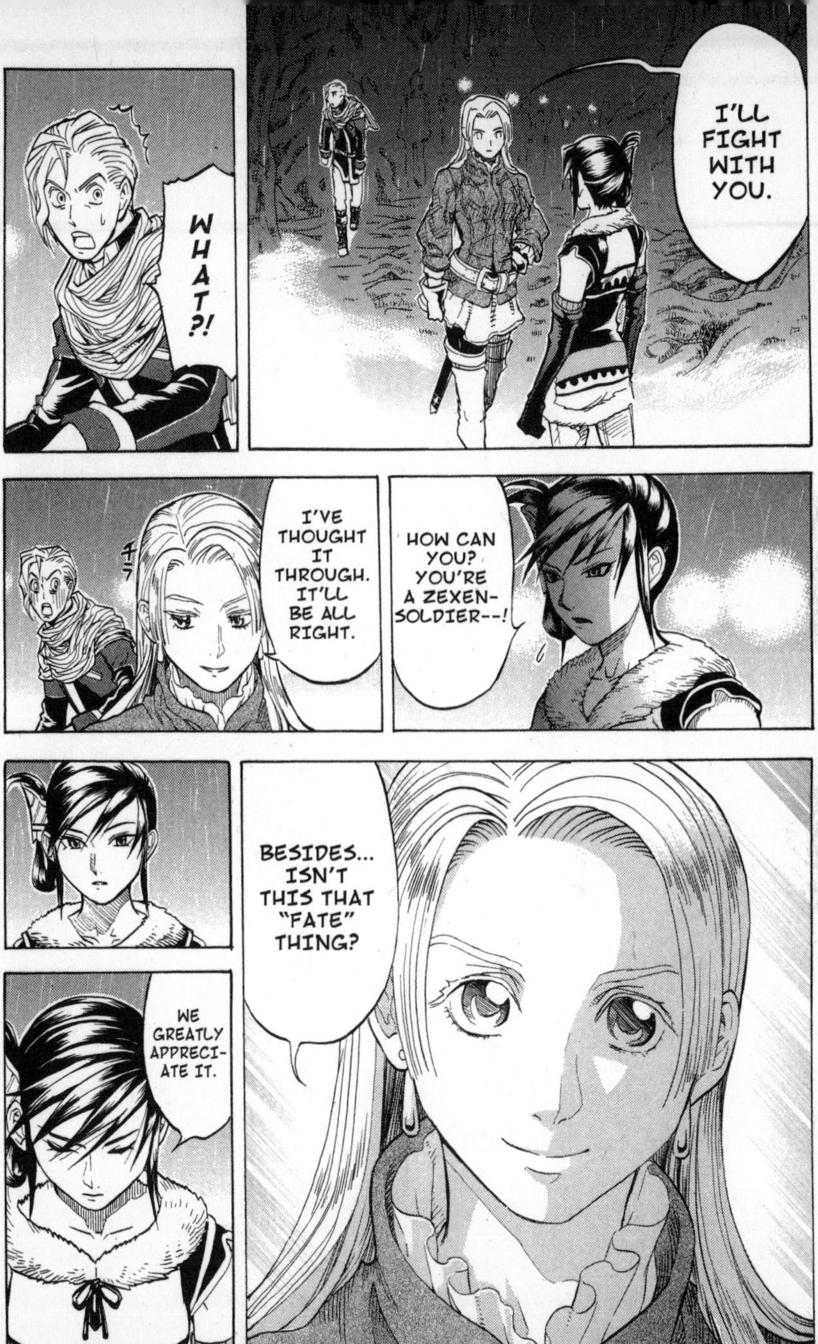
I'LL FIGHT WITH YOU.
WHAT?!
HOW CAN YOU? YOU'RE A ZEXEN-SOLDIER--!
I'VE THOUGHT IT THROUGH. IT'LL BE ALL RIGHT.
BESIDES... ISN'T THIS THAT "FATE" THING?
WE GREATLY APPRECI-ATE IT.

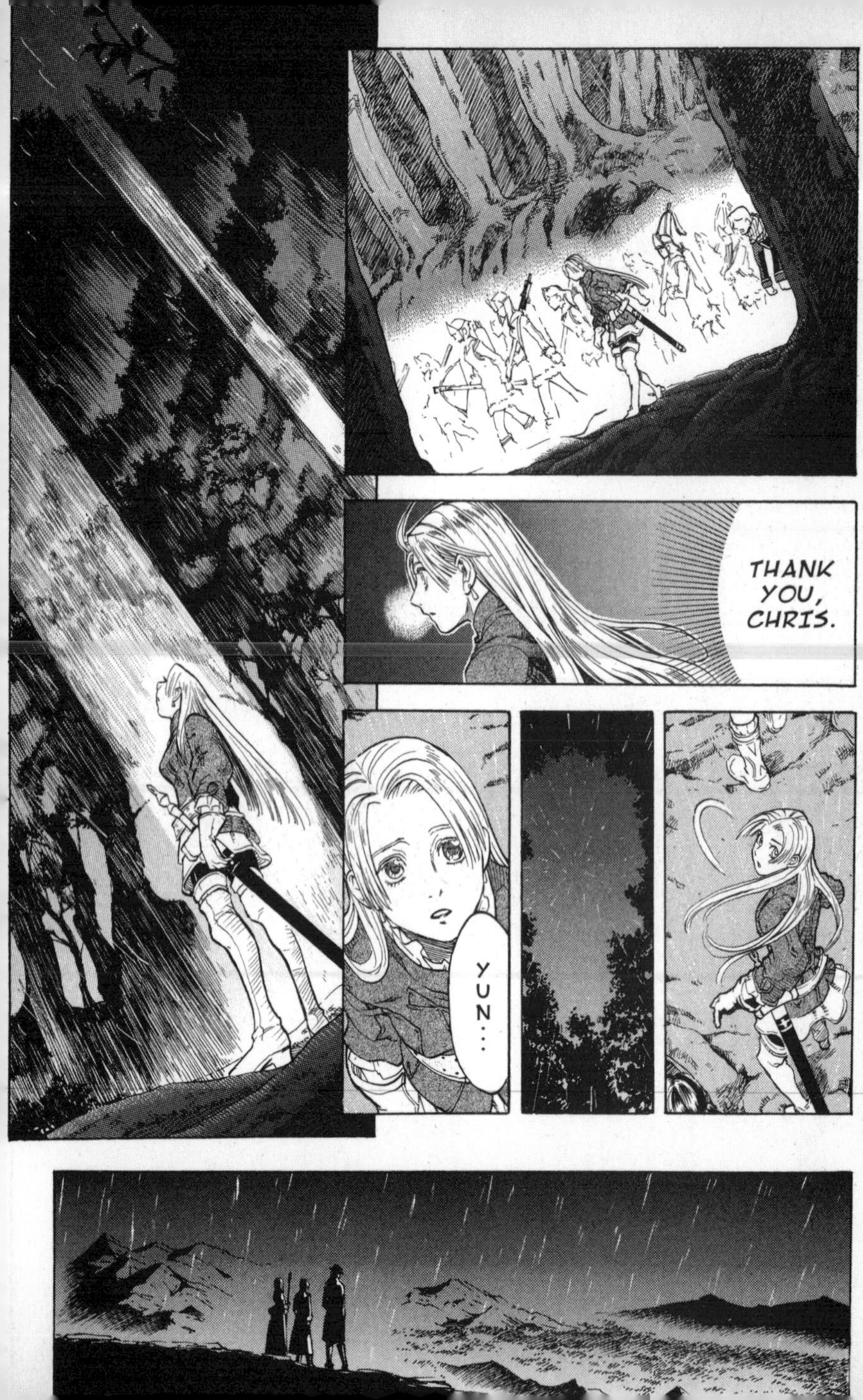
THANK YOU, CHRIS.
YUN...

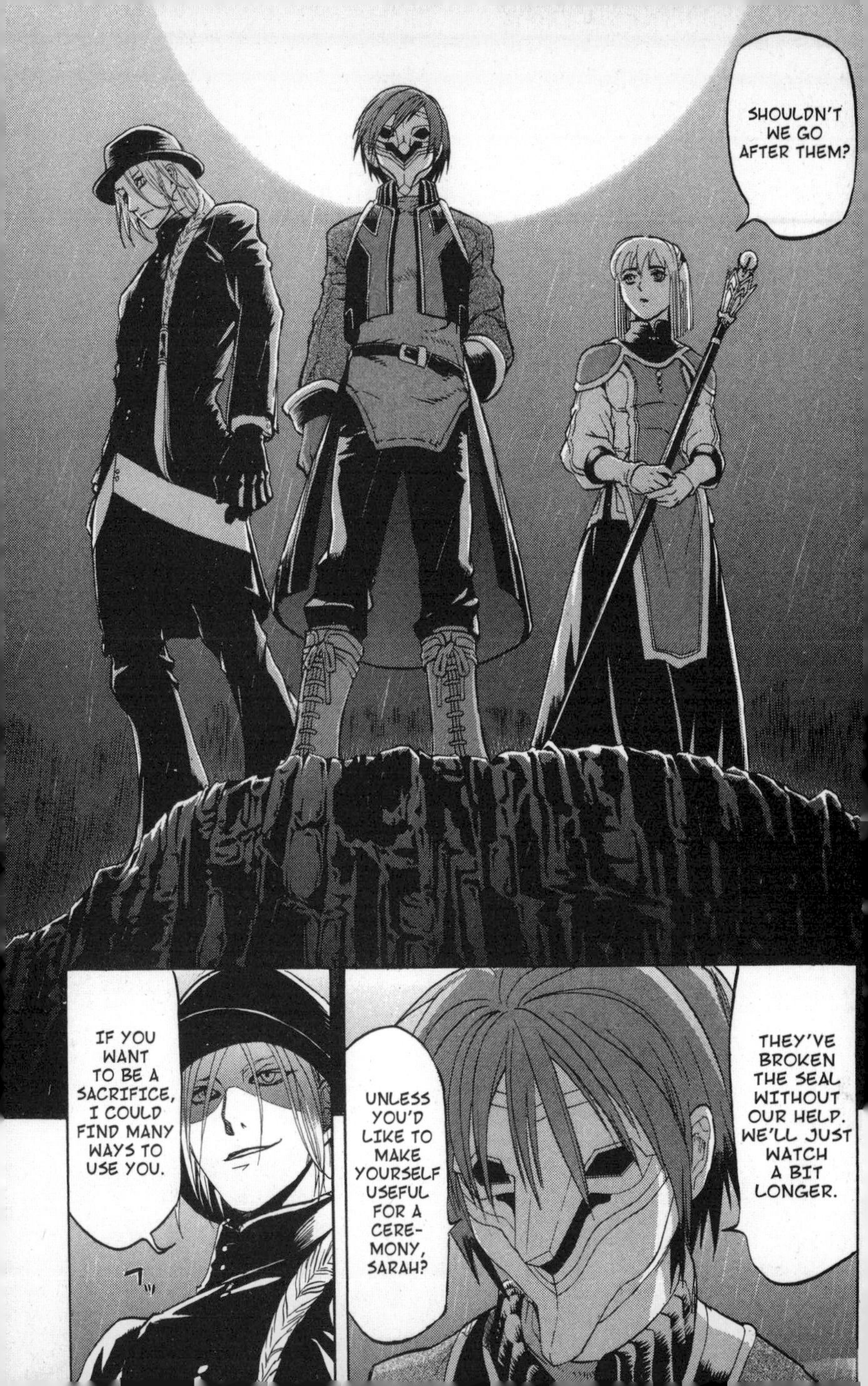
SHOULDN'T WE GO AFTER THEM?
THEY'VE BROKEN THE SEAL WITHOUT OUR HELP. WE'LL JUST WATCH A BIT LONGER.
UNLESS YOU'D LIKE TO MAKE YOURSELF USEFUL FOR A CERE-MONY, SARAH?
IF YOU WANT TO BE A SACRIFICE, I COULD FIND MANY WAYS TO USE YOU.

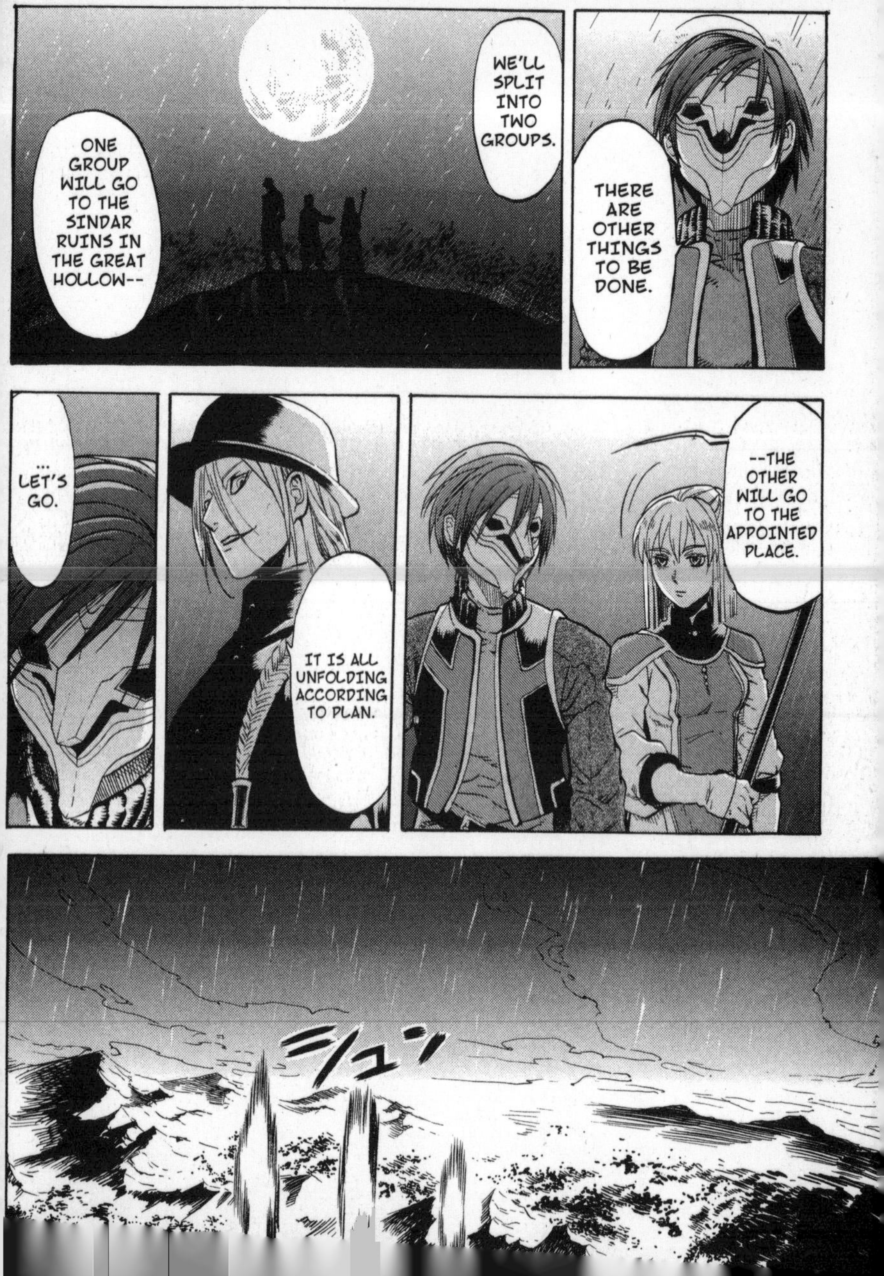
THERE ARE OTHER THINGS TO BE DONE.
WE'LL SPLIT INTO TWO GROUPS.
ONE GROUP WILL GO TO THE SINDAR RUINS IN THE GREAT HOLLOW--
--THE OTHER WILL GO TO THE APPOINTED PLACE.
IT IS ALL UNFOLDING ACCORDING TO PLAN.
... LET'S GO.
シュン

Can one tell
if destiny has been
changed or not...?

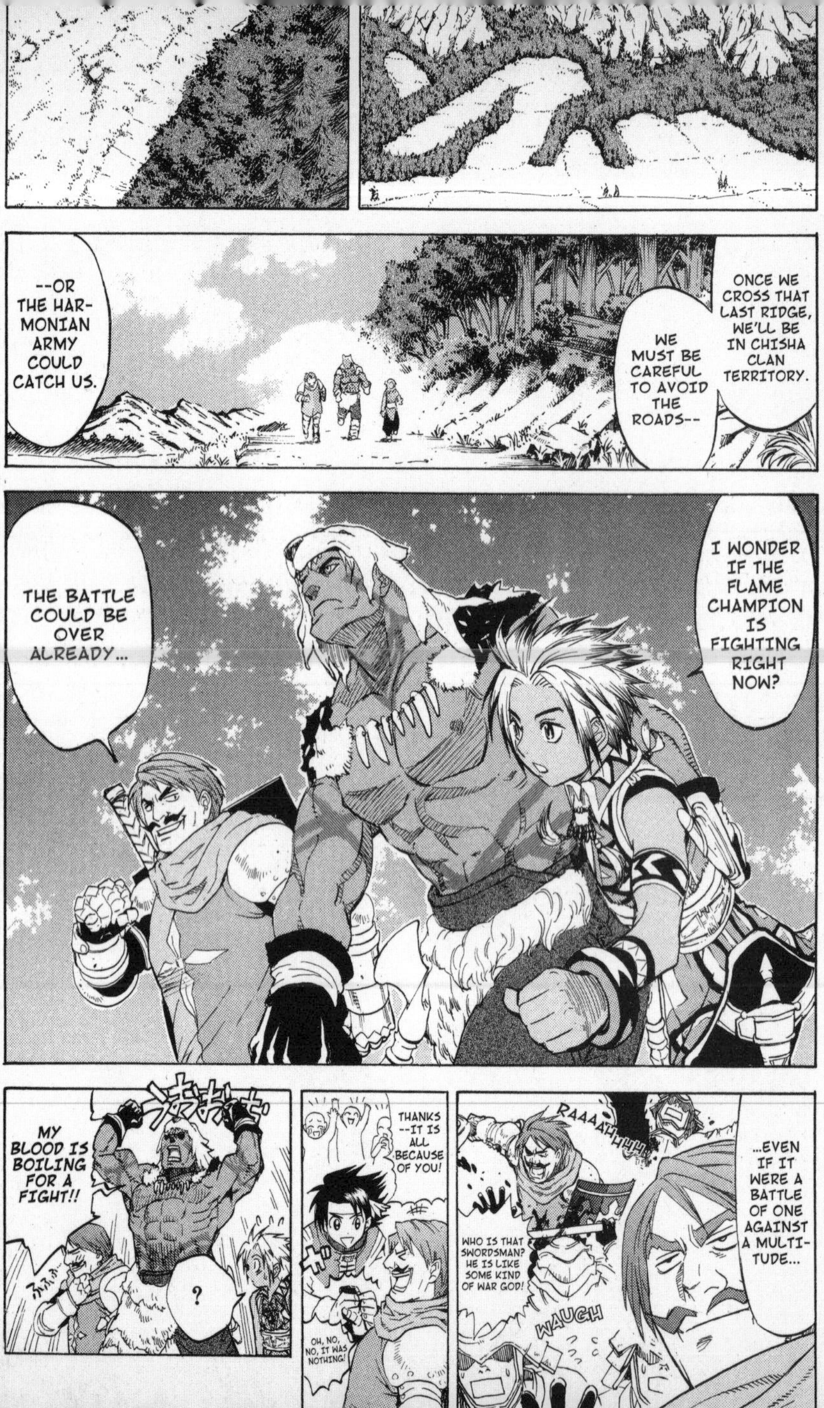
ONCE WE CROSS THAT LAST RIDGE, WE'LL BE IN CHISHA CLAN TERRITORY.
WE MUST BE CAREFUL TO AVOID THE ROADS--
--OR THE HAR-MONIAN ARMY COULD CATCH US.
I WONDER IF THE FLAME CHAMPION IS FIGHTING RIGHT NOW?
THE BATTLE COULD BE OVER ALREADY...
...EVEN IF IT WERE A BATTLE OF ONE AGAINST A MULTI-TUDE...
RAAAAHHHH
WHO IS THAT SWORDSMAN? HE IS LIKE SOME KIND OF WAR GOD!
WAUGH
THANKS --IT IS ALL BECAUSE OF YOU!
OH, NO, NO, IT WAS NOTHING!
MY BLOOD IS BOILING FOR A FIGHT!!
?

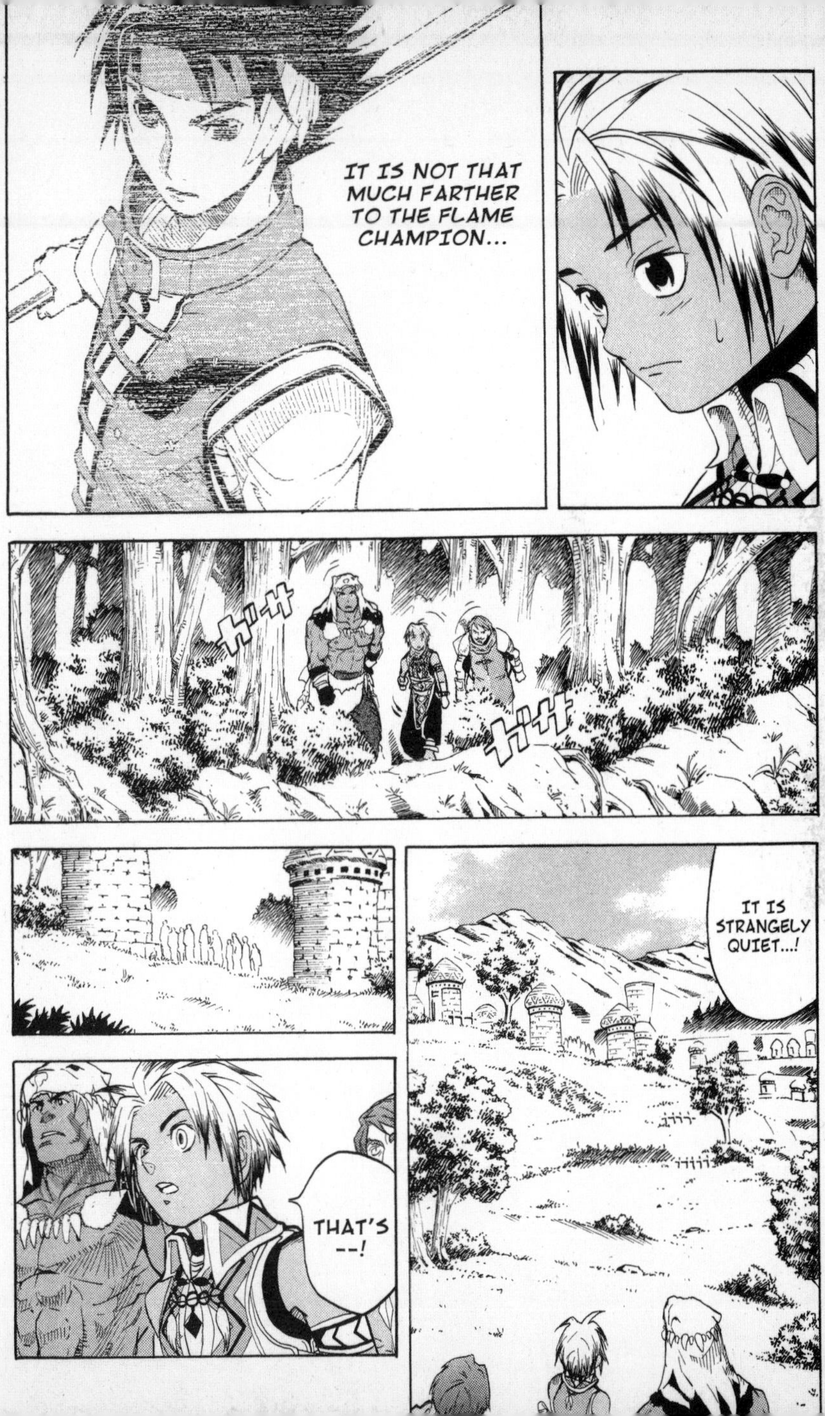
IT IS NOT THAT MUCH FARTHER TO THE FLAME CHAMPION...
IT IS STRANGELY QUIET...!
THAT'S --!

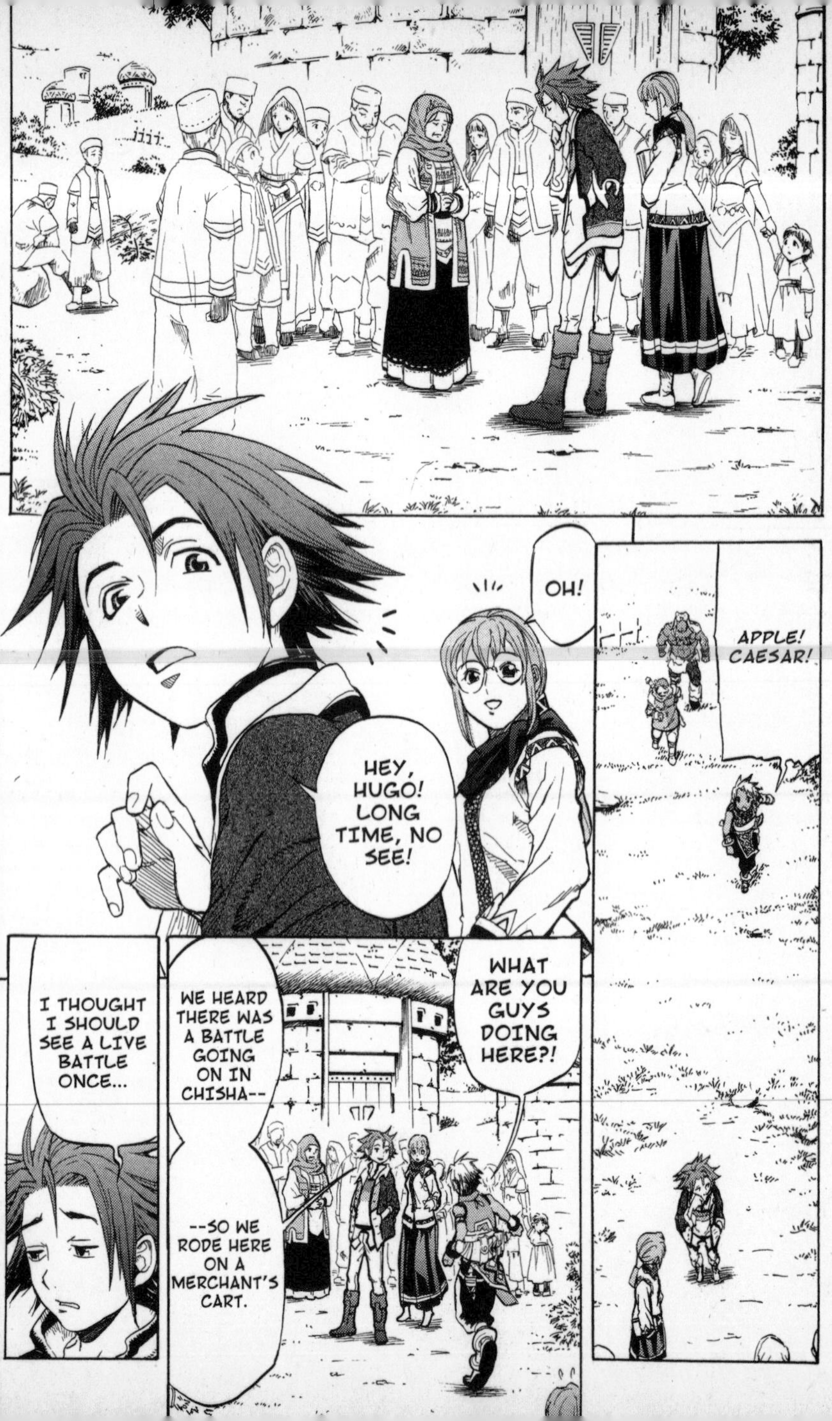
APPLE! CAESAR!
OH!
HEY, HUGO! LONG TIME, NO SEE!
WHAT ARE YOU GUYS DOING HERE?!
WE HEARD THERE WAS A BATTLE GOING ON IN CHISHA--
--SO WE RODE HERE ON A MERCHANT'S CART.
I THOUGHT I SHOULD SEE A LIVE BATTLE ONCE...

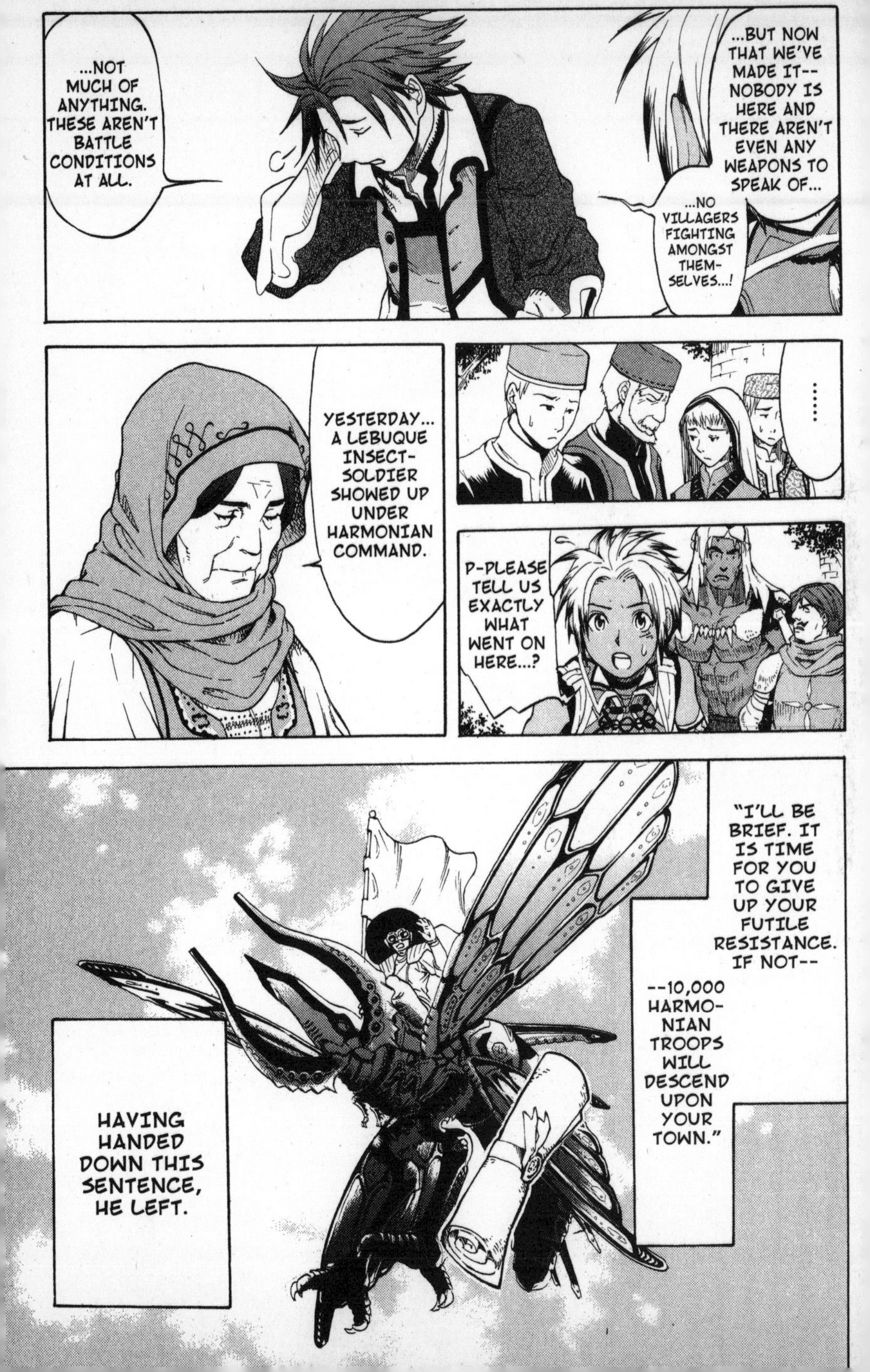
...BUT NOW THAT WE'VE MADE IT-- NOBODY IS HERE AND THERE AREN'T EVEN ANY WEAPONS TO SPEAK OF...
...NO VILLAGERS FIGHTING AMONGST THEM-SELVES...!
...NOT MUCH OF ANYTHING. THESE AREN'T BATTLE CONDITIONS AT ALL.
......
P-PLEASE TELL US EXACTLY WHAT WENT ON HERE...?
YESTERDAY... A LEBUQUE INSECT-SOLDIER SHOWED UP UNDER HARMONIAN COMMAND.
"I'LL BE BRIEF. IT IS TIME FOR YOU TO GIVE UP YOUR FUTILE RESISTANCE. IF NOT--
--10,000 HARMO-NIAN TROOPS WILL DESCEND UPON YOUR TOWN."
HAVING HANDED DOWN THIS SENTENCE, HE LEFT.

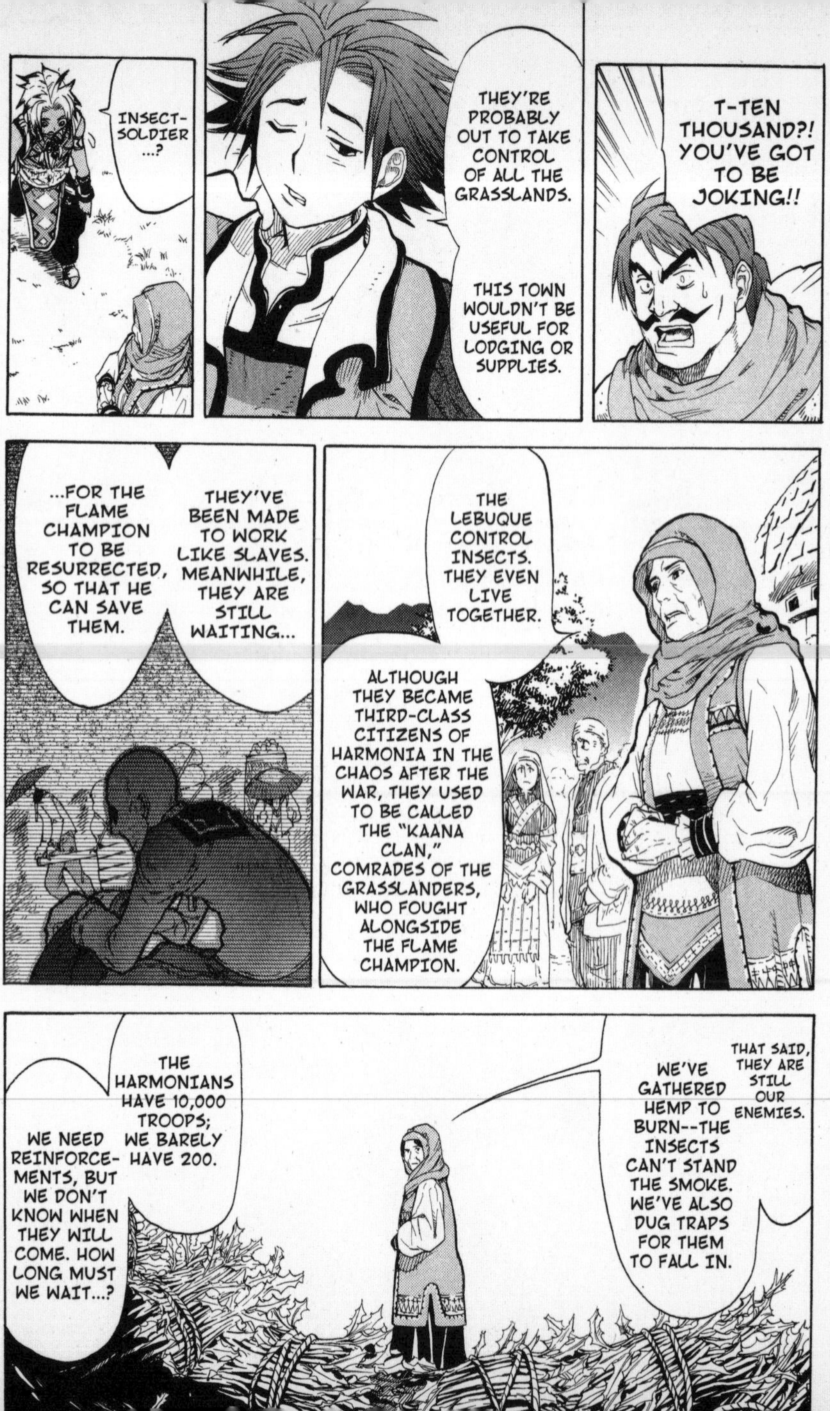
T-TEN THOUSAND?! YOU'VE GOT TO BE JOKING!!
THEY'RE PROBABLY OUT TO TAKE CONTROL OF ALL THE GRASSLANDS.
THIS TOWN WOULDN'T BE USEFUL FOR LODGING OR SUPPLIES.
INSECT-SOLDIER ...?
THE LEBUQUE CONTROL INSECTS. THEY EVEN LIVE TOGETHER.
ALTHOUGH THEY BECAME THIRD-CLASS CITIZENS OF HARMONIA IN THE CHAOS AFTER THE WAR, THEY USED TO BE CALLED THE "KAANA CLAN," COMRADES OF THE GRASSLANDERS, WHO FOUGHT ALONGSIDE THE FLAME CHAMPION.
THEY'VE BEEN MADE TO WORK LIKE SLAVES. MEANWHILE, THEY ARE STILL WAITING...
...FOR THE FLAME CHAMPION TO BE RESURRECTED, SO THAT HE CAN SAVE THEM.
THAT SAID, THEY ARE STILL OUR ENEMIES.
WE'VE GATHERED HEMP TO BURN--THE INSECTS CAN'T STAND THE SMOKE. WE'VE ALSO DUG TRAPS FOR THEM TO FALL IN.
THE HARMONIANS HAVE 10,000 TROOPS; WE BARELY HAVE 200.
WE NEED REINFORCE-MENTS, BUT WE DON'T KNOW WHEN THEY WILL COME. HOW LONG MUST WE WAIT...?

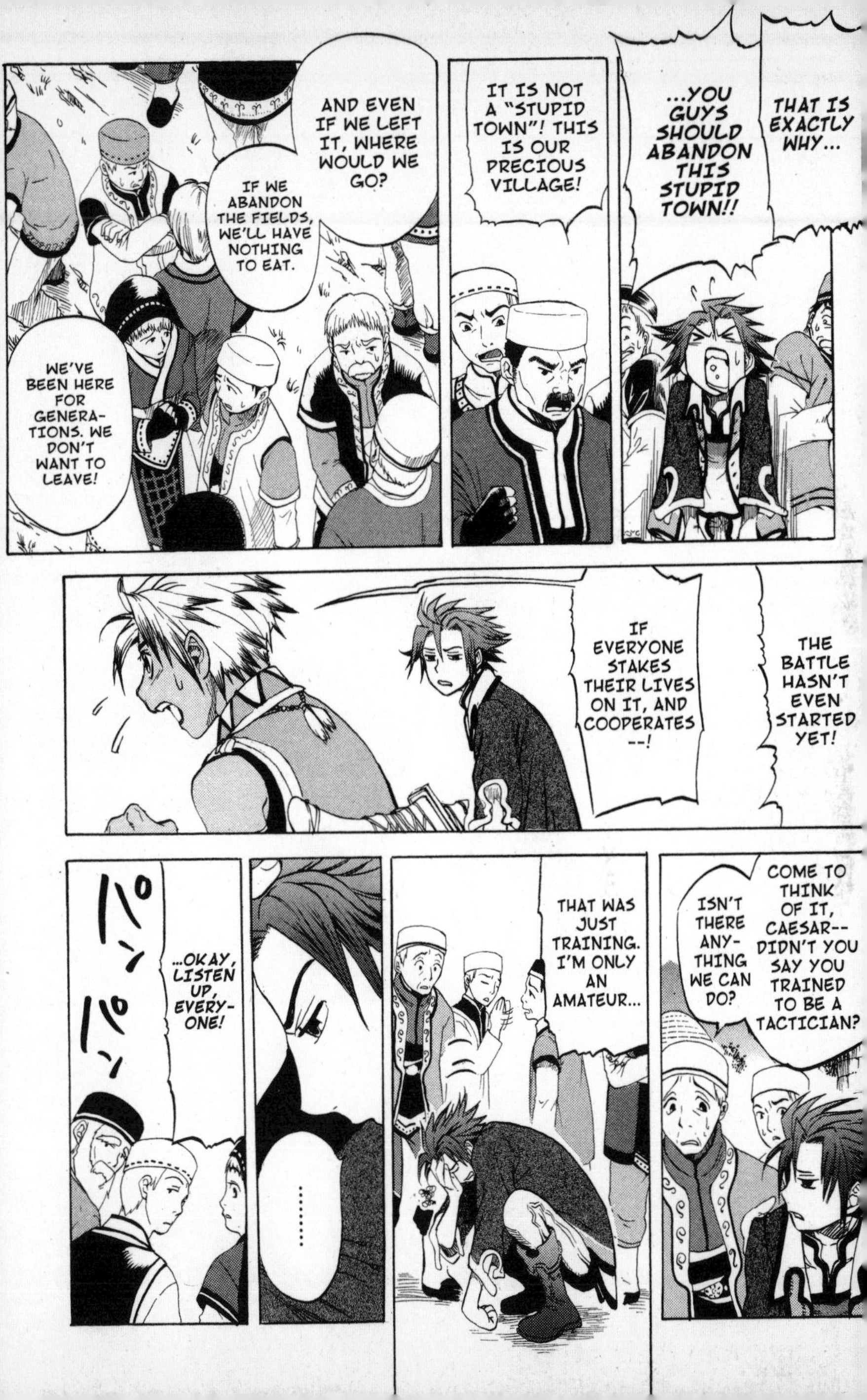
THAT IS EXACTLY WHY...
...YOU GUYS SHOULD ABANDON THIS STUPID TOWN!!
IT IS NOT A "STUPID TOWN"! THIS IS OUR PRECIOUS VILLAGE!
AND EVEN IF WE LEFT IT, WHERE WOULD WE GO?
IF WE ABANDON THE FIELDS, WE'LL HAVE NOTHING TO EAT.
WE'VE BEEN HERE FOR GENERATIONS. WE DON'T WANT TO LEAVE!
THE BATTLE HASN'T EVEN STARTED YET!
IF EVERYONE STAKES THEIR LIVES ON IT, AND COOPERATES--!
COME TO THINK OF IT, CAESAR--DIDN'T YOU SAY YOU TRAINED TO BE A TACTICIAN?
ISN'T THERE ANYTHING WE CAN DO?
THAT WAS JUST TRAINING. I'M ONLY AN AMATEUR...
......
パン パン
...OKAY, LISTEN UP, EVERYONE!

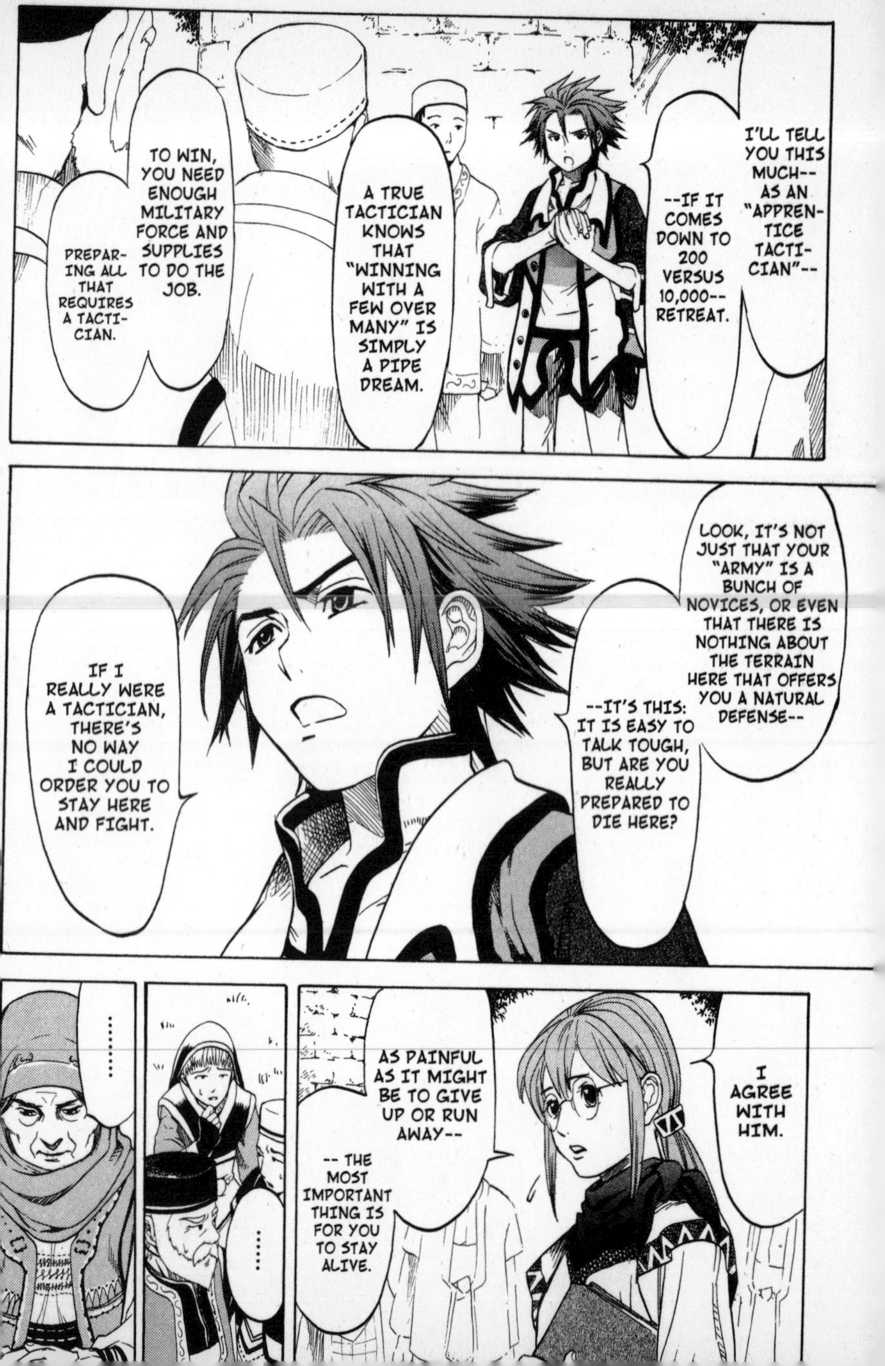
I'LL TELL YOU THIS MUCH-- AS AN "APPRENTICE TACTICIAN"--
--IF IT COMES DOWN TO 200 VERSUS 10,000-- RETREAT.
A TRUE TACTICIAN KNOWS THAT "WINNING WITH A FEW OVER MANY" IS SIMPLY A PIPE DREAM.
TO WIN, YOU NEED ENOUGH MILITARY FORCE AND SUPPLIES TO DO THE JOB.
PREPARING ALL THAT REQUIRES A TACTICIAN.
LOOK, IT'S NOT JUST THAT YOUR "ARMY" IS A BUNCH OF NOVICES, OR EVEN THAT THERE IS NOTHING ABOUT THE TERRAIN HERE THAT OFFERS YOU A NATURAL DEFENSE--
--IT'S THIS: IT IS EASY TO TALK TOUGH, BUT ARE YOU REALLY PREPARED TO DIE HERE?
IF I REALLY WERE A TACTICIAN, THERE'S NO WAY I COULD ORDER YOU TO STAY HERE AND FIGHT.
I AGREE WITH HIM.
AS PAINFUL AS IT MIGHT BE TO GIVE UP OR RUN AWAY--
-- THE MOST IMPORTANT THING IS FOR YOU TO STAY ALIVE.
......
......
......

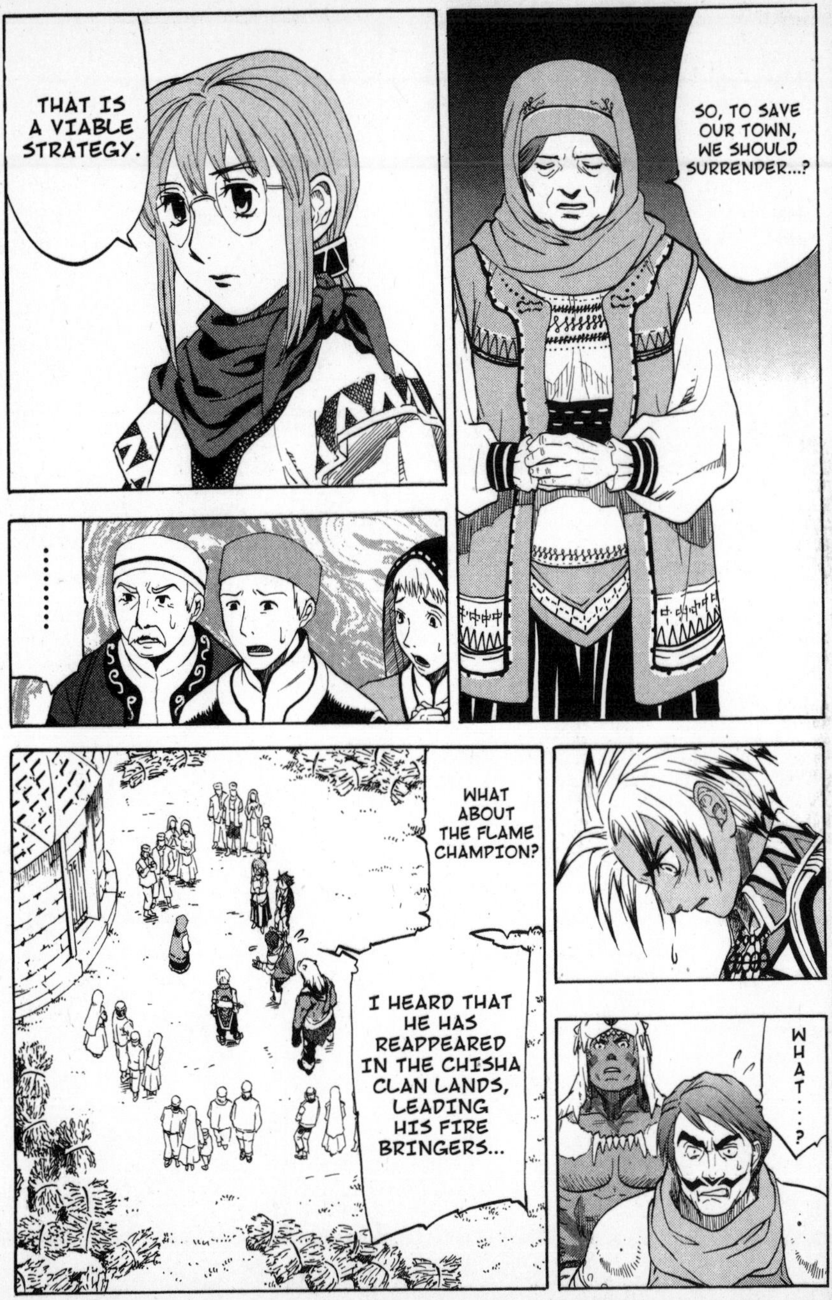
SO, TO SAVE OUR TOWN, WE SHOULD SURRENDER...?
THAT IS A VIABLE STRATEGY.
......
WHAT...?
WHAT ABOUT THE FLAME CHAMPION?
I HEARD THAT HE HAS REAPPEARED IN THE CHISHA CLAN LANDS, LEADING HIS FIRE BRINGERS...

IT HAS TO BE A RUMOR.

I'M SORRY... I'M AFRAID THAT IS NOT TRUE.

WHA...

おおお‥‥‥

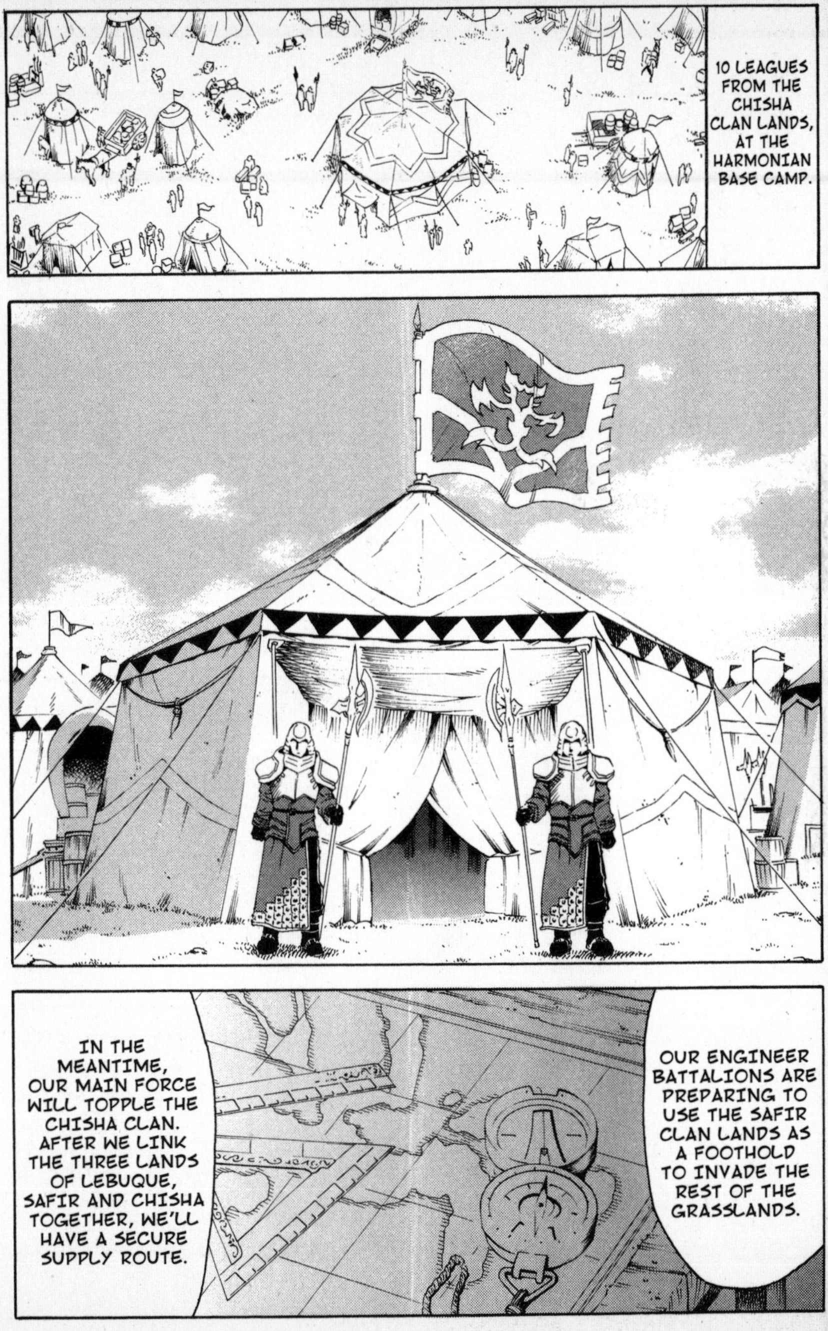
10 LEAGUES FROM THE CHISHA CLAN LANDS, AT THE HARMONIAN BASE CAMP.
OUR ENGINEER BATTALIONS ARE PREPARING TO USE THE SAFIR CLAN LANDS AS A FOOTHOLD TO INVADE THE REST OF THE GRASSLANDS.
IN THE MEANTIME, OUR MAIN FORCE WILL TOPPLE THE CHISHA CLAN. AFTER WE LINK THE THREE LANDS OF LEBUQUE, SAFIR AND CHISHA TOGETHER, WE'LL HAVE A SECURE SUPPLY ROUTE.

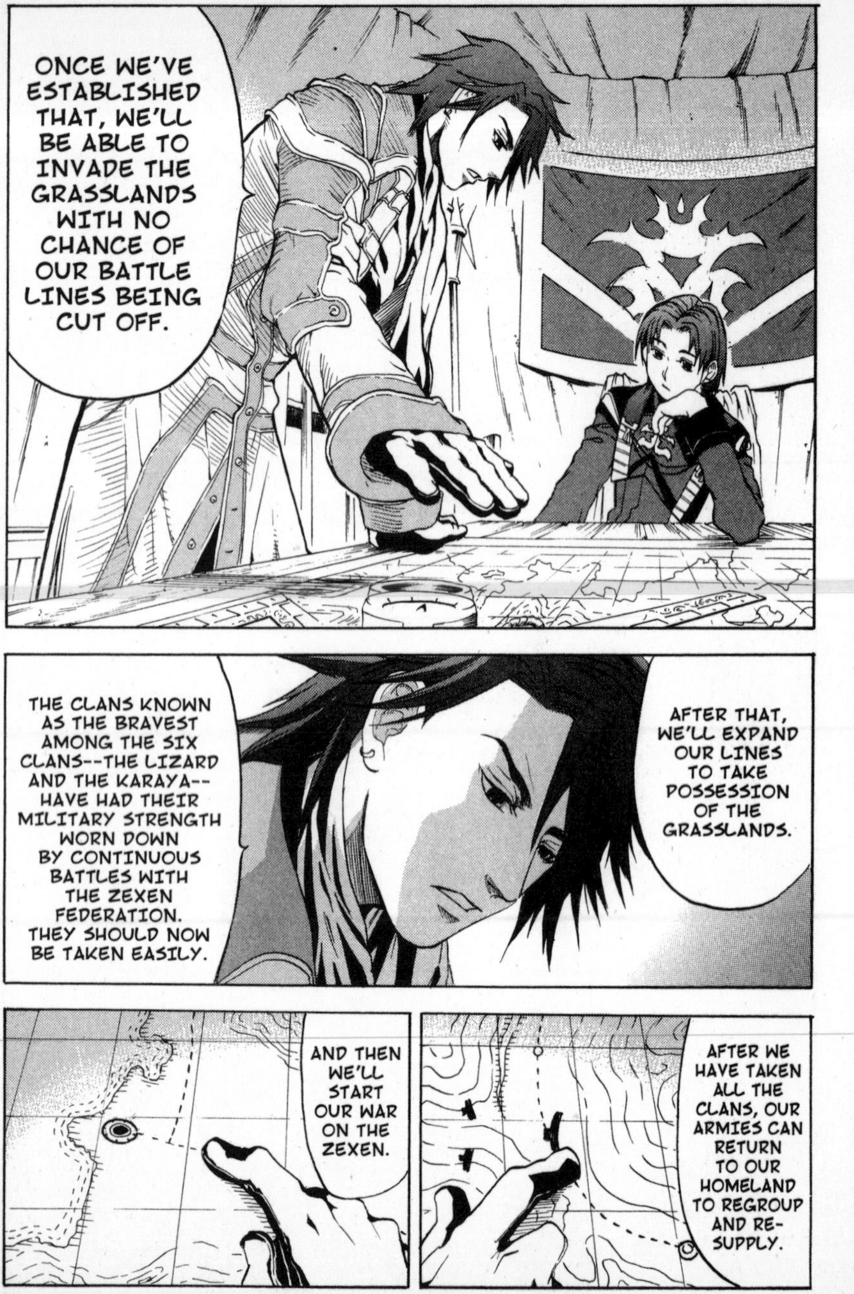
ONCE WE'VE ESTABLISHED THAT, WE'LL BE ABLE TO INVADE THE GRASSLANDS WITH NO CHANCE OF OUR BATTLE LINES BEING CUT OFF.
AFTER THAT, WE'LL EXPAND OUR LINES TO TAKE POSSESSION OF THE GRASSLANDS.
THE CLANS KNOWN AS THE BRAVEST AMONG THE SIX CLANS--THE LIZARD AND THE KARAYA--HAVE HAD THEIR MILITARY STRENGTH WORN DOWN BY CONTINUOUS BATTLES WITH THE ZEXEN FEDERATION. THEY SHOULD NOW BE TAKEN EASILY.
AFTER WE HAVE TAKEN ALL THE CLANS, OUR ARMIES CAN RETURN TO OUR HOMELAND TO REGROUP AND RE-SUPPLY.
AND THEN WE'LL START OUR WAR ON THE ZEXEN.

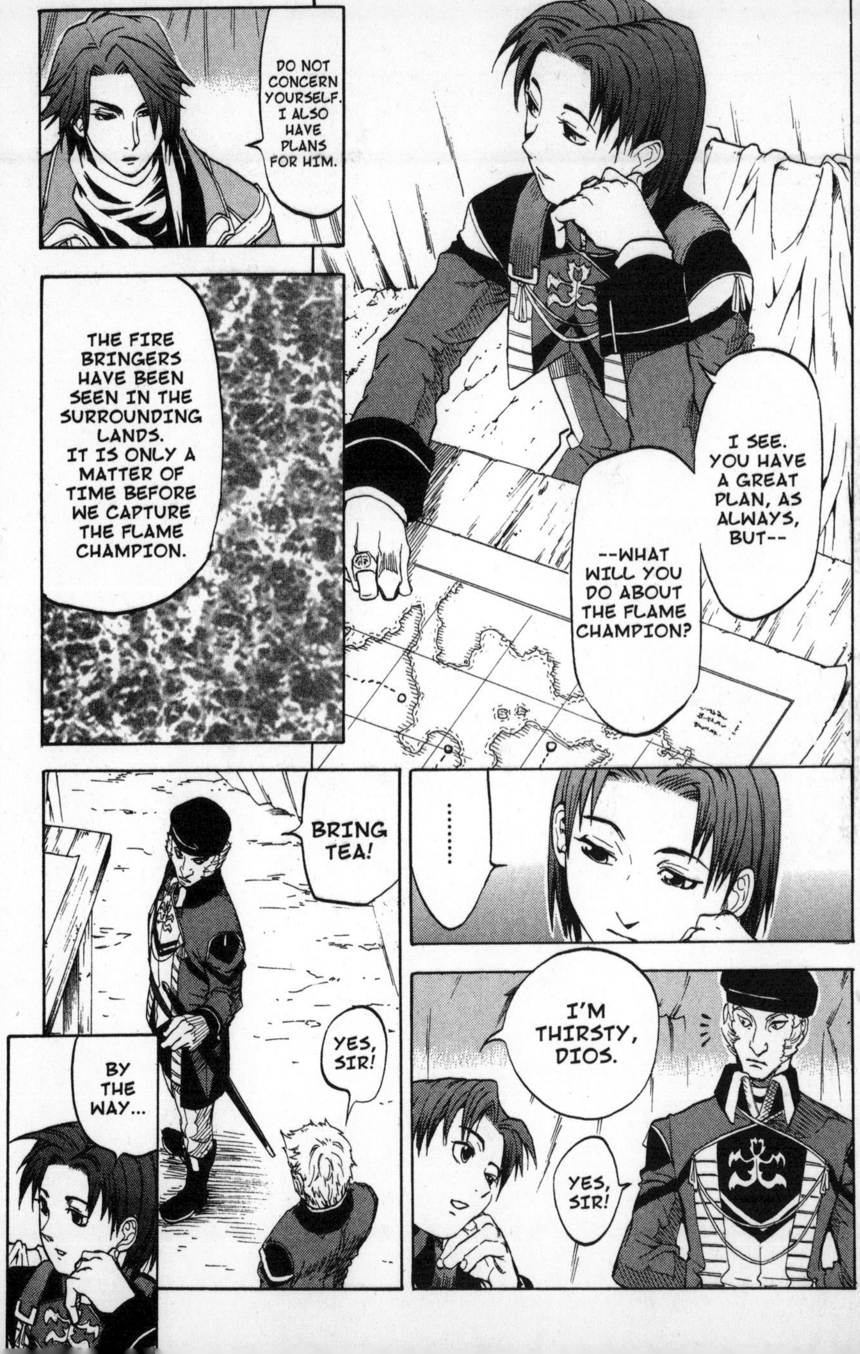
I SEE. YOU HAVE A GREAT PLAN, AS ALWAYS, BUT--
--WHAT WILL YOU DO ABOUT THE FLAME CHAMPION?
DO NOT CONCERN YOURSELF. I ALSO HAVE PLANS FOR HIM.
THE FIRE BRINGERS HAVE BEEN SEEN IN THE SURROUNDING LANDS. IT IS ONLY A MATTER OF TIME BEFORE WE CAPTURE THE FLAME CHAMPION.
....
I'M THIRSTY, DIOS.
YES, SIR!
BRING TEA!
YES, SIR!
BY THE WAY...

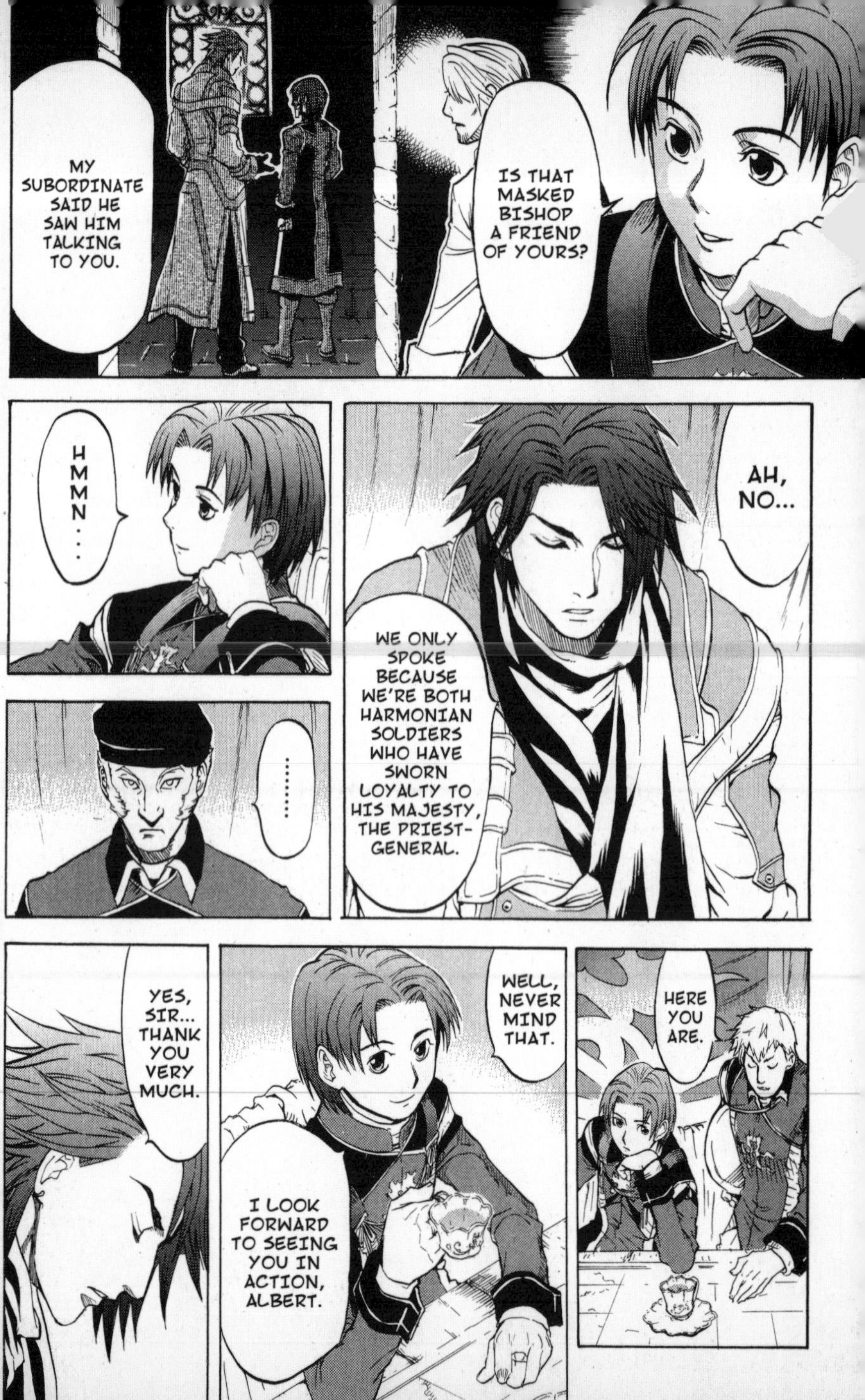
IS THAT MASKED BISHOP A FRIEND OF YOURS?
MY SUBORDINATE SAID HE SAW HIM TALKING TO YOU.
AH, NO...
WE ONLY SPOKE BECAUSE WE'RE BOTH HARMONIAN SOLDIERS WHO HAVE SWORN LOYALTY TO HIS MAJESTY, THE PRIEST-GENERAL.
HMMN...
......
HERE YOU ARE.
WELL, NEVER MIND THAT.
I LOOK FORWARD TO SEEING YOU IN ACTION, ALBERT.
YES, SIR... THANK YOU VERY MUCH.

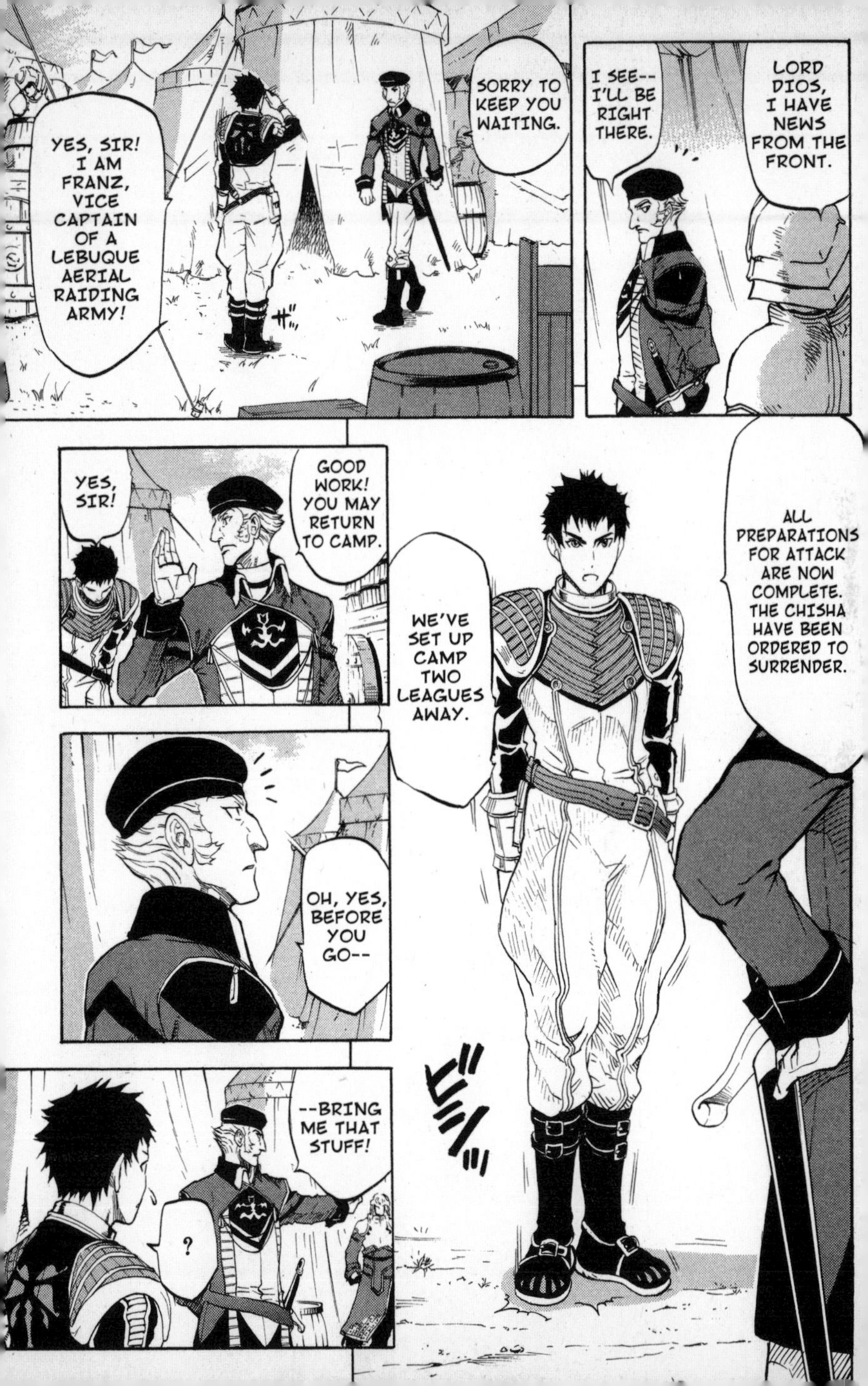
LORD DIOS, I HAVE NEWS FROM THE FRONT.
I SEE-- I'LL BE RIGHT THERE.
SORRY TO KEEP YOU WAITING.
YES, SIR! I AM FRANZ, VICE CAPTAIN OF A LEBUQUE AERIAL RAIDING ARMY!
ALL PREPARATIONS FOR ATTACK ARE NOW COMPLETE. THE CHISHA HAVE BEEN ORDERED TO SURRENDER.
WE'VE SET UP CAMP TWO LEAGUES AWAY.
GOOD WORK! YOU MAY RETURN TO CAMP.
YES, SIR!
OH, YES, BEFORE YOU GO--
--BRING ME THAT STUFF!
?

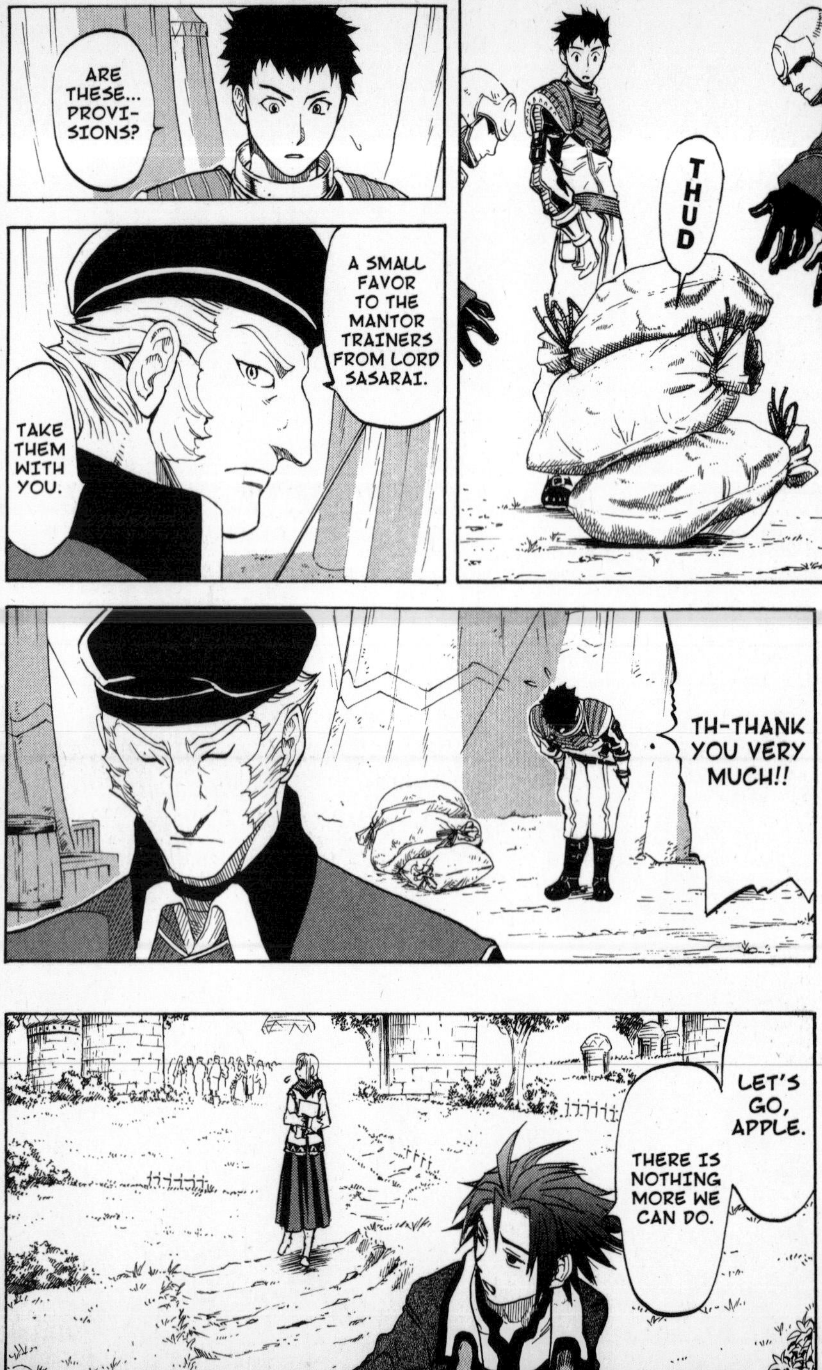
THUD
ARE THESE... PROVISIONS?
A SMALL FAVOR TO THE MANTOR TRAINERS FROM LORD SASARAI.
TAKE THEM WITH YOU.
TH-THANK YOU VERY MUCH!!
LET'S GO, APPLE.
THERE IS NOTHING MORE WE CAN DO.

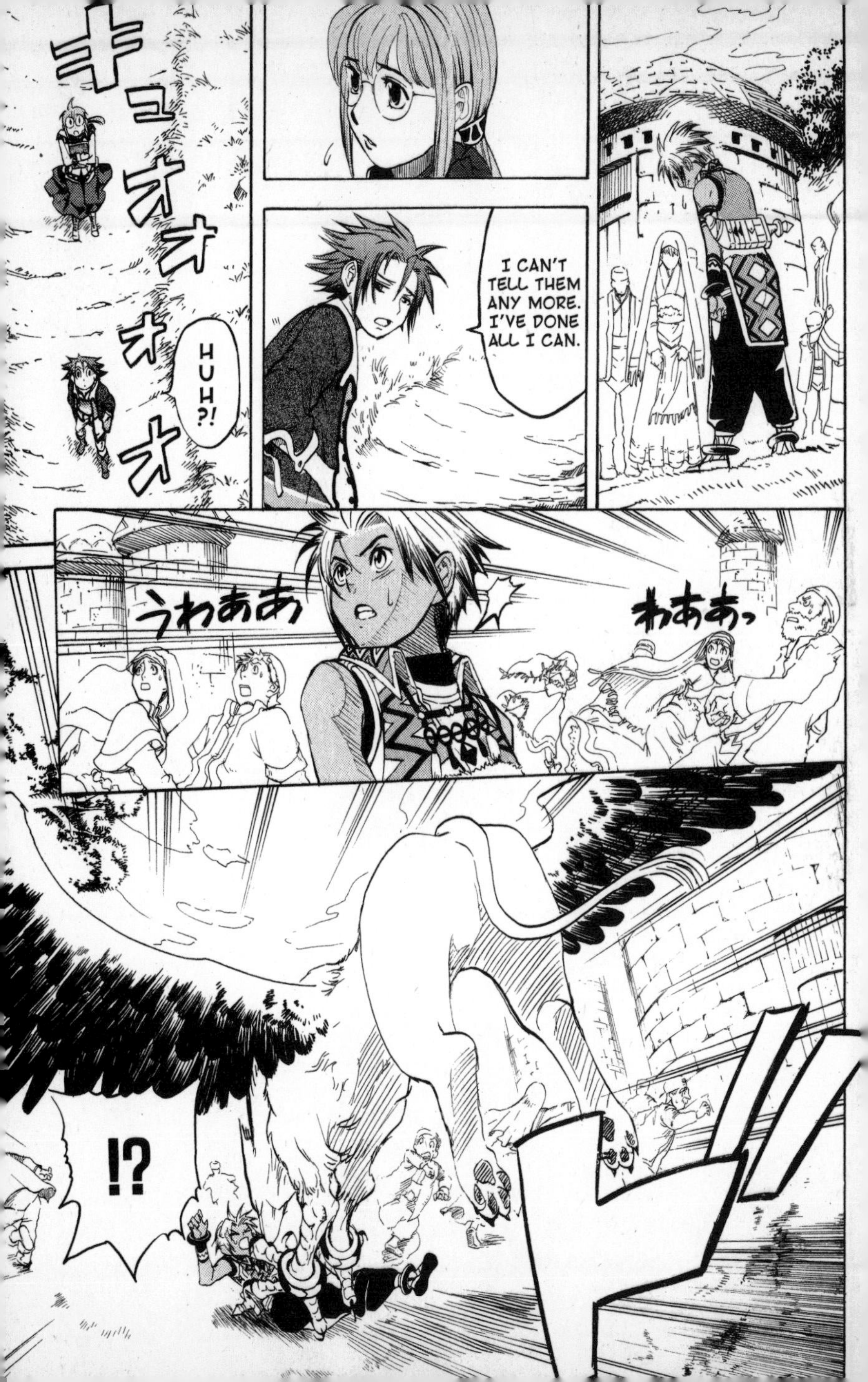
I CAN'T TELL THEM ANY MORE. I'VE DONE ALL I CAN.
キュオオオオ
HUH?!
わあぁっ
うわあぁ
!?

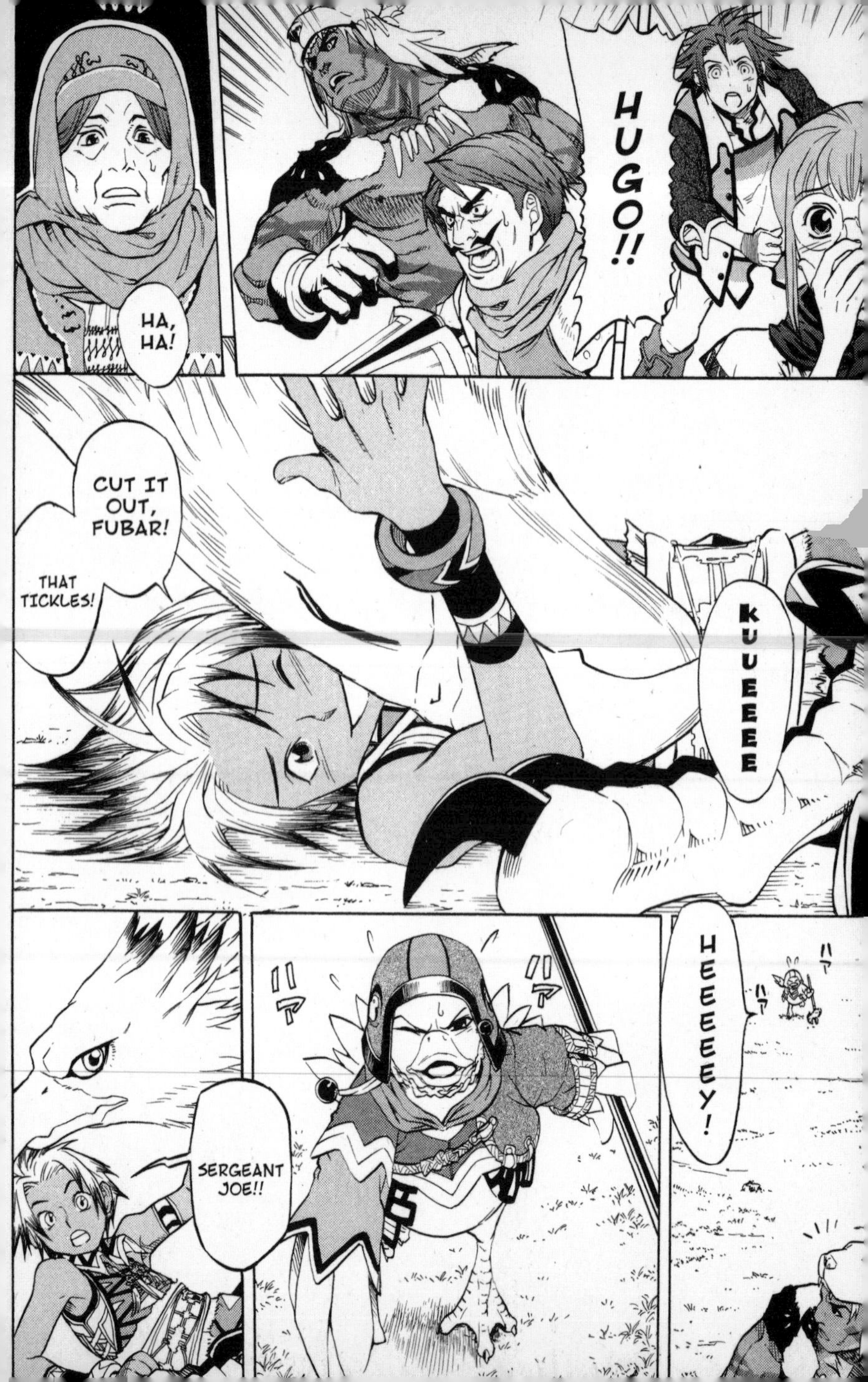
HUGO!!
HA, HA!
KUUEEEE
CUT IT OUT, FUBAR!
THAT TICKLES!
HEEEEEY!
ハァ ハァ
ハァ
ハァ
SERGEANT JOE!!

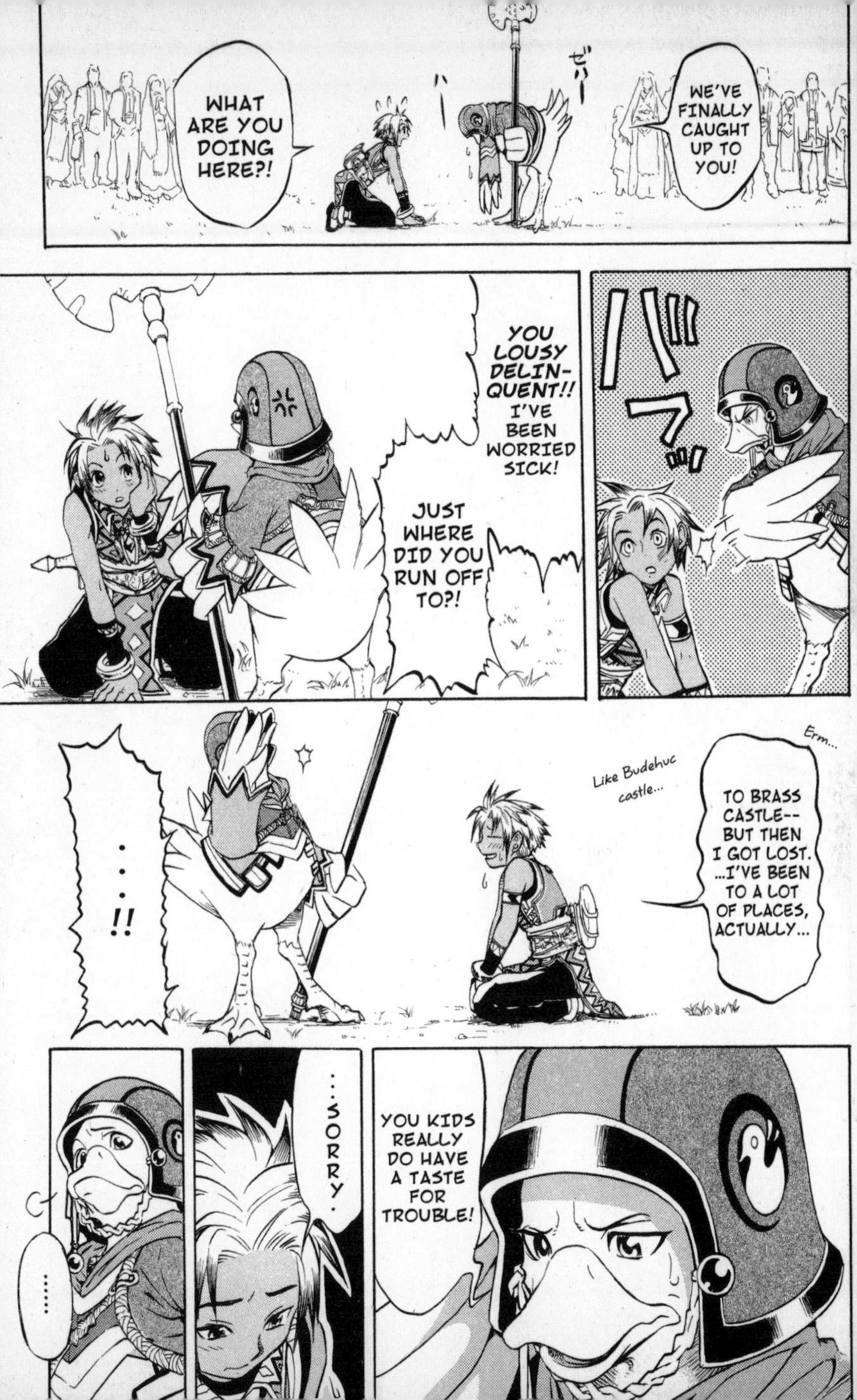
ゼハー
WE'VE FINALLY CAUGHT UP TO YOU!
ハー
WHAT ARE YOU DOING HERE?!
YOU LOUSY DELIN-QUENT!! I'VE BEEN WORRIED SICK!
JUST WHERE DID YOU RUN OFF TO?!
Erm...
TO BRASS CASTLE--BUT THEN I GOT LOST. ...I'VE BEEN TO A LOT OF PLACES, ACTUALLY...
Like Budehuc castle...
....!!
YOU KIDS REALLY DO HAVE A TASTE FOR TROUBLE!
...SORRY.
......

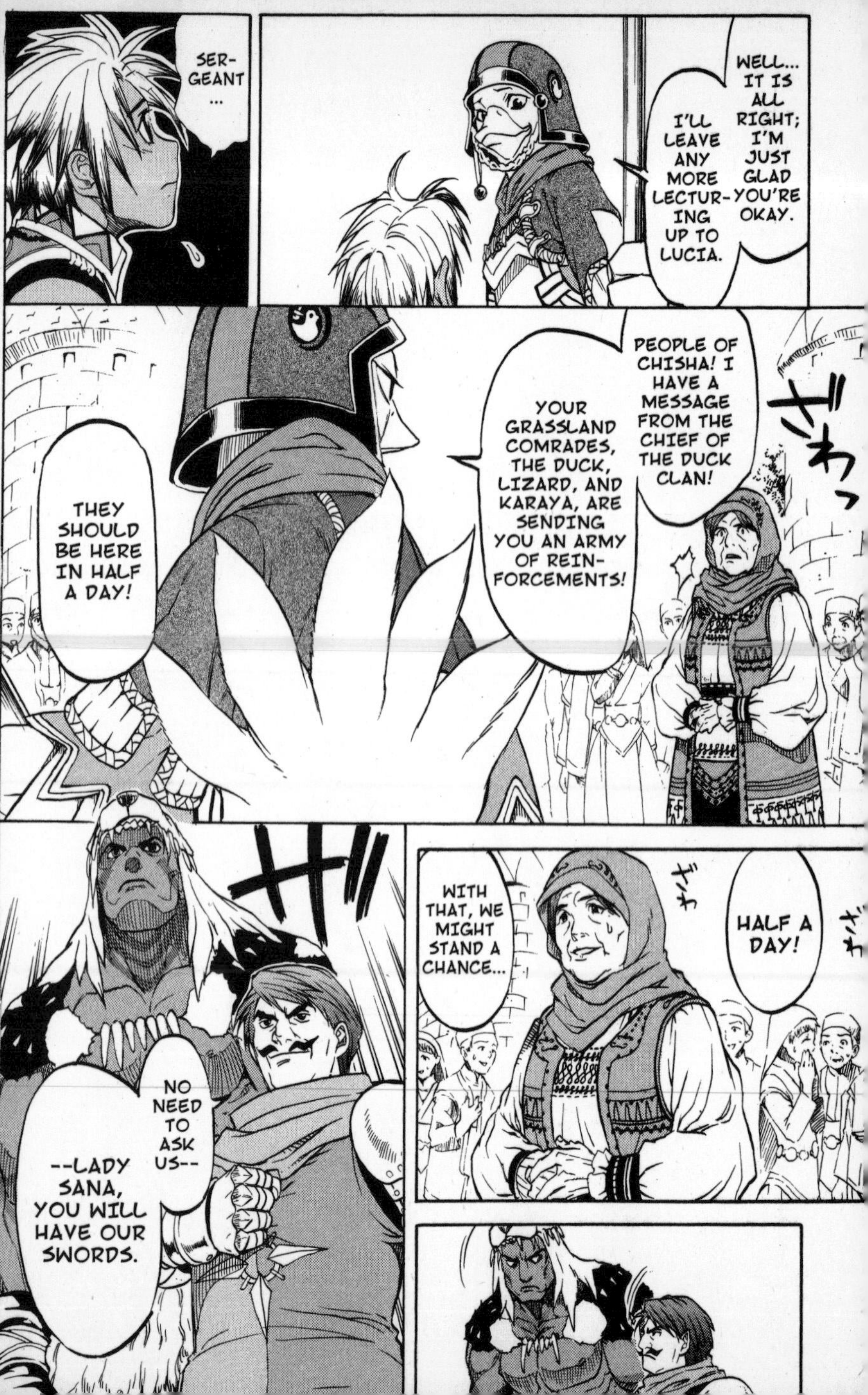
WELL... IT IS ALL RIGHT; I'M JUST GLAD YOU'RE OKAY.
I'LL LEAVE ANY MORE LECTURING UP TO LUCIA.
SER-GEANT...
ざわっ
PEOPLE OF CHISHA! I HAVE A MESSAGE FROM THE CHIEF OF THE DUCK CLAN!
YOUR GRASSLAND COMRADES, THE DUCK, LIZARD, AND KARAYA, ARE SENDING YOU AN ARMY OF REIN-FORCEMENTS!
THEY SHOULD BE HERE IN HALF A DAY!
ざわ
HALF A DAY!
ざわ
WITH THAT, WE MIGHT STAND A CHANCE...
NO NEED TO ASK US--
--LADY SANA, YOU WILL HAVE OUR SWORDS.

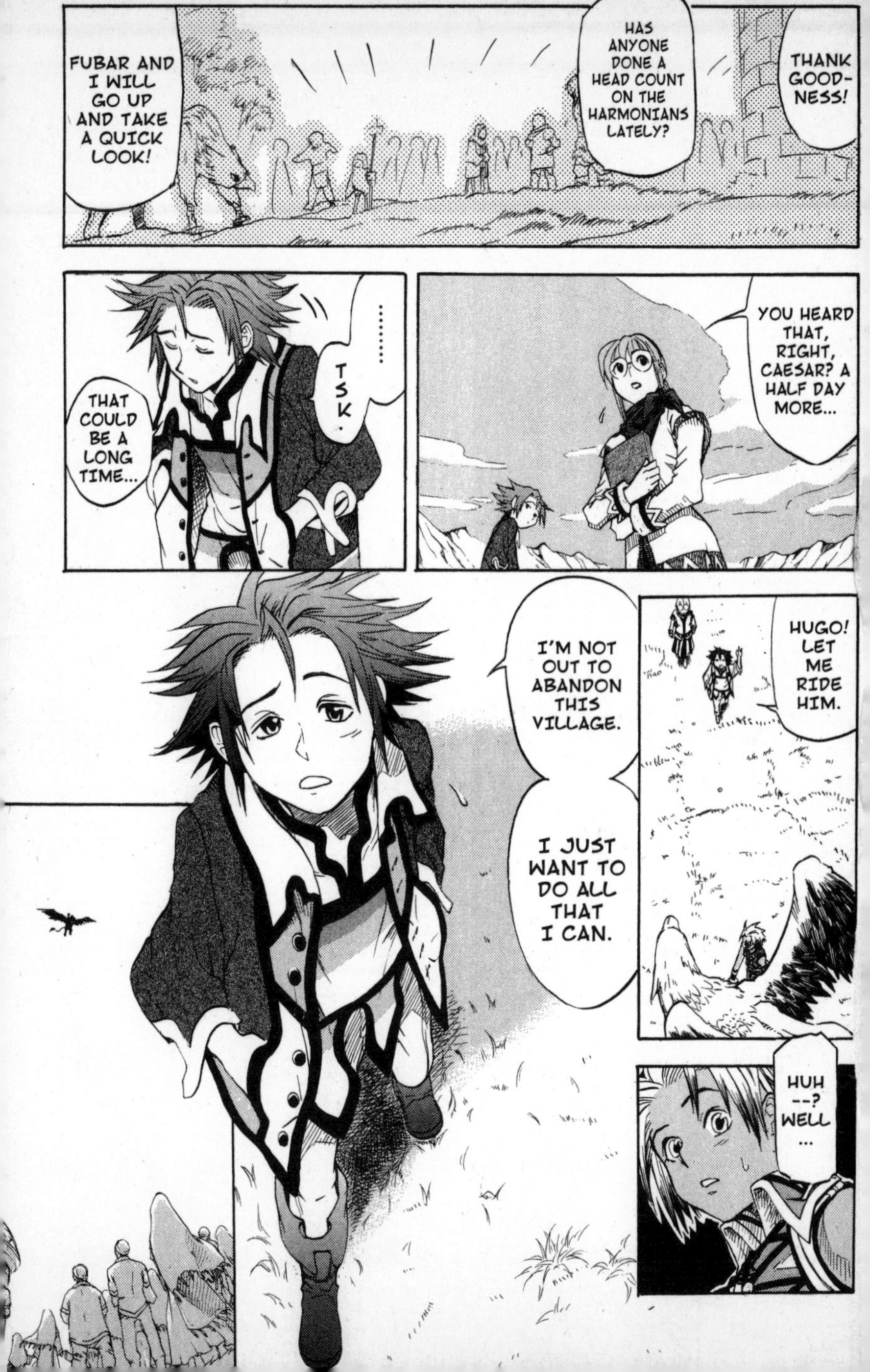
THANK GOODNESS!
HAS ANYONE DONE A HEAD COUNT ON THE HARMONIANS LATELY?
FUBAR AND I WILL GO UP AND TAKE A QUICK LOOK!
YOU HEARD THAT, RIGHT, CAESAR? A HALF DAY MORE...
....
TSK.
THAT COULD BE A LONG TIME...
HUGO! LET ME RIDE HIM.
HUH--? WELL...
I'M NOT OUT TO ABANDON THIS VILLAGE.
I JUST WANT TO DO ALL THAT I CAN.

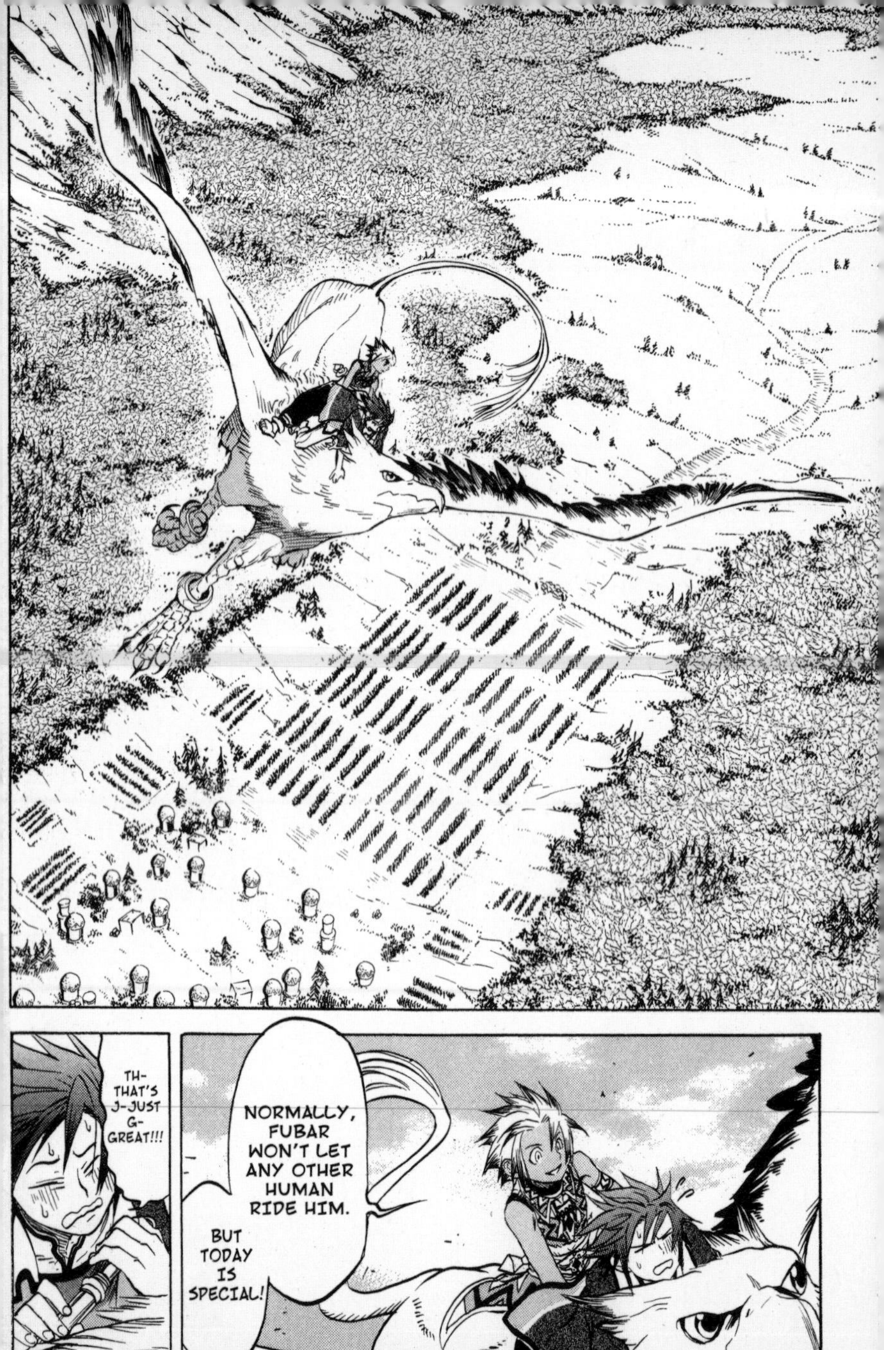
NORMALLY, FUBAR WON'T LET ANY OTHER HUMAN RIDE HIM.
BUT TODAY IS SPECIAL!
TH-THAT'S J-JUST G-GREAT!!!

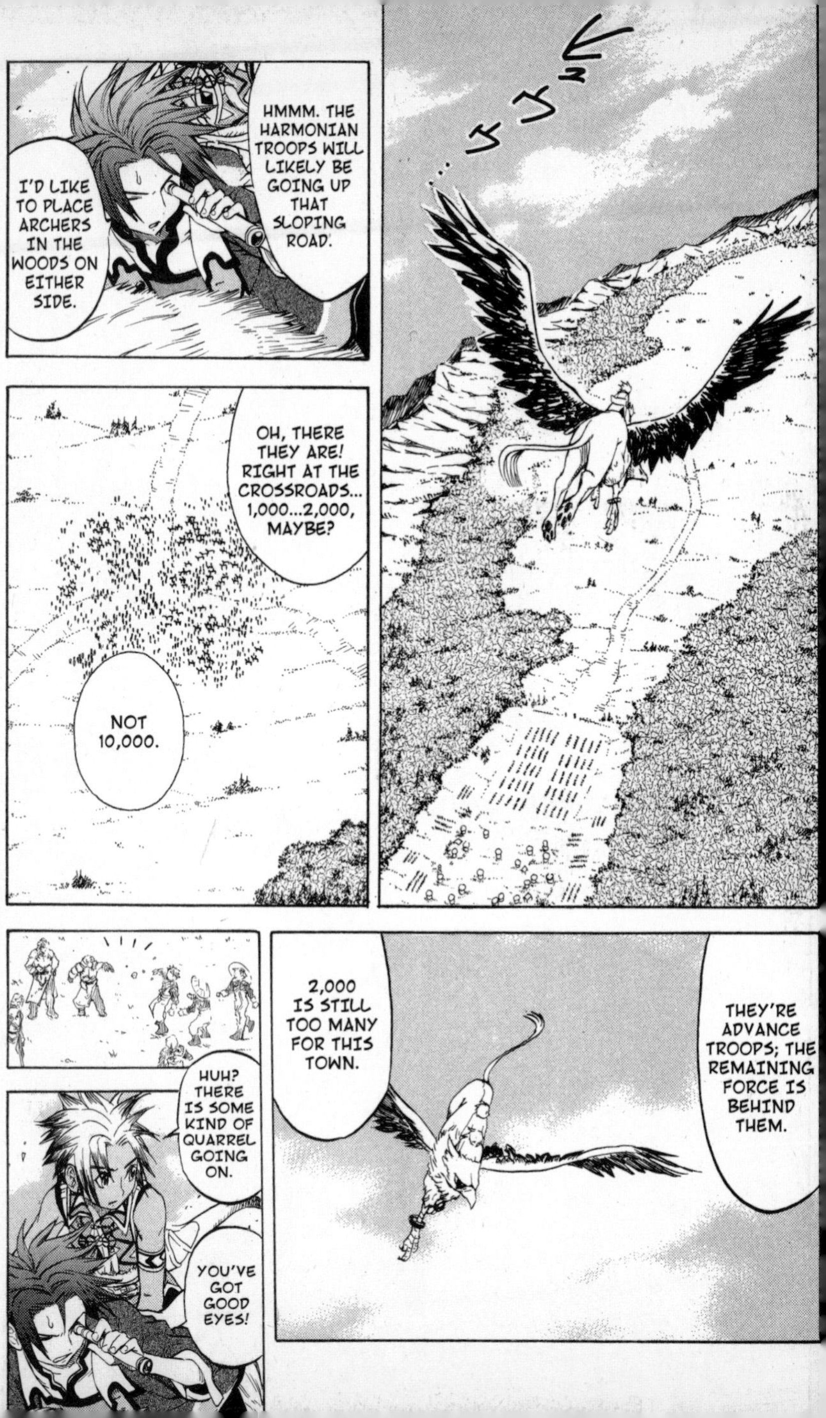
HMMM. THE HARMONIAN TROOPS WILL LIKELY BE GOING UP THAT SLOPING ROAD.
I'D LIKE TO PLACE ARCHERS IN THE WOODS ON EITHER SIDE.
OH, THERE THEY ARE! RIGHT AT THE CROSSROADS... 1,000...2,000, MAYBE?
NOT 10,000.
THEY'RE ADVANCE TROOPS; THE REMAINING FORCE IS BEHIND THEM.
2,000 IS STILL TOO MANY FOR THIS TOWN.
HUH? THERE IS SOME KIND OF QUARREL GOING ON.
YOU'VE GOT GOOD EYES!

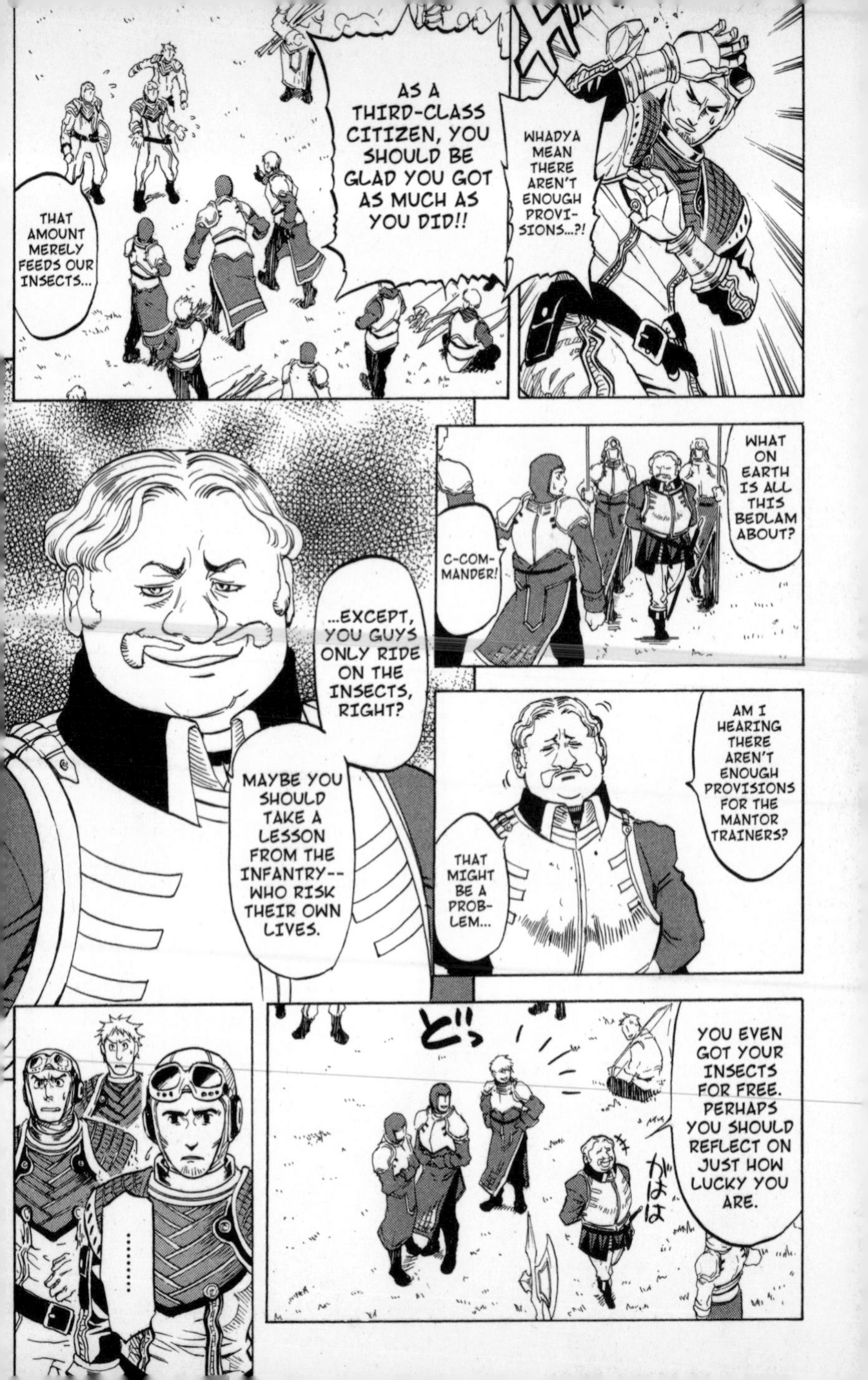
WHADYA MEAN THERE AREN'T ENOUGH PROVISIONS...?!
AS A THIRD-CLASS CITIZEN, YOU SHOULD BE GLAD YOU GOT AS MUCH AS YOU DID!!
THAT AMOUNT MERELY FEEDS OUR INSECTS...
WHAT ON EARTH IS ALL THIS BEDLAM ABOUT?
C-COMMANDER!
AM I HEARING THERE AREN'T ENOUGH PROVISIONS FOR THE MANTOR TRAINERS?
THAT MIGHT BE A PROBLEM...
...EXCEPT, YOU GUYS ONLY RIDE ON THE INSECTS, RIGHT?
MAYBE YOU SHOULD TAKE A LESSON FROM THE INFANTRY-- WHO RISK THEIR OWN LIVES.
YOU EVEN GOT YOUR INSECTS FOR FREE. PERHAPS YOU SHOULD REFLECT ON JUST HOW LUCKY YOU ARE.
どっ
がはは
....

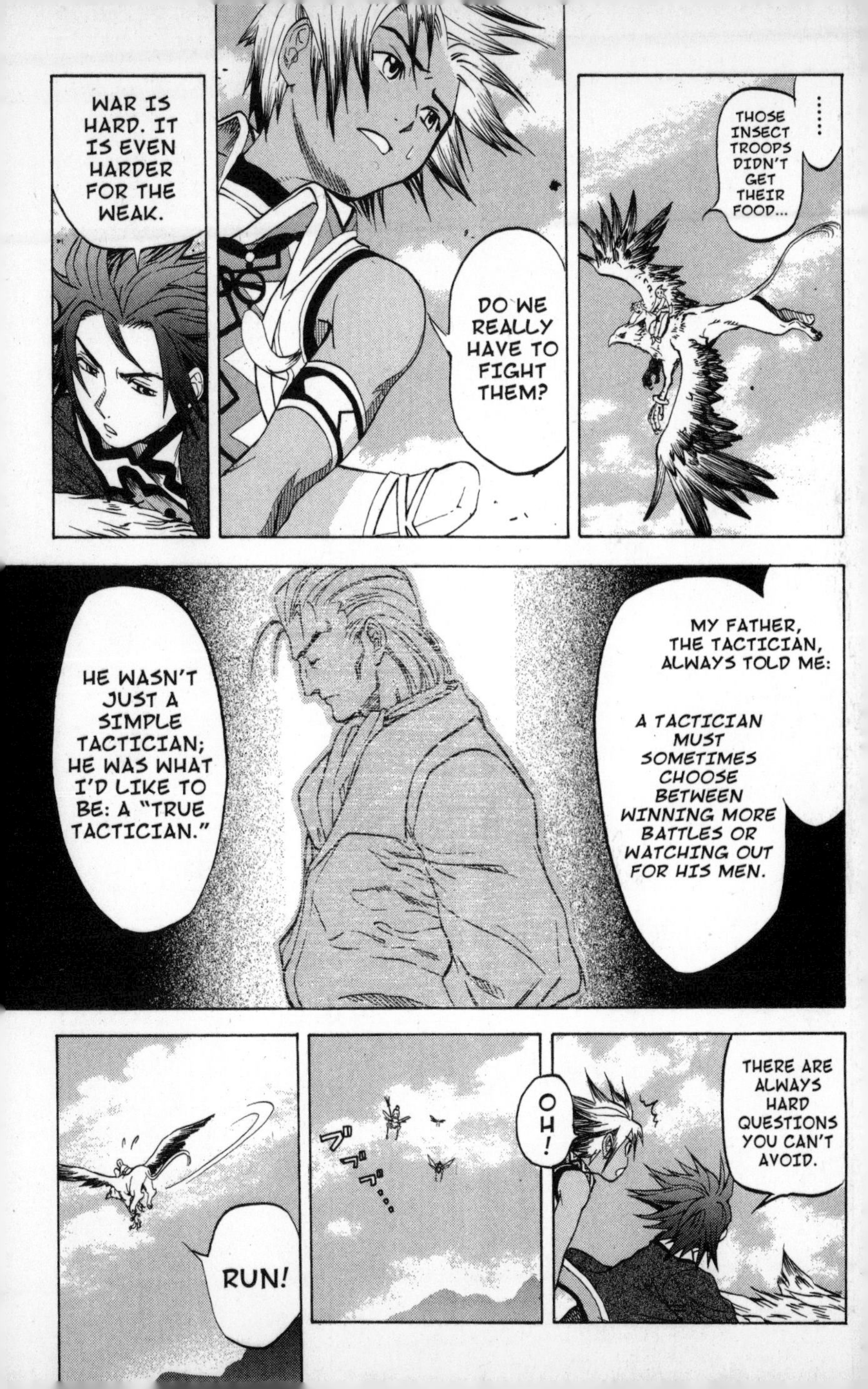
......
THOSE INSECT TROOPS DIDN'T GET THEIR FOOD...
DO WE REALLY HAVE TO FIGHT THEM?
WAR IS HARD. IT IS EVEN HARDER FOR THE WEAK.
MY FATHER, THE TACTICIAN, ALWAYS TOLD ME:
A TACTICIAN MUST SOMETIMES CHOOSE BETWEEN WINNING MORE BATTLES OR WATCHING OUT FOR HIS MEN.
HE WASN'T JUST A SIMPLE TACTICIAN; HE WAS WHAT I'D LIKE TO BE: A "TRUE TACTICIAN."
THERE ARE ALWAYS HARD QUESTIONS YOU CAN'T AVOID.
OH!
RUN!

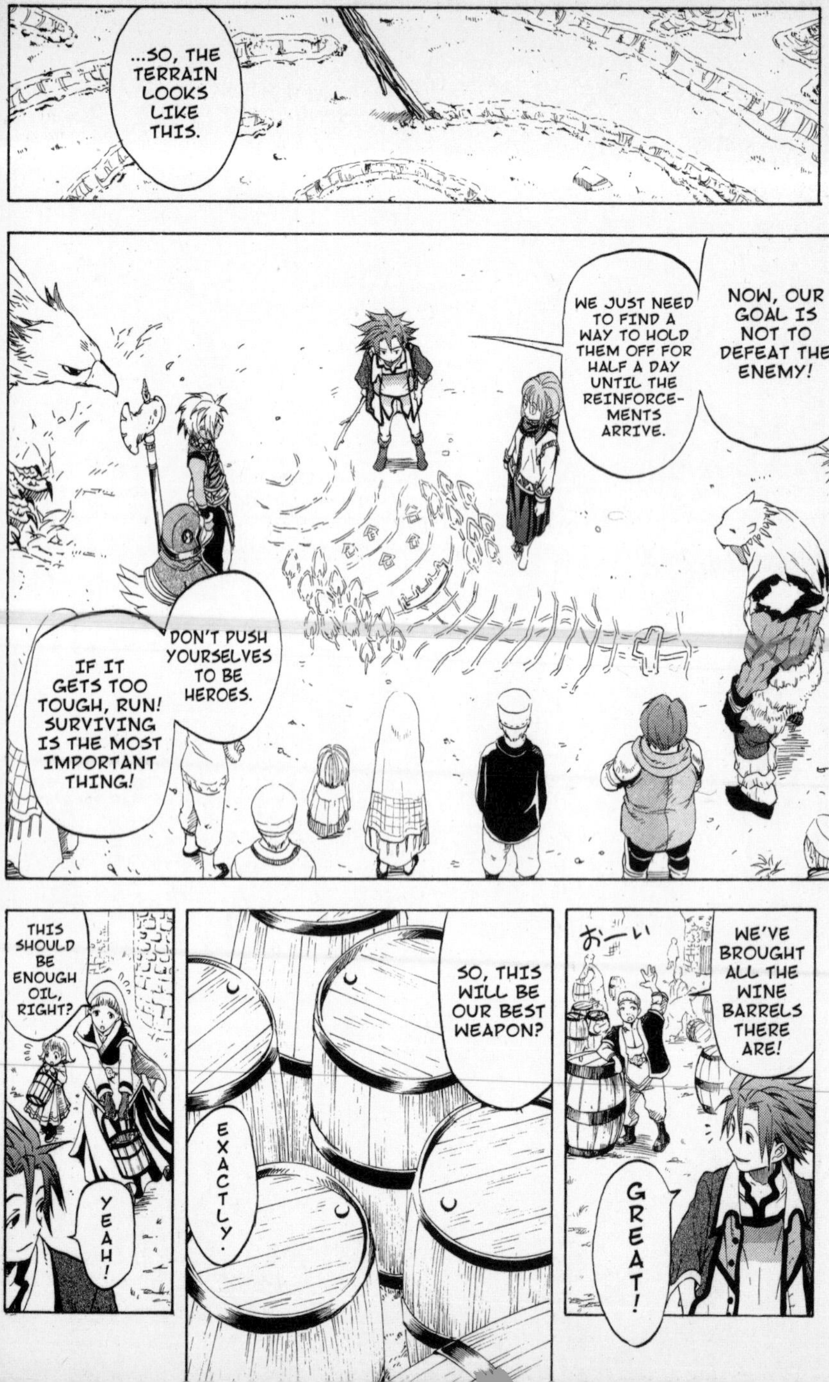
...SO, THE TERRAIN LOOKS LIKE THIS.
NOW, OUR GOAL IS NOT TO DEFEAT THE ENEMY!
WE JUST NEED TO FIND A WAY TO HOLD THEM OFF FOR HALF A DAY UNTIL THE REINFORCEMENTS ARRIVE.
DON'T PUSH YOURSELVES TO BE HEROES.
IF IT GETS TOO TOUGH, RUN! SURVIVING IS THE MOST IMPORTANT THING!
おーい
WE'VE BROUGHT ALL THE WINE BARRELS THERE ARE!
GREAT!
SO, THIS WILL BE OUR BEST WEAPON?
EXACTLY.
THIS SHOULD BE ENOUGH OIL, RIGHT?
YEAH!

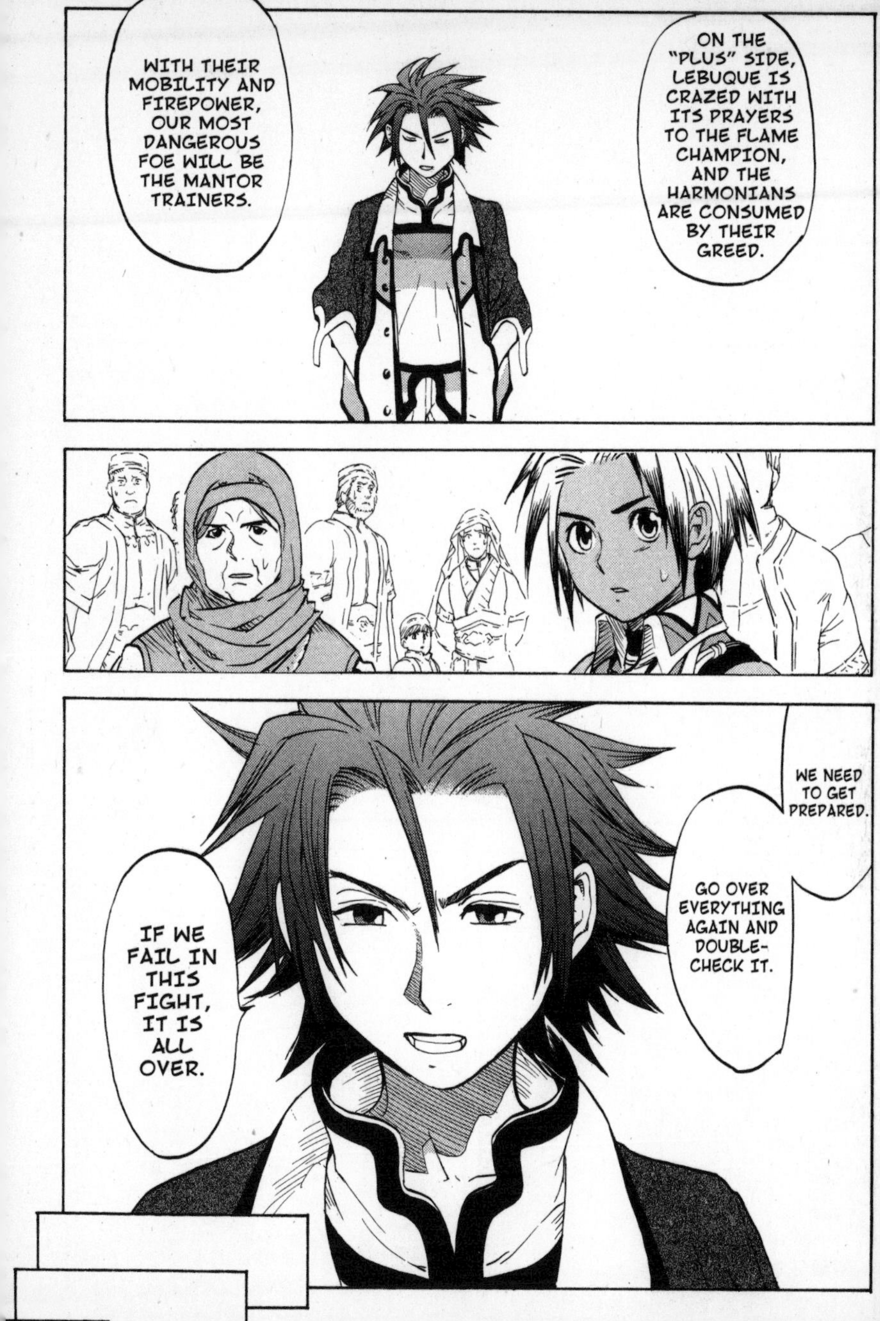
WITH THEIR MOBILITY AND FIREPOWER, OUR MOST DANGEROUS FOE WILL BE THE MANTOR TRAINERS.
ON THE "PLUS" SIDE, LEBUQUE IS CRAZED WITH ITS PRAYERS TO THE FLAME CHAMPION, AND THE HARMONIANS ARE CONSUMED BY THEIR GREED.
IF WE FAIL IN THIS FIGHT, IT IS ALL OVER.
WE NEED TO GET PREPARED.
GO OVER EVERYTHING AGAIN AND DOUBLE-CHECK IT.

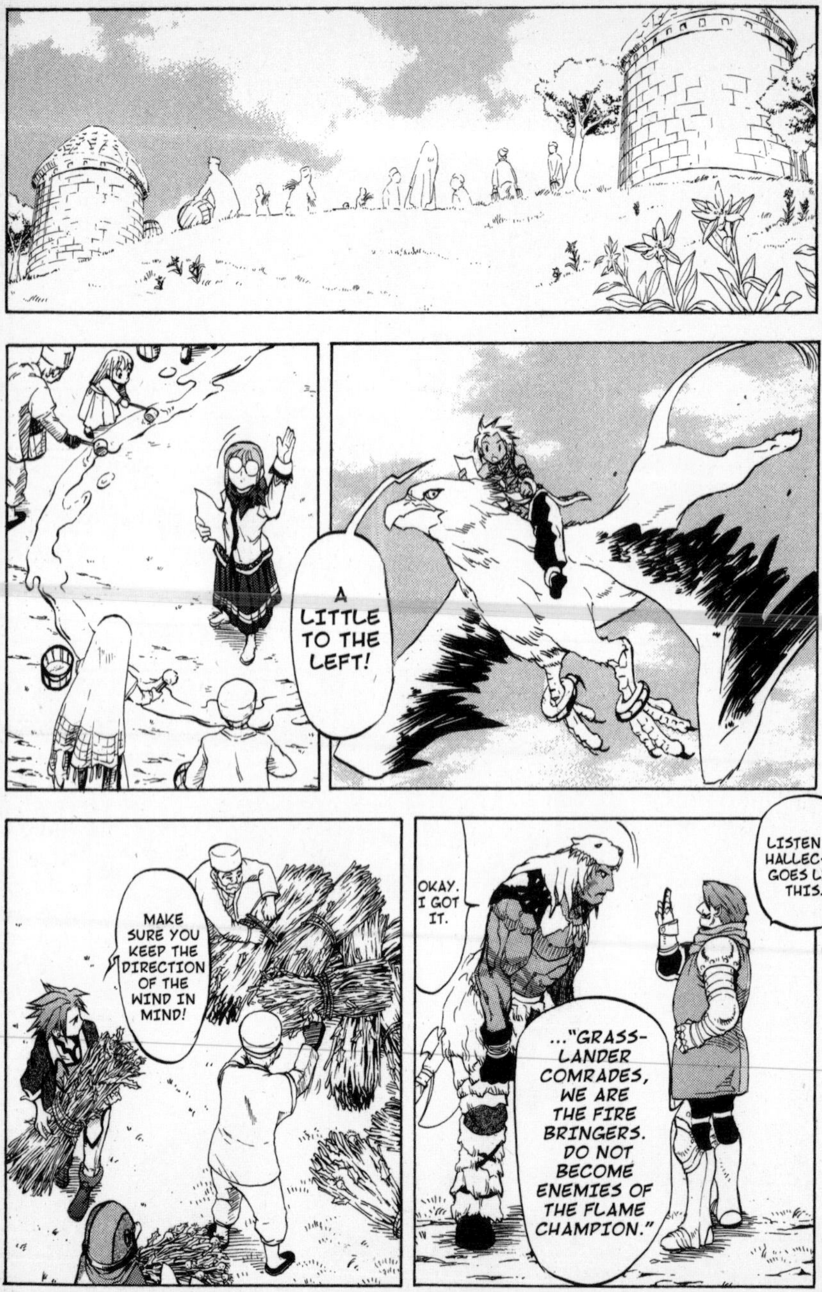
A LITTLE TO THE LEFT!
LISTEN UP, HALLEC--IT GOES LIKE THIS...
OKAY. I GOT IT.
..."GRASS-LANDER COMRADES, WE ARE THE FIRE BRINGERS. DO NOT BECOME ENEMIES OF THE FLAME CHAMPION."
MAKE SURE YOU KEEP THE DIRECTION OF THE WIND IN MIND!

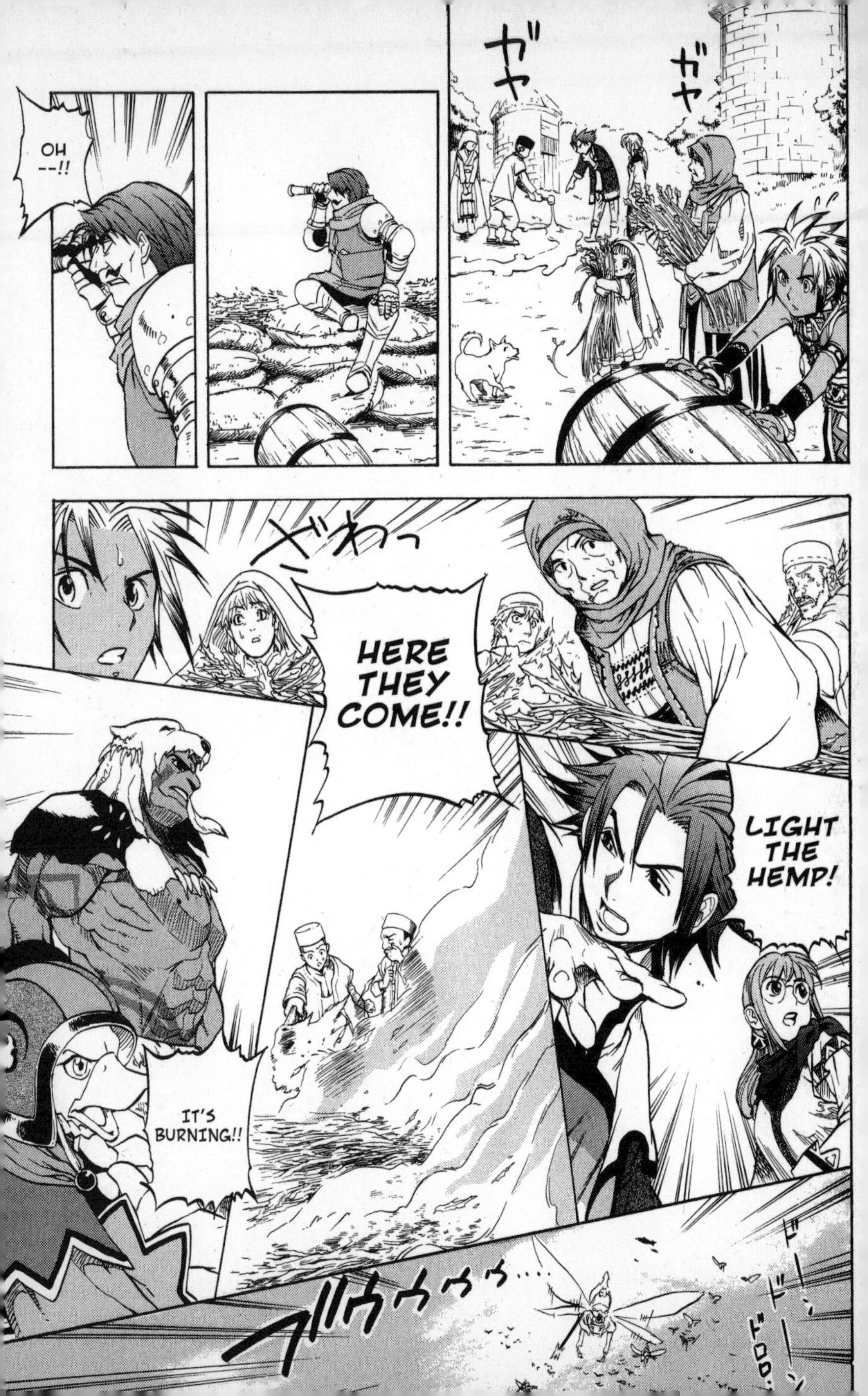
ガヤ
ガヤ
OH --!!
ざわっ
HERE THEY COME!!
LIGHT THE HEMP!
IT'S BURNING!!

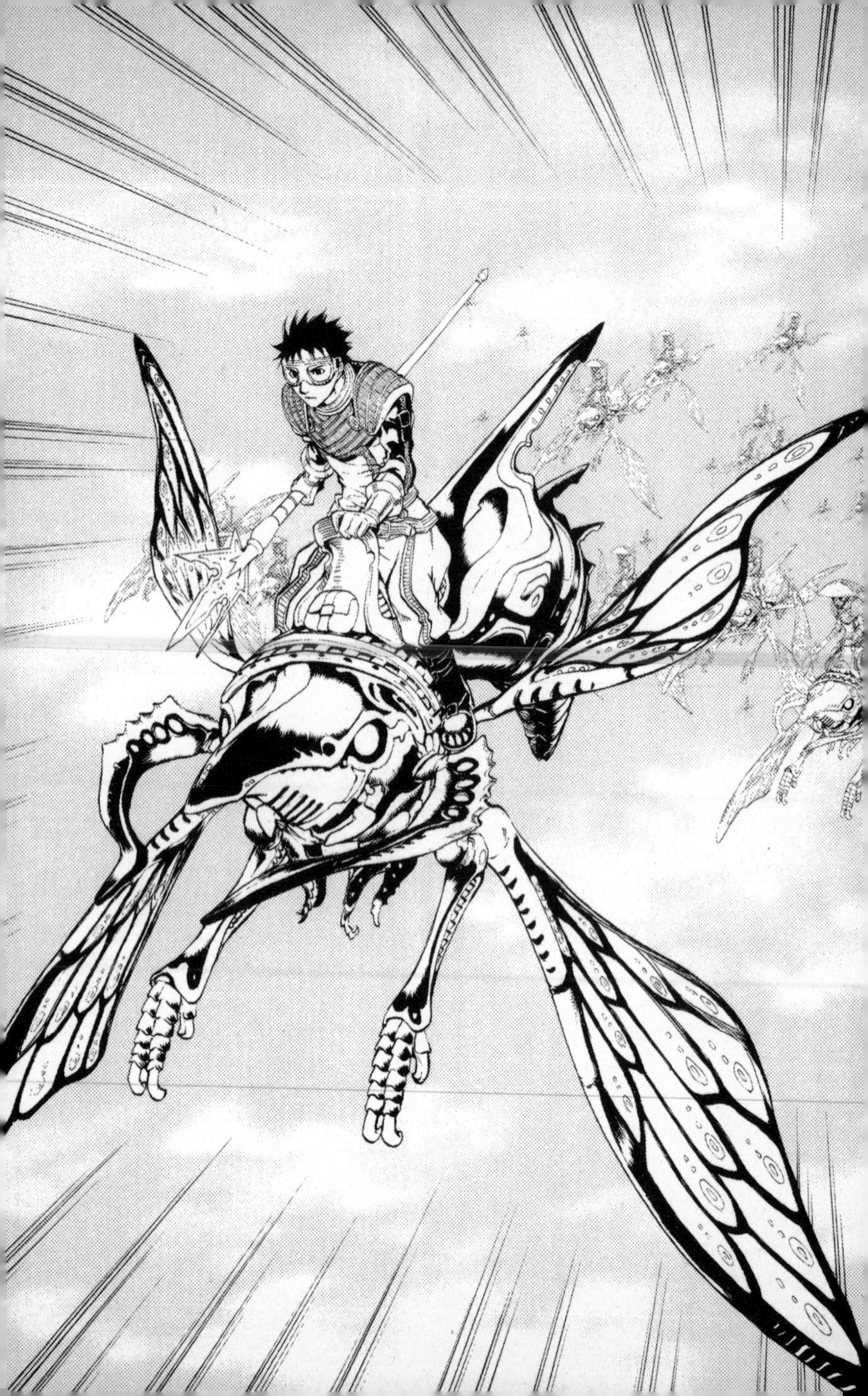

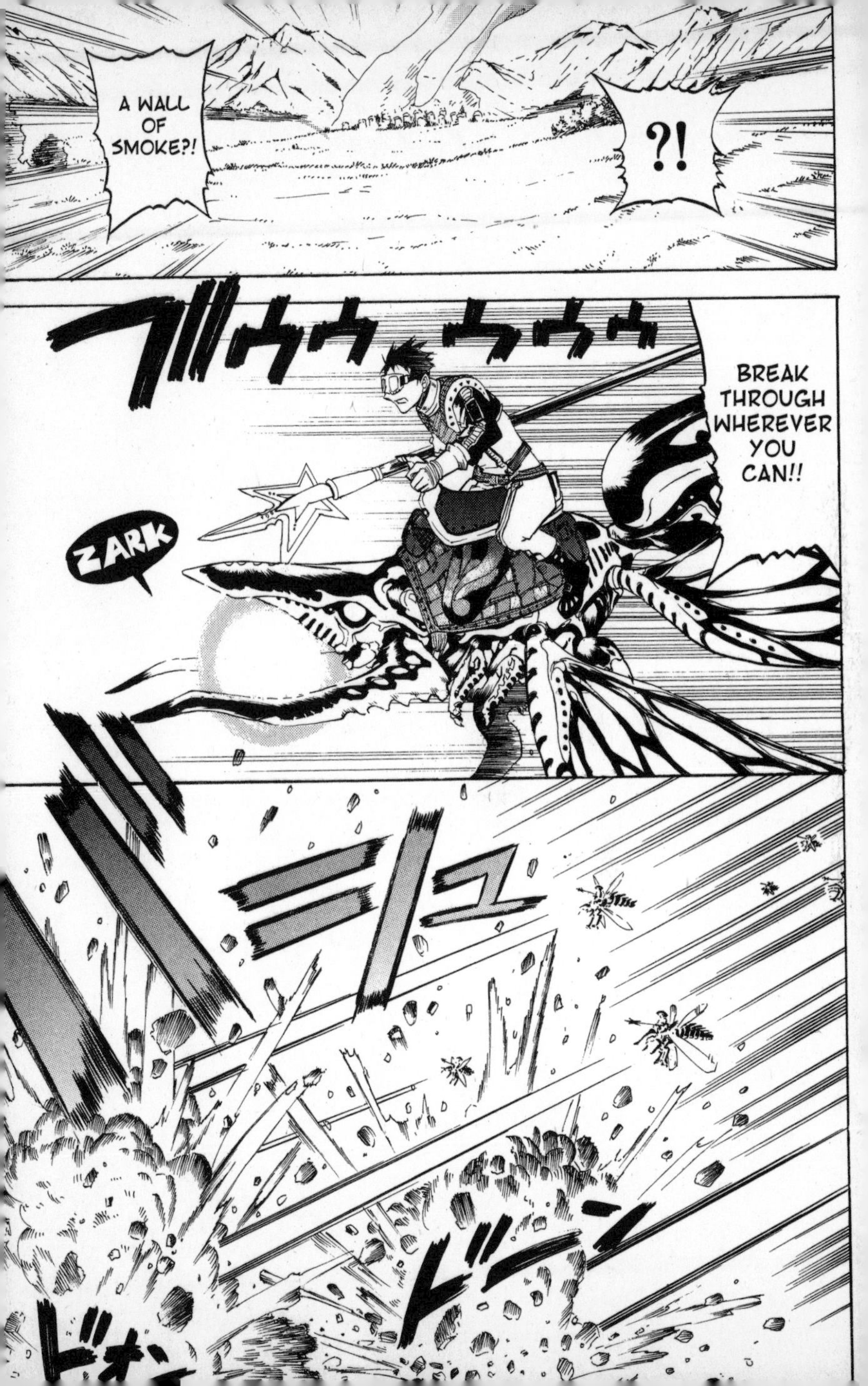
?!
A WALL OF SMOKE?!
BREAK THROUGH WHEREVER YOU CAN!!
ZARK

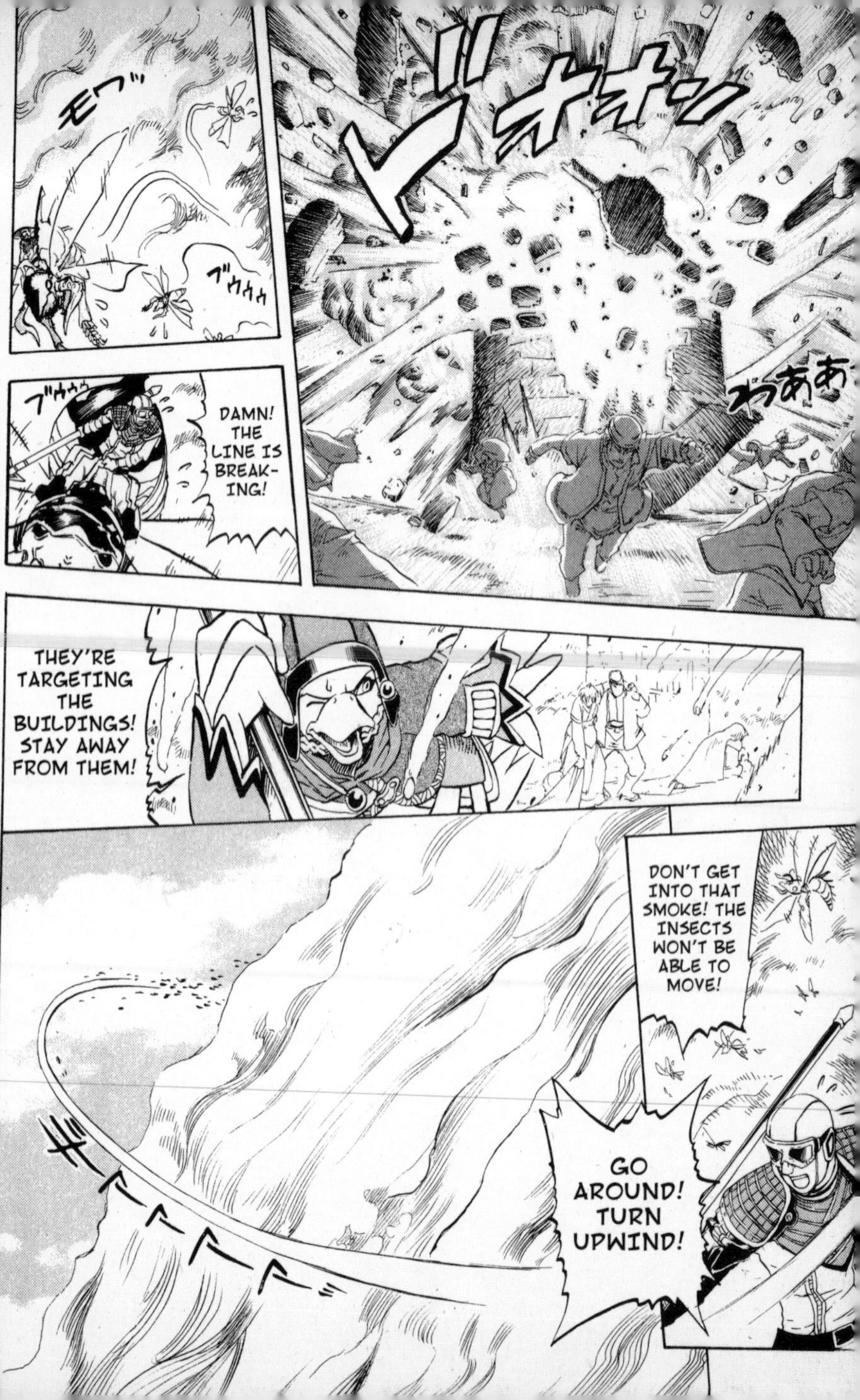
わああ
モワ
ブウウウ
ブウウウ
DAMN! THE LINE IS BREAK-ING!
THEY'RE TARGETING THE BUILDINGS! STAY AWAY FROM THEM!
DON'T GET INTO THAT SMOKE! THE INSECTS WON'T BE ABLE TO MOVE!
GO AROUND! TURN UPWIND!

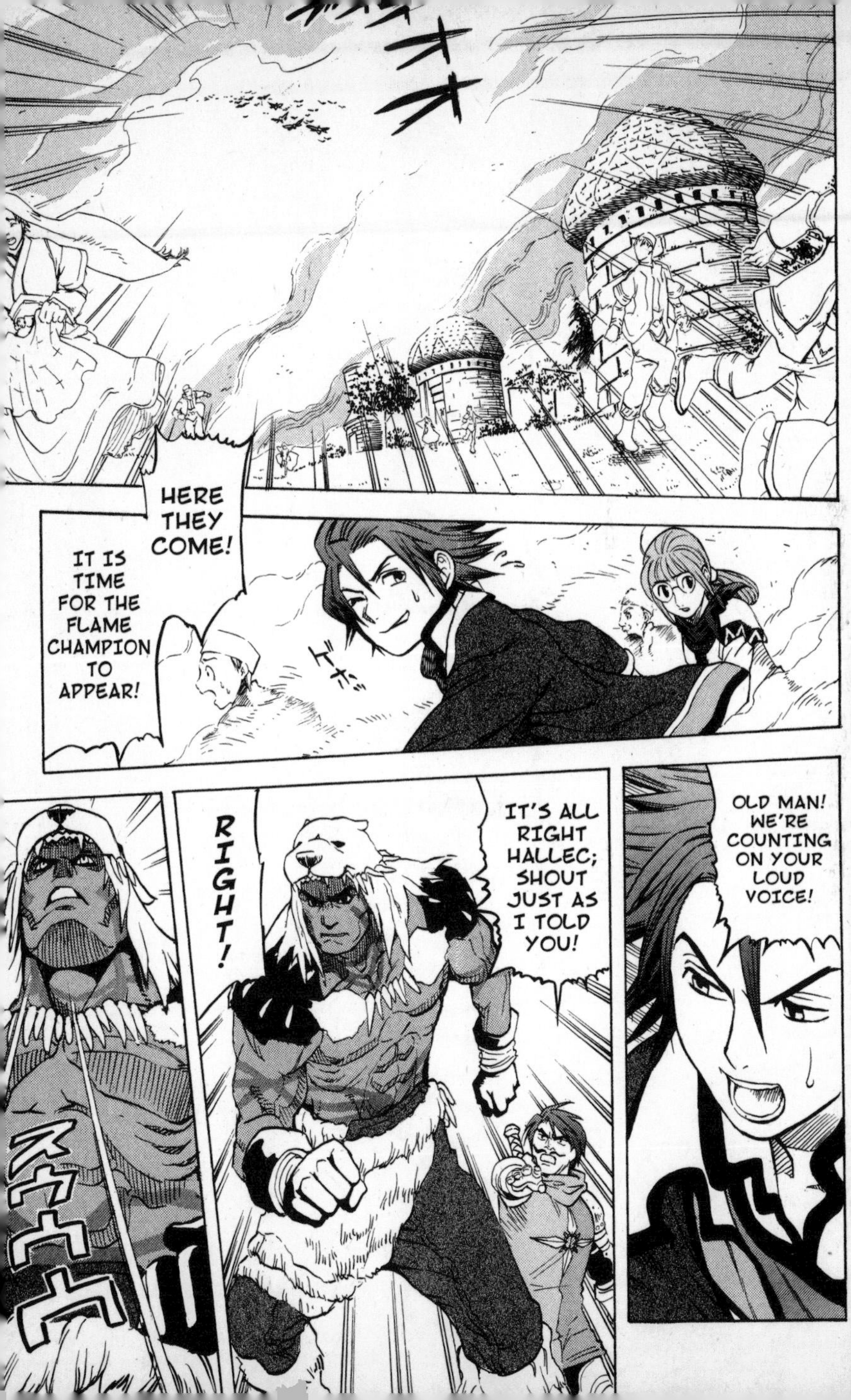
HERE THEY COME!
IT IS TIME FOR THE FLAME CHAMPION TO APPEAR!
OLD MAN! WE'RE COUNTING ON YOUR LOUD VOICE!
IT'S ALL RIGHT HALLEC; SHOUT JUST AS I TOLD YOU!
RIGHT!

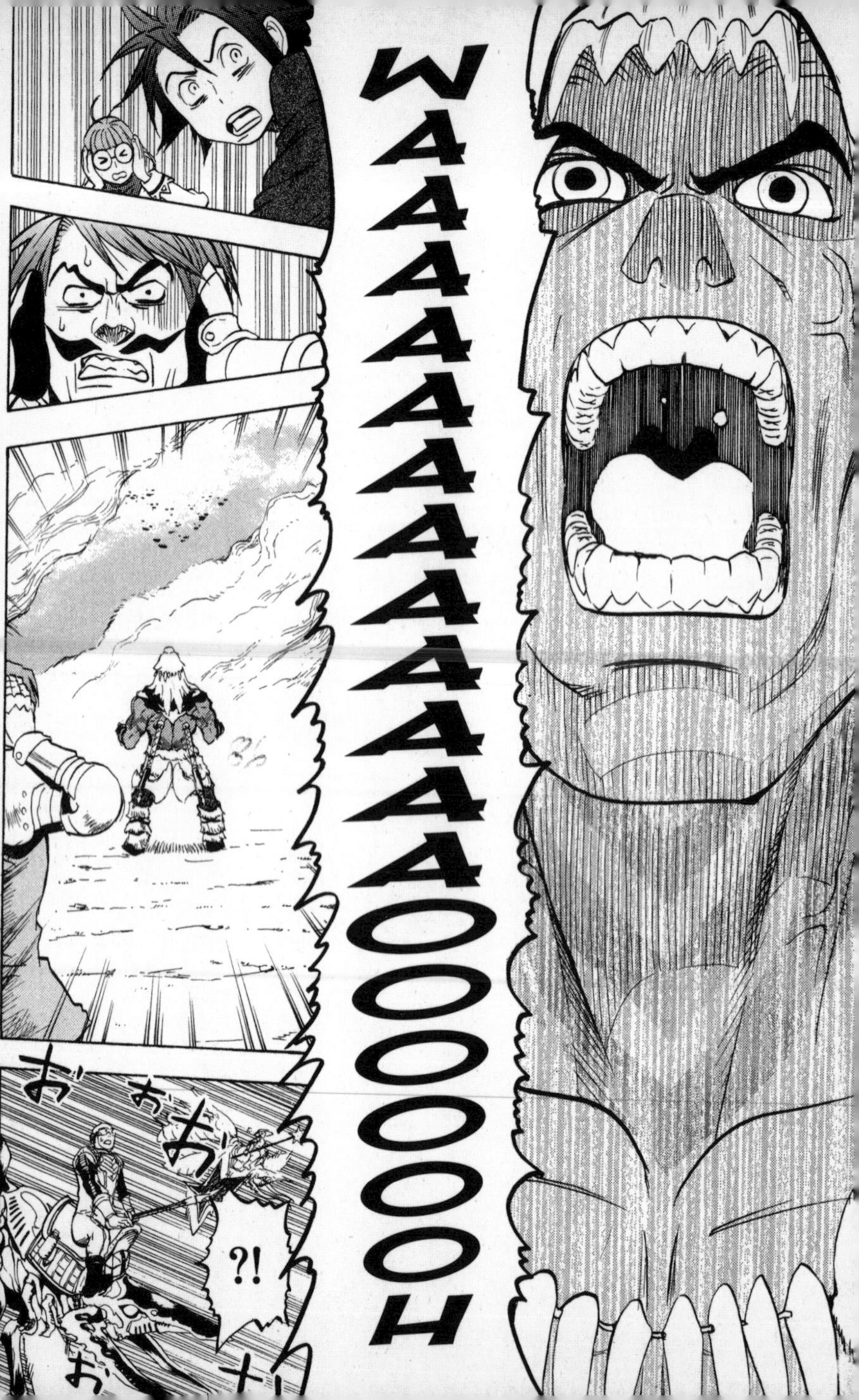
WAAAAAAAAAAOOOOOH
?!

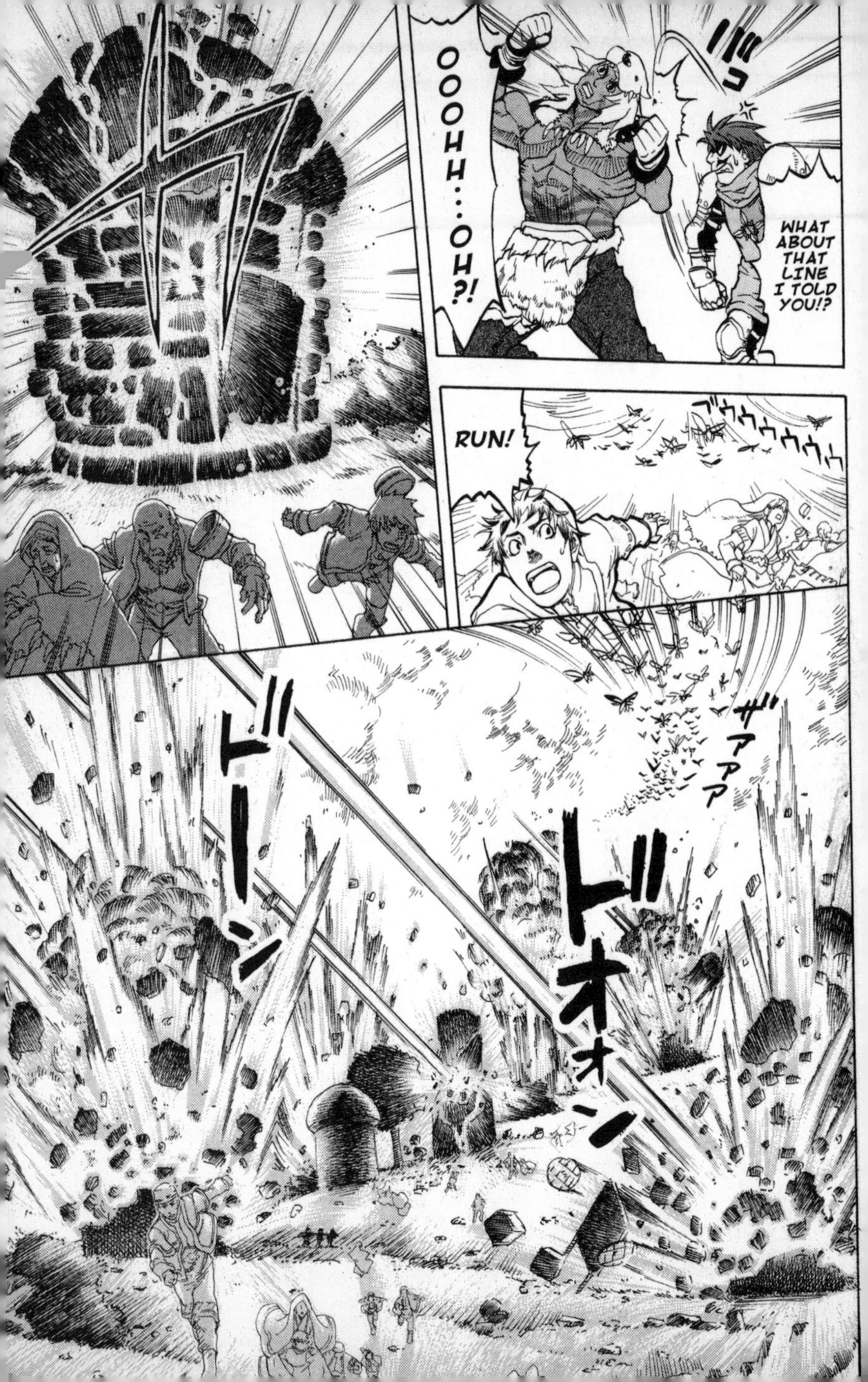
OOOHH...OH?!
WHAT ABOUT THAT LINE I TOLD YOU!?
RUN!
ブウウウウウウ
ザアアア
ドオォン
ドーン

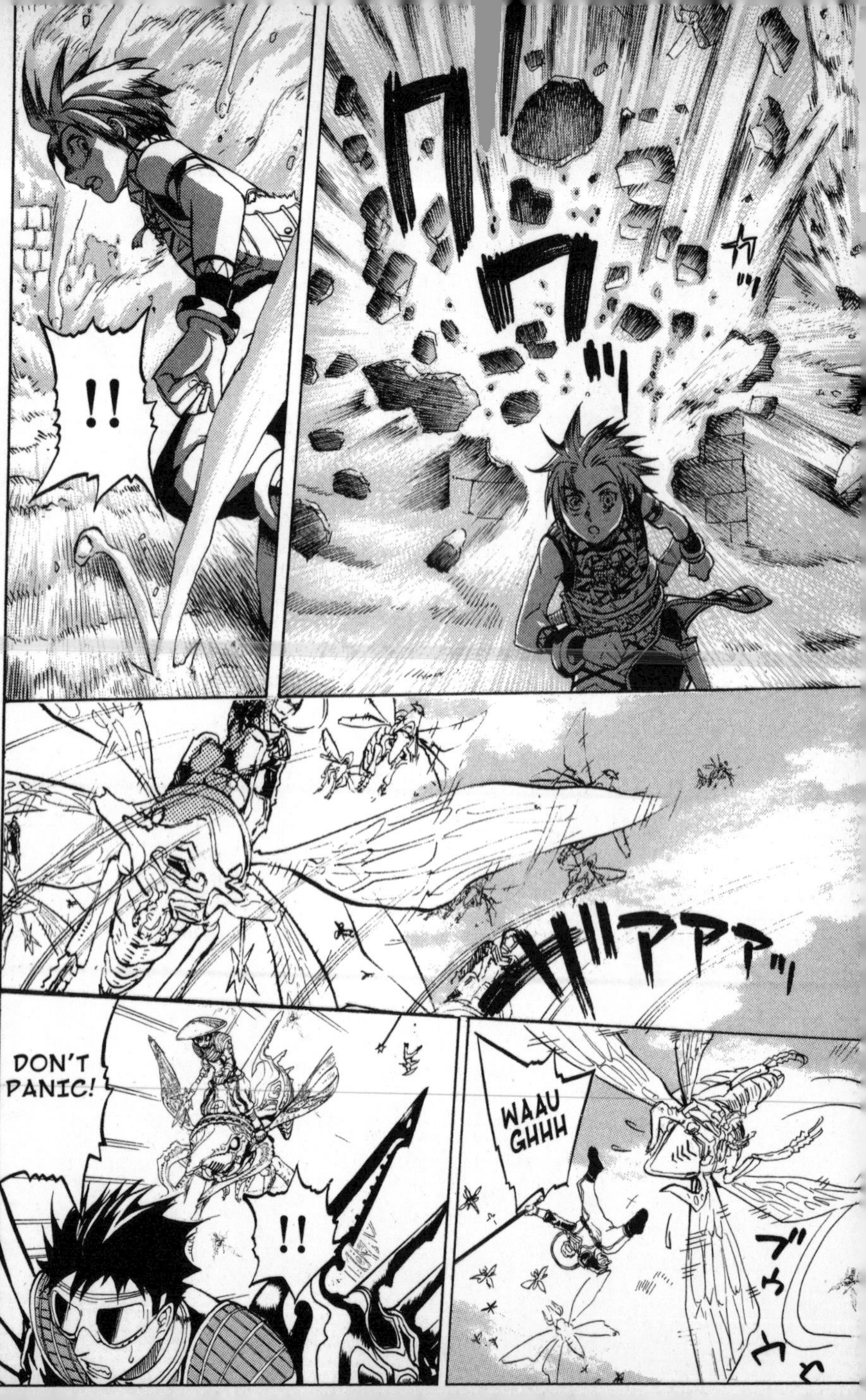
!!
WAAU GHHH
DON'T PANIC!
!!

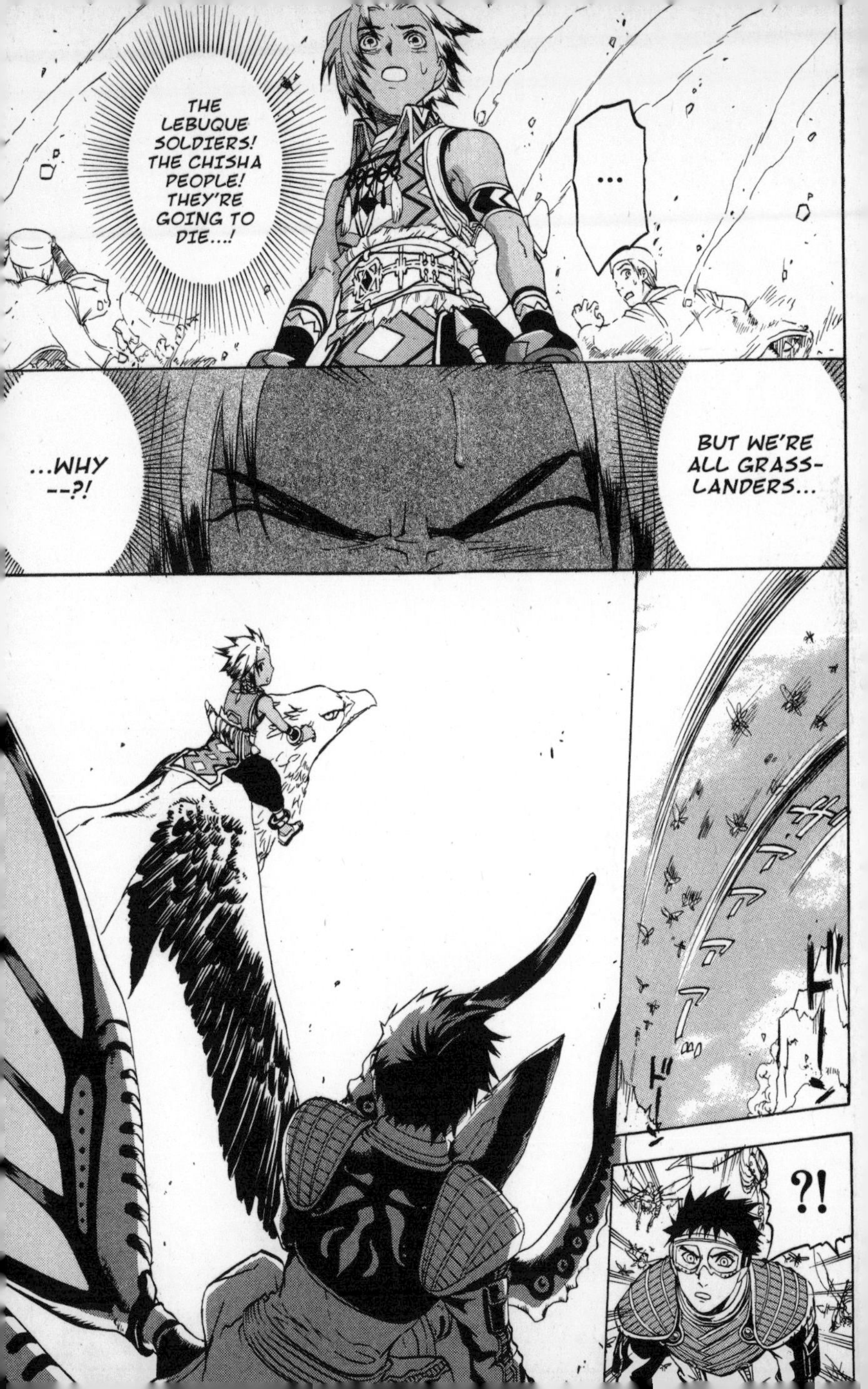
...
THE LEBUQUE SOLDIERS! THE CHISHA PEOPLE! THEY'RE GOING TO DIE...!
BUT WE'RE ALL GRASS-LANDERS...
...WHY --?!
?!

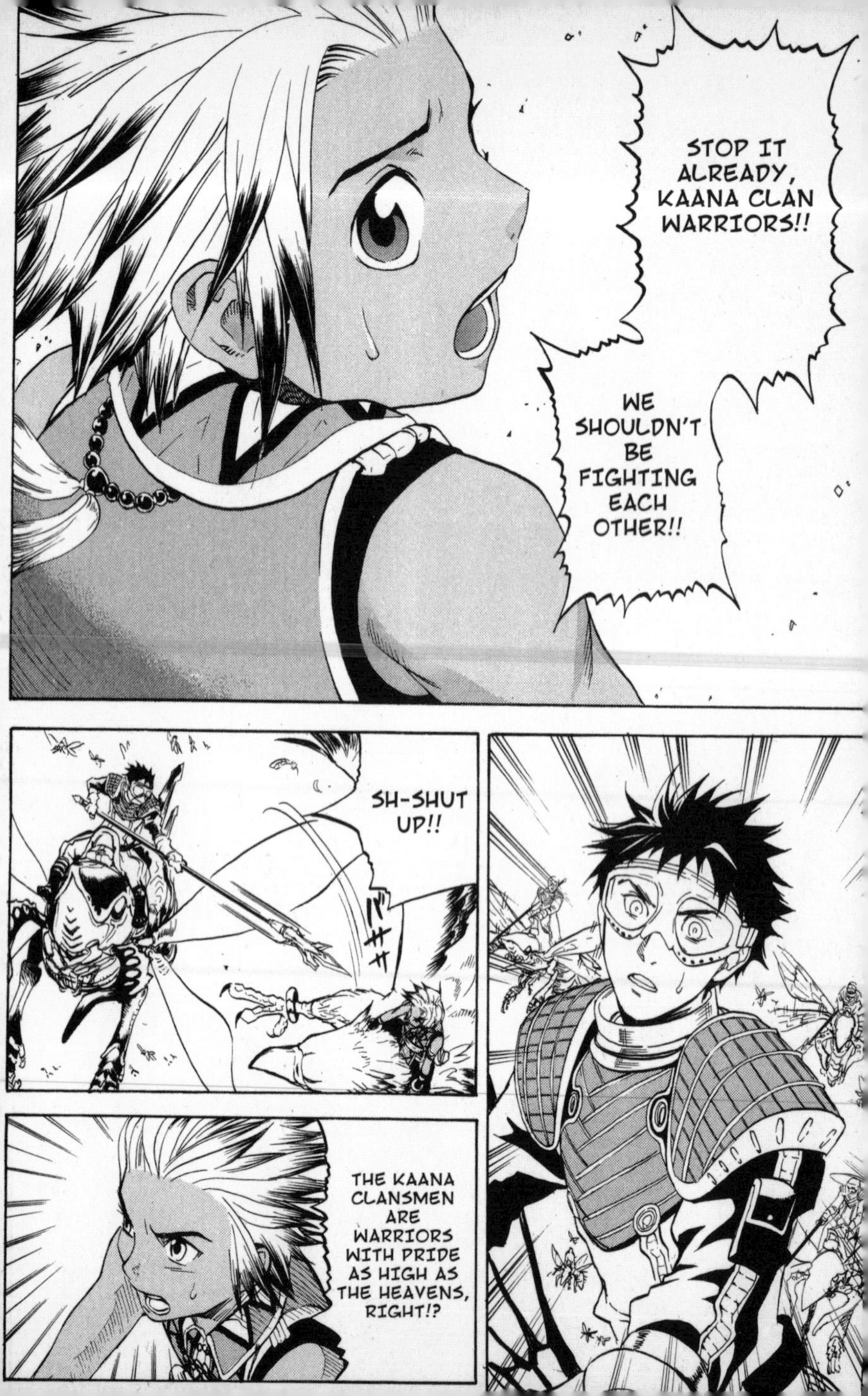
STOP IT ALREADY, KAANA CLAN WARRIORS!!
WE SHOULDN'T BE FIGHTING EACH OTHER!!
SH-SHUT UP!!
バッ
THE KAANA CLANSMEN ARE WARRIORS WITH PRIDE AS HIGH AS THE HEAVENS, RIGHT!?

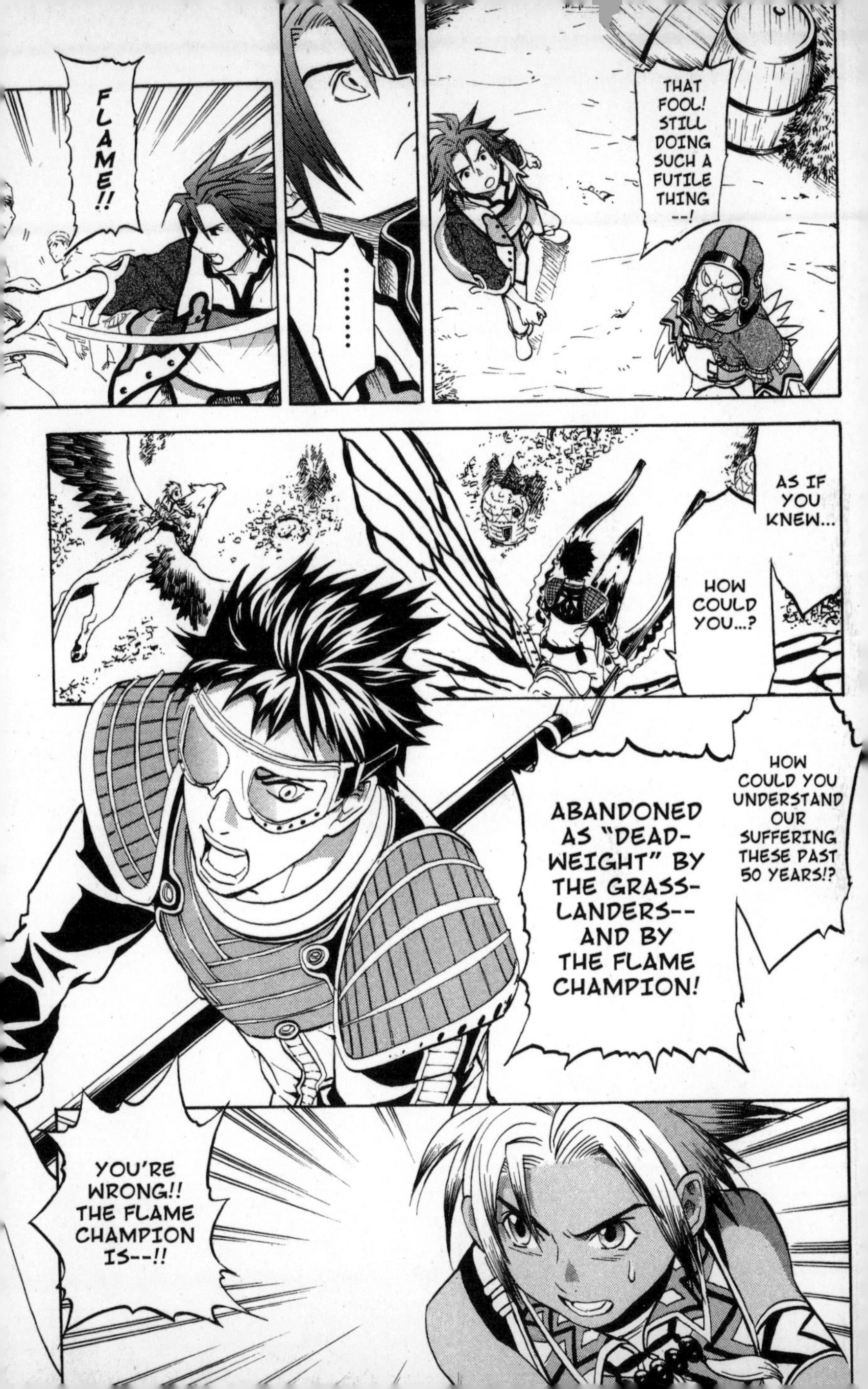
THAT FOOL! STILL DOING SUCH A FUTILE THING --!
......
FLAME!!
AS IF YOU KNEW...
HOW COULD YOU...?
HOW COULD YOU UNDERSTAND OUR SUFFERING THESE PAST 50 YEARS!?
ABANDONED AS "DEAD-WEIGHT" BY THE GRASS-LANDERS-- AND BY THE FLAME CHAMPION!
YOU'RE WRONG!! THE FLAME CHAMPION IS--!!

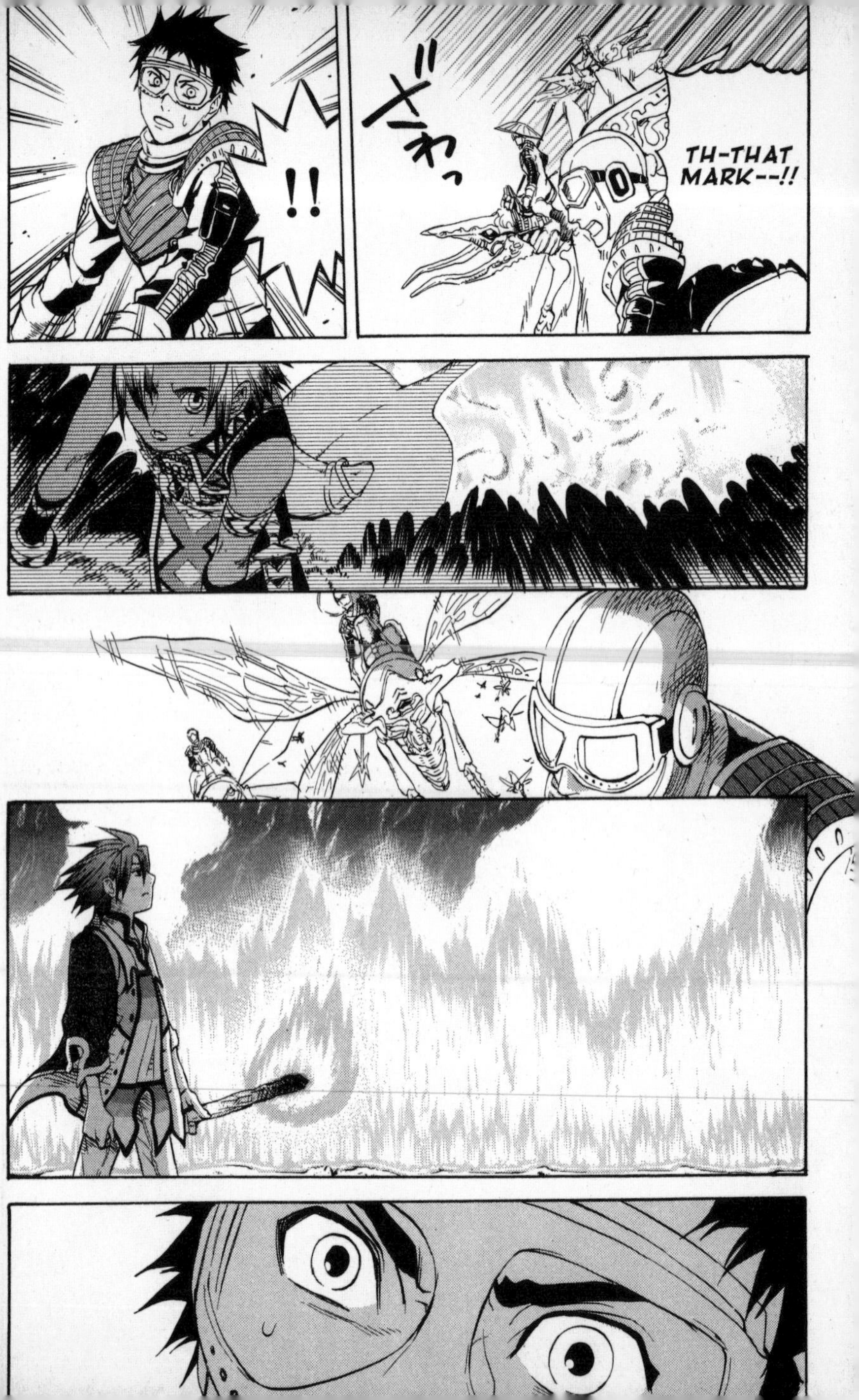
ざわっ
TH-THAT MARK--!!
!!

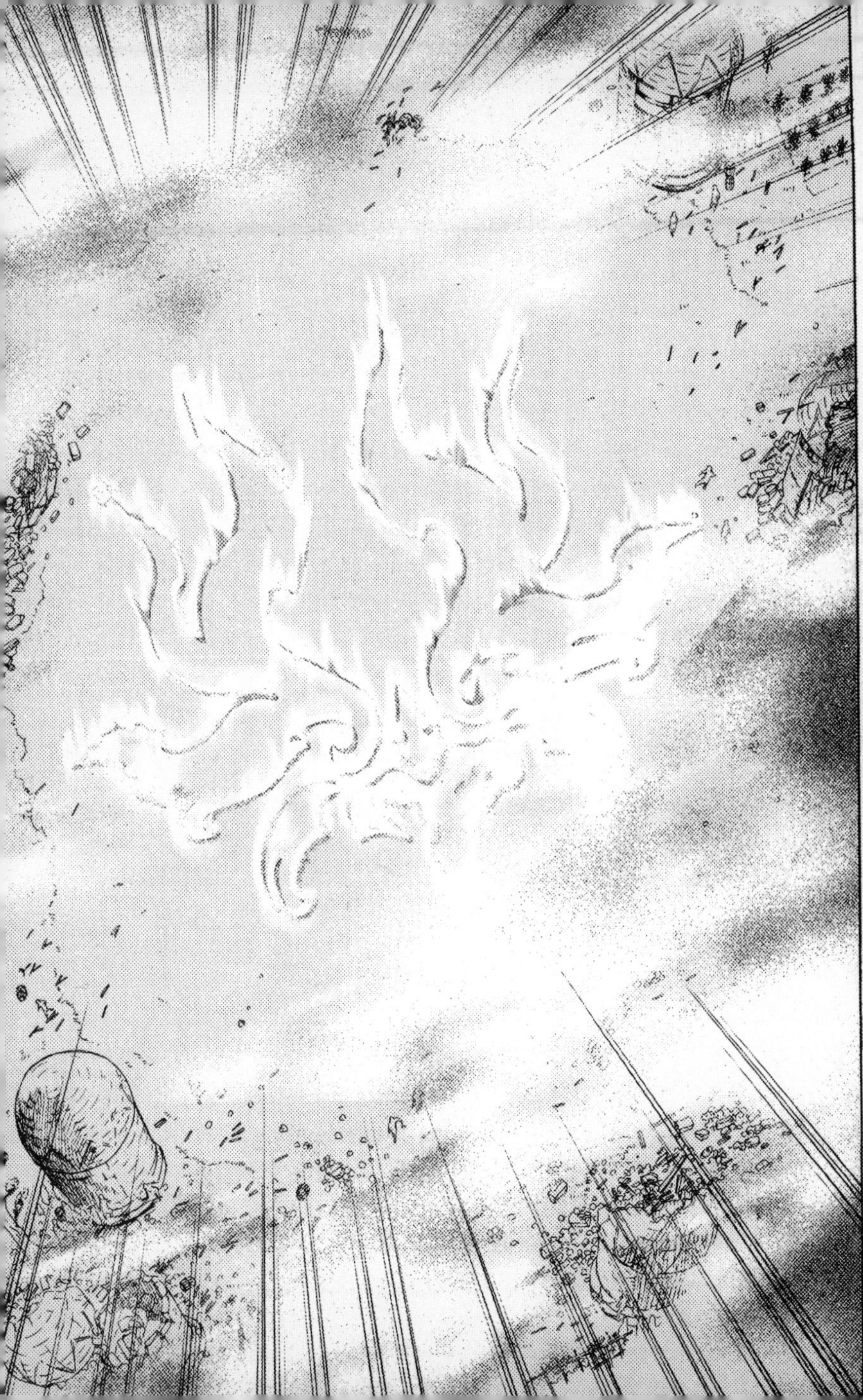

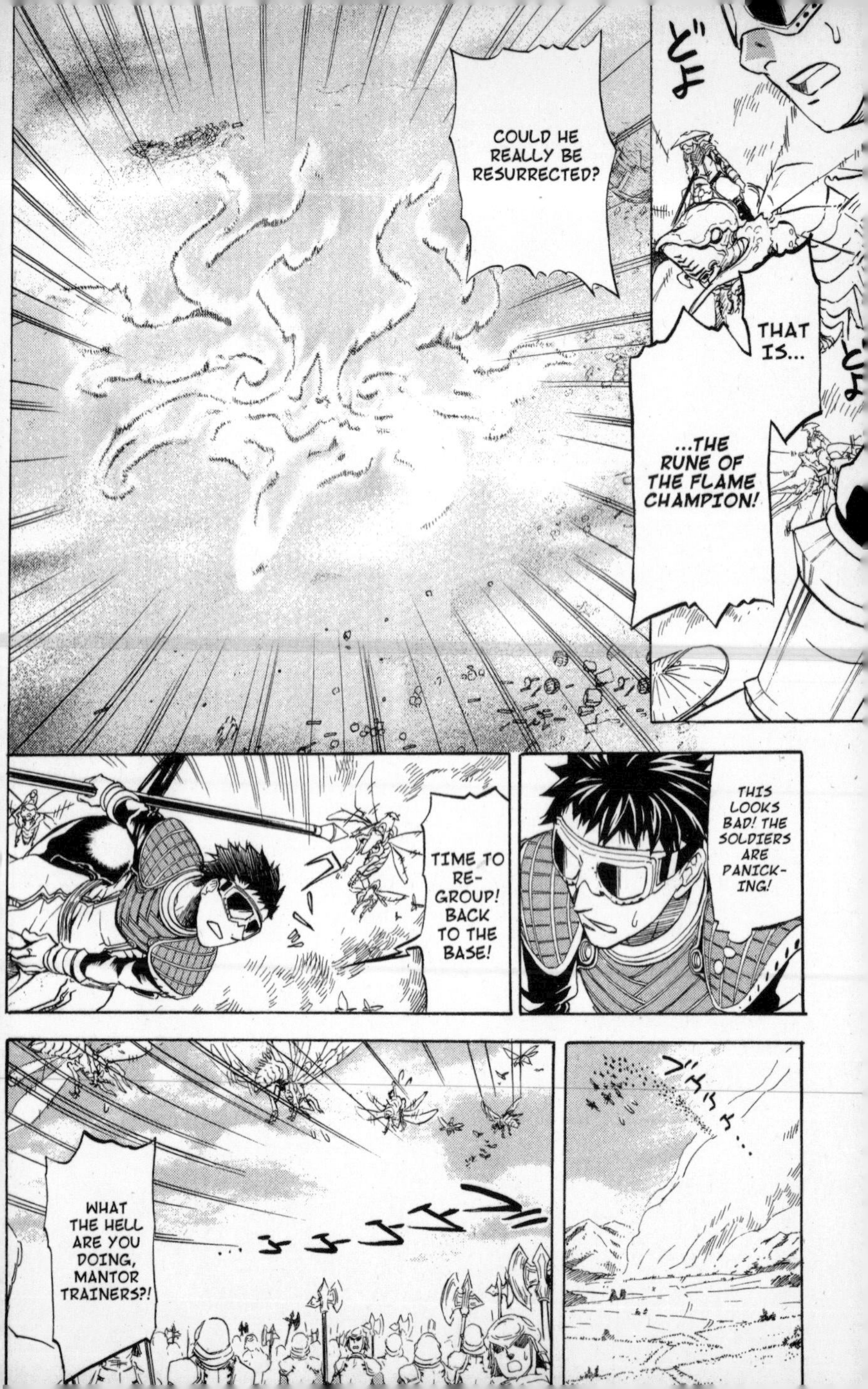
どよ
THAT IS...
...THE RUNE OF THE FLAME CHAMPION!
どよ
COULD HE REALLY BE RESURRECTED?
THIS LOOKS BAD! THE SOLDIERS ARE PANICK-ING!
TIME TO RE-GROUP! BACK TO THE BASE!
WHAT THE HELL ARE YOU DOING, MANTOR TRAINERS?!

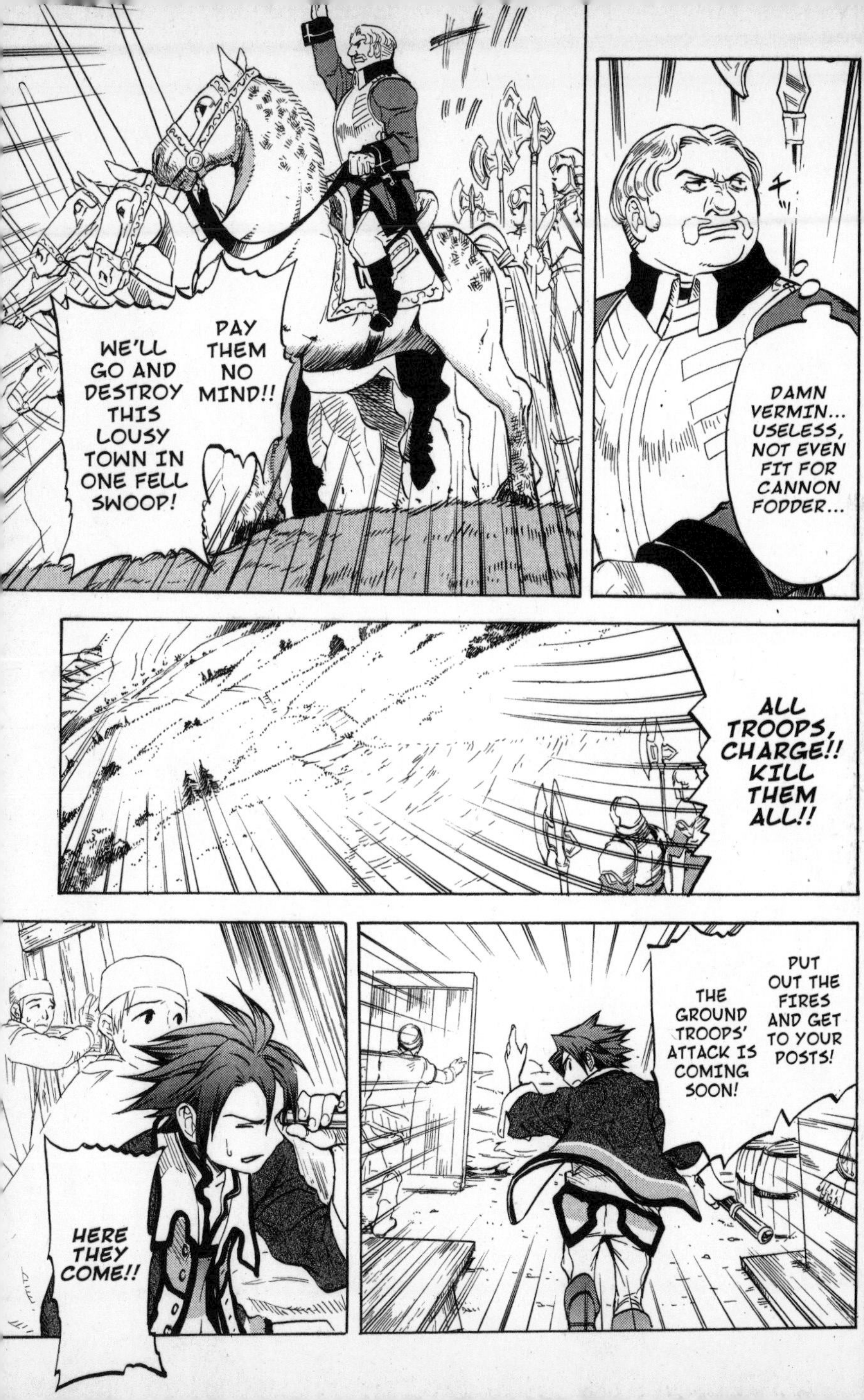
DAMN VERMIN... USELESS, NOT EVEN FIT FOR CANNON FODDER...
PAY THEM NO MIND!!
WE'LL GO AND DESTROY THIS LOUSY TOWN IN ONE FELL SWOOP!
ALL TROOPS, CHARGE!! KILL THEM ALL!!
PUT OUT THE FIRES AND GET TO YOUR POSTS!
THE GROUND TROOPS' ATTACK IS COMING SOON!
HERE THEY COME!!

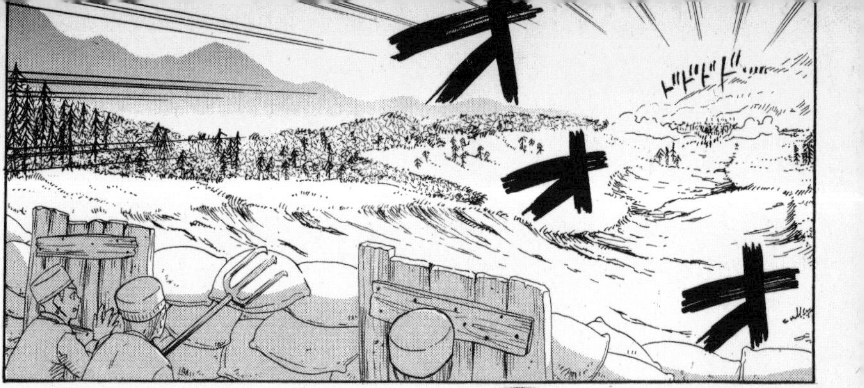
オオオ
ドドドド…
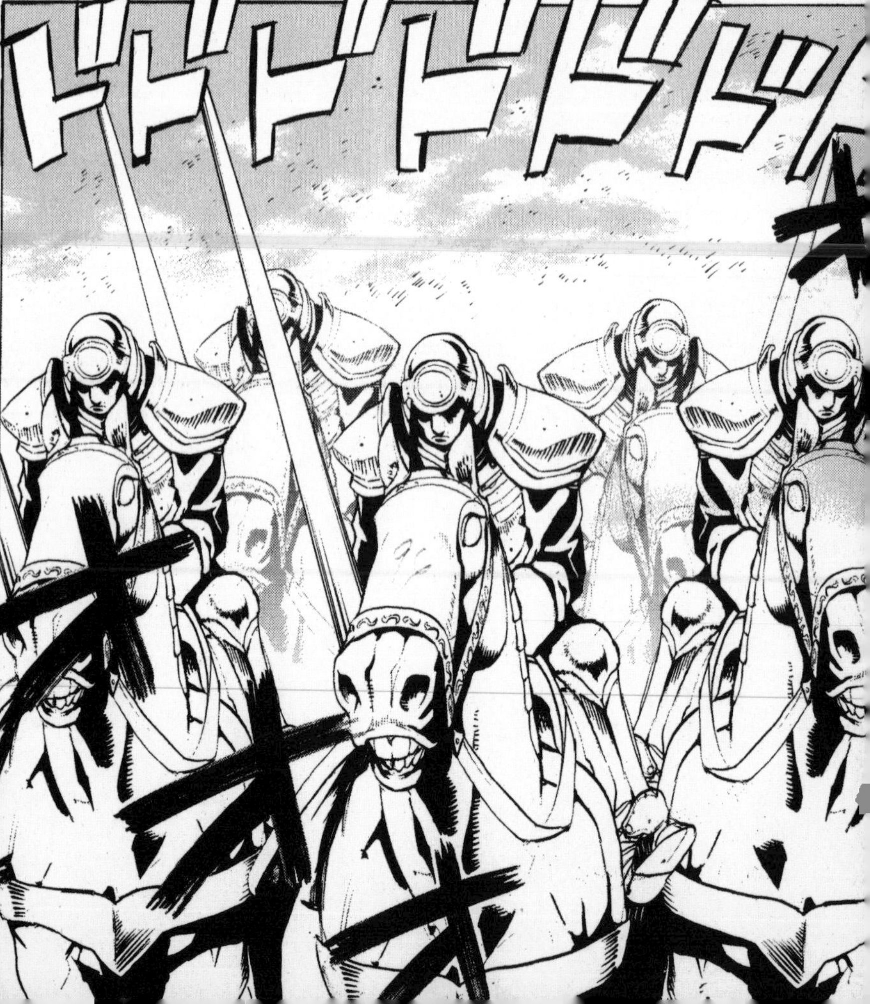
ドドドドドド
オオ

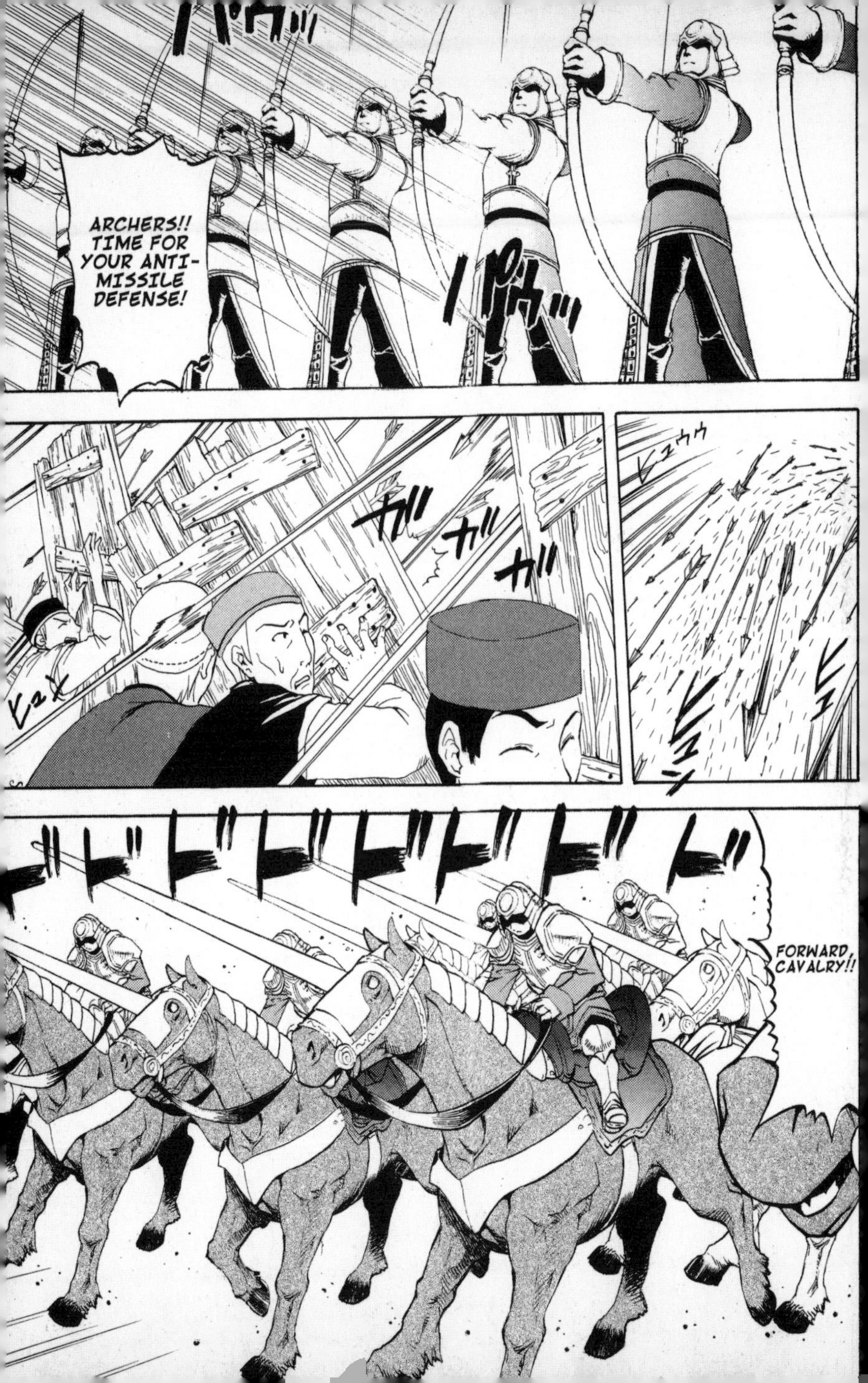
ARCHERS!! TIME FOR YOUR ANTI-MISSILE DEFENSE!
FORWARD CAVALRY!!

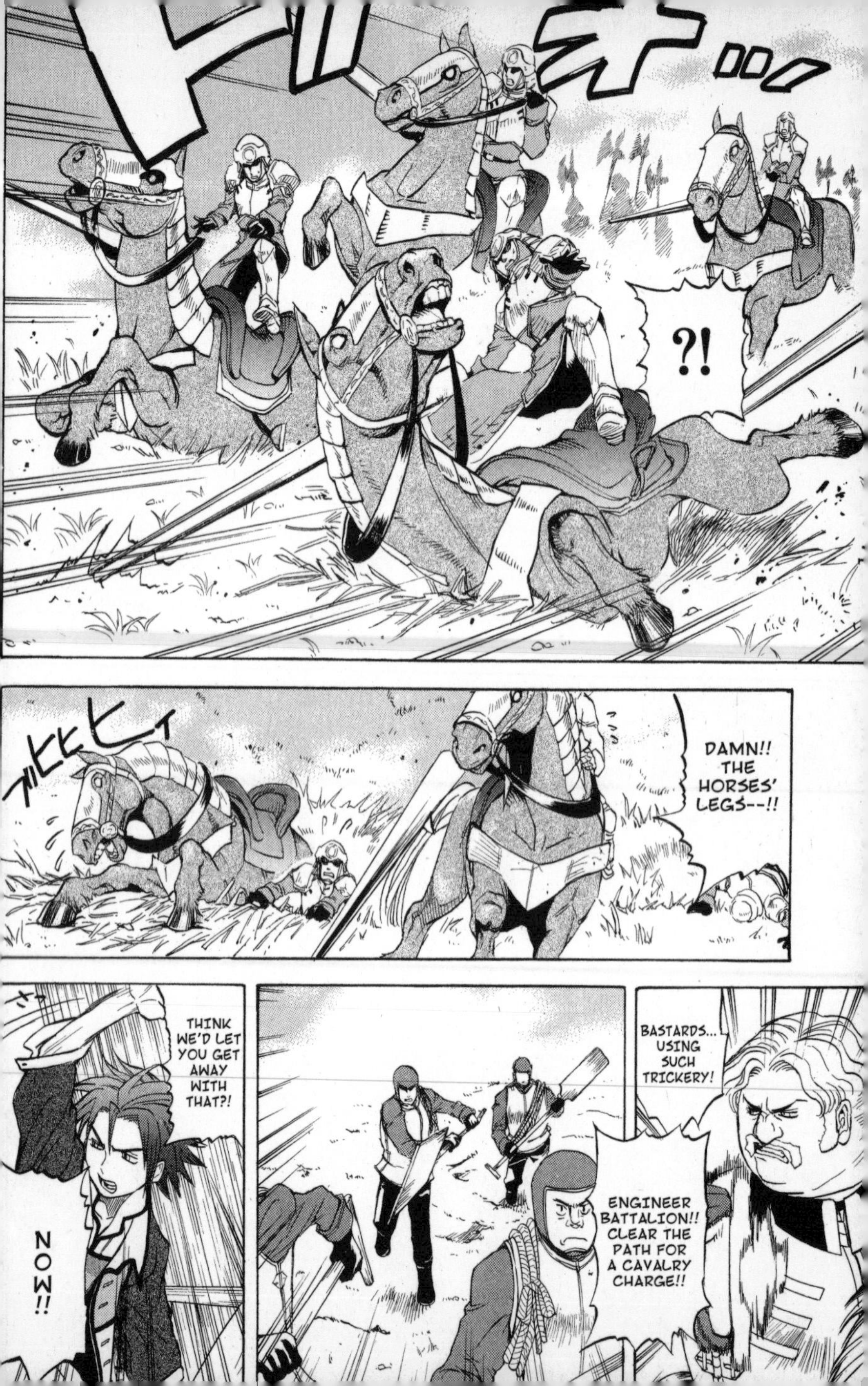
?!
DAMN!! THE HORSES' LEGS--!!
BASTARDS... USING SUCH TRICKERY!
ENGINEER BATTALION!! CLEAR THE PATH FOR A CAVALRY CHARGE!!
THINK WE'D LET YOU GET AWAY WITH THAT?!
NOW!!

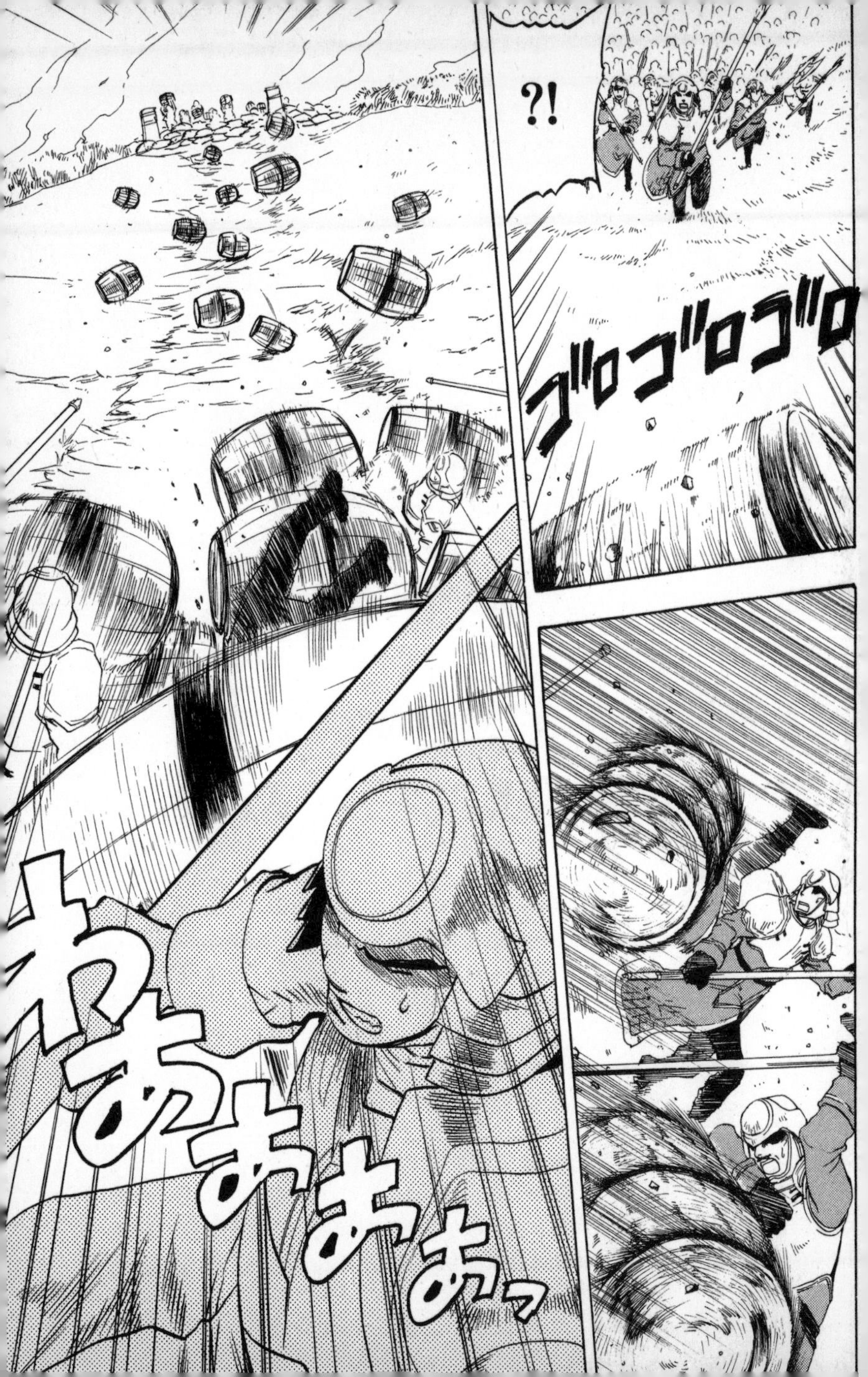
?!
ゴロゴロ
わぁぁぁぁっ

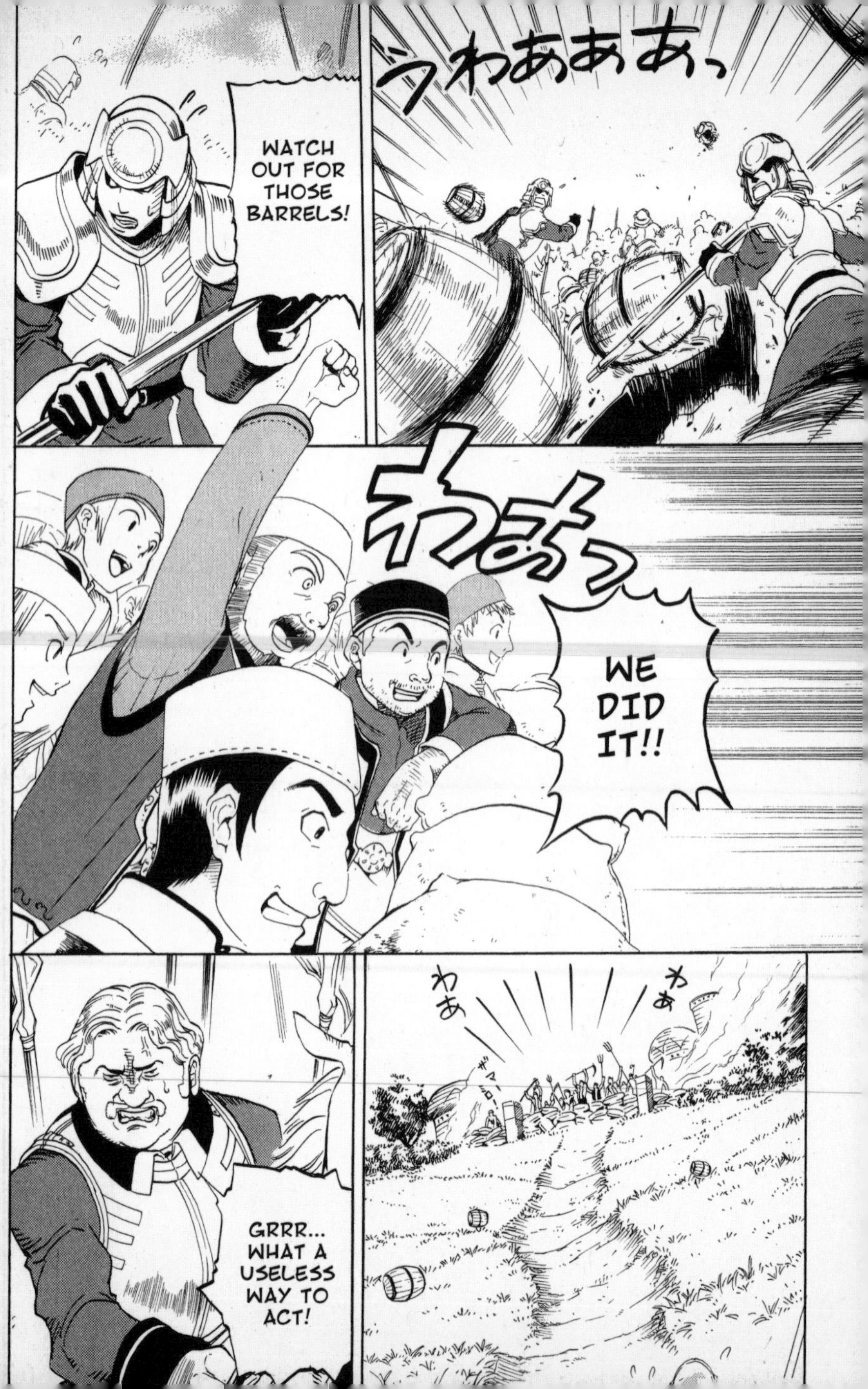
うわあああっ
WATCH OUT FOR THOSE BARRELS!
わあっ
WE DID IT!!
わあ
わあ
ザマーミロ!
GRRR... WHAT A USELESS WAY TO ACT!

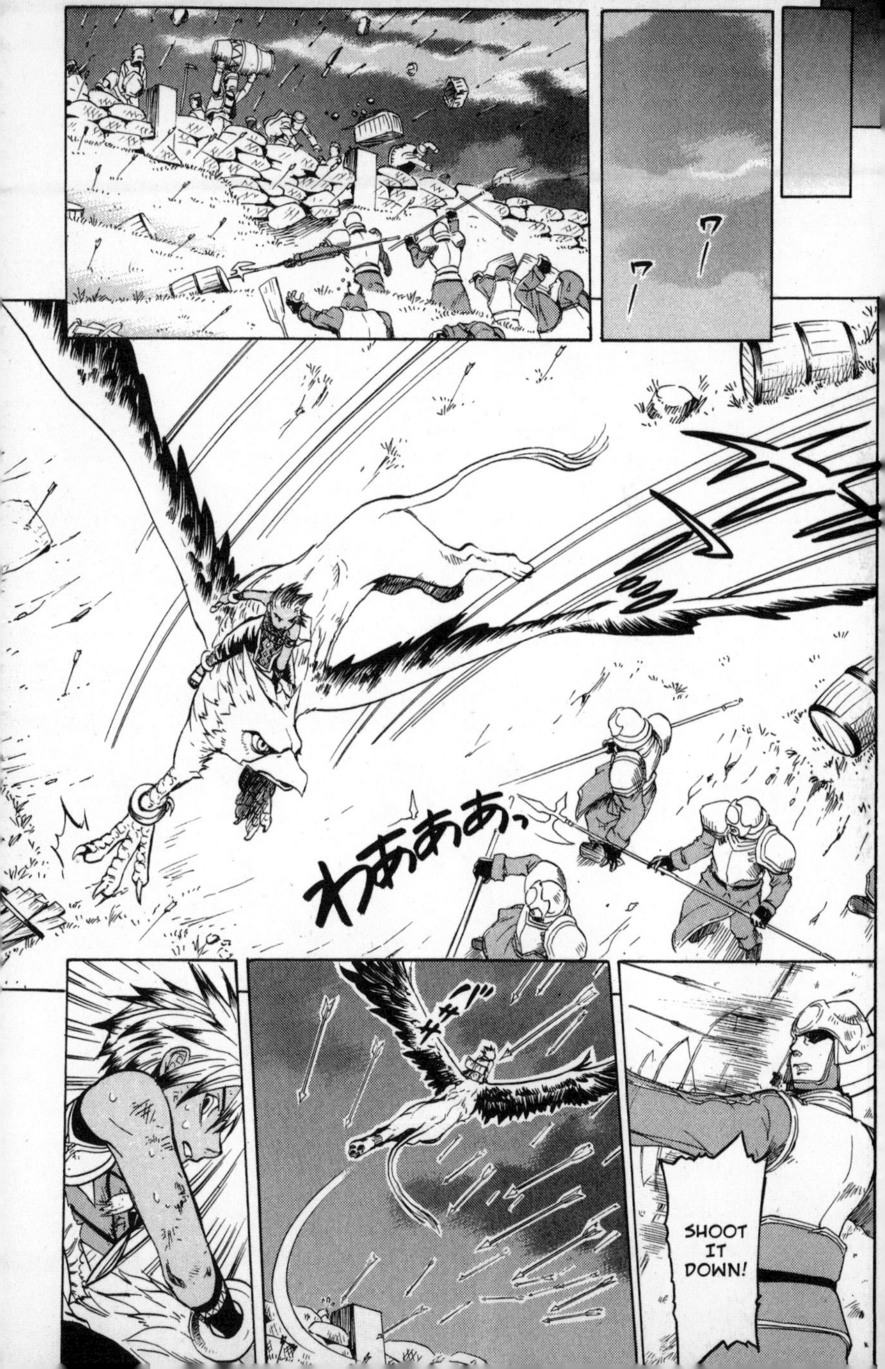
ワー
ワー
わあああっ
SHOOT IT DOWN!

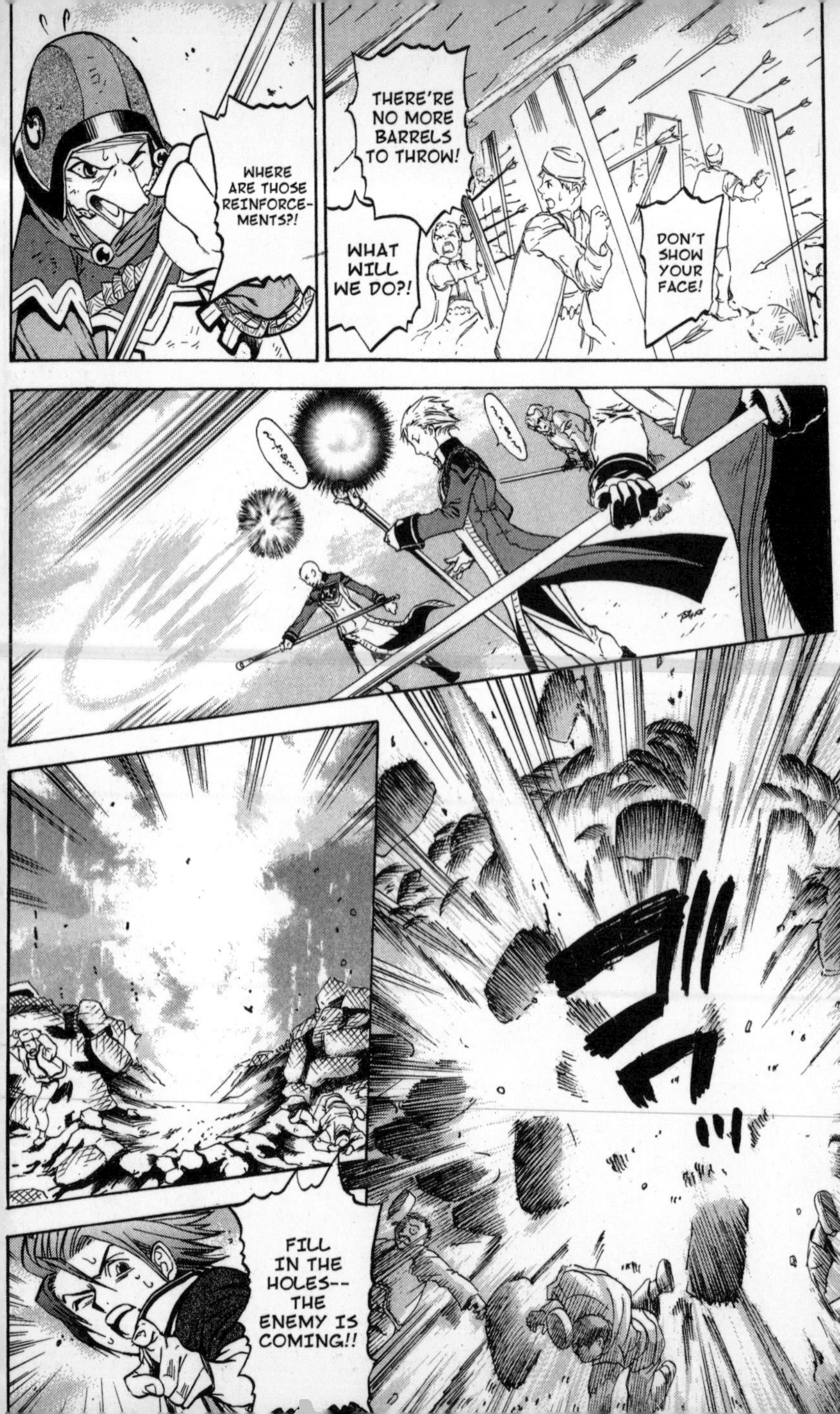
THERE'RE NO MORE BARRELS TO THROW!
DON'T SHOW YOUR FACE!
WHAT WILL WE DO?!
WHERE ARE THOSE REINFORCEMENTS?!
FILL IN THE HOLES-- THE ENEMY IS COMING!!

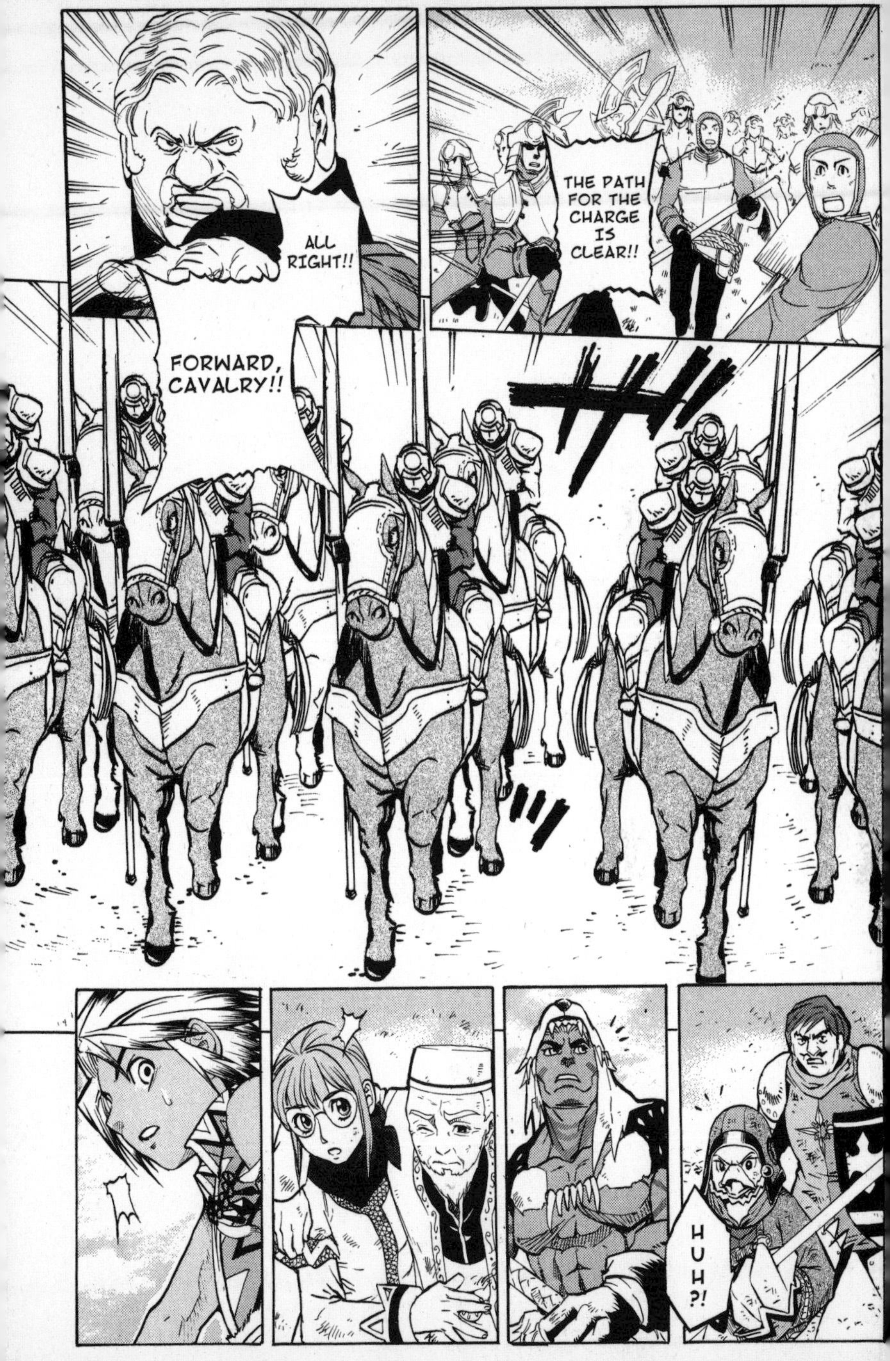
THE PATH FOR THE CHARGE IS CLEAR!!
ALL RIGHT!!
FORWARD, CAVALRY!!
HUH?!

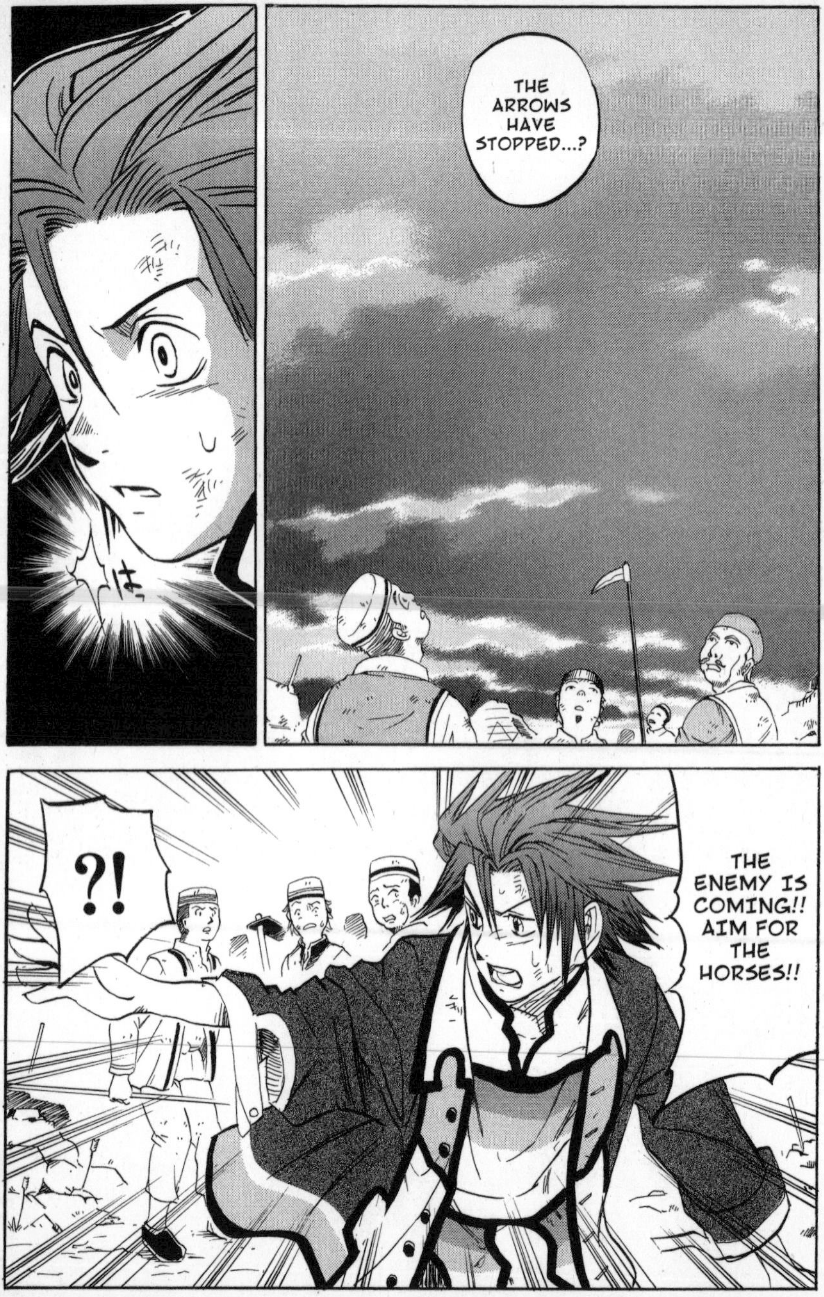
THE ARROWS HAVE STOPPED...?
THE ENEMY IS COMING!! AIM FOR THE HORSES!!
?!

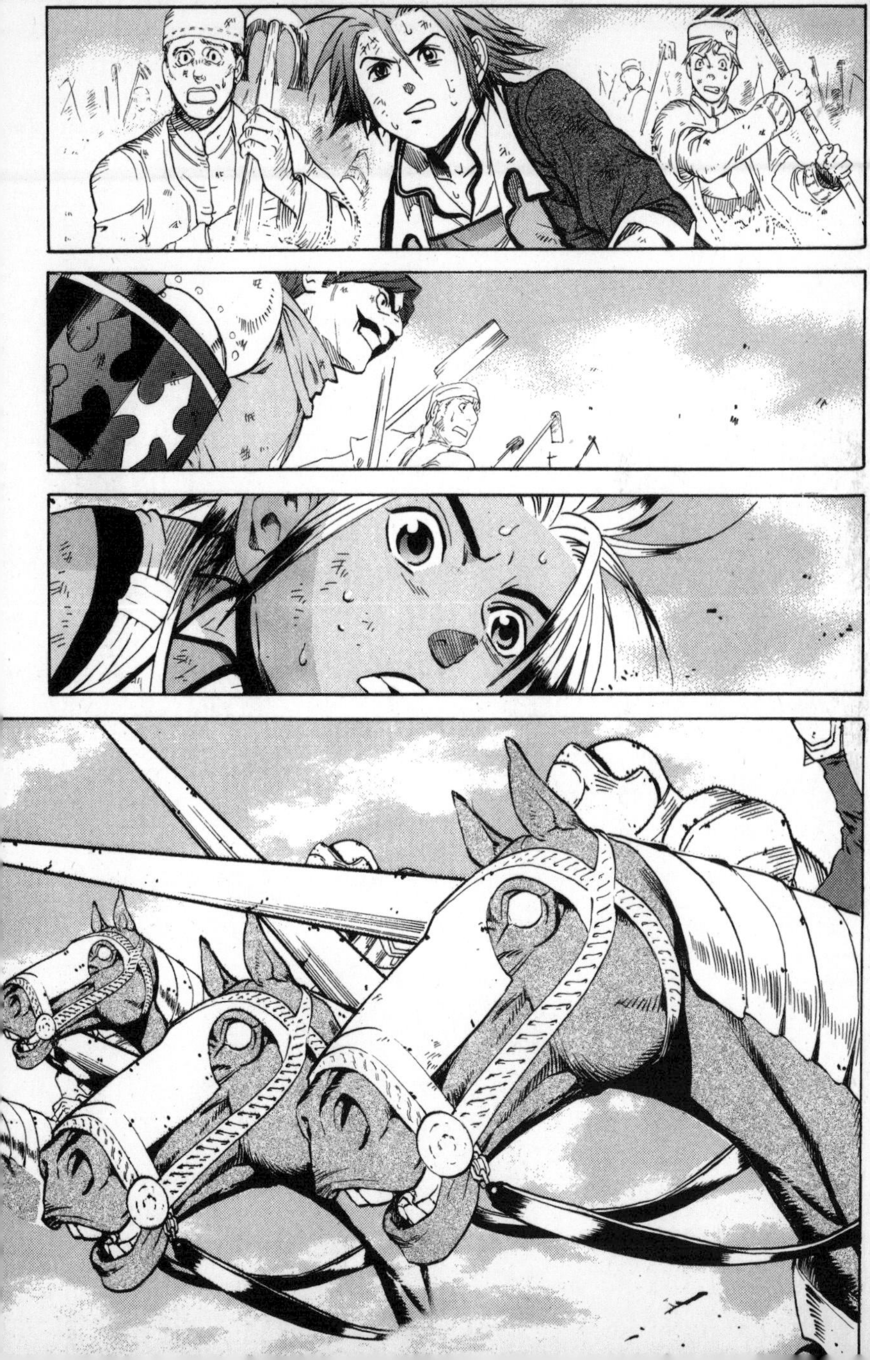

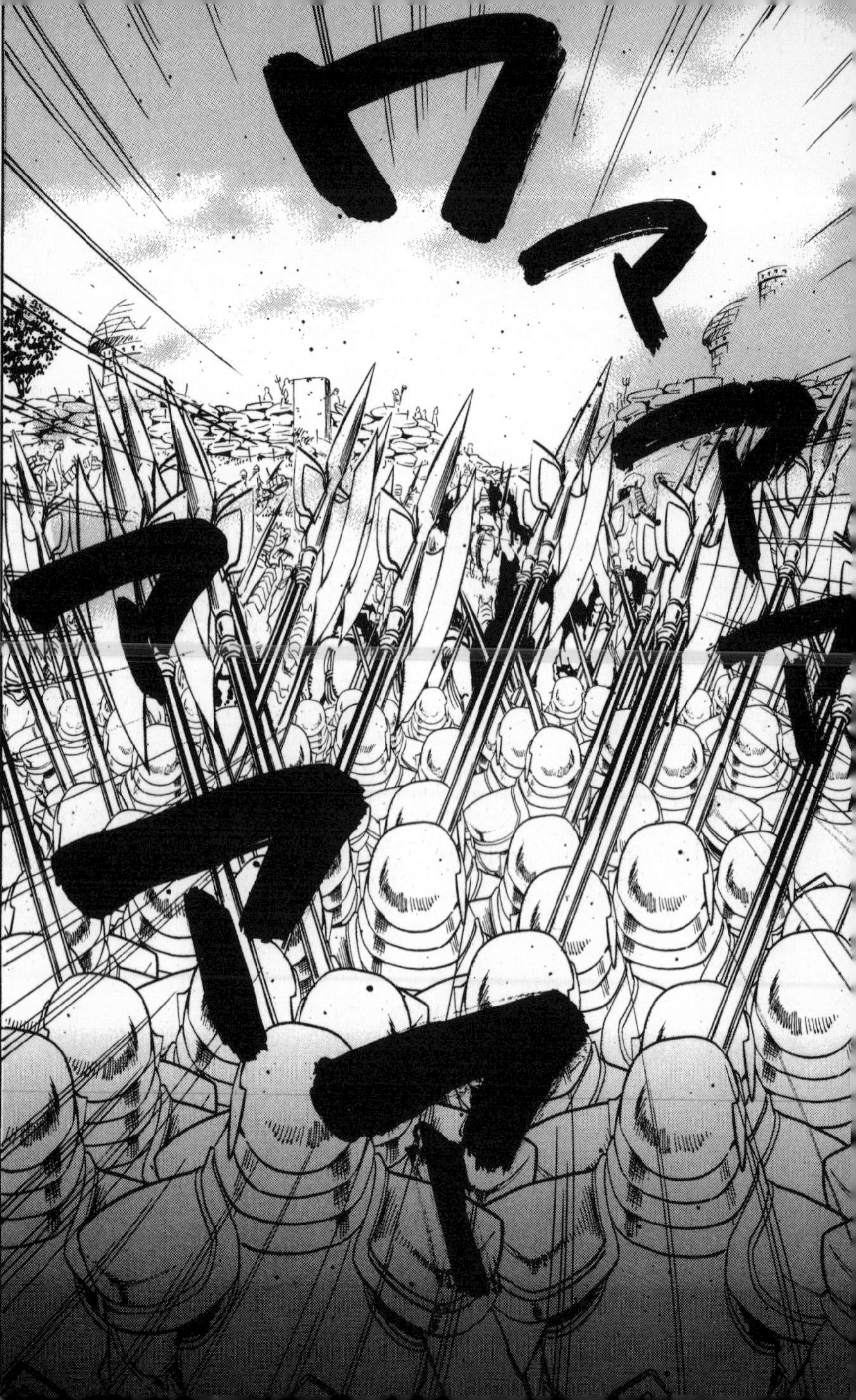
ワァアァアアア

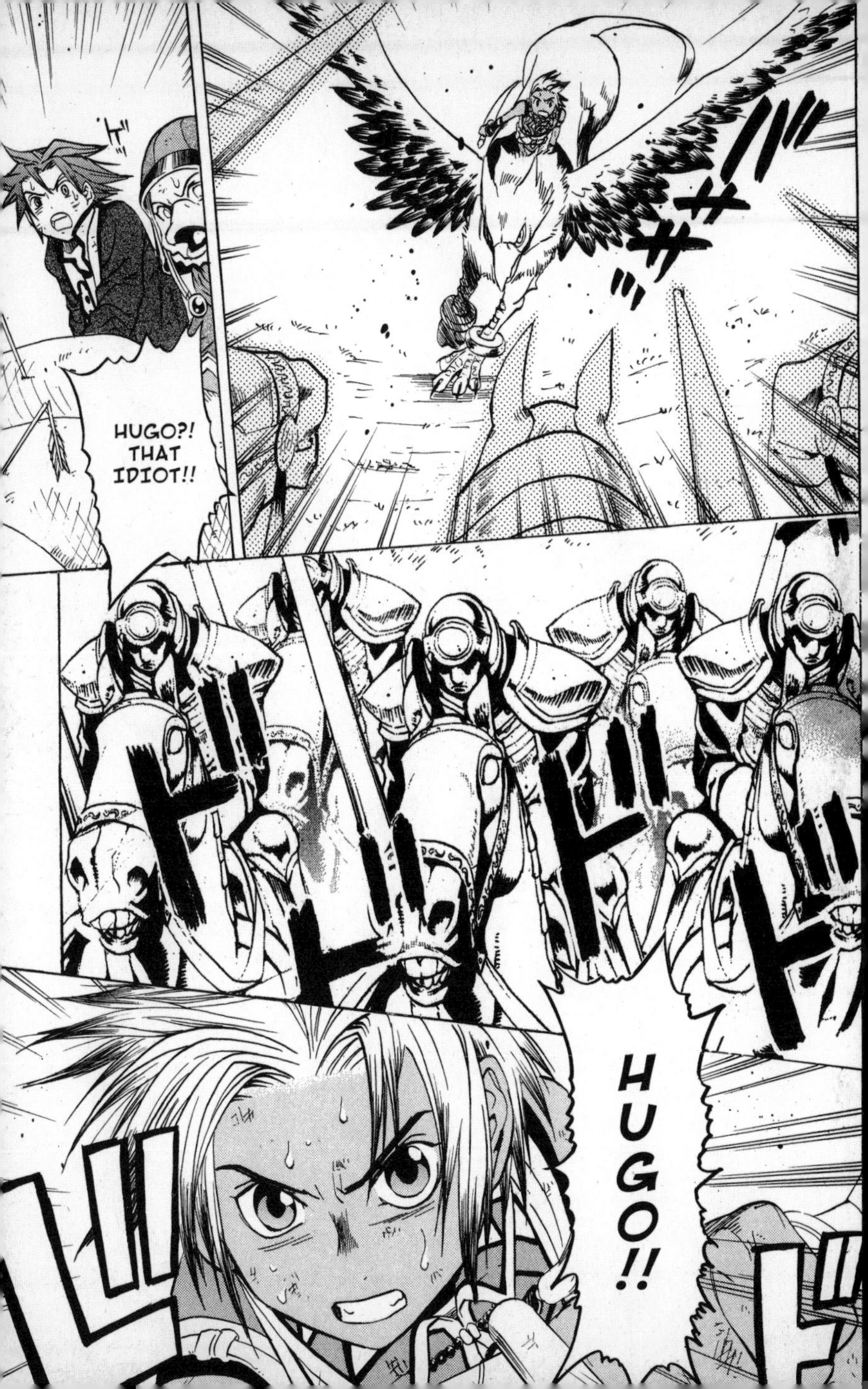

HUGO?! THAT IDIOT!!
HUGO!!

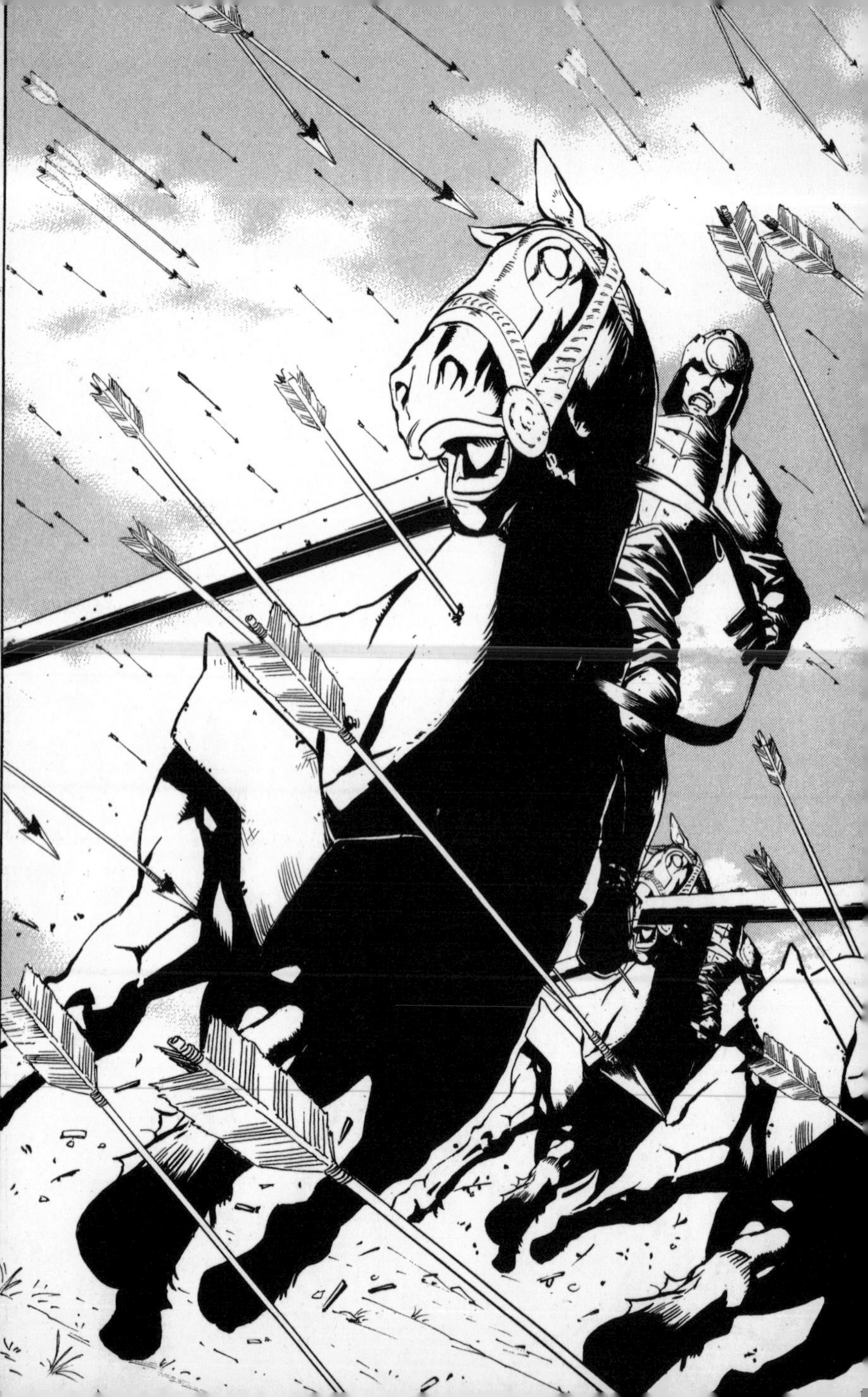

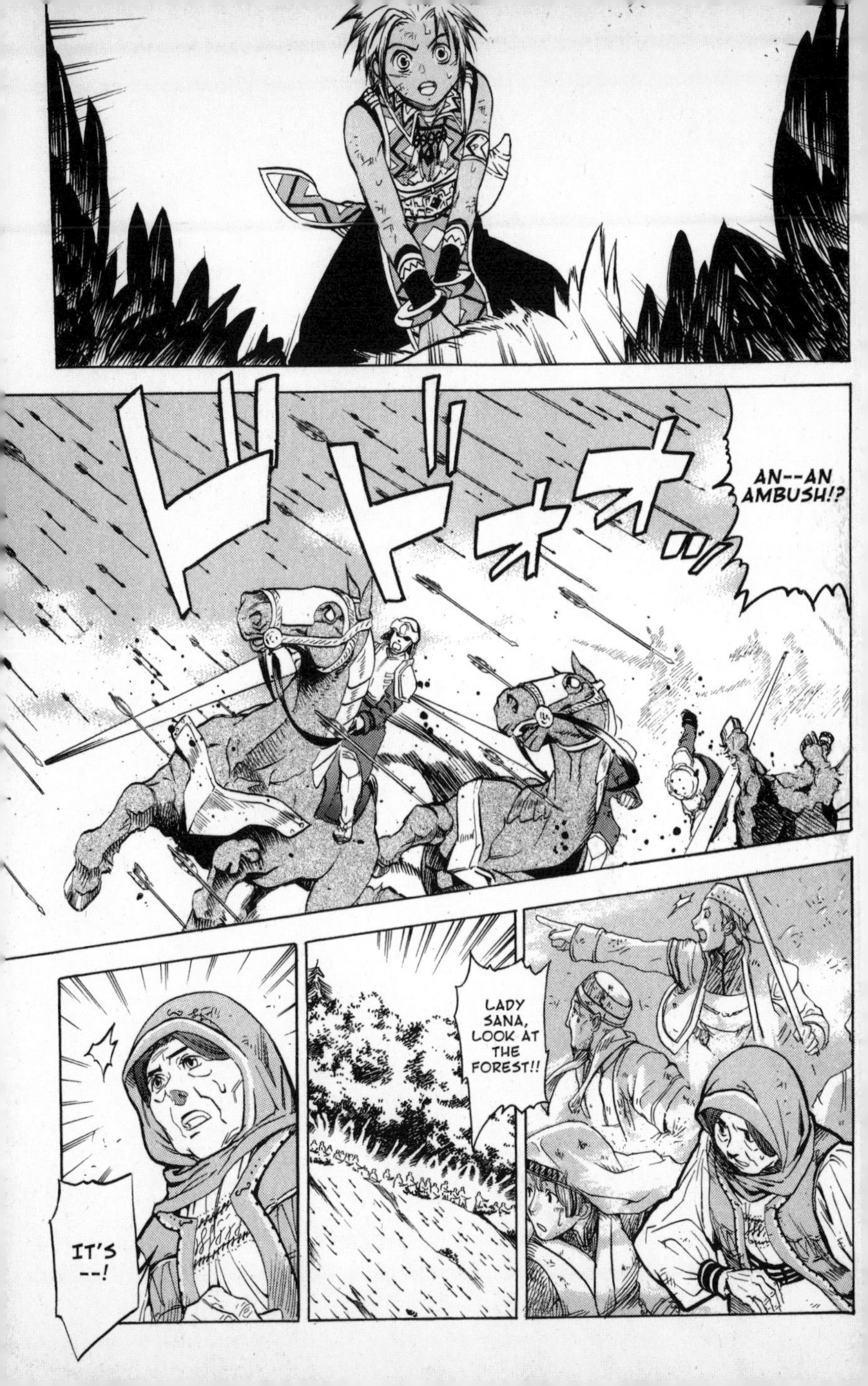
AN--AN AMBUSH!?
LADY SANA, LOOK AT THE FOREST!!
IT'S --!

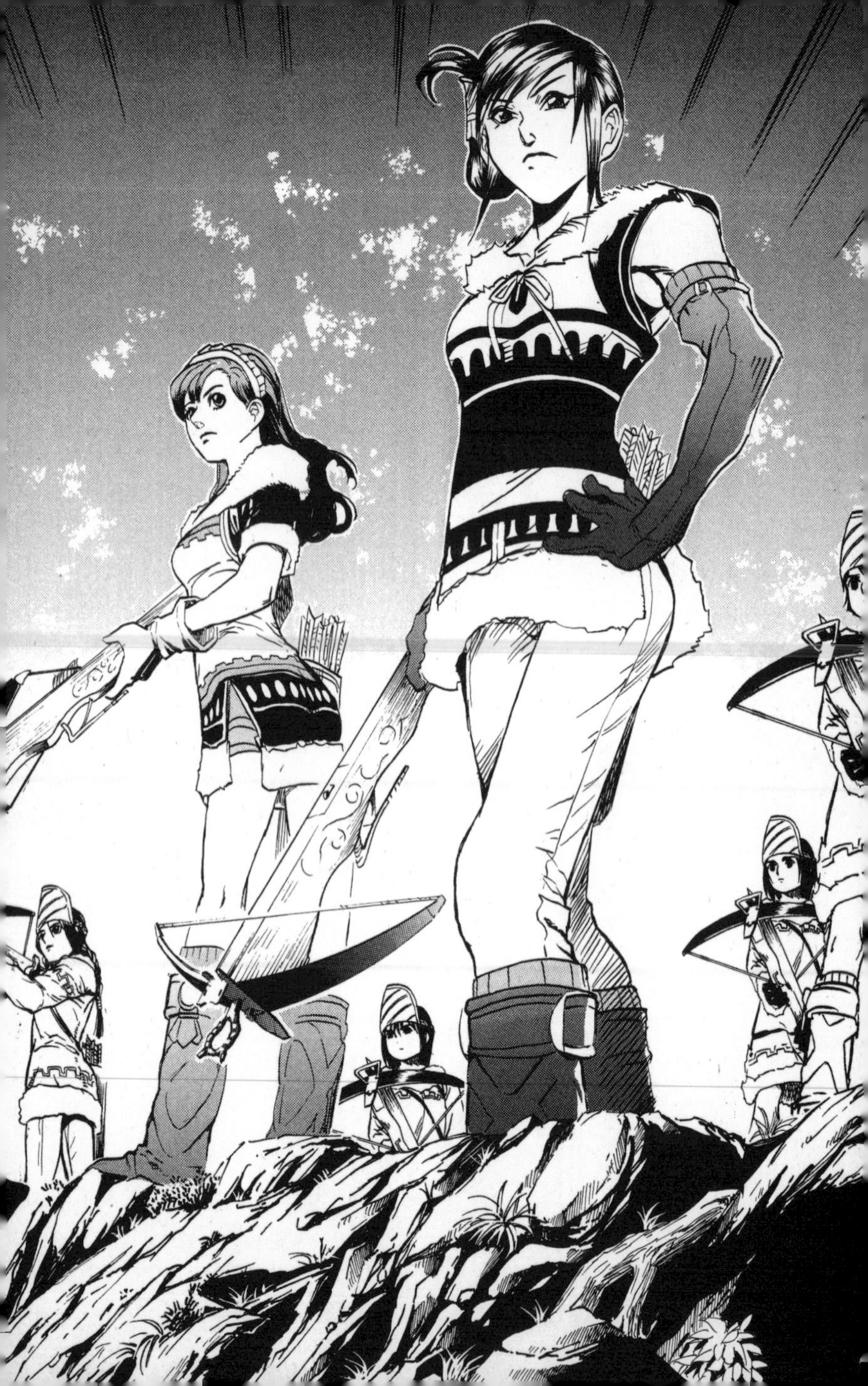

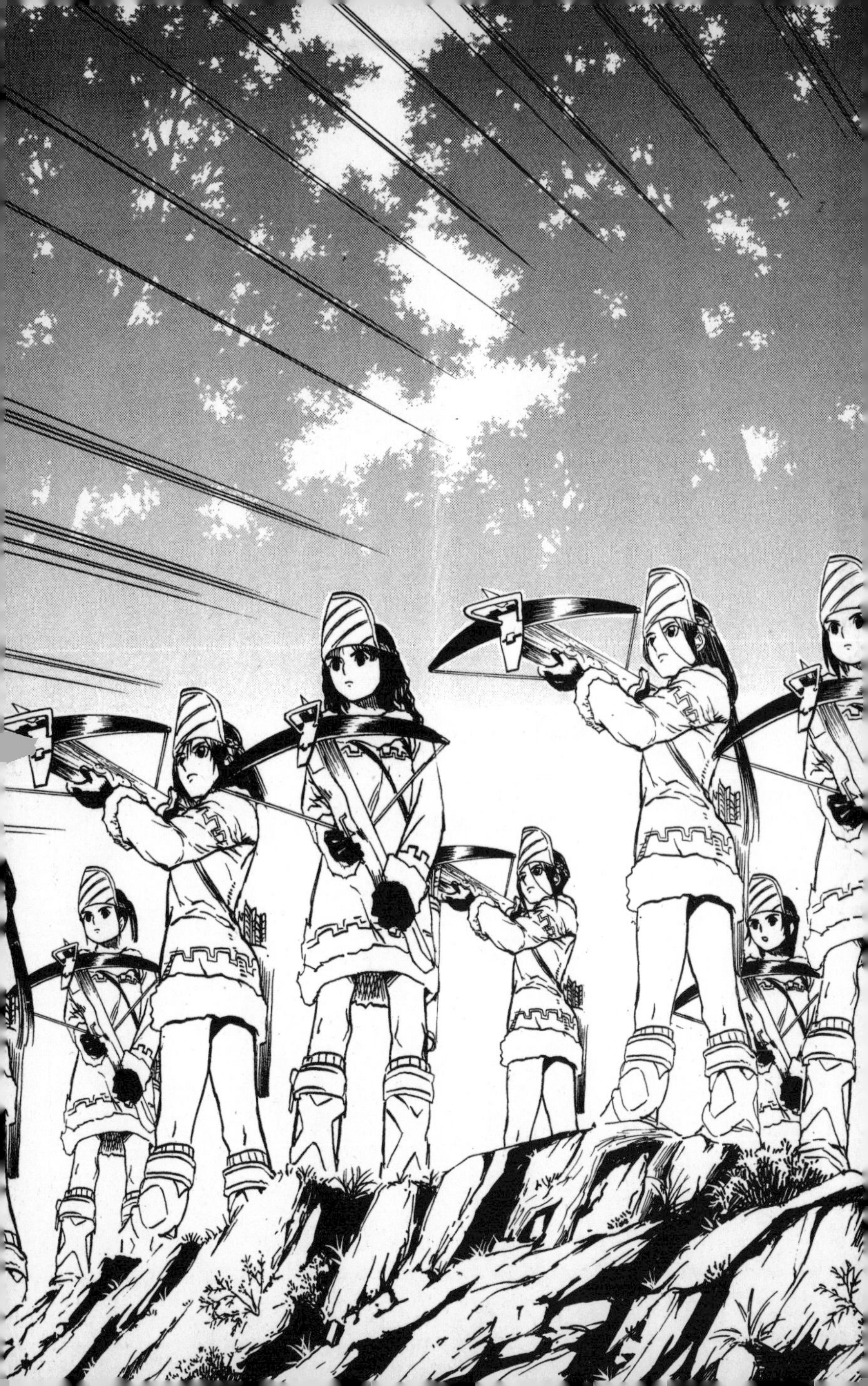

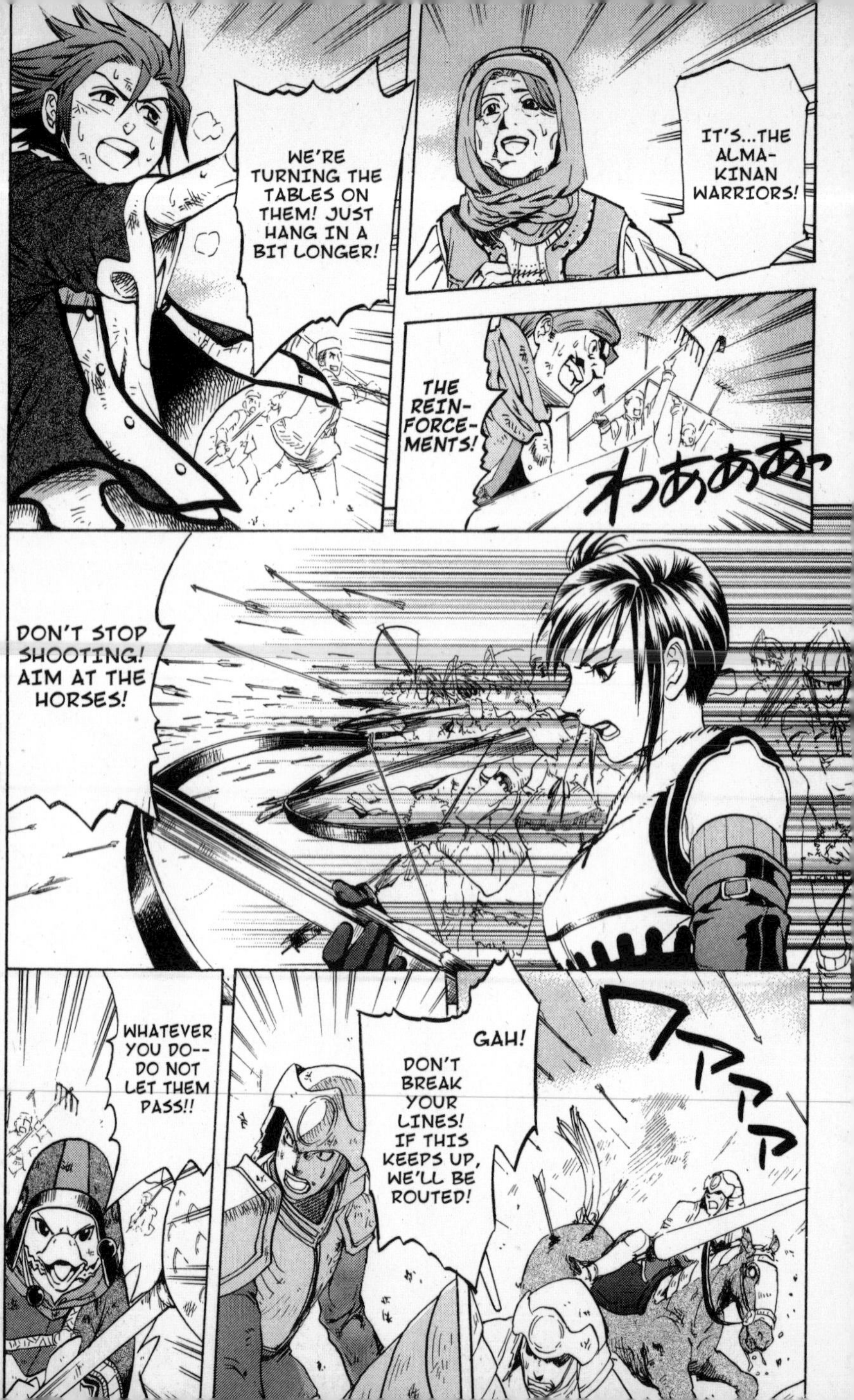
IT'S...THE ALMA-KINAN WARRIORS!
THE REIN-FORCE-MENTS!
わあああぁ
WE'RE TURNING THE TABLES ON THEM! JUST HANG IN A BIT LONGER!
DON'T STOP SHOOTING! AIM AT THE HORSES!
ワァァァ
GAH!
DON'T BREAK YOUR LINES! IF THIS KEEPS UP, WE'LL BE ROUTED!
WHATEVER YOU DO-- DO NOT LET THEM PASS!!

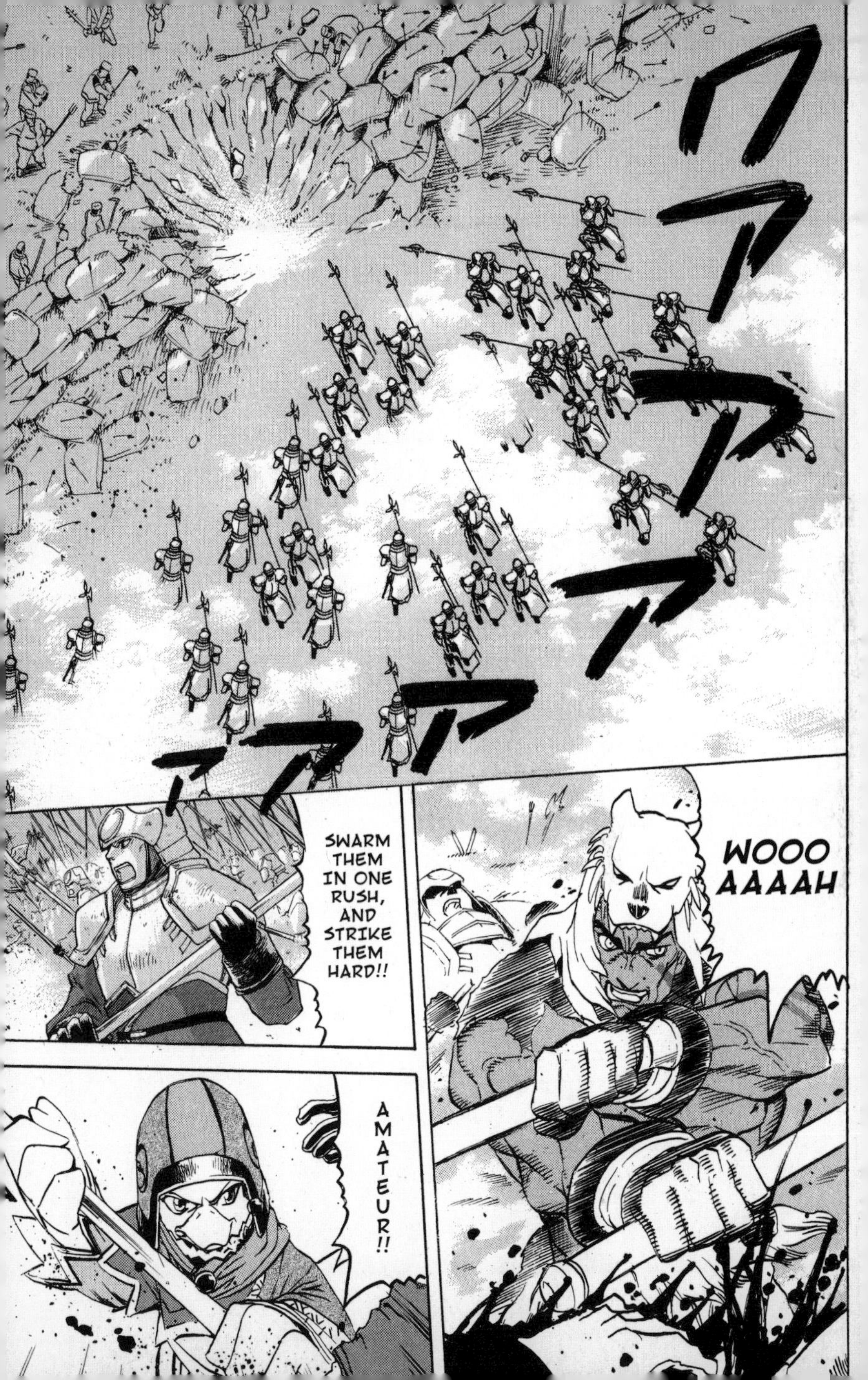
ワアアアアア
WOOO AAAAH
SWARM THEM IN ONE RUSH, AND STRIKE THEM HARD!!
AMATEUR!!

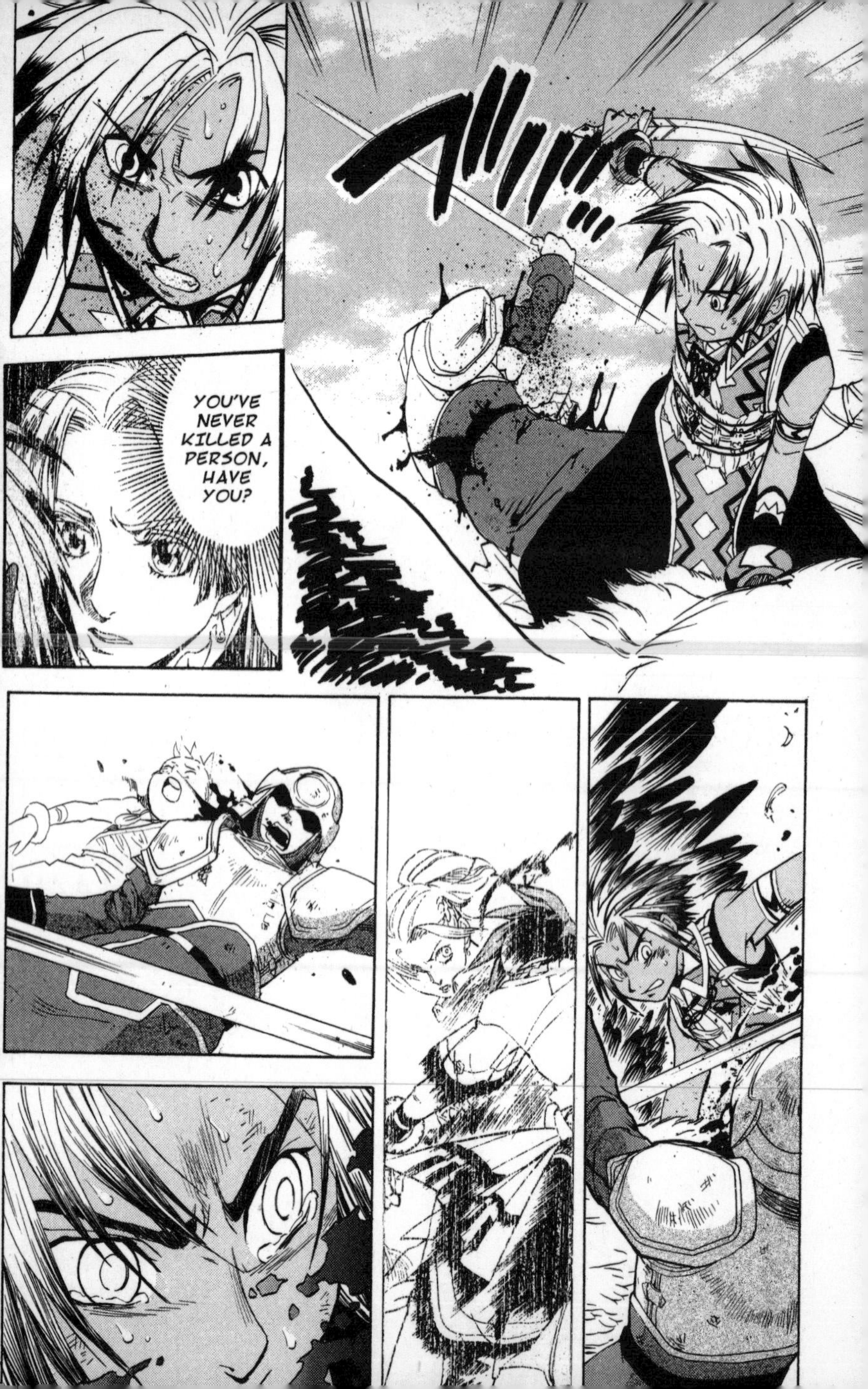
YOU'VE NEVER KILLED A PERSON, HAVE YOU?

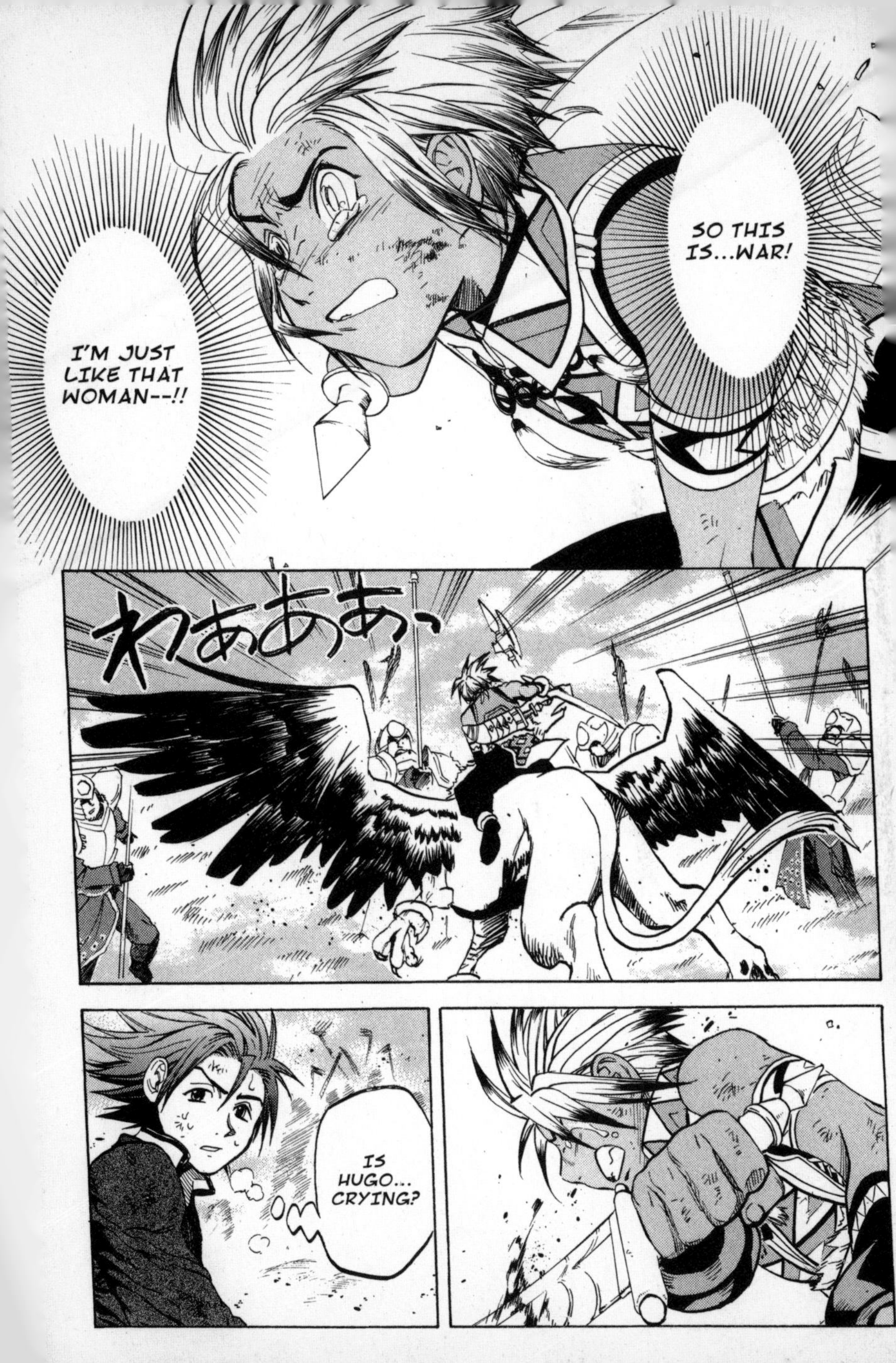
SO THIS IS...WAR!
I'M JUST LIKE THAT WOMAN--!!
わあああ
IS HUGO... CRYING?

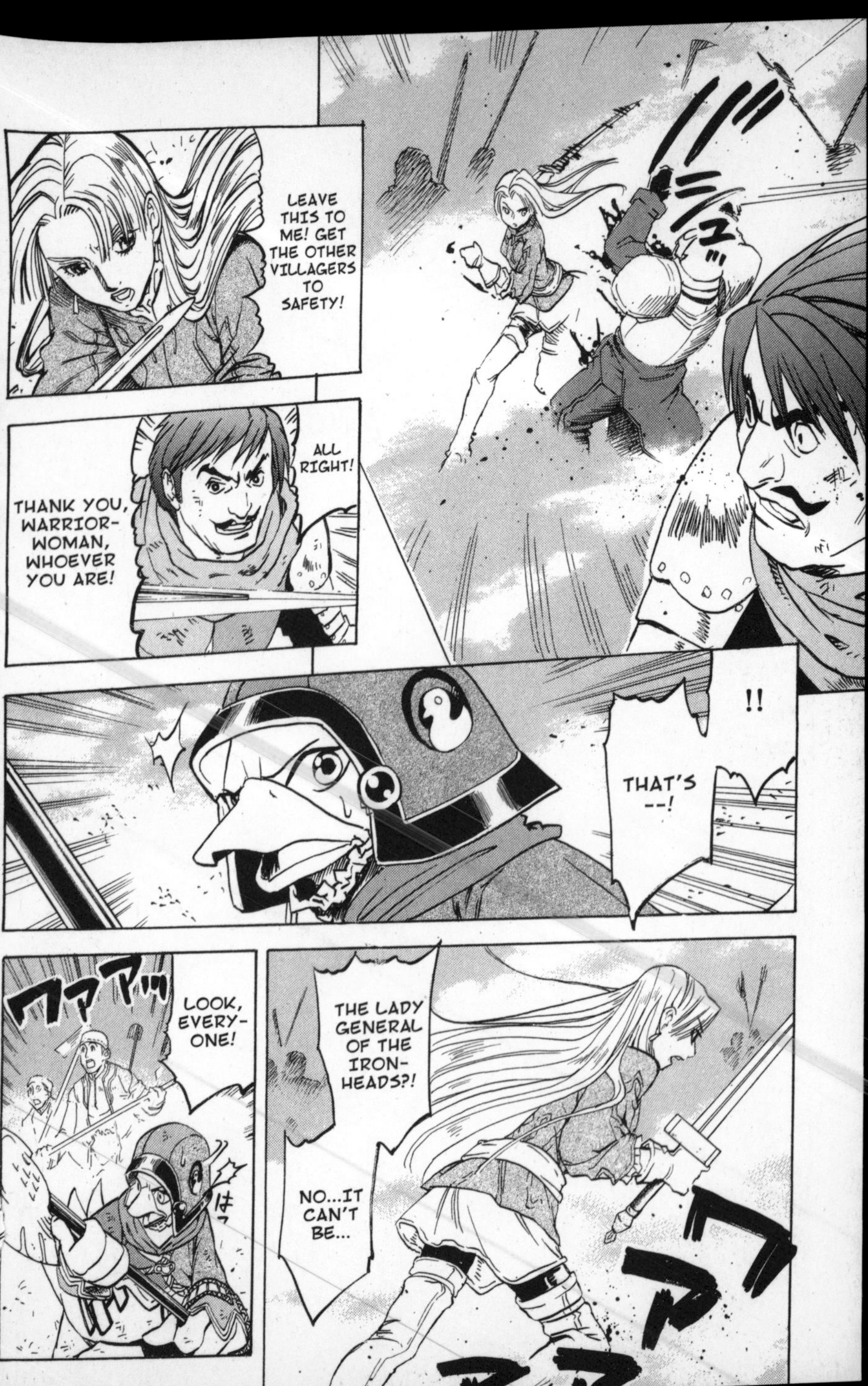
LEAVE THIS TO ME! GET THE OTHER VILLAGERS TO SAFETY!
ALL RIGHT!
THANK YOU, WARRIOR-WOMAN, WHOEVER YOU ARE!
!!
THAT'S --!
THE LADY GENERAL OF THE IRON-HEADS?!
NO...IT CAN'T BE...
LOOK, EVERY-ONE!
はっ

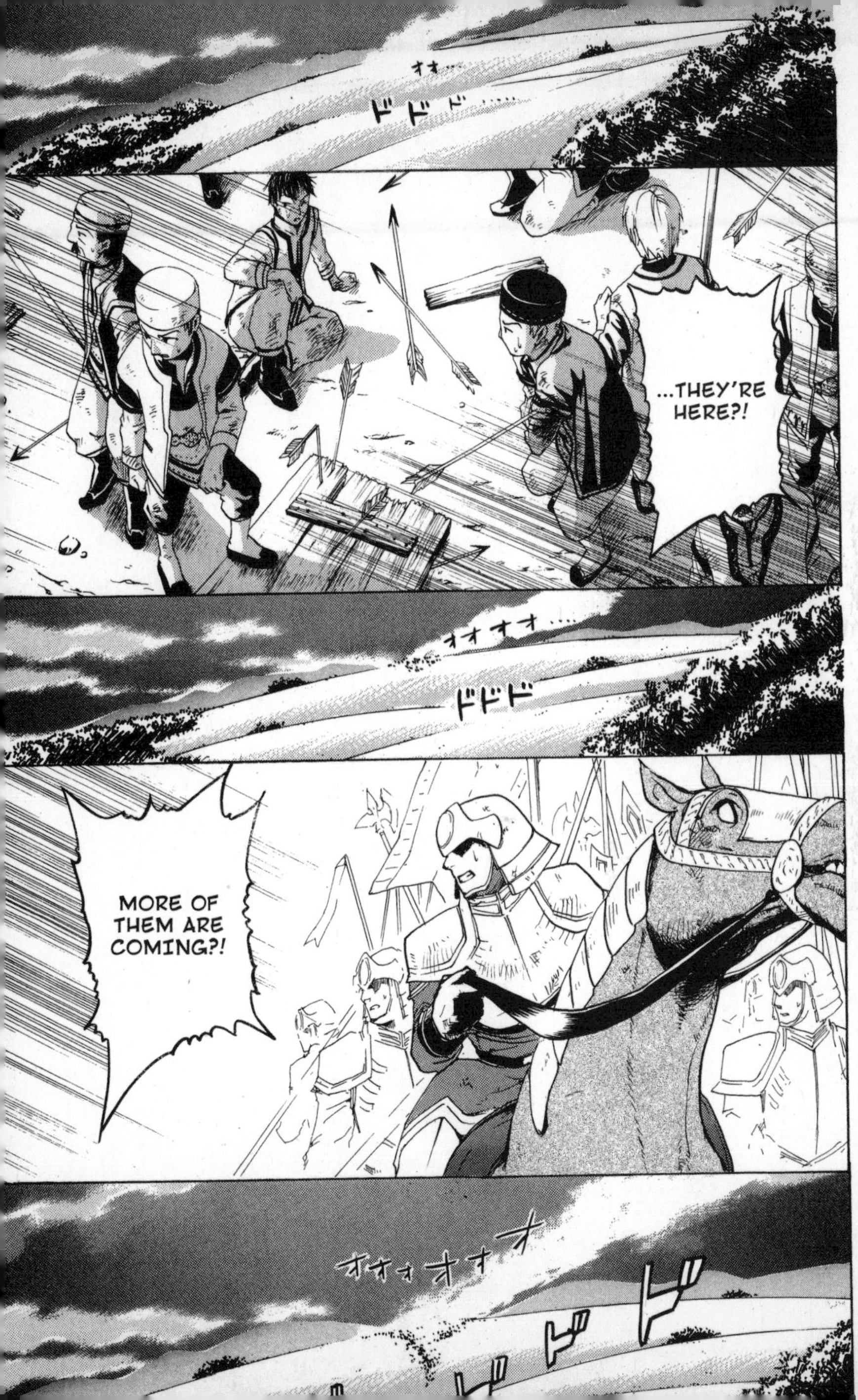
オオ…
ドドド……
…THEY'RE HERE?!
オオオオ……
ドドド
MORE OF THEM ARE COMING?!
オオォオオオ
ドドドド

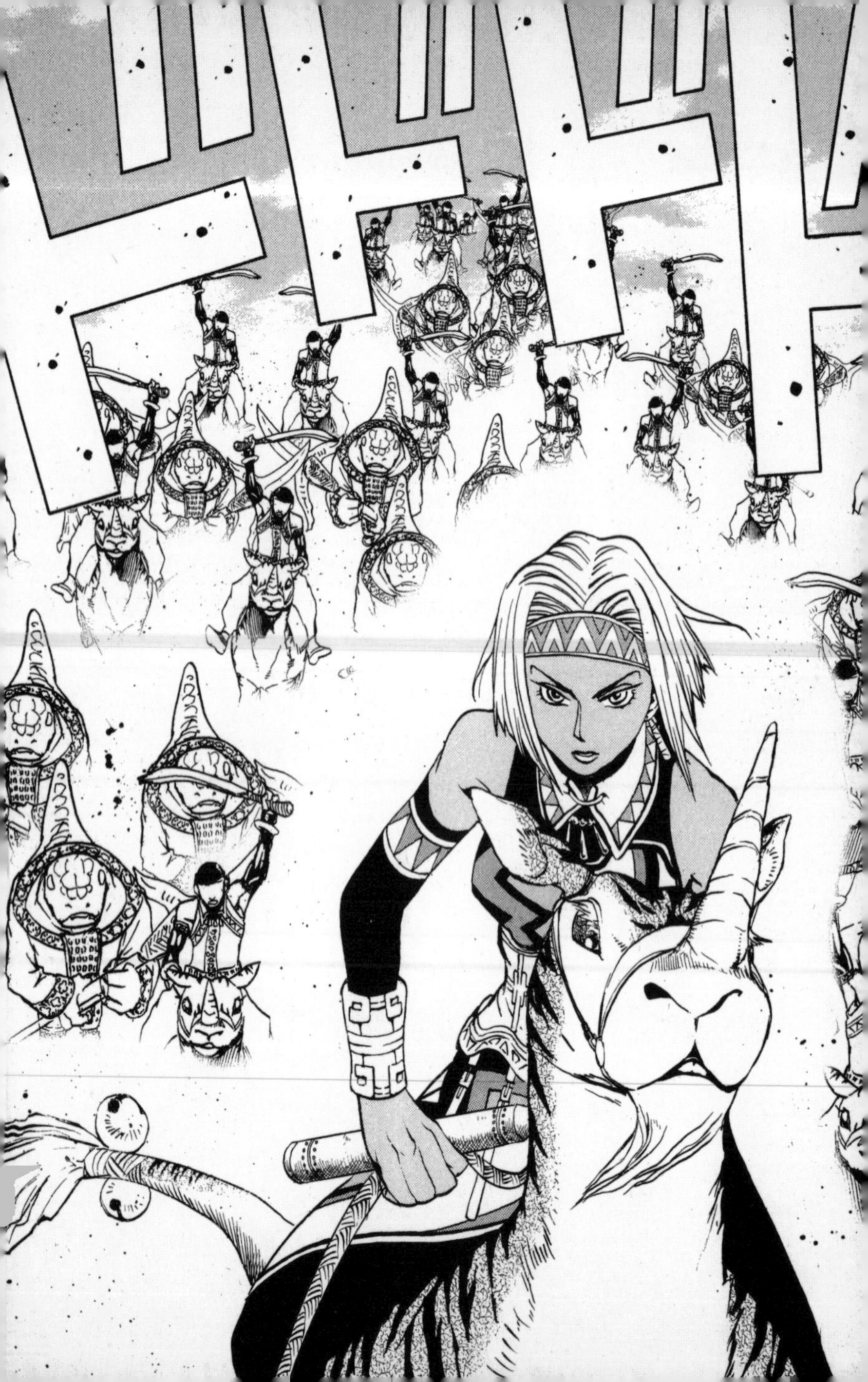

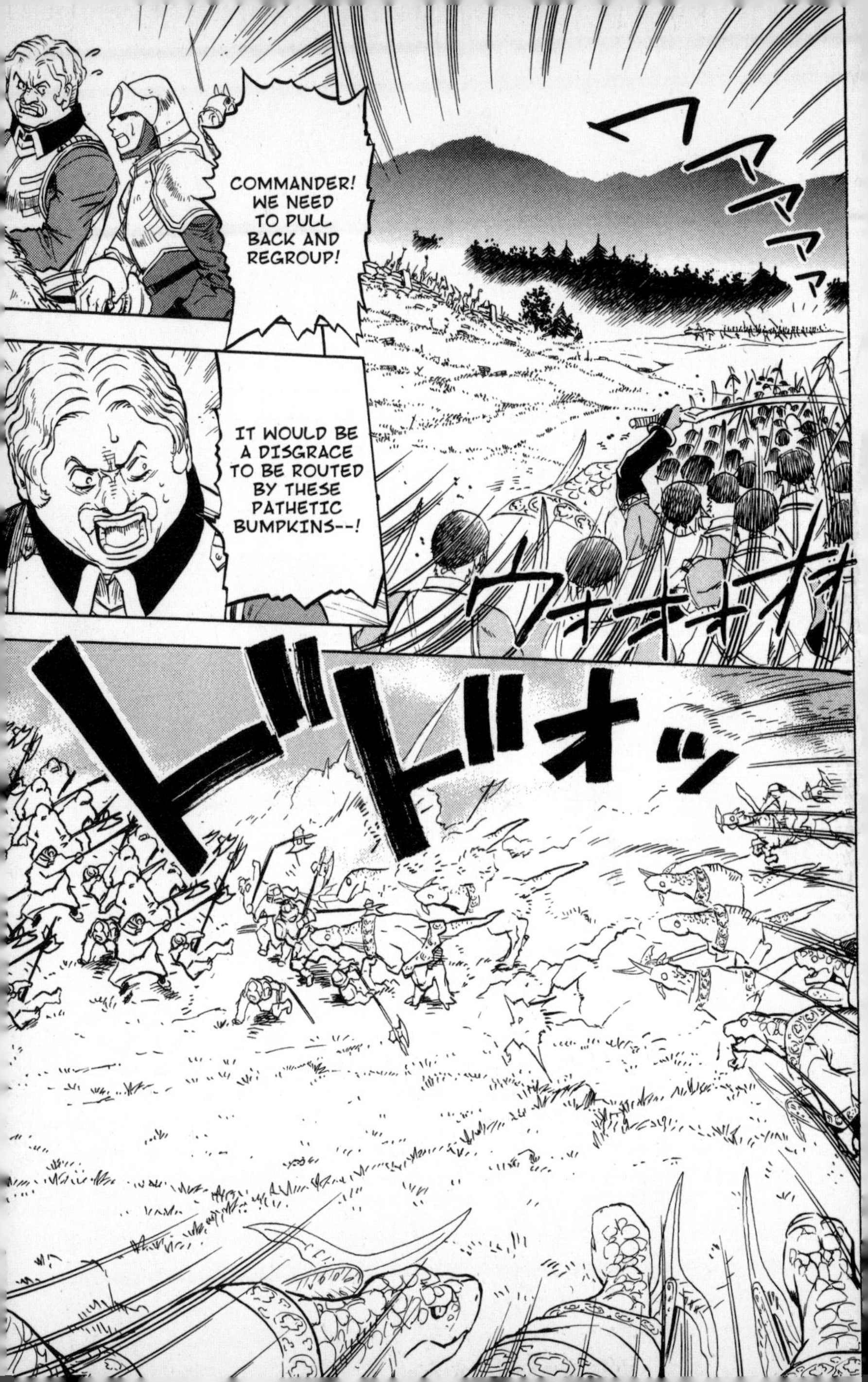
COMMANDER! WE NEED TO PULL BACK AND REGROUP!
IT WOULD BE A DISGRACE TO BE ROUTED BY THESE PATHETIC BUMPKINS--!
ドドオッ

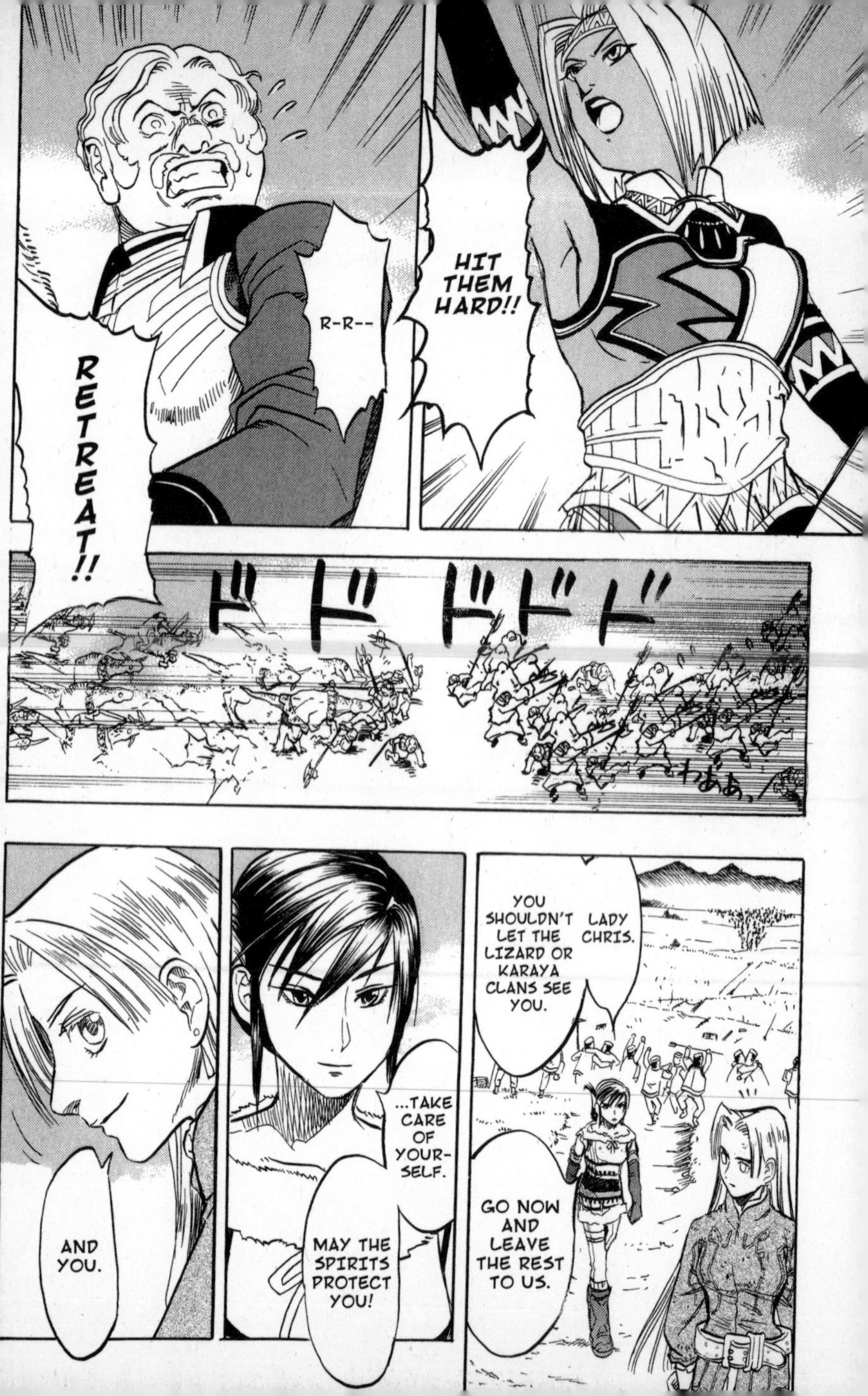
HIT THEM HARD!!
R-R--
RETREAT!!
ドド ドドド
LADY CHRIS.
YOU SHOULDN'T LET THE LIZARD OR KARAYA CLANS SEE YOU.
GO NOW AND LEAVE THE REST TO US.
...TAKE CARE OF YOUR-SELF.
MAY THE SPIRITS PROTECT YOU!
AND YOU.

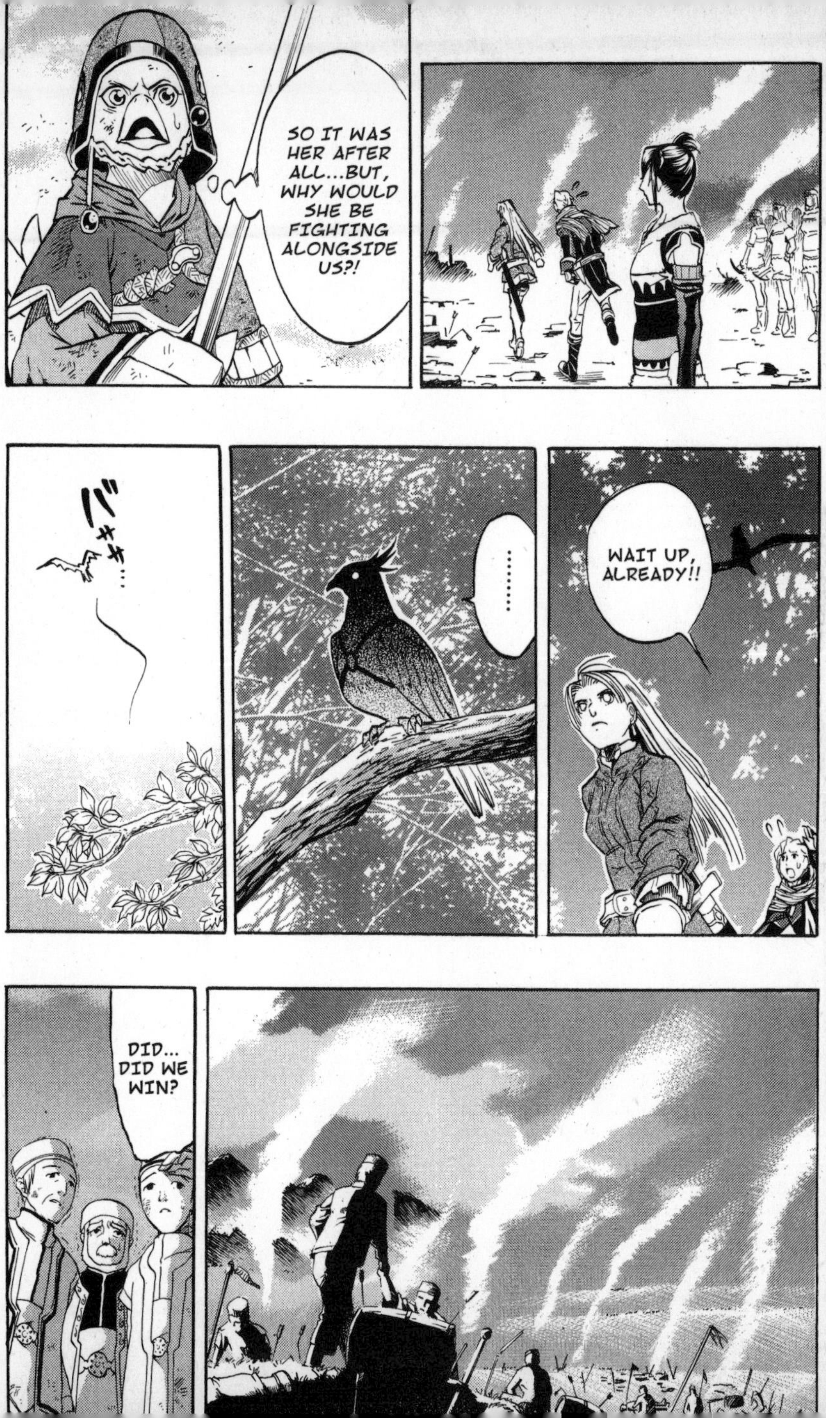
SO IT WAS HER AFTER ALL...BUT, WHY WOULD SHE BE FIGHTING ALONGSIDE US?!
WAIT UP, ALREADY!!
......
バキキ...
DID... DID WE WIN?

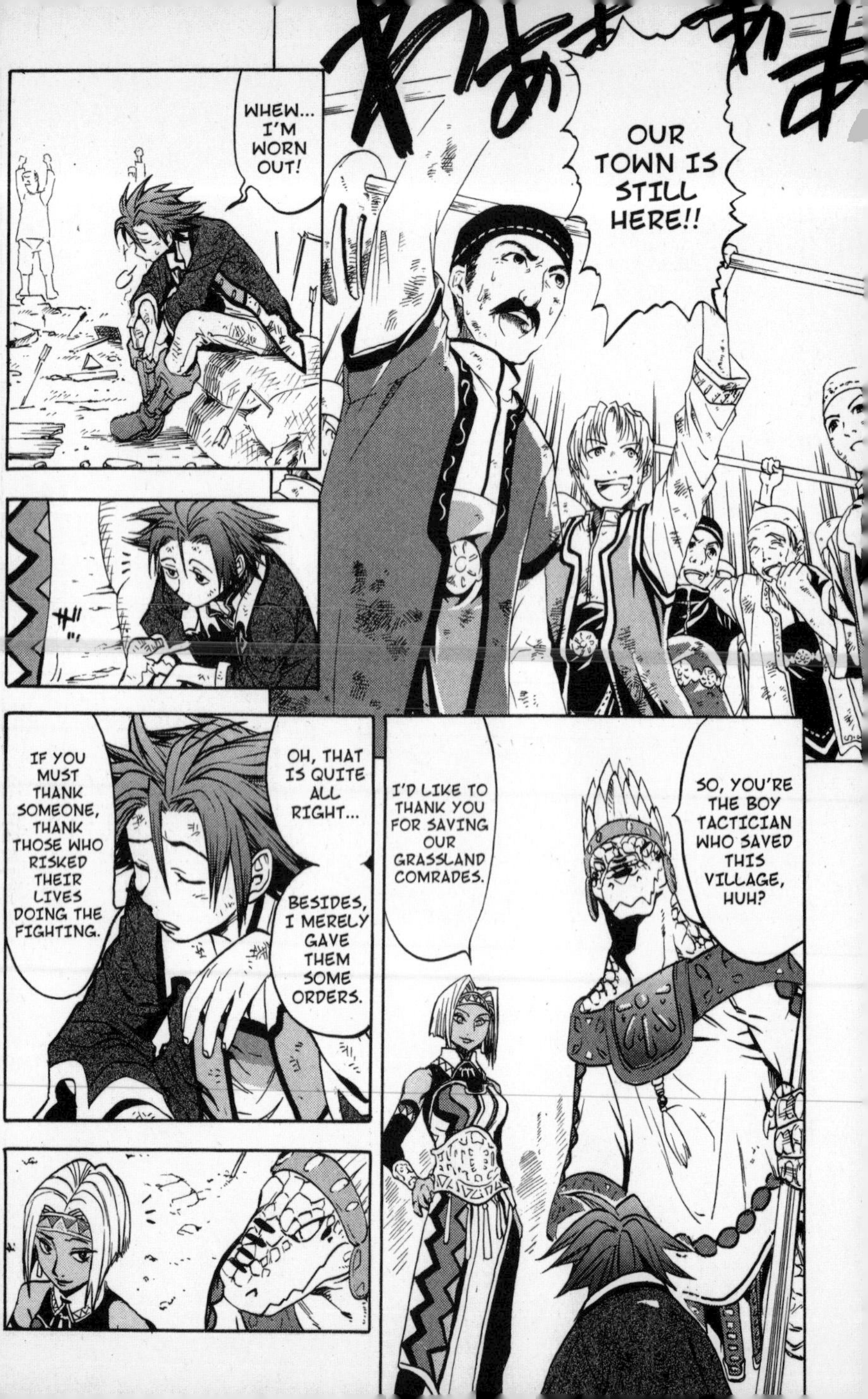

OUR TOWN IS STILL HERE!!
WHEW... I'M WORN OUT!
SO, YOU'RE THE BOY TACTICIAN WHO SAVED THIS VILLAGE, HUH?
I'D LIKE TO THANK YOU FOR SAVING OUR GRASSLAND COMRADES.
OH, THAT IS QUITE ALL RIGHT...
BESIDES, I MERELY GAVE THEM SOME ORDERS.
IF YOU MUST THANK SOMEONE, THANK THOSE WHO RISKED THEIR LIVES DOING THE FIGHTING.

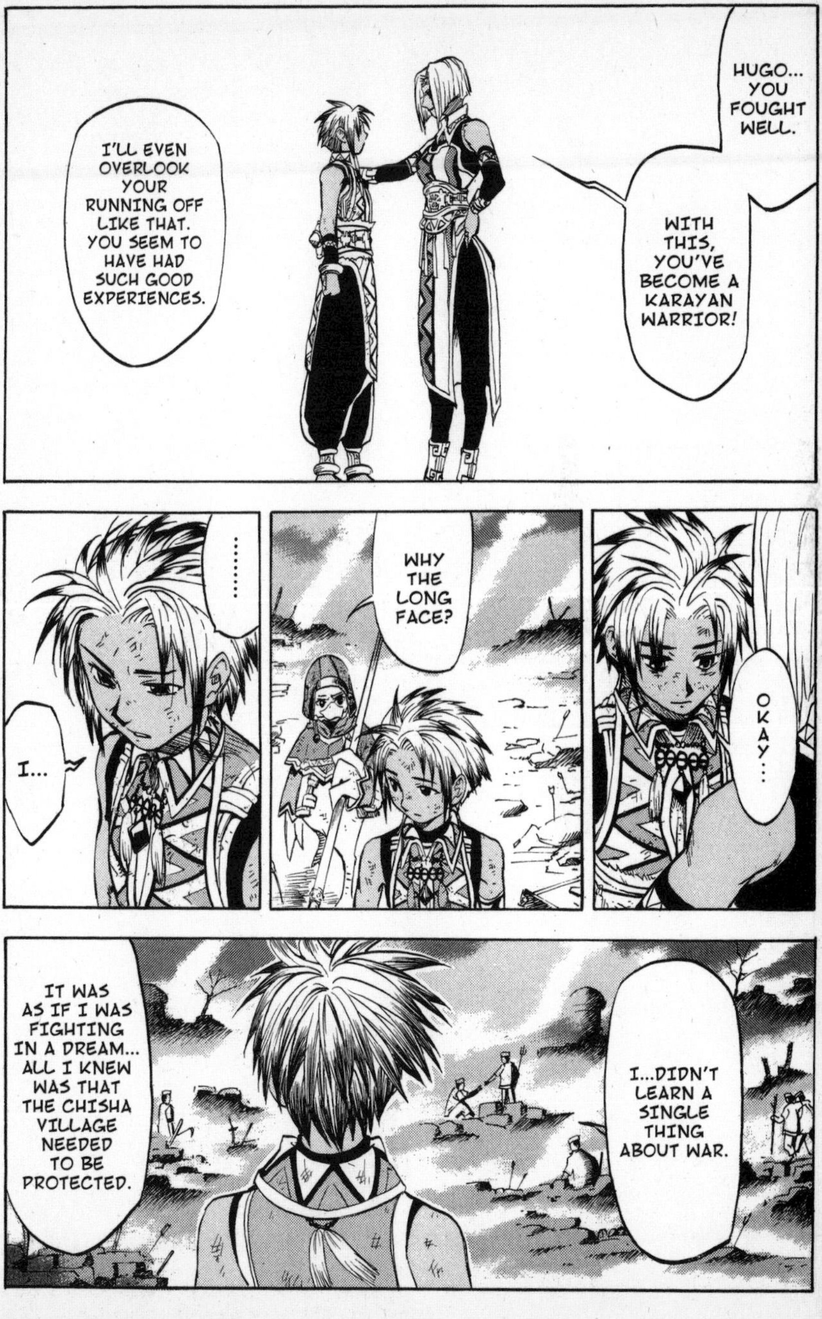
HUGO... YOU FOUGHT WELL.
WITH THIS, YOU'VE BECOME A KARAYAN WARRIOR!
I'LL EVEN OVERLOOK YOUR RUNNING OFF LIKE THAT. YOU SEEM TO HAVE HAD SUCH GOOD EXPERIENCES.
OKAY...
WHY THE LONG FACE?
......
I...
I...DIDN'T LEARN A SINGLE THING ABOUT WAR.
IT WAS AS IF I WAS FIGHTING IN A DREAM... ALL I KNEW WAS THAT THE CHISHA VILLAGE NEEDED TO BE PROTECTED.

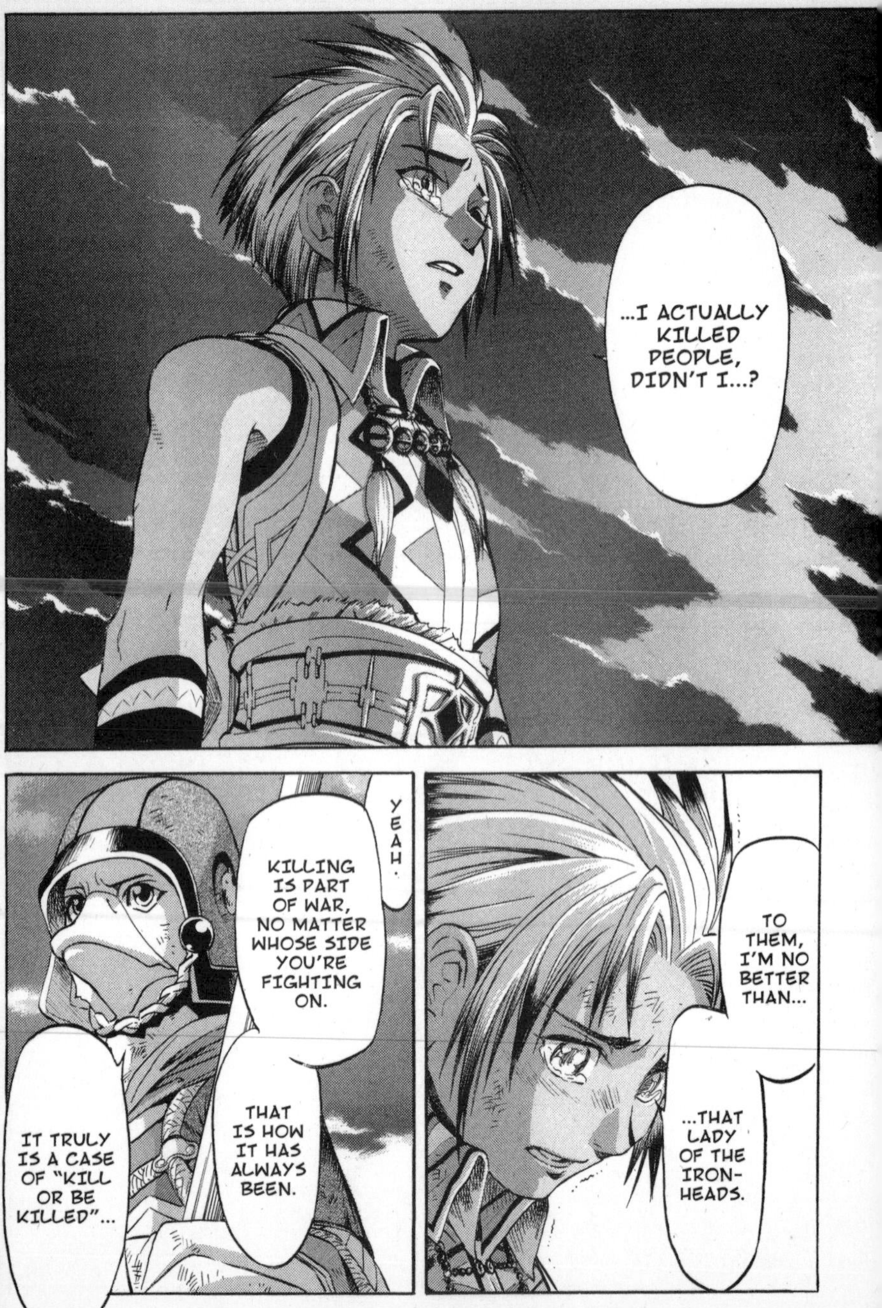
...I ACTUALLY KILLED PEOPLE, DIDN'T I...?
TO THEM, I'M NO BETTER THAN...
...THAT LADY OF THE IRON-HEADS.
YEAH.
KILLING IS PART OF WAR, NO MATTER WHOSE SIDE YOU'RE FIGHTING ON.
THAT IS HOW IT HAS ALWAYS BEEN.
IT TRULY IS A CASE OF "KILL OR BE KILLED"...

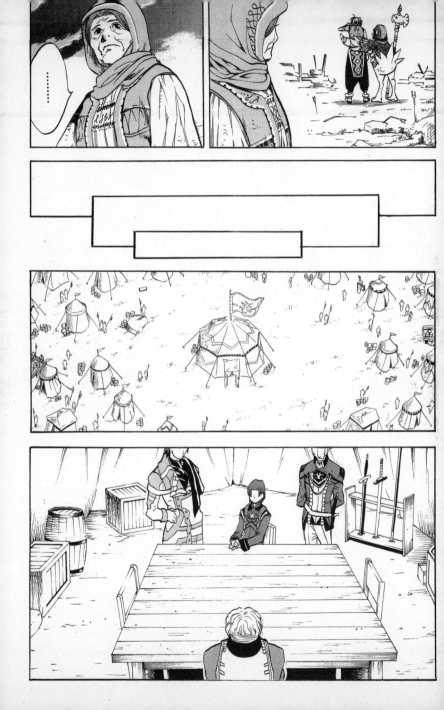

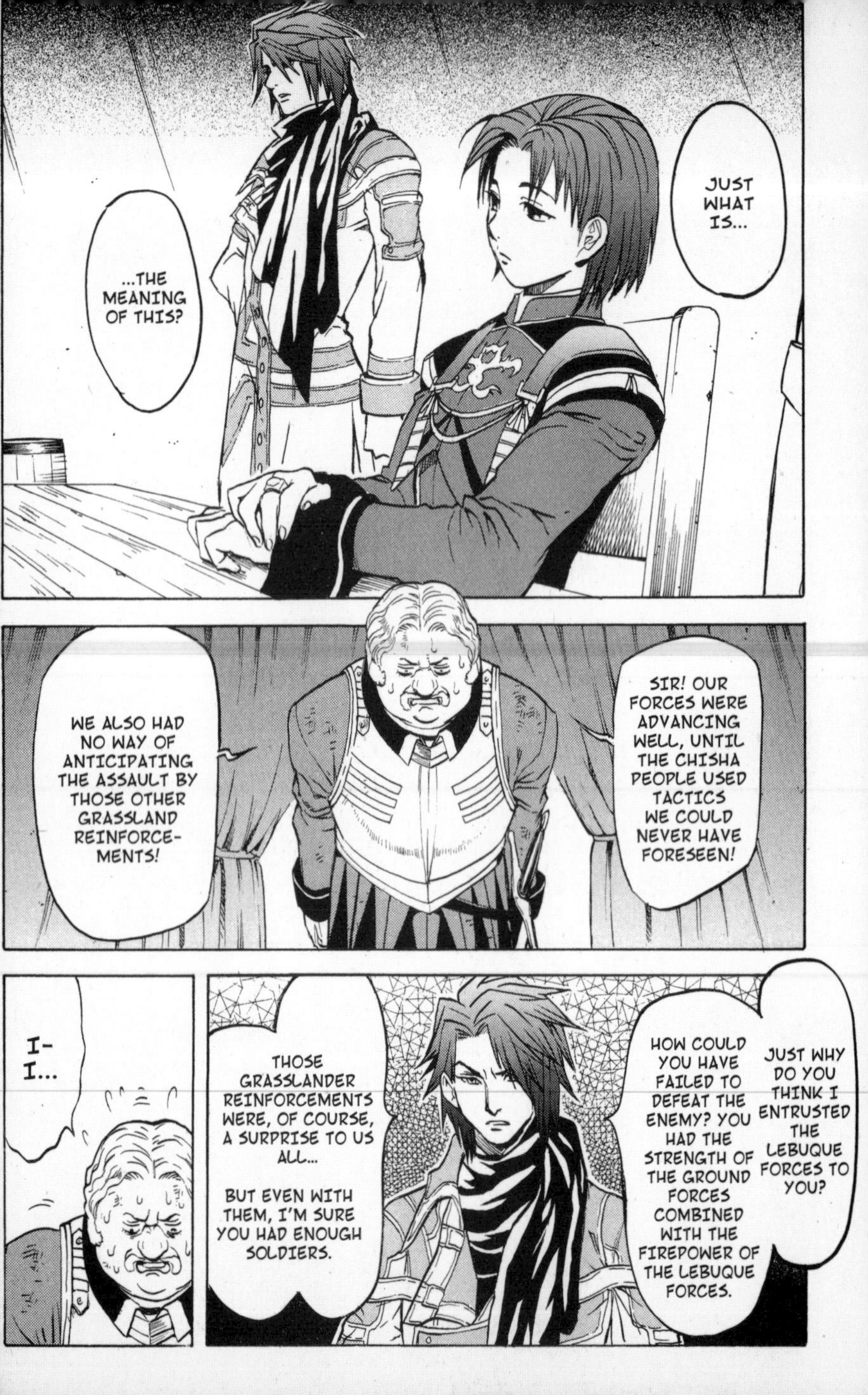
JUST WHAT IS...
...THE MEANING OF THIS?
SIR! OUR FORCES WERE ADVANCING WELL, UNTIL THE CHISHA PEOPLE USED TACTICS WE COULD NEVER HAVE FORESEEN!
WE ALSO HAD NO WAY OF ANTICIPATING THE ASSAULT BY THOSE OTHER GRASSLAND REINFORCE-MENTS!
JUST WHY DO YOU THINK I ENTRUSTED THE LEBUQUE FORCES TO YOU?
HOW COULD YOU HAVE FAILED TO DEFEAT THE ENEMY? YOU HAD THE STRENGTH OF THE GROUND FORCES COMBINED WITH THE FIREPOWER OF THE LEBUQUE FORCES.
THOSE GRASSLANDER REINFORCEMENTS WERE, OF COURSE, A SURPRISE TO US ALL...
BUT EVEN WITH THEM, I'M SURE YOU HAD ENOUGH SOLDIERS.
I-I...

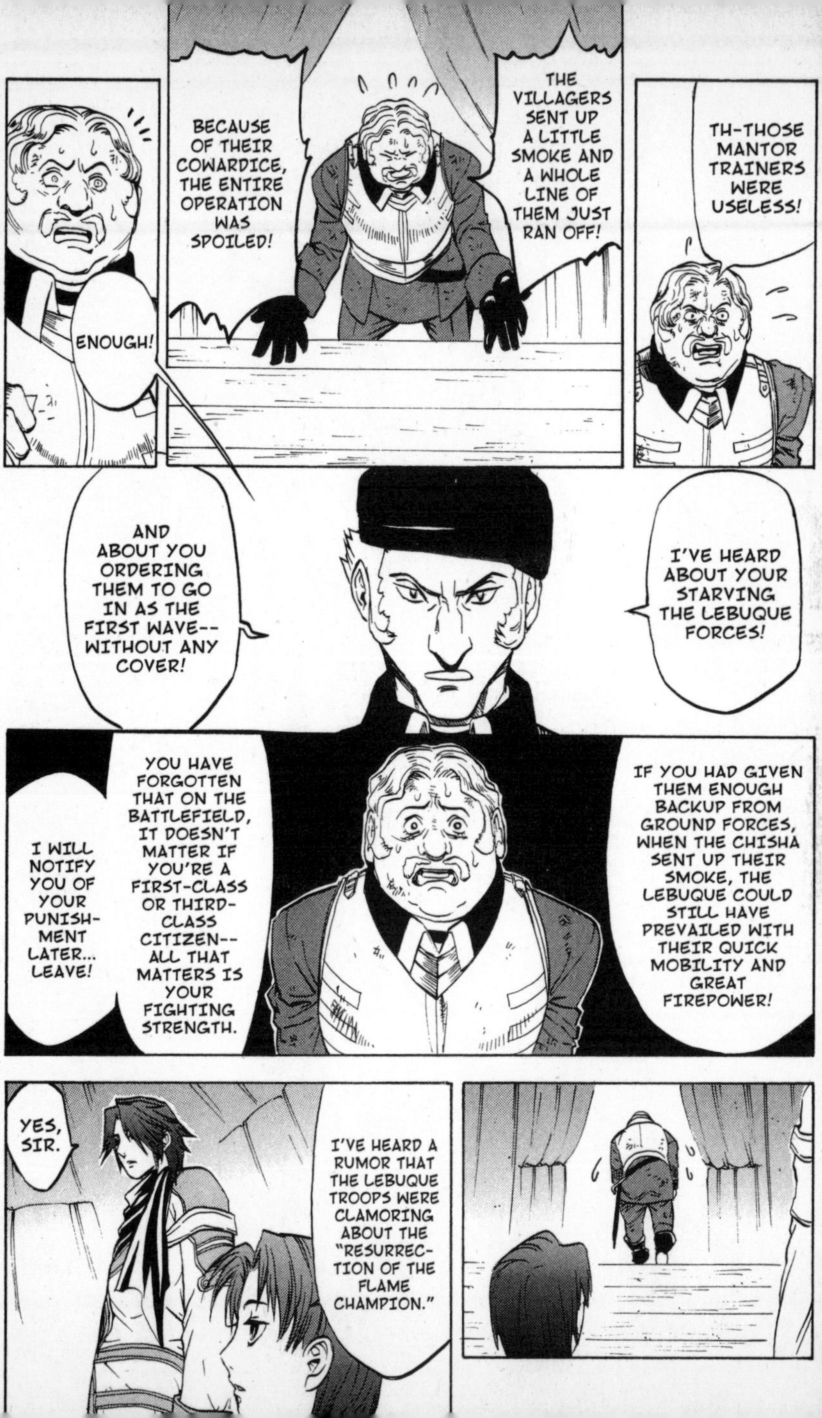
TH-THOSE MANTOR TRAINERS WERE USELESS!
THE VILLAGERS SENT UP A LITTLE SMOKE AND A WHOLE LINE OF THEM JUST RAN OFF!
BECAUSE OF THEIR COWARDICE, THE ENTIRE OPERATION WAS SPOILED!
ENOUGH!
I'VE HEARD ABOUT YOUR STARVING THE LEBUQUE FORCES!
AND ABOUT YOU ORDERING THEM TO GO IN AS THE FIRST WAVE--WITHOUT ANY COVER!
IF YOU HAD GIVEN THEM ENOUGH BACKUP FROM GROUND FORCES, WHEN THE CHISHA SENT UP THEIR SMOKE, THE LEBUQUE COULD STILL HAVE PREVAILED WITH THEIR QUICK MOBILITY AND GREAT FIREPOWER!
YOU HAVE FORGOTTEN THAT ON THE BATTLEFIELD, IT DOESN'T MATTER IF YOU'RE A FIRST-CLASS OR THIRD-CLASS CITIZEN--ALL THAT MATTERS IS YOUR FIGHTING STRENGTH.
I WILL NOTIFY YOU OF YOUR PUNISHMENT LATER... LEAVE!
I'VE HEARD A RUMOR THAT THE LEBUQUE TROOPS WERE CLAMORING ABOUT THE "RESURRECTION OF THE FLAME CHAMPION."
YES, SIR.

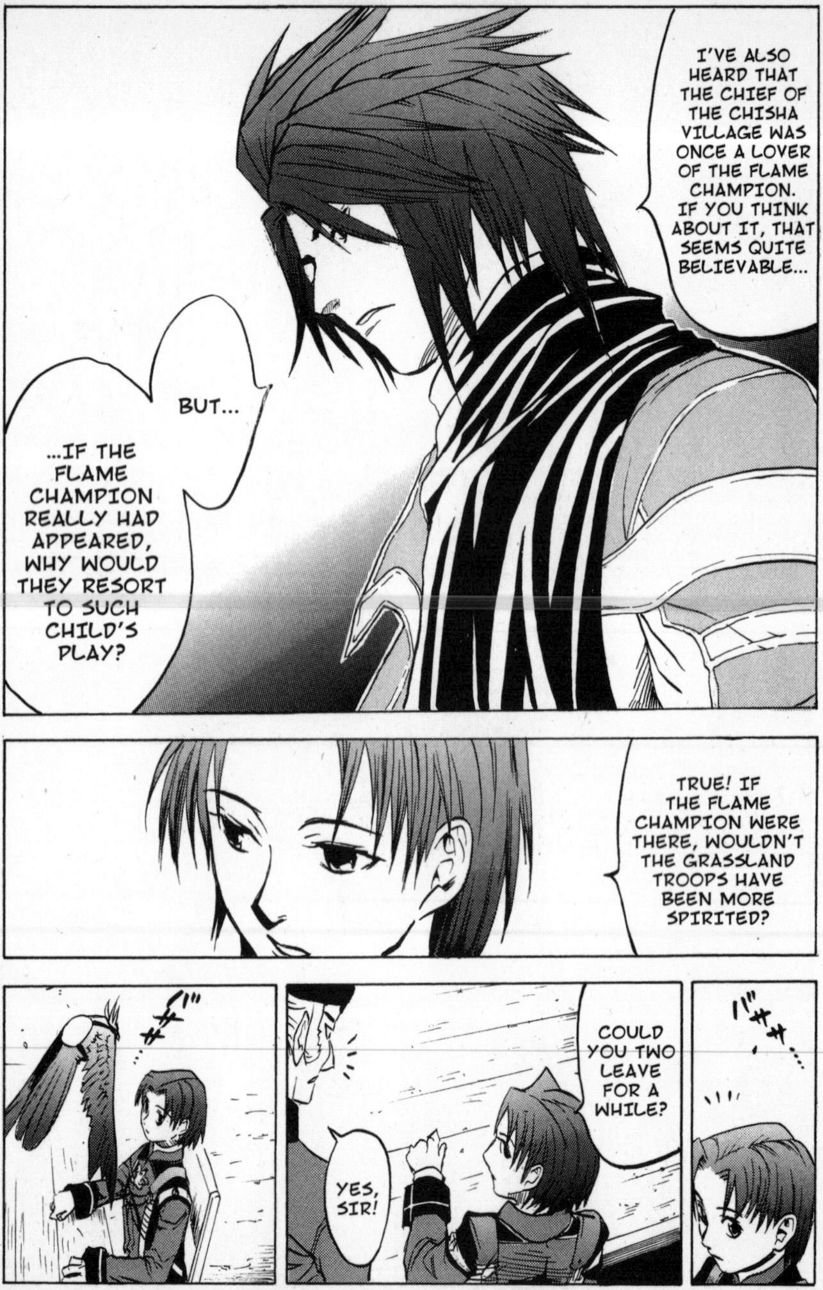
I'VE ALSO HEARD THAT THE CHIEF OF THE CHISHA VILLAGE WAS ONCE A LOVER OF THE FLAME CHAMPION. IF YOU THINK ABOUT IT, THAT SEEMS QUITE BELIEVABLE...
BUT...
...IF THE FLAME CHAMPION REALLY HAD APPEARED, WHY WOULD THEY RESORT TO SUCH CHILD'S PLAY?
TRUE! IF THE FLAME CHAMPION WERE THERE, WOULDN'T THE GRASSLAND TROOPS HAVE BEEN MORE SPIRITED?
COULD YOU TWO LEAVE FOR A WHILE?
YES, SIR!

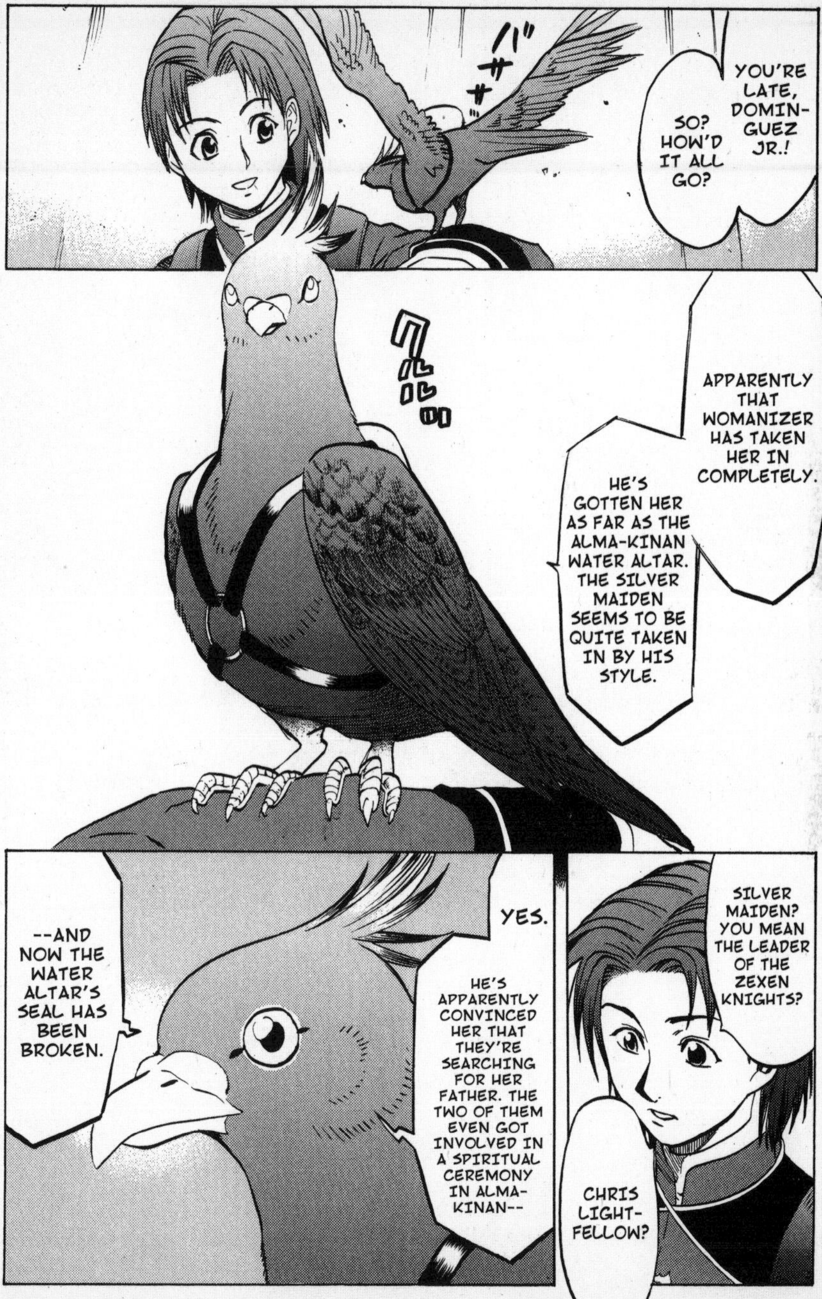
YOU'RE LATE, DOMIN-GUEZ JR.!
SO? HOW'D IT ALL GO?
APPARENTLY THAT WOMANIZER HAS TAKEN HER IN COMPLETELY.
HE'S GOTTEN HER AS FAR AS THE ALMA-KINAN WATER ALTAR. THE SILVER MAIDEN SEEMS TO BE QUITE TAKEN IN BY HIS STYLE.
SILVER MAIDEN? YOU MEAN THE LEADER OF THE ZEXEN KNIGHTS?
CHRIS LIGHT-FELLOW?
YES.
HE'S APPARENTLY CONVINCED HER THAT THEY'RE SEARCHING FOR HER FATHER. THE TWO OF THEM EVEN GOT INVOLVED IN A SPIRITUAL CEREMONY IN ALMA-KINAN--
--AND NOW THE WATER ALTAR'S SEAL HAS BEEN BROKEN.

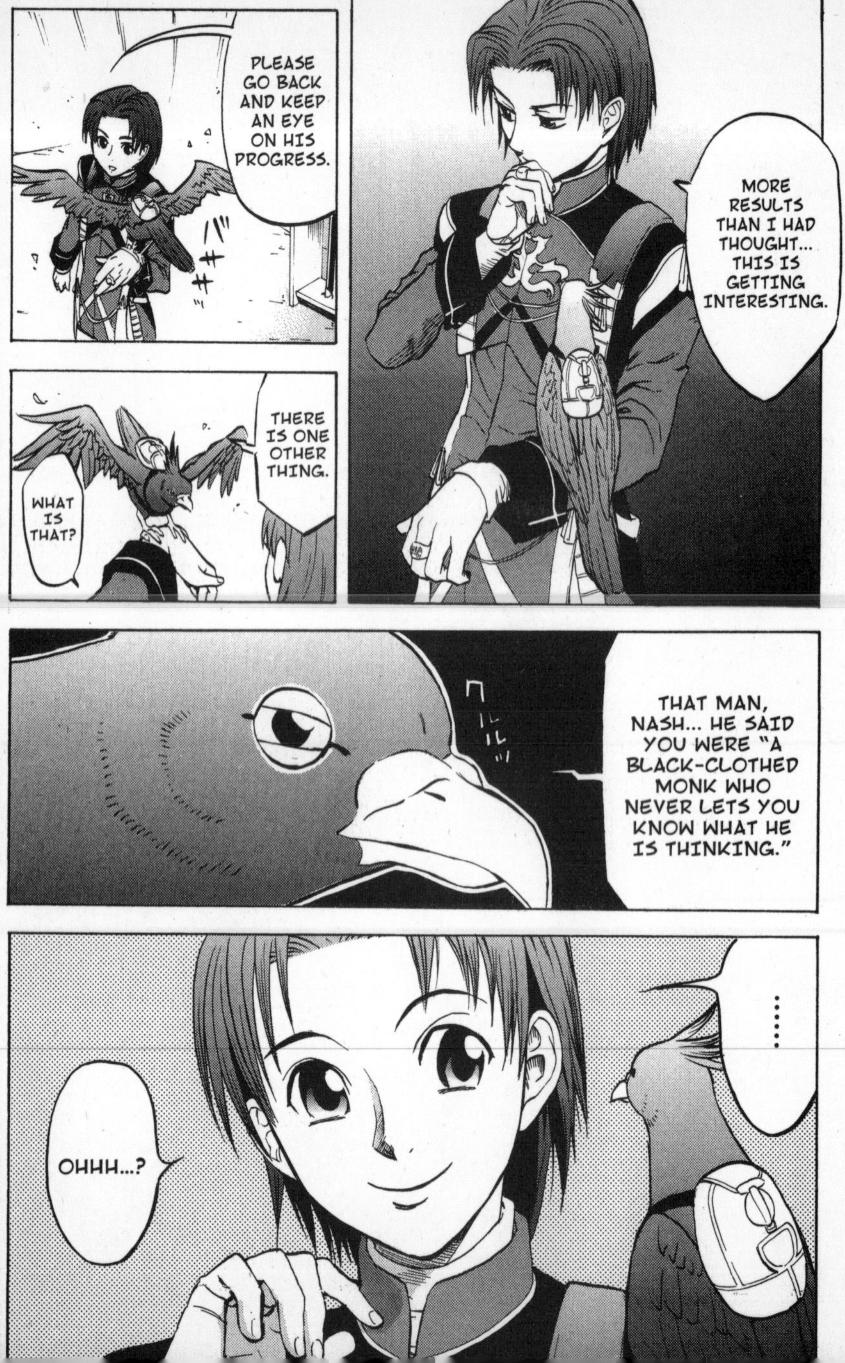
MORE RESULTS THAN I HAD THOUGHT... THIS IS GETTING INTERESTING.
PLEASE GO BACK AND KEEP AN EYE ON HIS PROGRESS.
THERE IS ONE OTHER THING.
WHAT IS THAT?
THAT MAN, NASH... HE SAID YOU WERE "A BLACK-CLOTHED MONK WHO NEVER LETS YOU KNOW WHAT HE IS THINKING."
......
OHHH...?

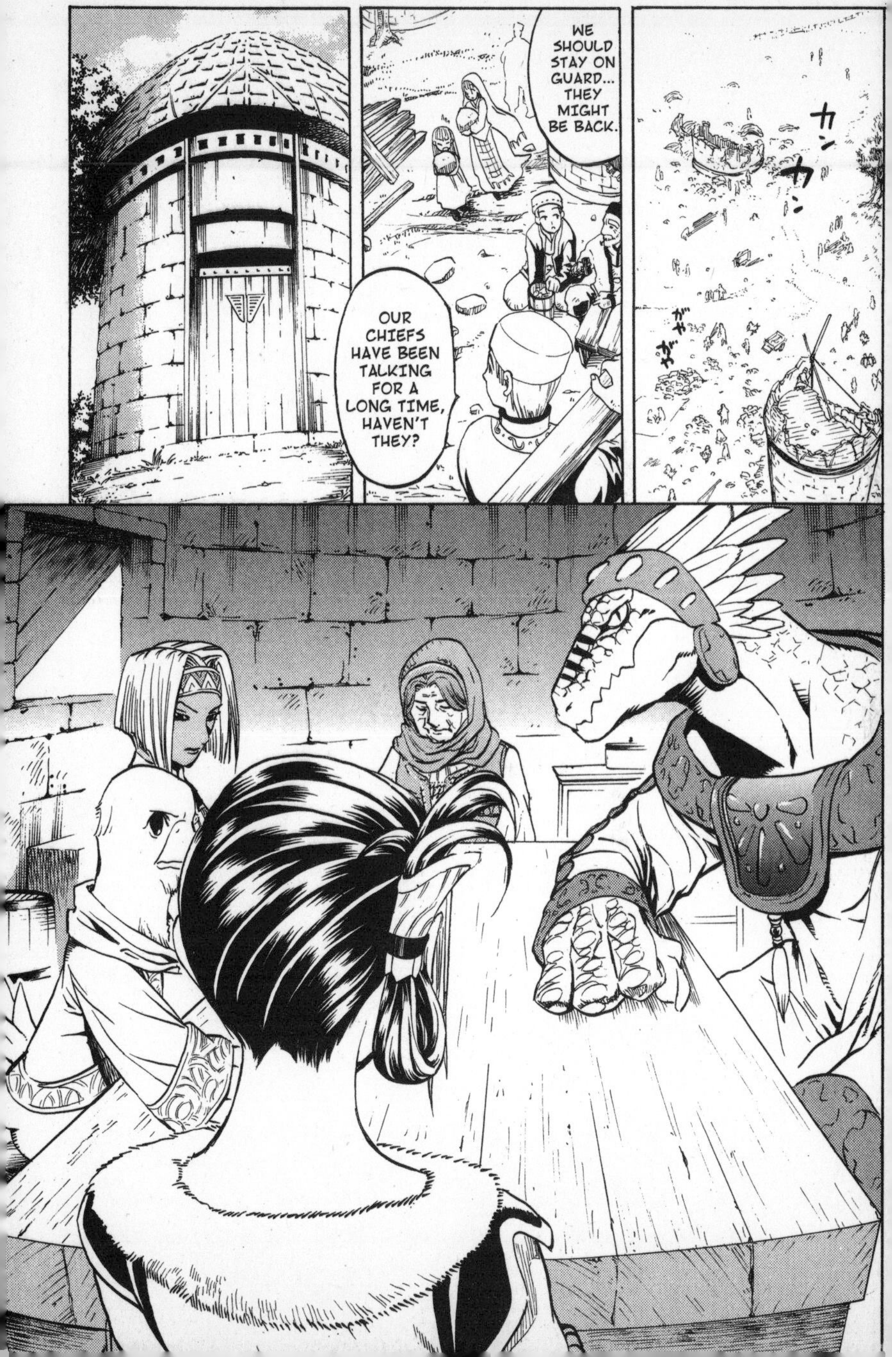
カン
カン
ガヤ
ガヤ
WE SHOULD STAY ON GUARD... THEY MIGHT BE BACK.
OUR CHIEFS HAVE BEEN TALKING FOR A LONG TIME, HAVEN'T THEY?

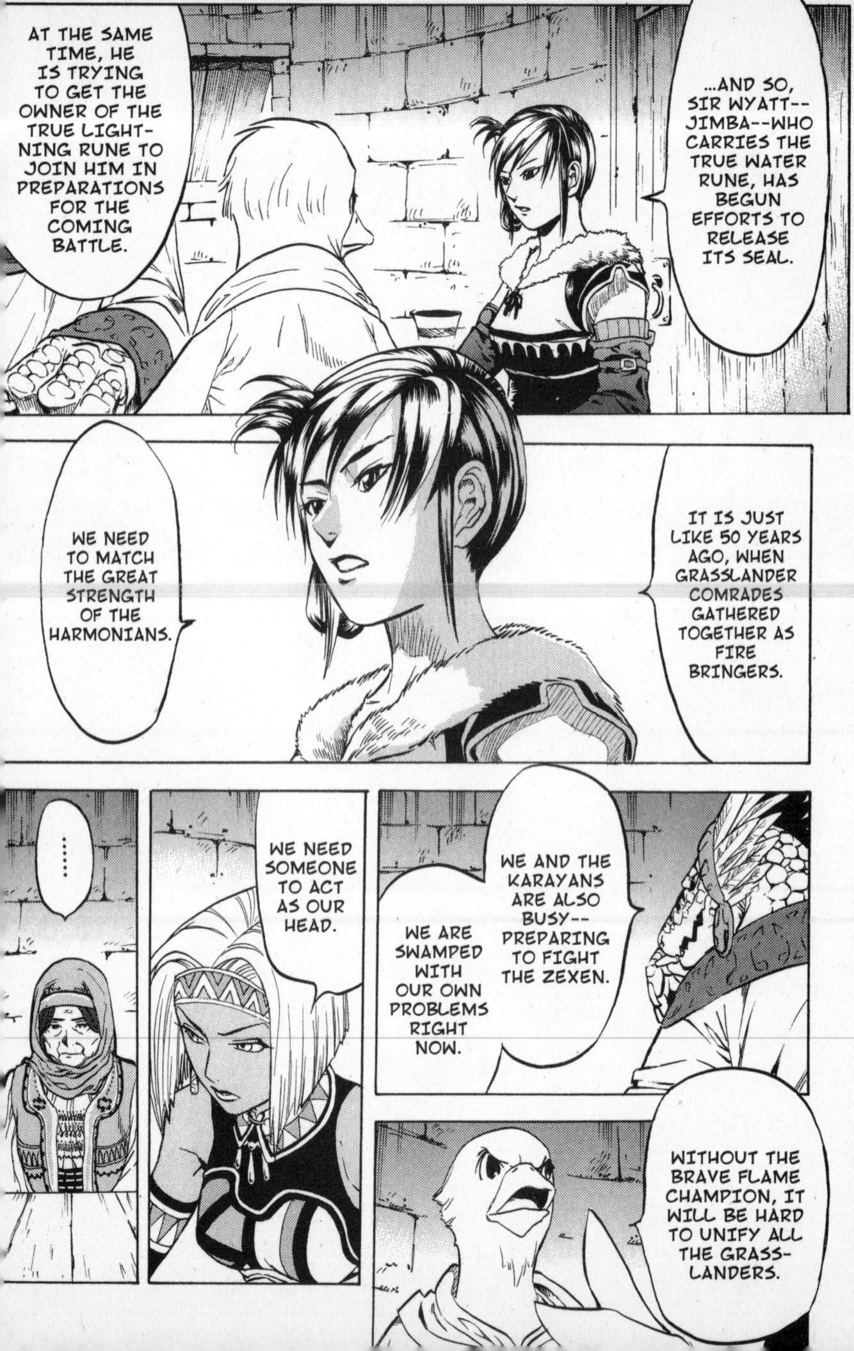
...AND SO, SIR WYATT--JIMBA--WHO CARRIES THE TRUE WATER RUNE, HAS BEGUN EFFORTS TO RELEASE ITS SEAL.
AT THE SAME TIME, HE IS TRYING TO GET THE OWNER OF THE TRUE LIGHTNING RUNE TO JOIN HIM IN PREPARATIONS FOR THE COMING BATTLE.
IT IS JUST LIKE 50 YEARS AGO, WHEN GRASSLANDER COMRADES GATHERED TOGETHER AS FIRE BRINGERS.
WE NEED TO MATCH THE GREAT STRENGTH OF THE HARMONIANS.
WE AND THE KARAYANS ARE ALSO BUSY--PREPARING TO FIGHT THE ZEXEN.
WE ARE SWAMPED WITH OUR OWN PROBLEMS RIGHT NOW.
WITHOUT THE BRAVE FLAME CHAMPION, IT WILL BE HARD TO UNIFY ALL THE GRASSLANDERS.
WE NEED SOMEONE TO ACT AS OUR HEAD.
......

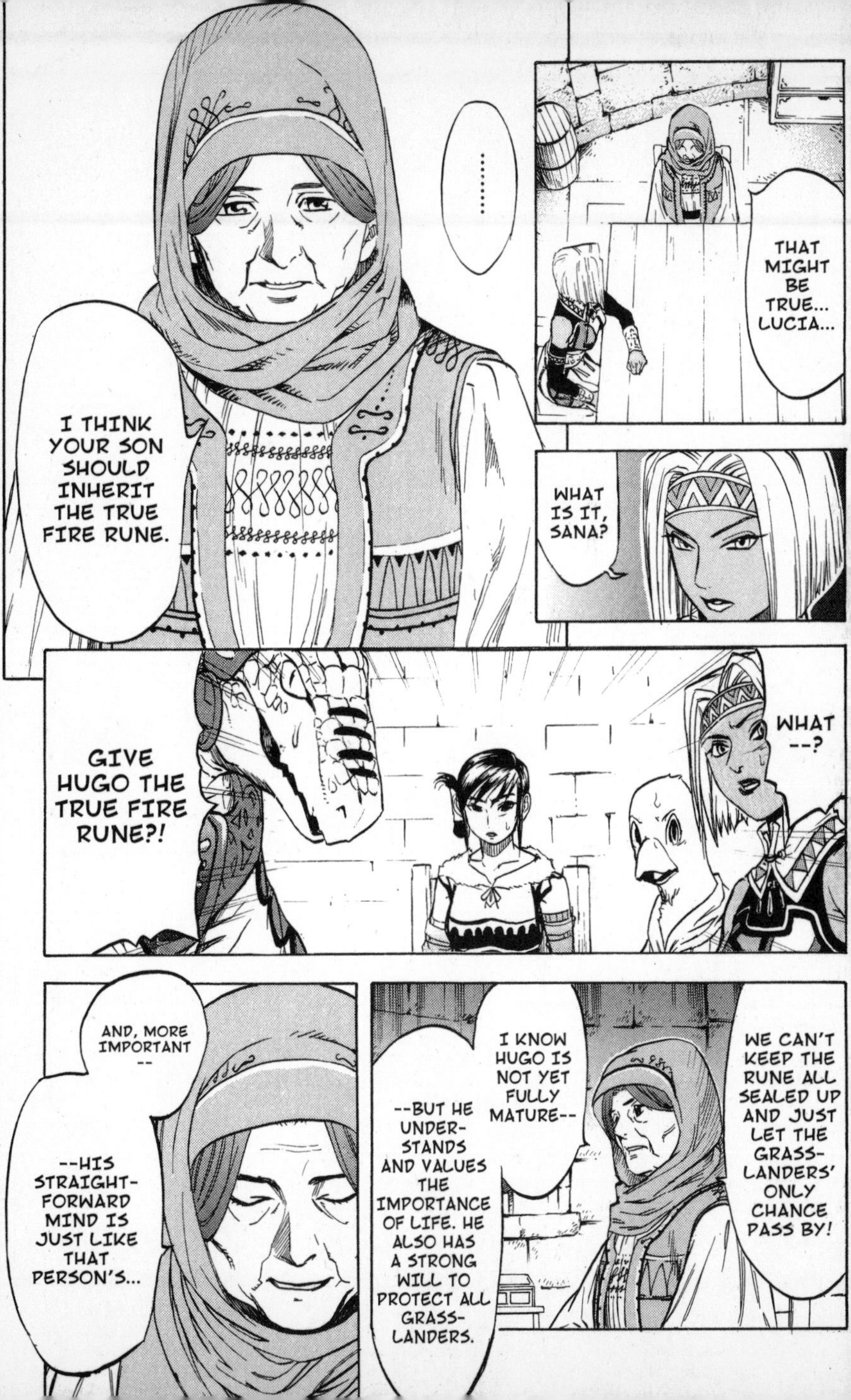

THAT MIGHT BE TRUE... LUCIA...
WHAT IS IT, SANA?
......
I THINK YOUR SON SHOULD INHERIT THE TRUE FIRE RUNE.
WHAT --?
GIVE HUGO THE TRUE FIRE RUNE?!
WE CAN'T KEEP THE RUNE ALL SEALED UP AND JUST LET THE GRASS-LANDERS' ONLY CHANCE PASS BY!
I KNOW HUGO IS NOT YET FULLY MATURE--
--BUT HE UNDER-STANDS AND VALUES THE IMPORTANCE OF LIFE. HE ALSO HAS A STRONG WILL TO PROTECT ALL GRASS-LANDERS.
AND, MORE IMPORTANT --
--HIS STRAIGHT-FORWARD MIND IS JUST LIKE THAT PERSON'S...

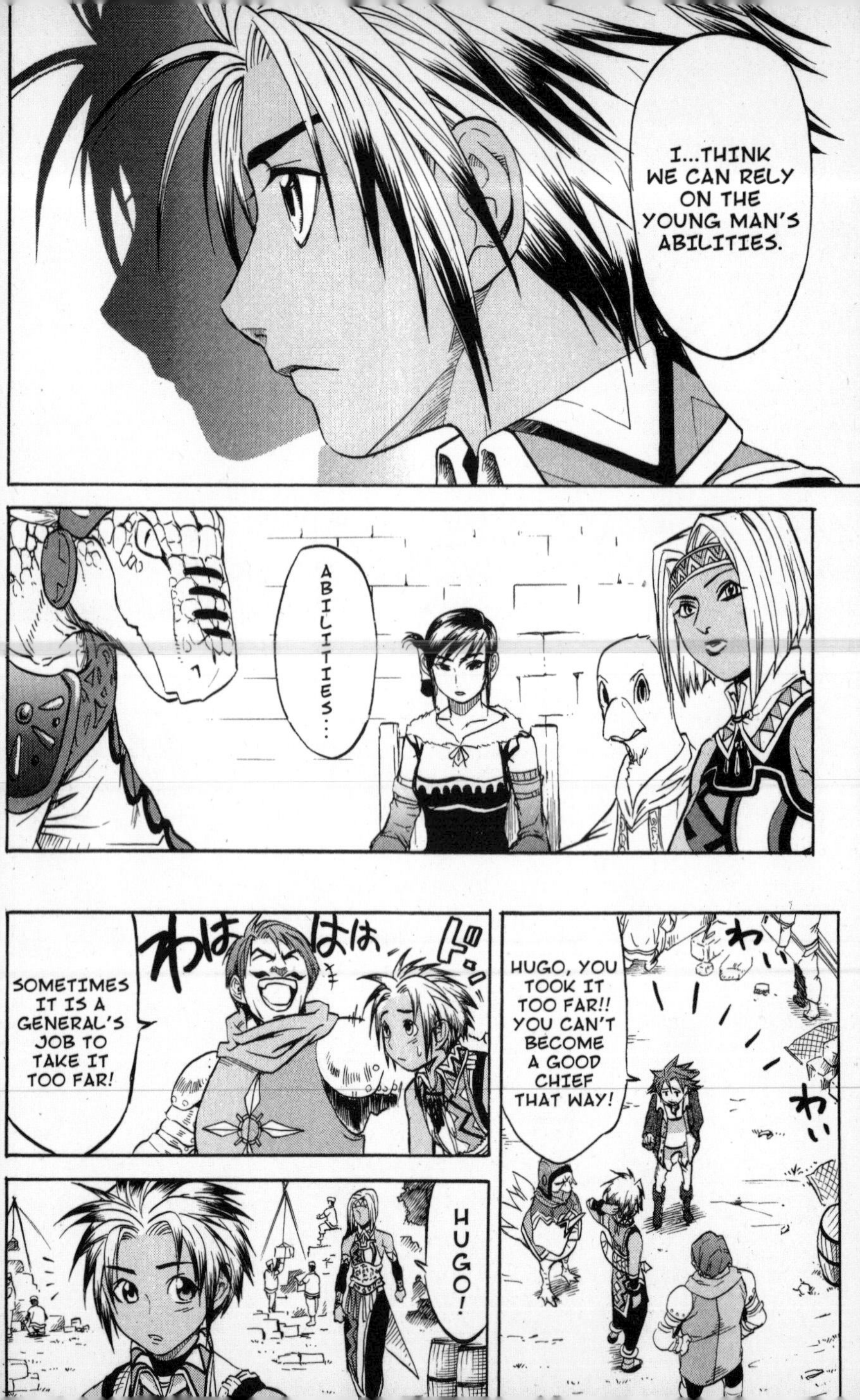
I...THINK WE CAN RELY ON THE YOUNG MAN'S ABILITIES.
ABILITIES...
HUGO, YOU TOOK IT TOO FAR!! YOU CAN'T BECOME A GOOD CHIEF THAT WAY!
わい
わい
わはははは
ド
SOMETIMES IT IS A GENERAL'S JOB TO TAKE IT TOO FAR!
HUGO!

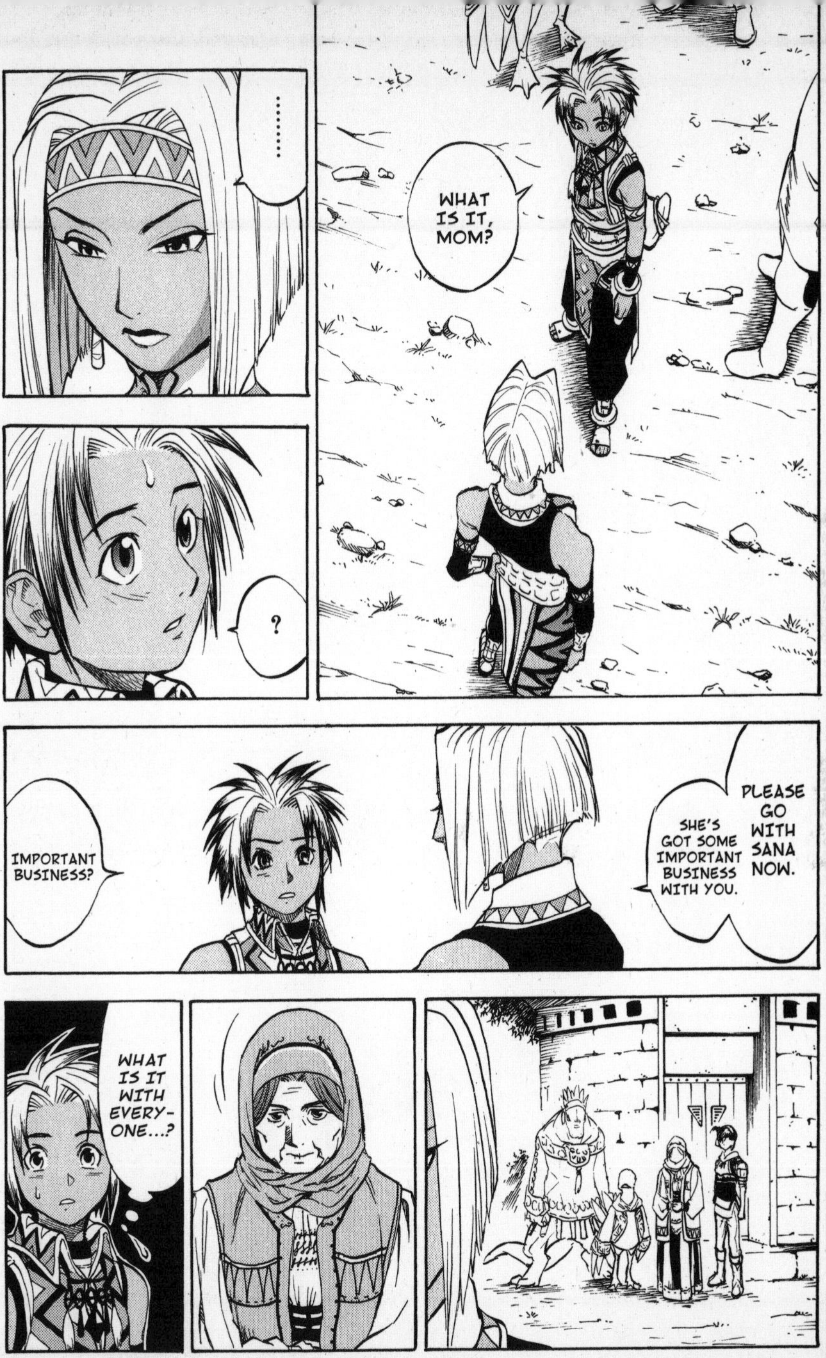
WHAT IS IT, MOM?
......
?
PLEASE GO WITH SANA NOW.
SHE'S GOT SOME IMPORTANT BUSINESS WITH YOU.
IMPORTANT BUSINESS?
WHAT IS IT WITH EVERY-ONE...?

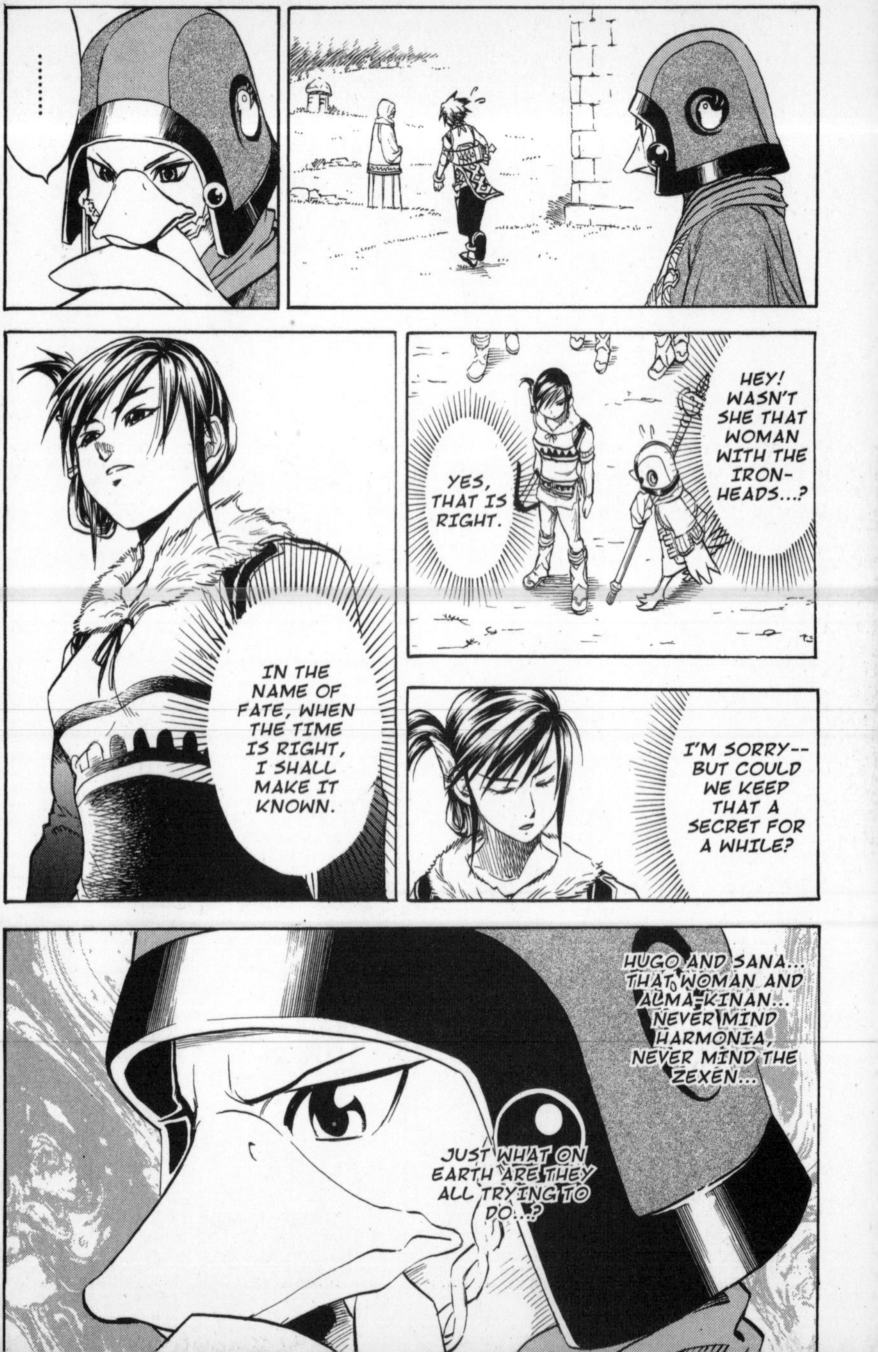
......
HEY! WASN'T SHE THAT WOMAN WITH THE IRON-HEADS...?
YES, THAT IS RIGHT.
I'M SORRY--BUT COULD WE KEEP THAT A SECRET FOR A WHILE?
IN THE NAME OF FATE, WHEN THE TIME IS RIGHT, I SHALL MAKE IT KNOWN.
HUGO AND SANA... THAT WOMAN AND ALMA-KINAN... NEVER MIND HARMONIA, NEVER MIND THE ZEXEN...
JUST WHAT ON EARTH ARE THEY ALL TRYING TO DO...?

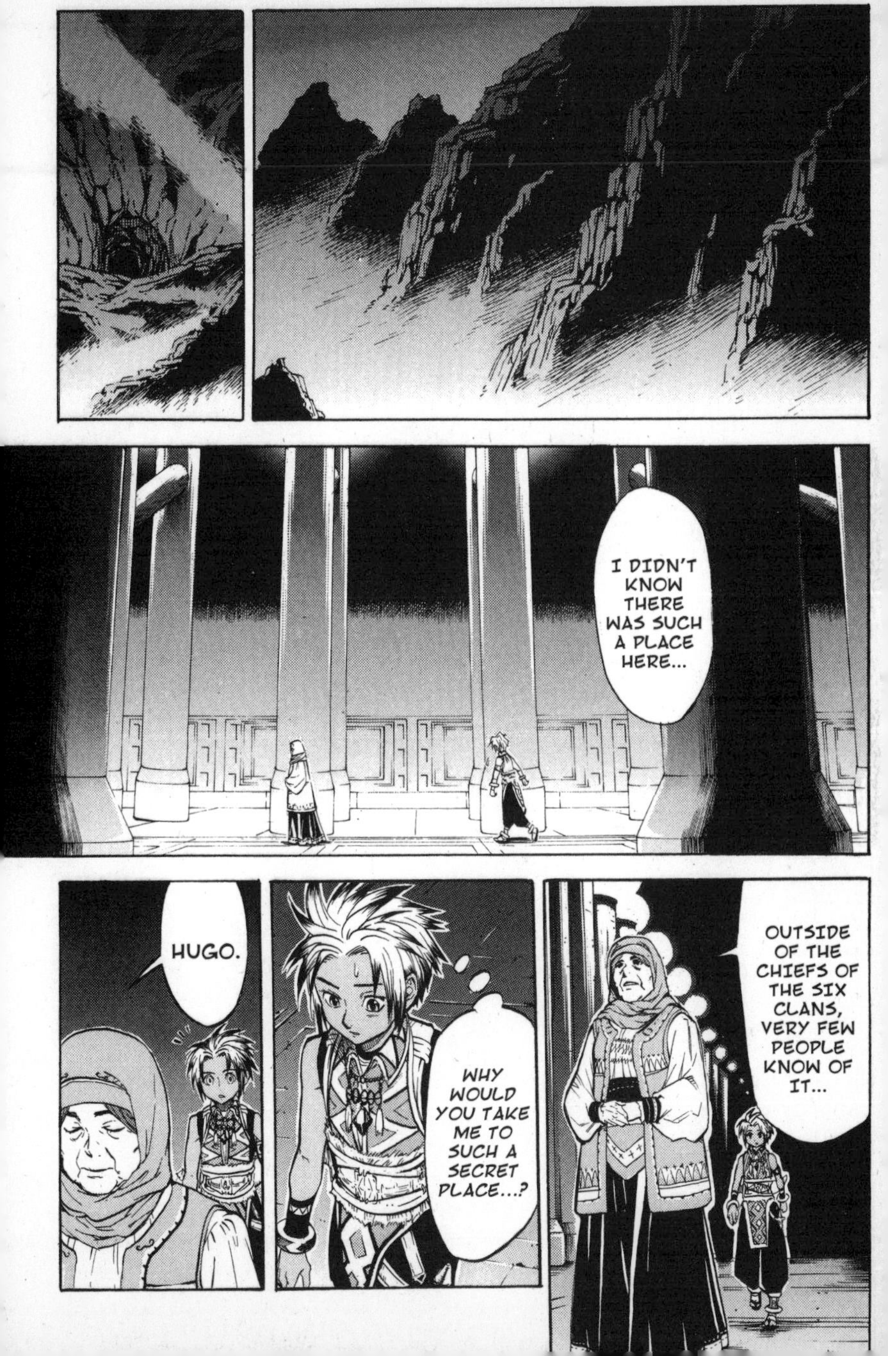
I DIDN'T KNOW THERE WAS SUCH A PLACE HERE...
OUTSIDE OF THE CHIEFS OF THE SIX CLANS, VERY FEW PEOPLE KNOW OF IT...
WHY WOULD YOU TAKE ME TO SUCH A SECRET PLACE...?
HUGO.

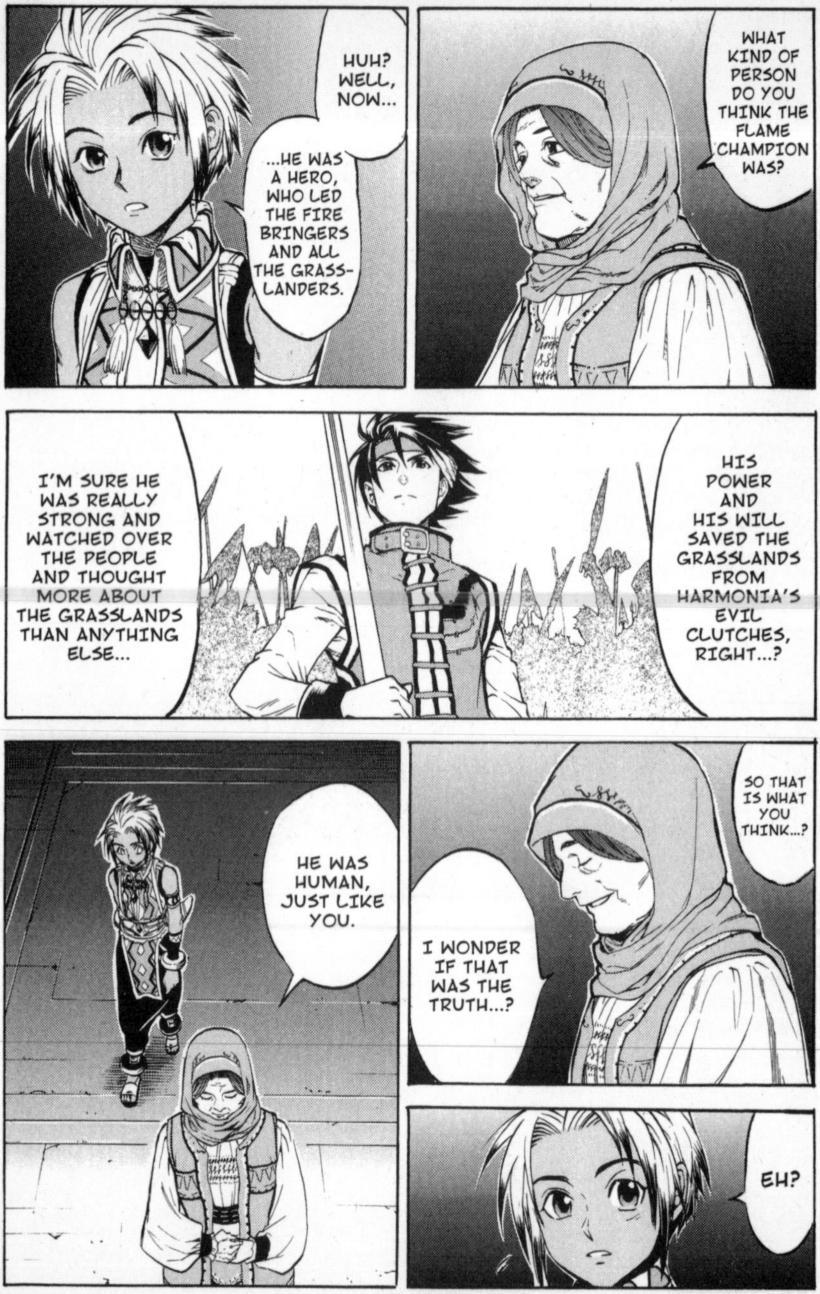

WHAT KIND OF PERSON DO YOU THINK THE FLAME CHAMPION WAS?
HUH? WELL, NOW...
...HE WAS A HERO, WHO LED THE FIRE BRINGERS AND ALL THE GRASS-LANDERS.
HIS POWER AND HIS WILL SAVED THE GRASSLANDS FROM HARMONIA'S EVIL CLUTCHES, RIGHT...?
I'M SURE HE WAS REALLY STRONG AND WATCHED OVER THE PEOPLE AND THOUGHT MORE ABOUT THE GRASSLANDS THAN ANYTHING ELSE...
SO THAT IS WHAT YOU THINK...?
I WONDER IF THAT WAS THE TRUTH...?
EH?
HE WAS HUMAN, JUST LIKE YOU.

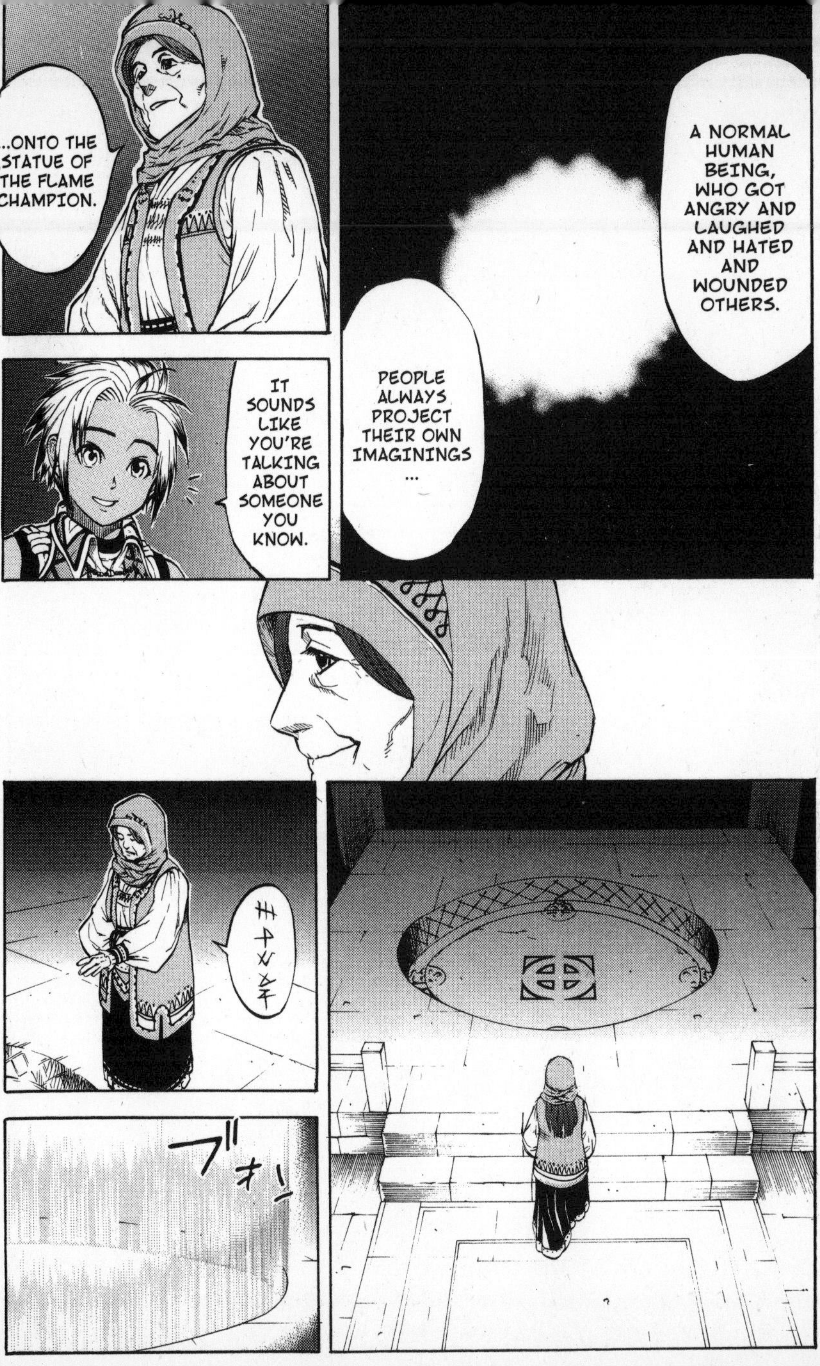
A NORMAL HUMAN BEING, WHO GOT ANGRY AND LAUGHED AND HATED AND WOUNDED OTHERS.
PEOPLE ALWAYS PROJECT THEIR OWN IMAGININGS ...
...ONTO THE STATUE OF THE FLAME CHAMPION.
IT SOUNDS LIKE YOU'RE TALKING ABOUT SOMEONE YOU KNOW.
ブオ!

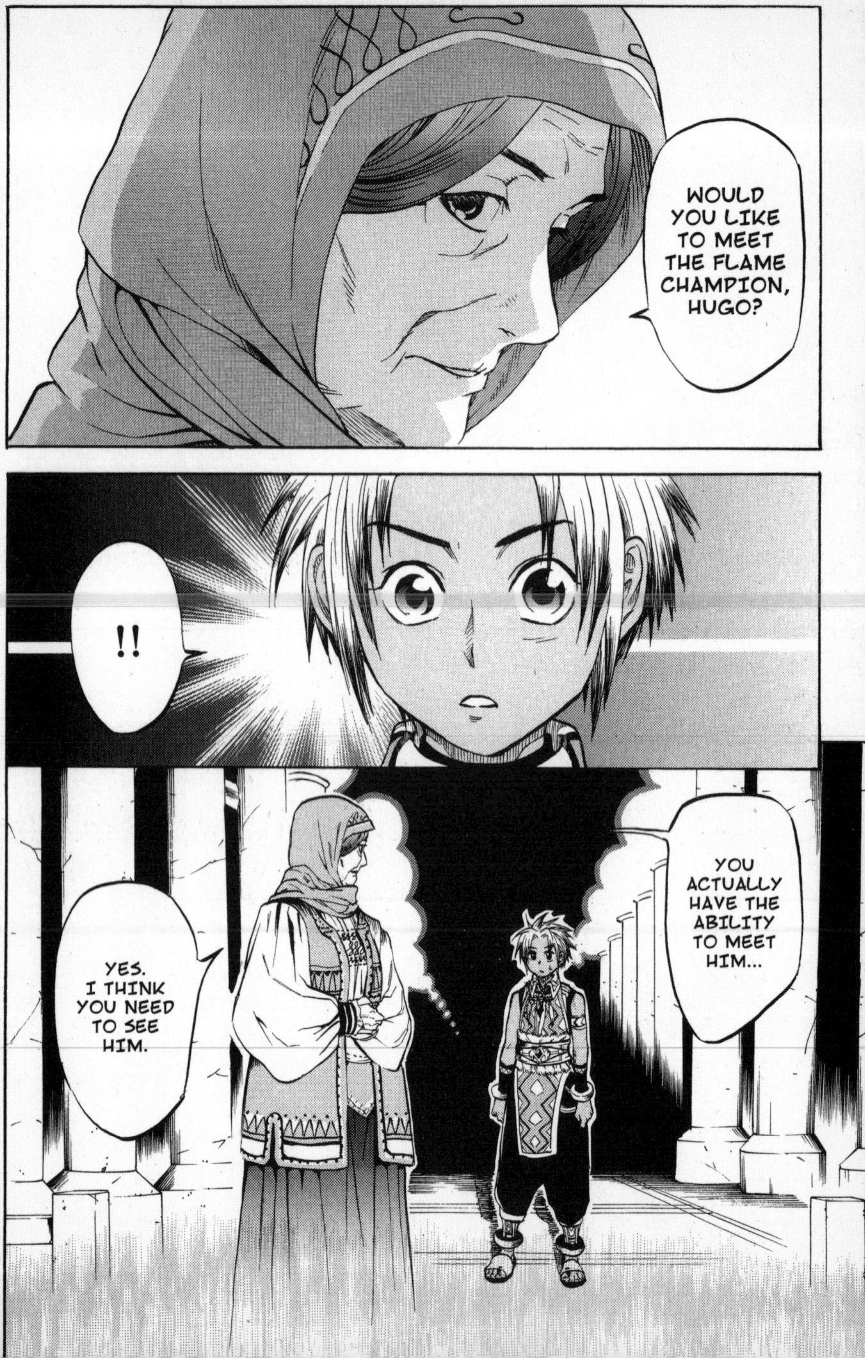
WOULD YOU LIKE TO MEET THE FLAME CHAMPION, HUGO?
!!
YOU ACTUALLY HAVE THE ABILITY TO MEET HIM...
YES. I THINK YOU NEED TO SEE HIM.

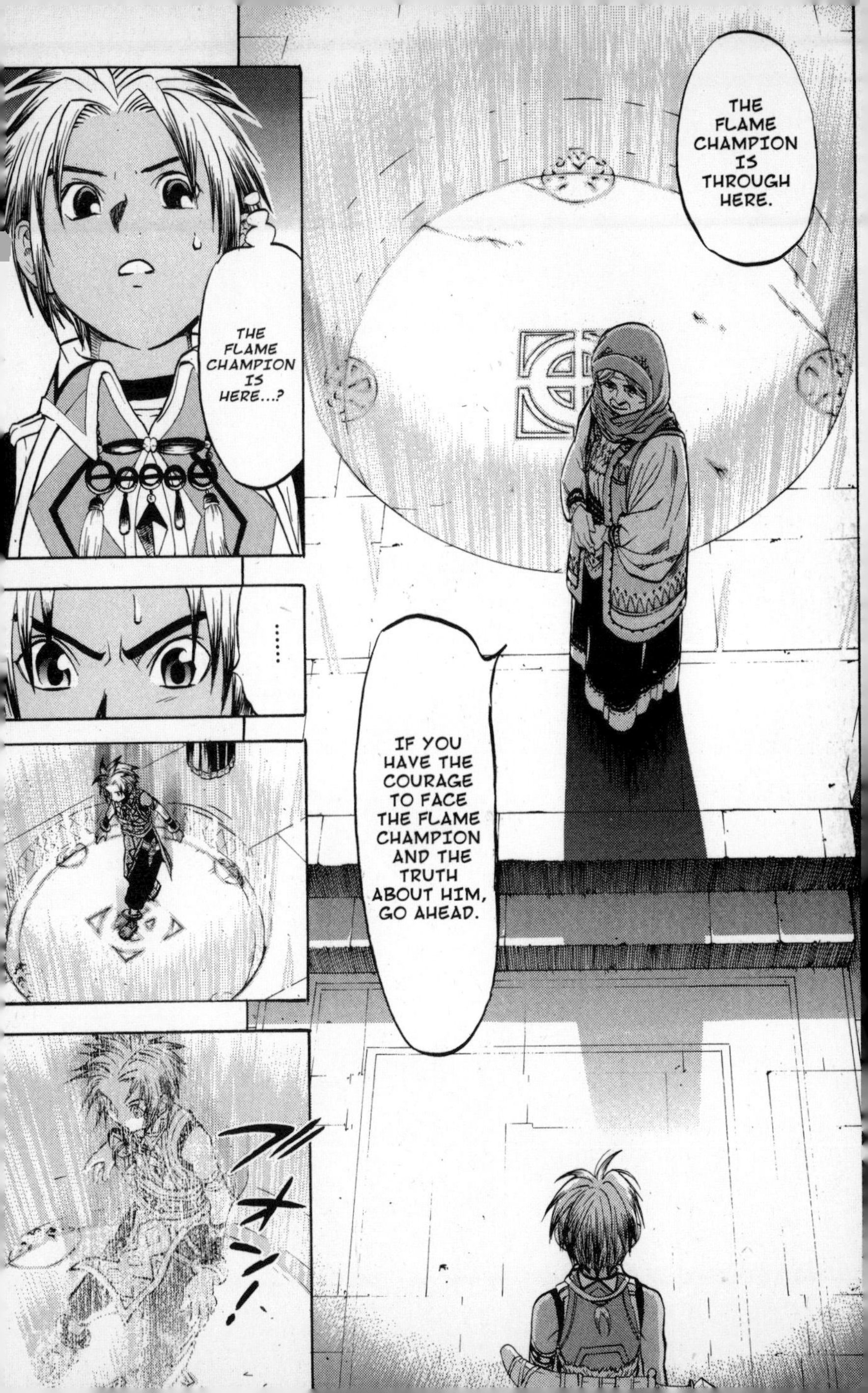
THE FLAME CHAMPION IS THROUGH HERE.
IF YOU HAVE THE COURAGE TO FACE THE FLAME CHAMPION AND THE TRUTH ABOUT HIM, GO AHEAD.
THE FLAME CHAMPION IS HERE...?
......

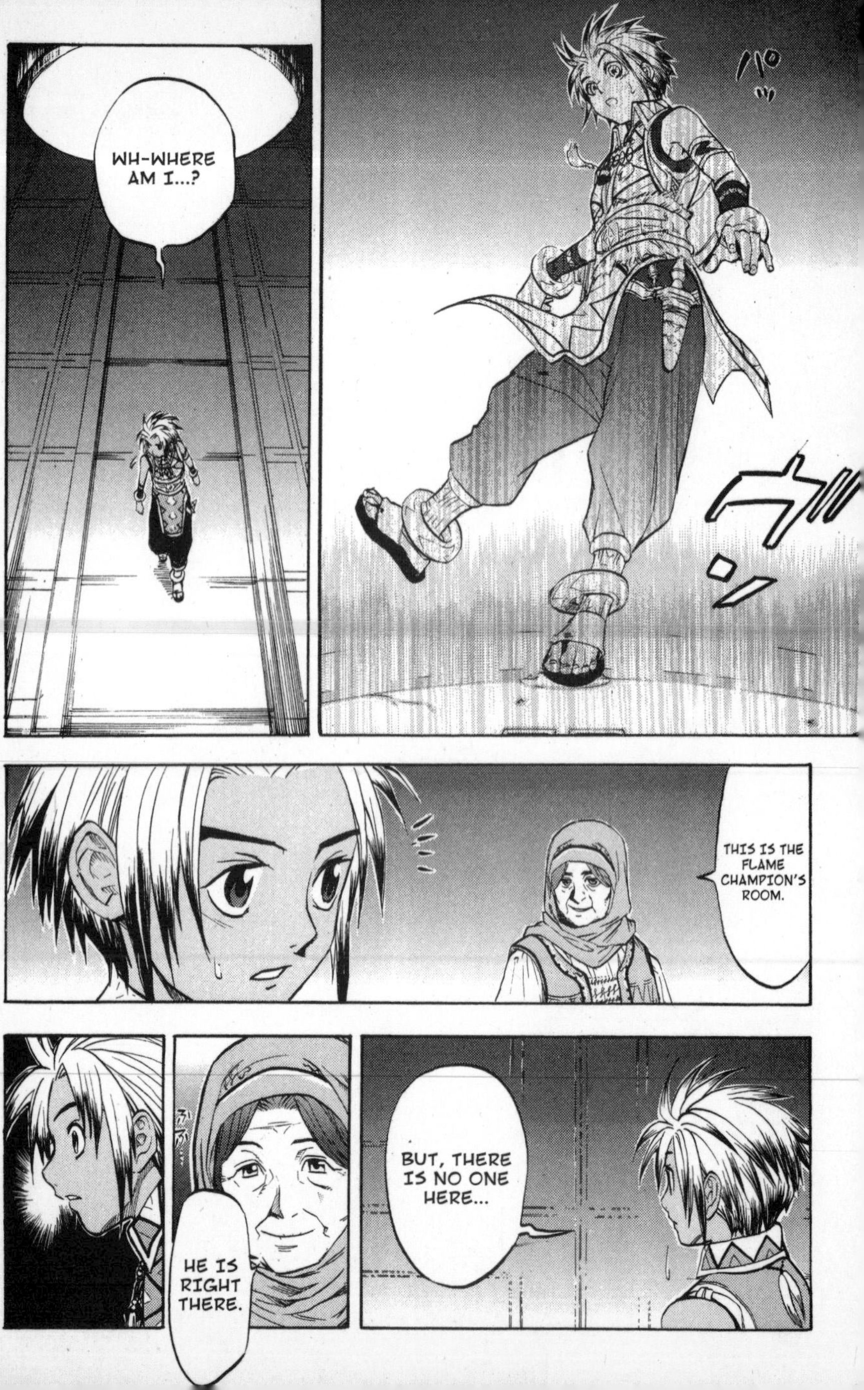
パッ
WH-WHERE AM I...?
THIS IS THE FLAME CHAMPION'S ROOM.
BUT, THERE IS NO ONE HERE...
HE IS RIGHT THERE.

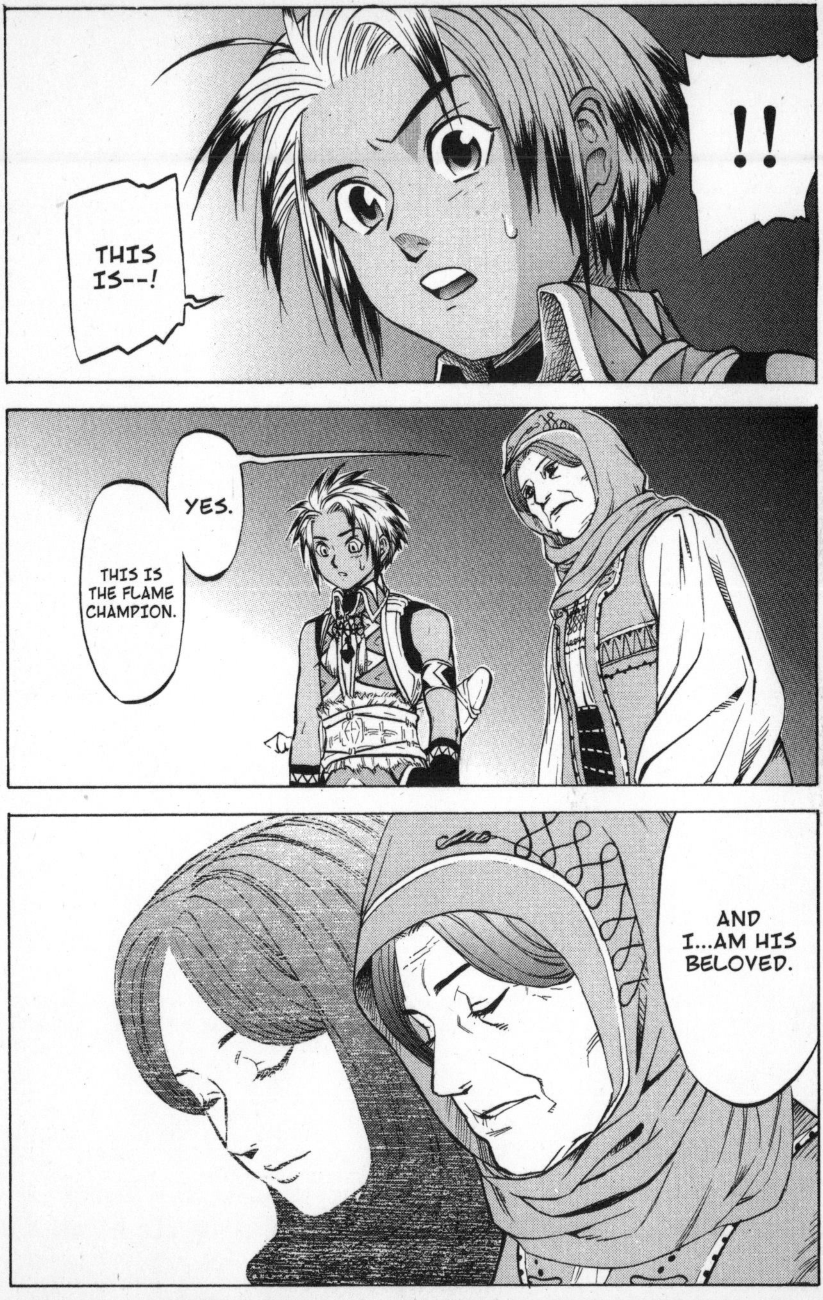
!!
THIS IS--!
YES.
THIS IS THE FLAME CHAMPION.
AND I...AM HIS BELOVED.

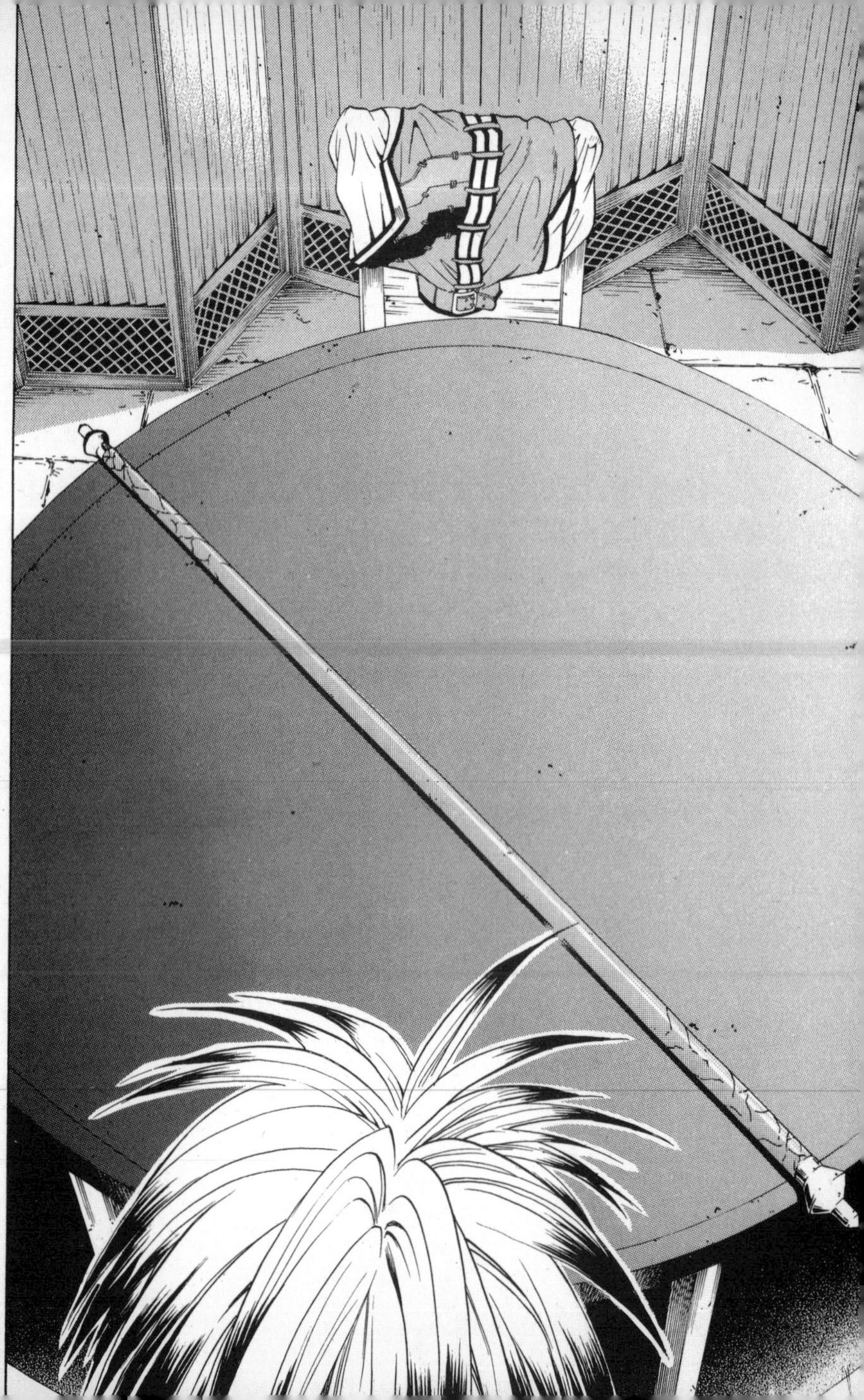

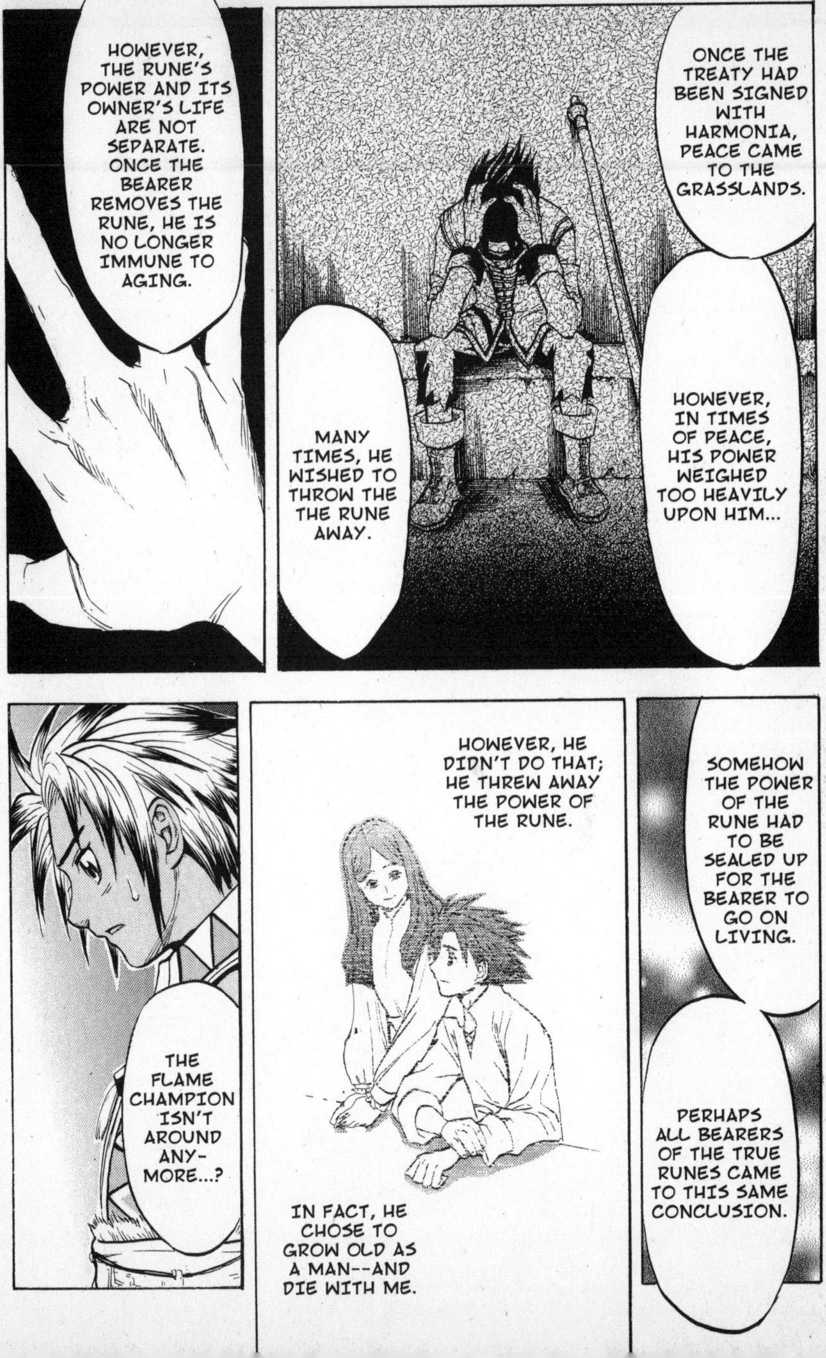
ONCE THE TREATY HAD BEEN SIGNED WITH HARMONIA, PEACE CAME TO THE GRASSLANDS.
HOWEVER, IN TIMES OF PEACE, HIS POWER WEIGHED TOO HEAVILY UPON HIM...
MANY TIMES, HE WISHED TO THROW THE THE RUNE AWAY.
HOWEVER, THE RUNE'S POWER AND ITS OWNER'S LIFE ARE NOT SEPARATE. ONCE THE BEARER REMOVES THE RUNE, HE IS NO LONGER IMMUNE TO AGING.
SOMEHOW THE POWER OF THE RUNE HAD TO BE SEALED UP FOR THE BEARER TO GO ON LIVING.
PERHAPS ALL BEARERS OF THE TRUE RUNES CAME TO THIS SAME CONCLUSION.
HOWEVER, HE DIDN'T DO THAT; HE THREW AWAY THE POWER OF THE RUNE.
IN FACT, HE CHOSE TO GROW OLD AS A MAN--AND DIE WITH ME.
THE FLAME CHAMPION ISN'T AROUND ANY-MORE...?

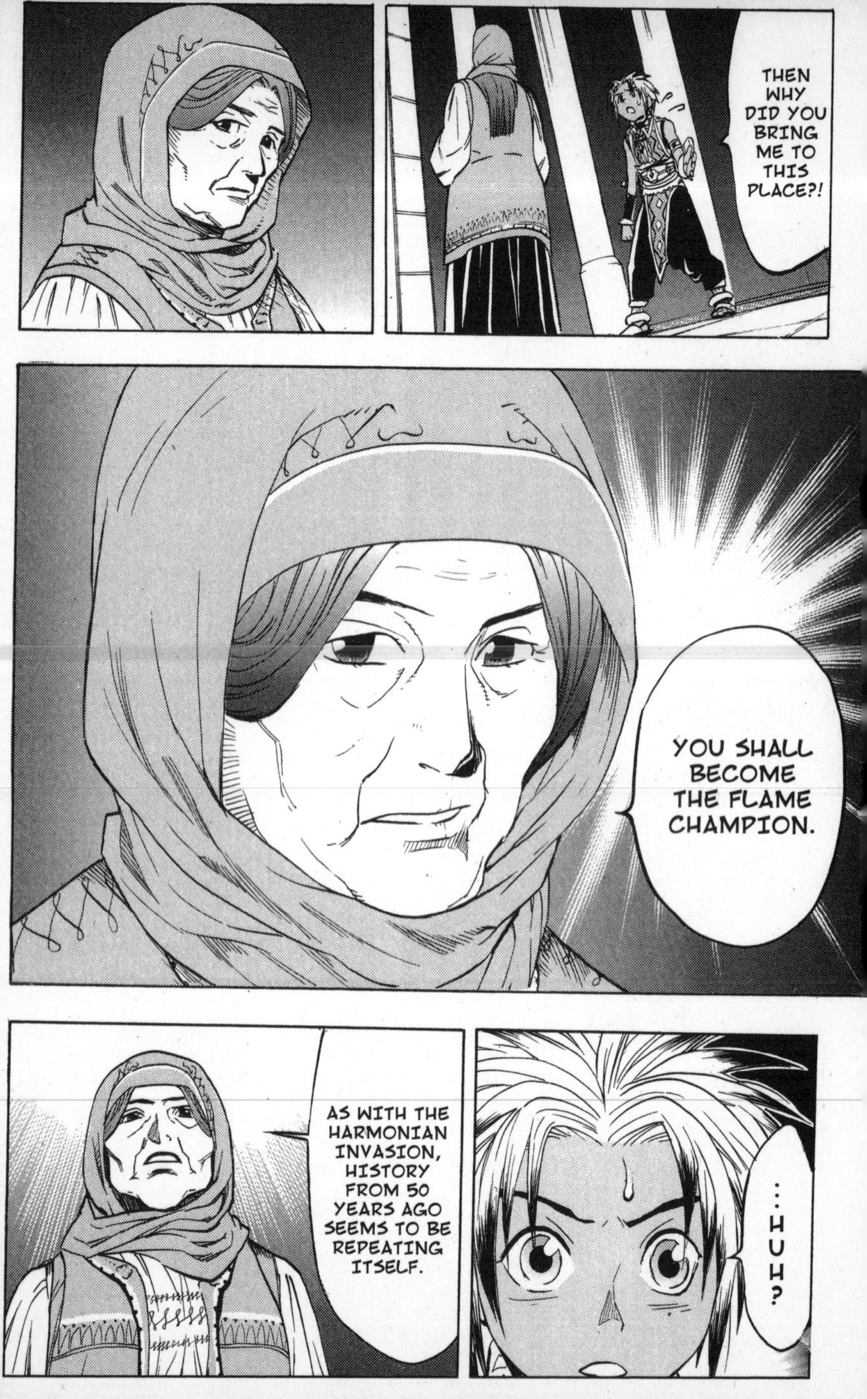
THEN WHY DID YOU BRING ME TO THIS PLACE?!
YOU SHALL BECOME THE FLAME CHAMPION.
...HUH?
AS WITH THE HARMONIAN INVASION, HISTORY FROM 50 YEARS AGO SEEMS TO BE REPEATING ITSELF.

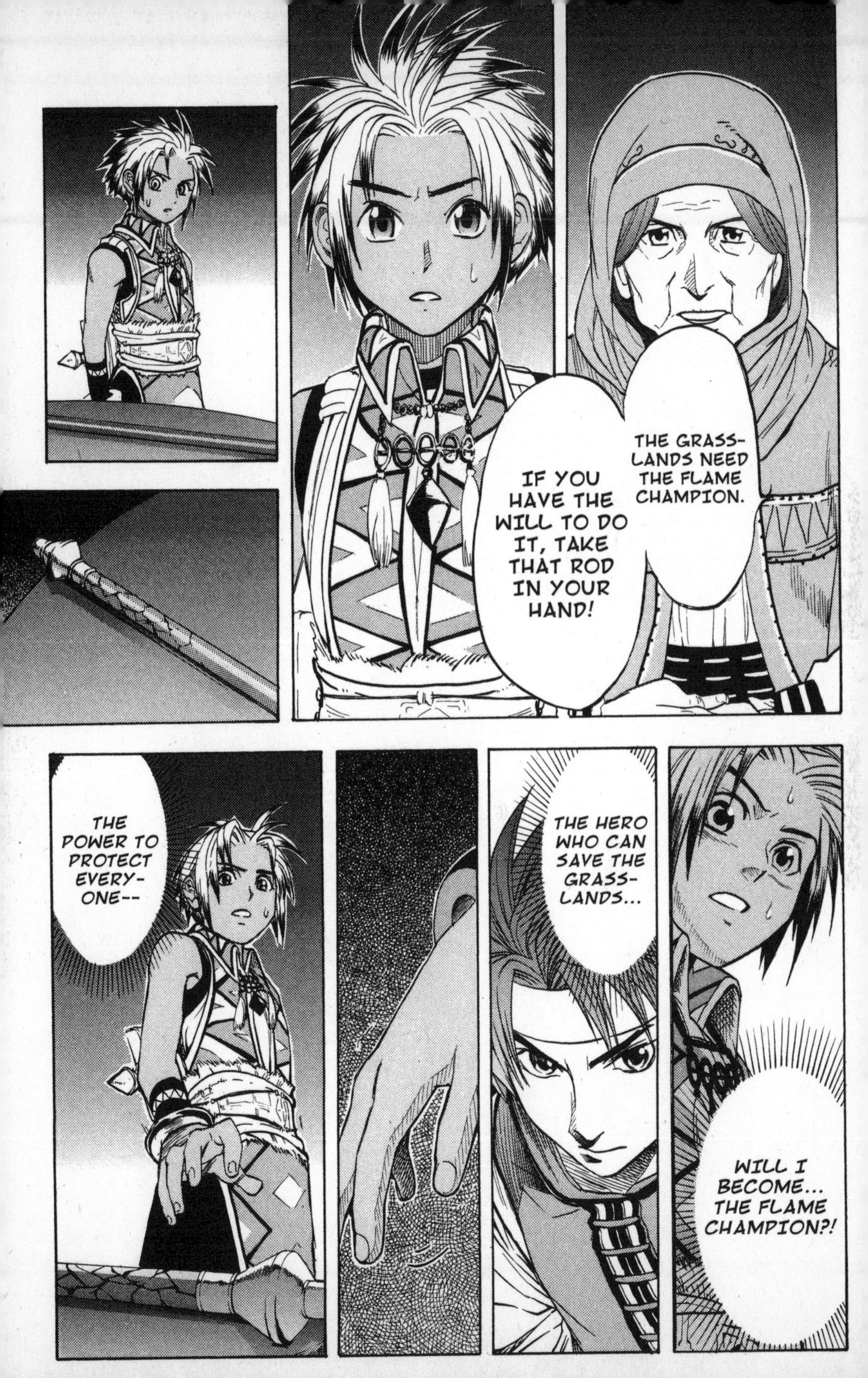
THE GRASS-LANDS NEED THE FLAME CHAMPION.
IF YOU HAVE THE WILL TO DO IT, TAKE THAT ROD IN YOUR HAND!
WILL I BECOME... THE FLAME CHAMPION?!
THE HERO WHO CAN SAVE THE GRASS-LANDS...
THE POWER TO PROTECT EVERY-ONE--

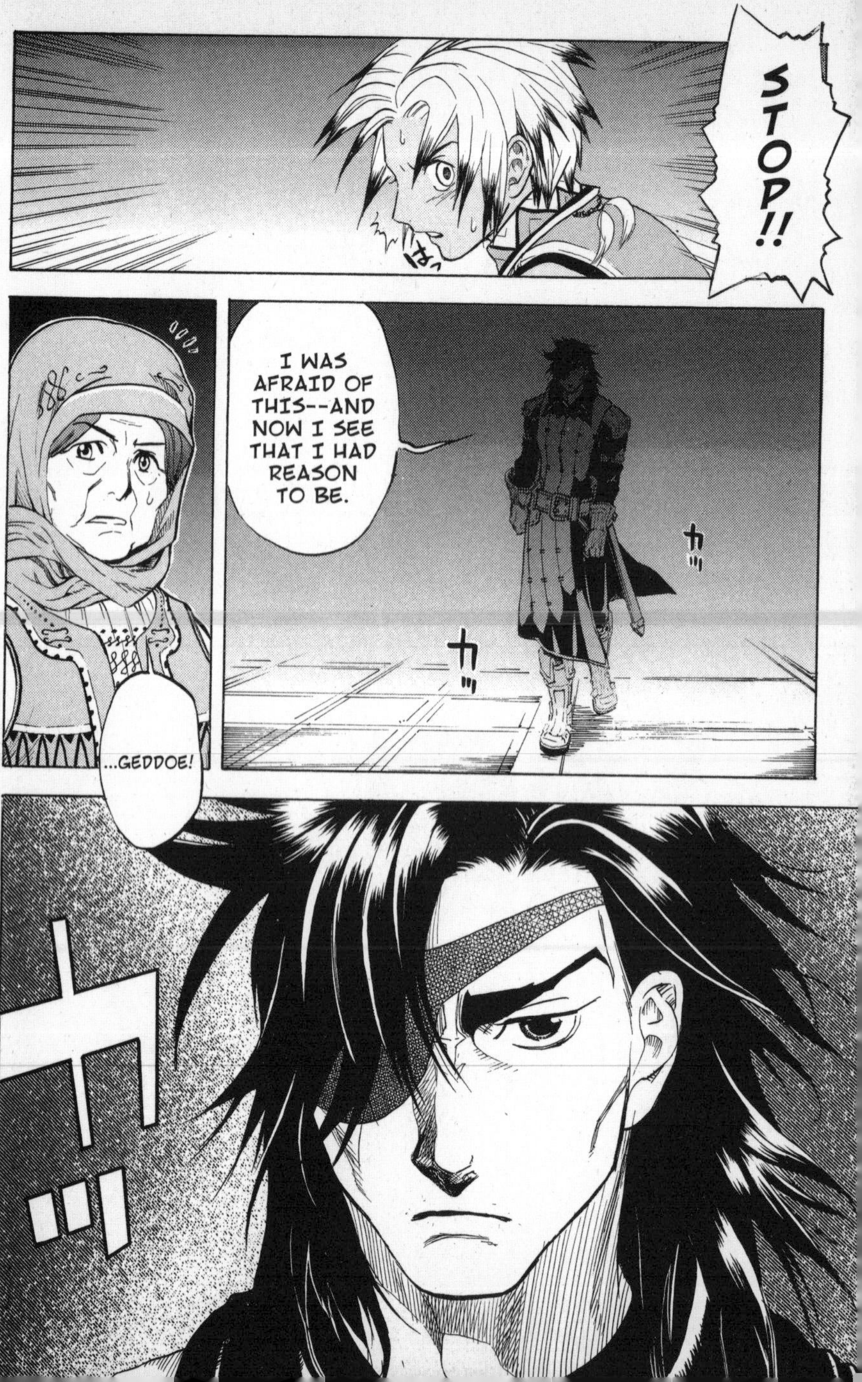
STOP!!
はっ
I WAS AFRAID OF THIS--AND NOW I SEE THAT I HAD REASON TO BE.
カッ
カッ
...GEDDOE!
カッ

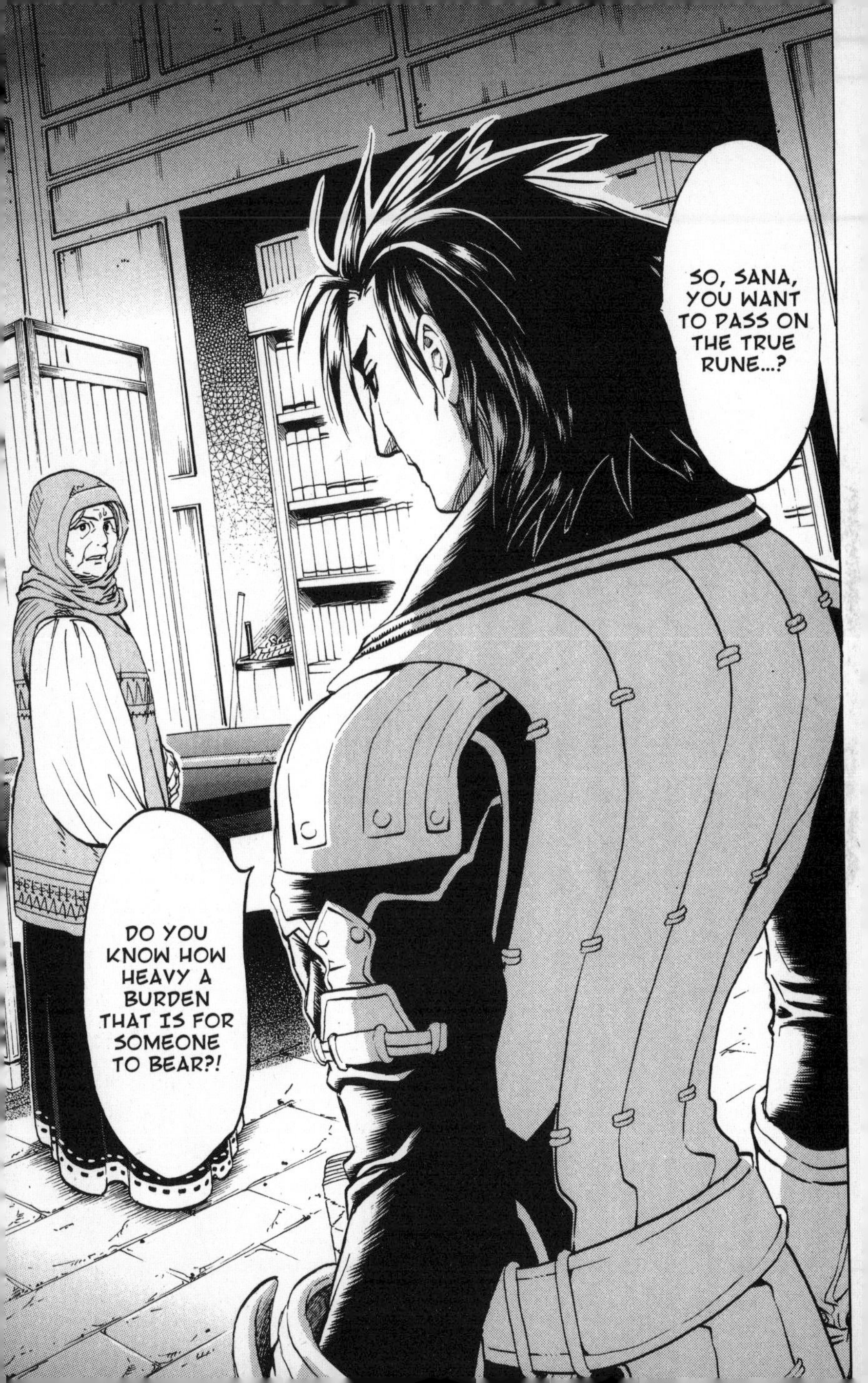
SO, SANA, YOU WANT TO PASS ON THE TRUE RUNE...?
DO YOU KNOW HOW HEAVY A BURDEN THAT IS FOR SOMEONE TO BEAR?!

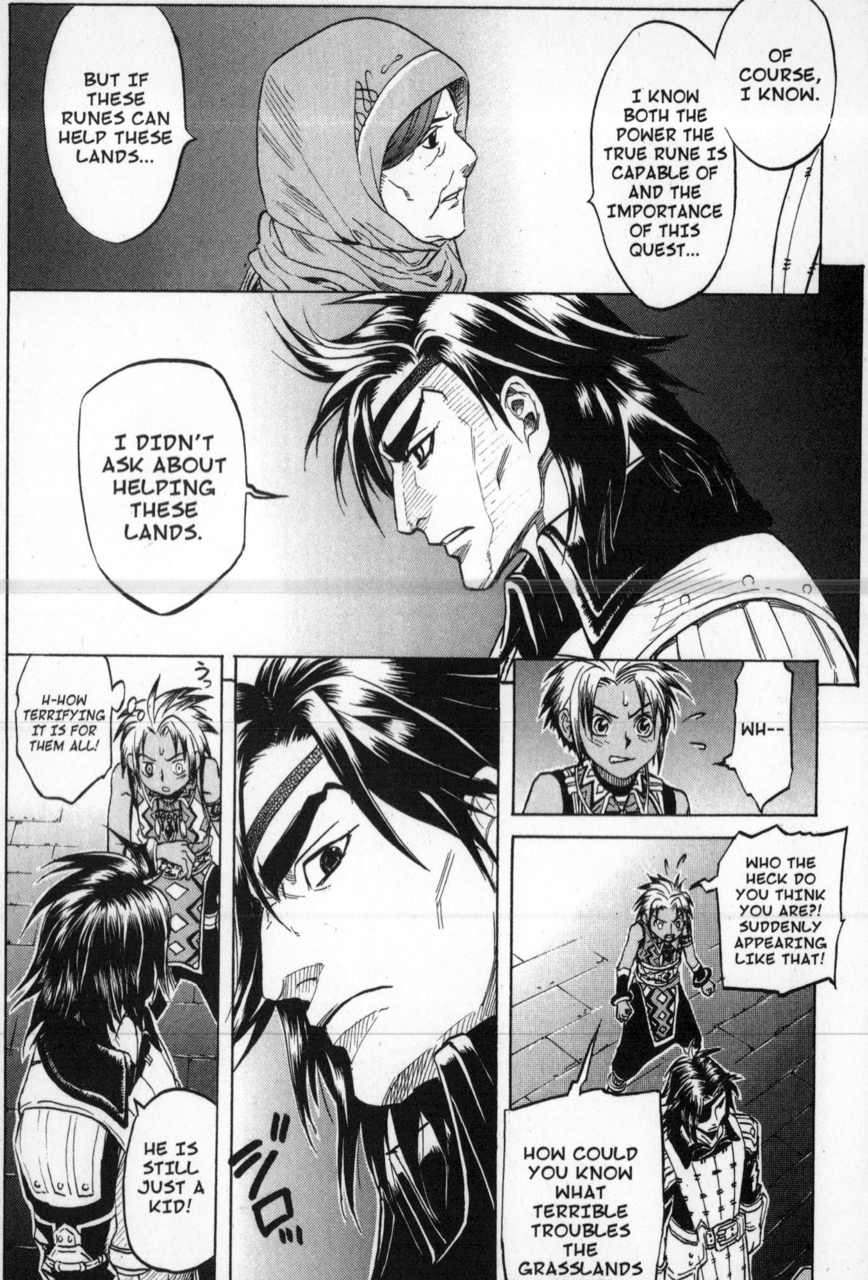
OF COURSE, I KNOW.
I KNOW BOTH THE POWER THE TRUE RUNE IS CAPABLE OF AND THE IMPORTANCE OF THIS QUEST...
BUT IF THESE RUNES CAN HELP THESE LANDS...
I DIDN'T ASK ABOUT HELPING THESE LANDS.
WH--
WHO THE HECK DO YOU THINK YOU ARE?! SUDDENLY APPEARING LIKE THAT!
HOW COULD YOU KNOW WHAT TERRIBLE TROUBLES THE GRASSLANDS FACE?!
H-HOW TERRIFYING IT IS FOR THEM ALL!
HE IS STILL JUST A KID!

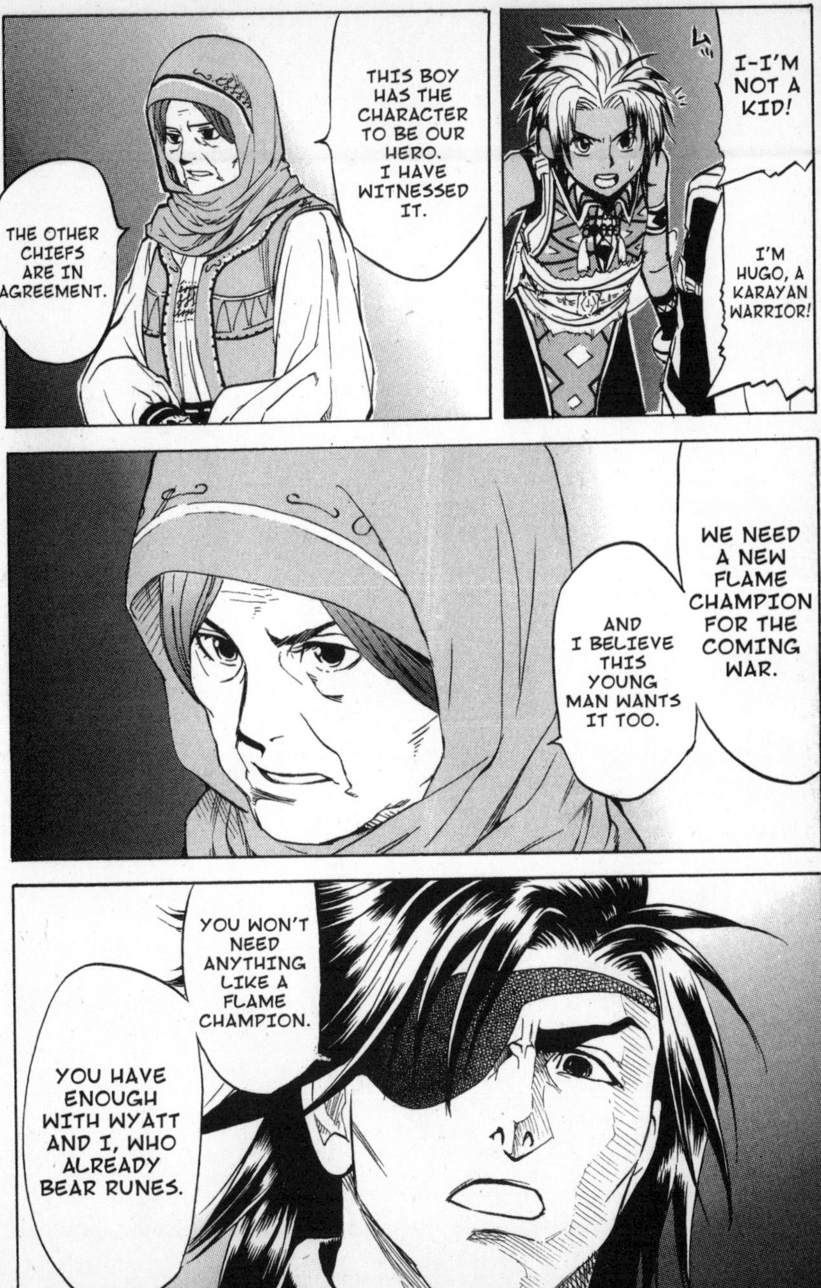
I-I'M NOT A KID!
I'M HUGO, A KARAYAN WARRIOR!
THIS BOY HAS THE CHARACTER TO BE OUR HERO. I HAVE WITNESSED IT.
THE OTHER CHIEFS ARE IN AGREEMENT.
WE NEED A NEW FLAME CHAMPION FOR THE COMING WAR.
AND I BELIEVE THIS YOUNG MAN WANTS IT TOO.
YOU WON'T NEED ANYTHING LIKE A FLAME CHAMPION.
YOU HAVE ENOUGH WITH WYATT AND I, WHO ALREADY BEAR RUNES.

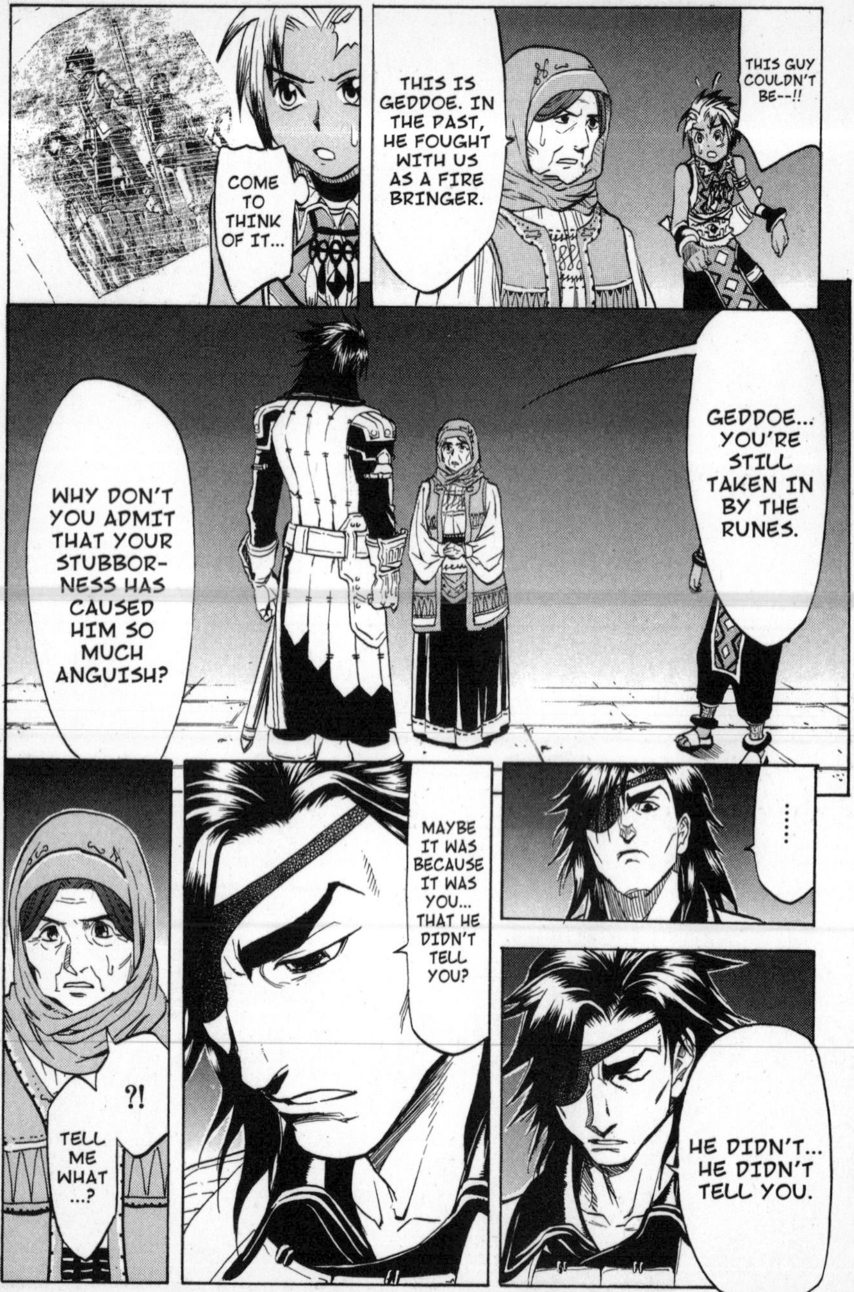
THIS GUY COULDN'T BE--!!
THIS IS GEDDOE. IN THE PAST, HE FOUGHT WITH US AS A FIRE BRINGER.
COME TO THINK OF IT...
GEDDOE... YOU'RE STILL TAKEN IN BY THE RUNES.
WHY DON'T YOU ADMIT THAT YOUR STUBBOR-NESS HAS CAUSED HIM SO MUCH ANGUISH?
......
HE DIDN'T... HE DIDN'T TELL YOU.
MAYBE IT WAS BECAUSE IT WAS YOU... THAT HE DIDN'T TELL YOU?
?!
TELL ME WHAT ...?

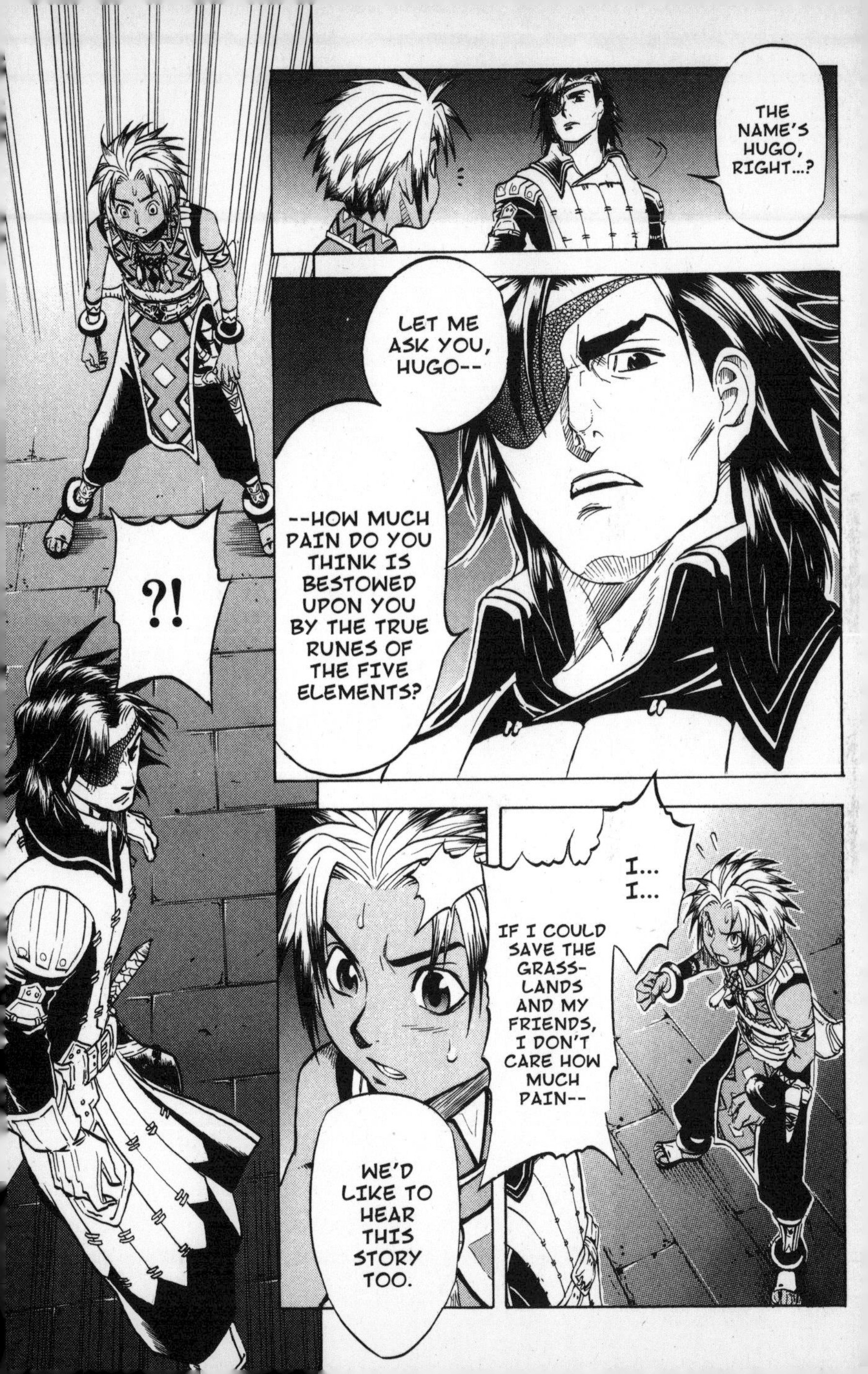
THE NAME'S HUGO, RIGHT...?
LET ME ASK YOU, HUGO--
--HOW MUCH PAIN DO YOU THINK IS BESTOWED UPON YOU BY THE TRUE RUNES OF THE FIVE ELEMENTS?
I... I...
IF I COULD SAVE THE GRASS-LANDS AND MY FRIENDS, I DON'T CARE HOW MUCH PAIN--
WE'D LIKE TO HEAR THIS STORY TOO.
?!

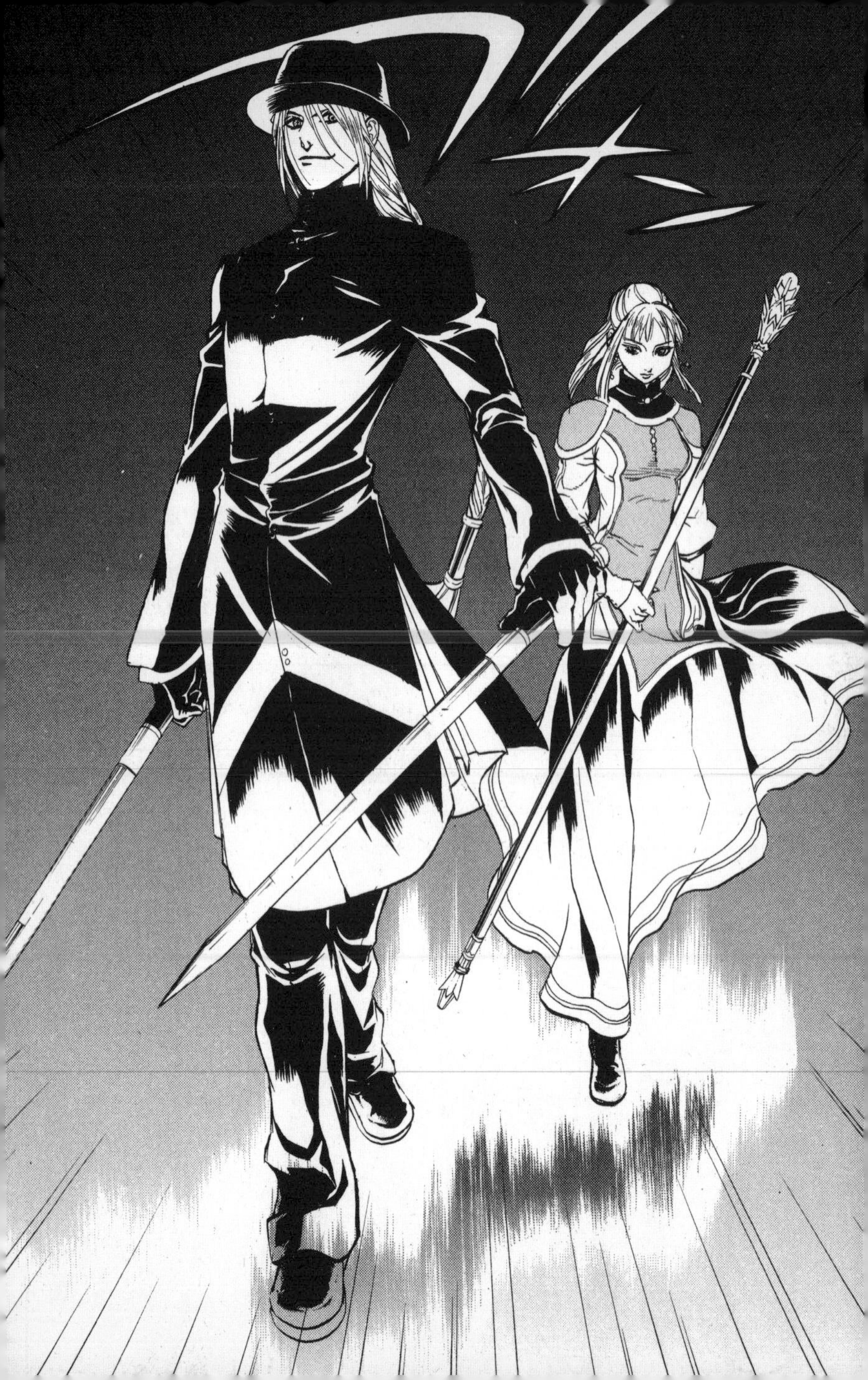

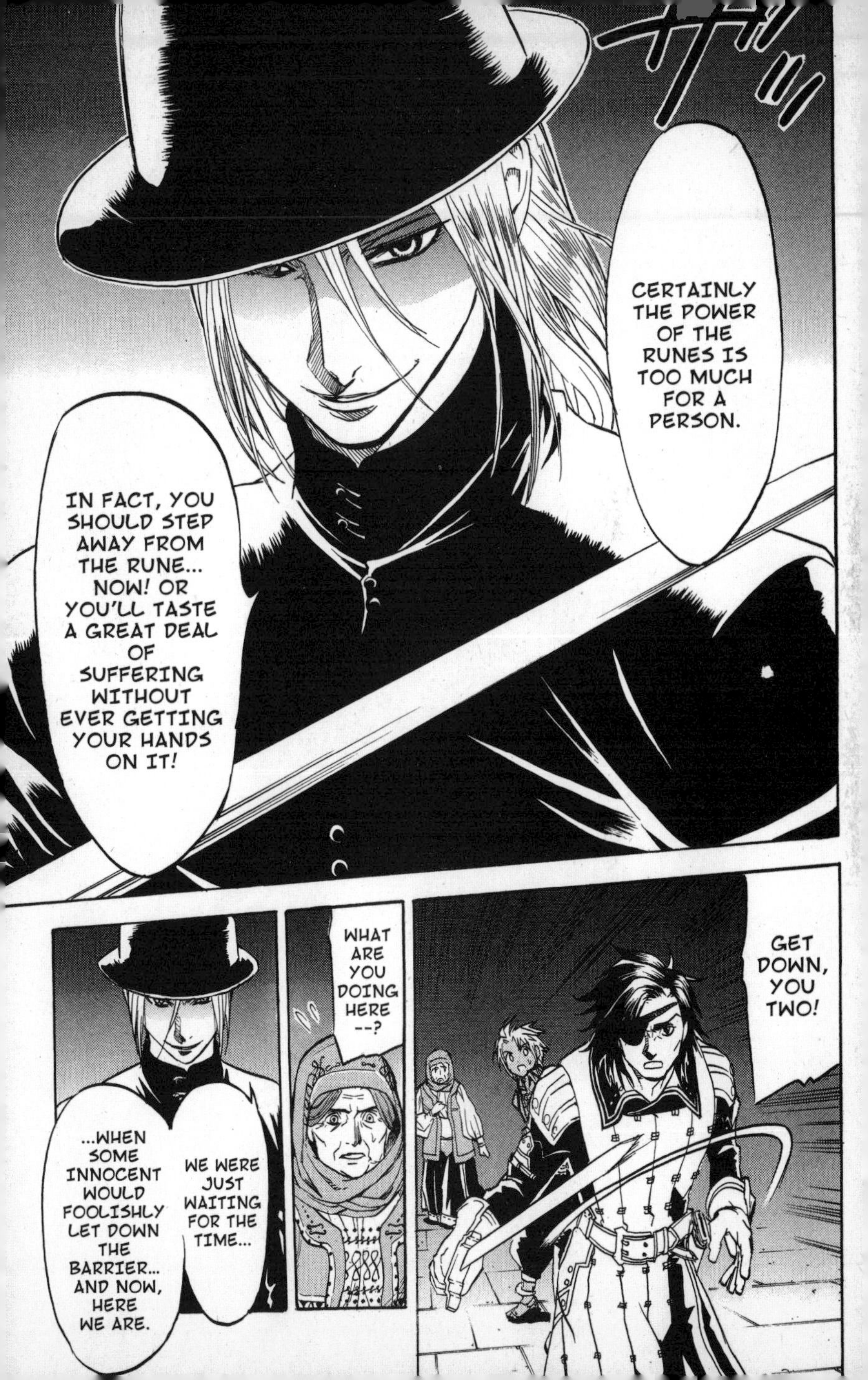
CERTAINLY THE POWER OF THE RUNES IS TOO MUCH FOR A PERSON.
IN FACT, YOU SHOULD STEP AWAY FROM THE RUNE... NOW! OR YOU'LL TASTE A GREAT DEAL OF SUFFERING WITHOUT EVER GETTING YOUR HANDS ON IT!
GET DOWN, YOU TWO!
WHAT ARE YOU DOING HERE --?
WE WERE JUST WAITING FOR THE TIME...
...WHEN SOME INNOCENT WOULD FOOLISHLY LET DOWN THE BARRIER... AND NOW, HERE WE ARE.

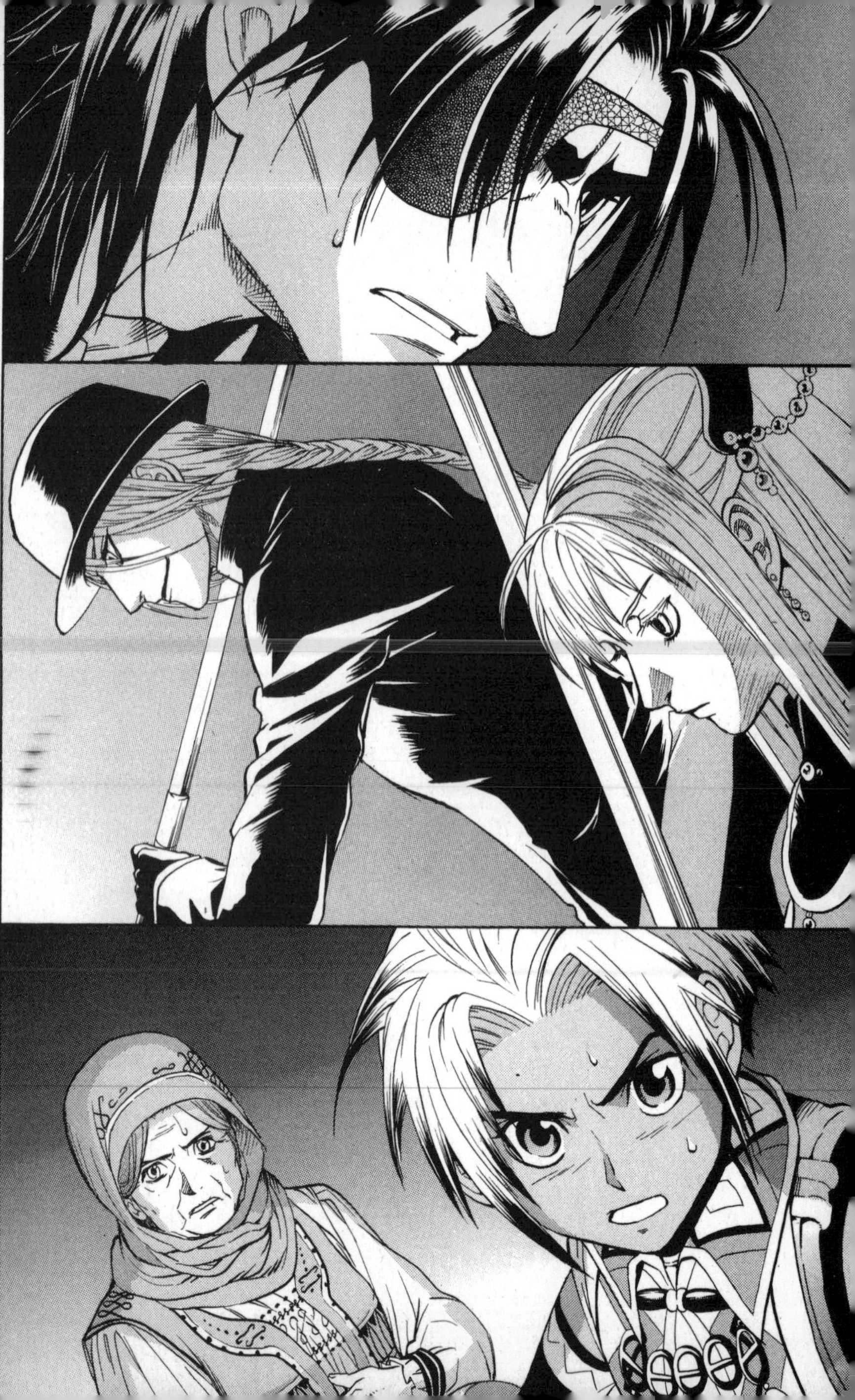

And if we should fan the
dying embers in the ashes...

Suikoden III
~~The Successor of Fate~~
Continued in Volume 5

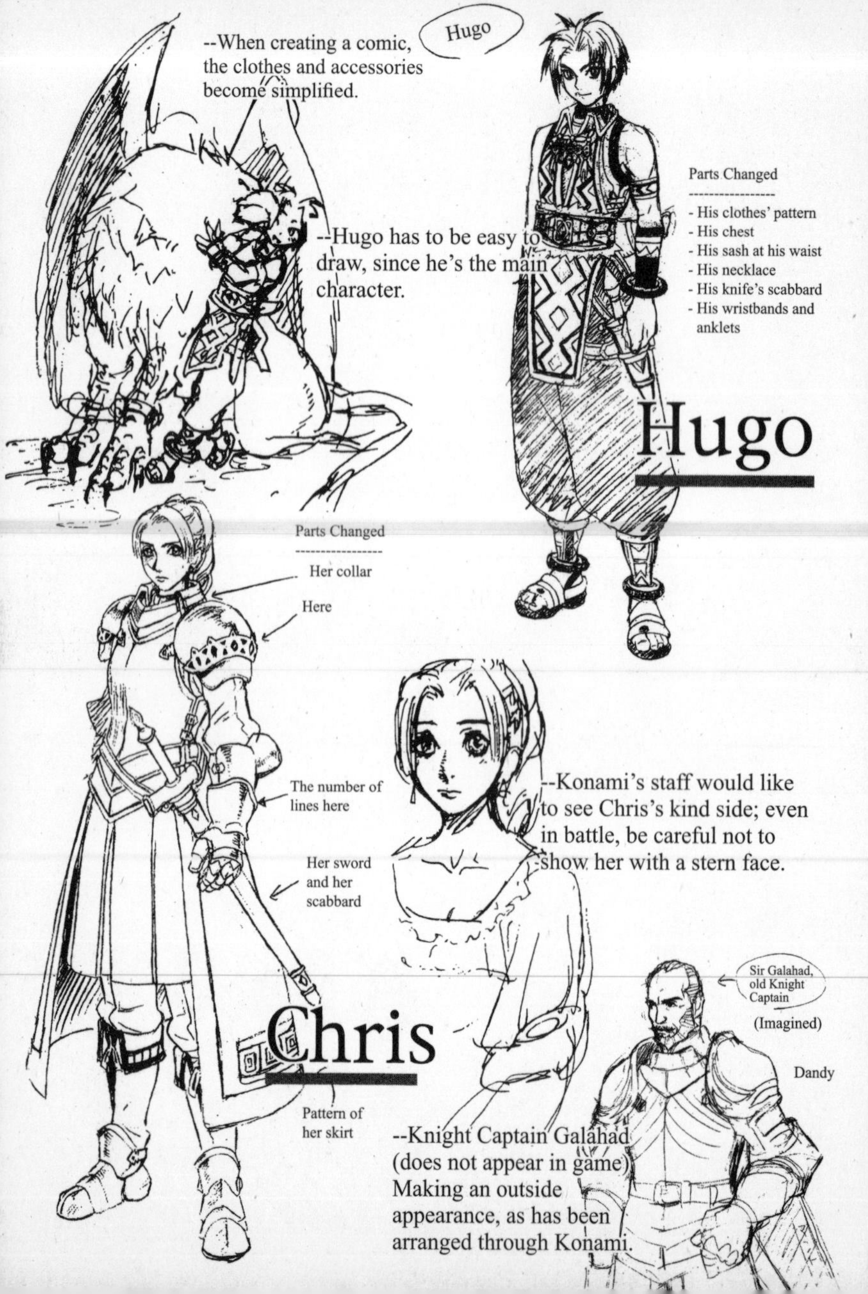
--When creating a comic, the clothes and accessories become simplified.
Hugo
--Hugo has to be easy to draw, since he's the main character.
Parts Changed
- His clothes' pattern
- His chest
- His sash at his waist
- His necklace
- His knife's scabbard
- His wristbands and anklets
Hugo
Parts Changed
Her collar
Here
The number of lines here
Her sword and her scabbard
--Konami's staff would like to see Chris's kind side; even in battle, be careful not to show her with a stern face.
Chris
Pattern of her skirt
Sir Galahad, old Knight Captain
(Imagined)
Dandy
--Knight Captain Galahad (does not appear in game) Making an outside appearance, as has been arranged through Konami.

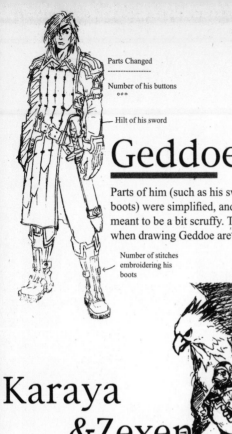

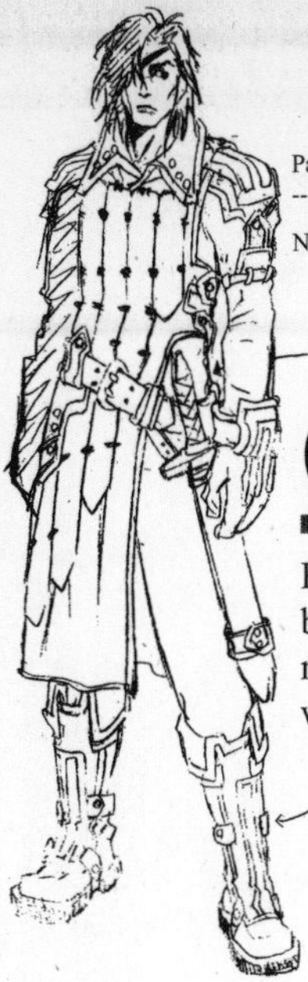
Parts Changed
Number of his buttons
ooo
Hilt of his sword
Number of stitches embroidering his boots

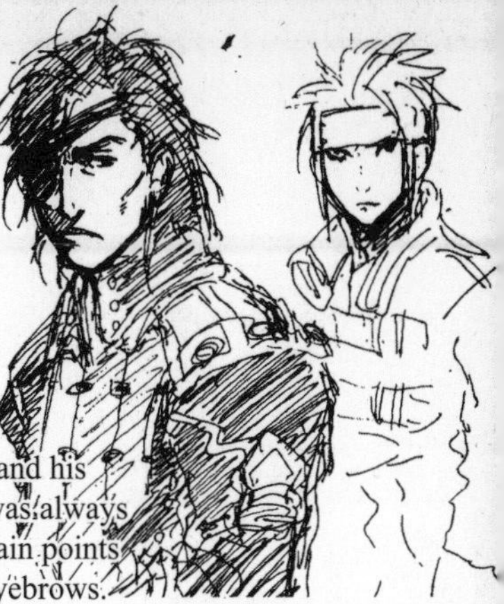

Geddoe

Parts of him (such as his sword and his boots) were simplified, and he was always meant to be a bit scruffy. The main points when drawing Geddoe are his eyebrows.

Karaya &Zexen

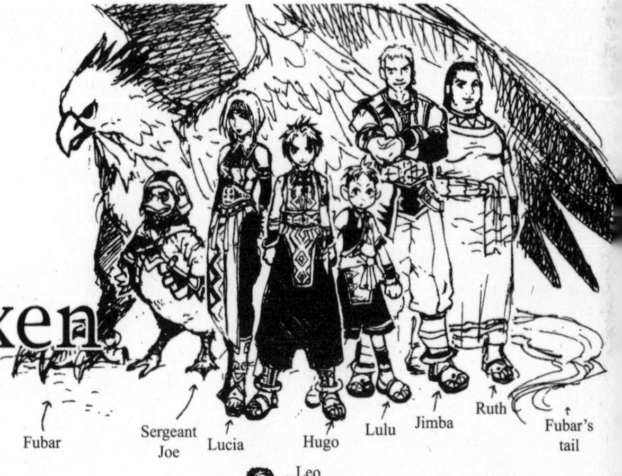
Fubar
Sergeant Joe
Lucia
Hugo
Lulu
Jimba
Ruth
Fubar's tail

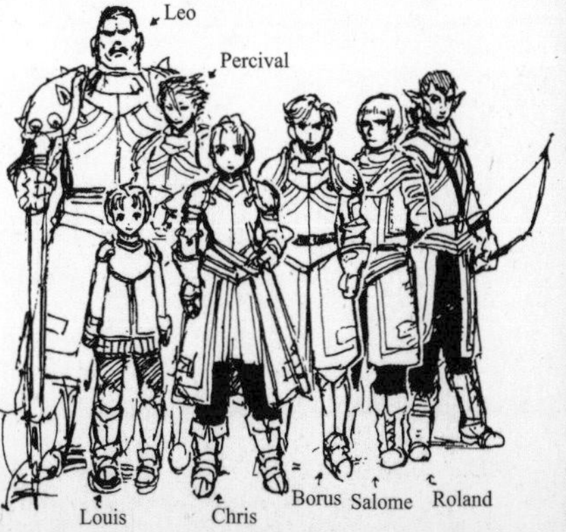
Leo
Percival
Louis
Chris
Borus
Salome
Roland

In the game, the main characters' statures are all set, but in the comic, there will be a number of changes in relation to their power.

The vast Grasslands, home to various people.

Long ago, the Six Clans gathered together to fight the
Zexen Federation
over border disputes. The Holy Kingdom of Harmonia also
sought control of all these lands. These three groups have
long been struggling with each other for power.

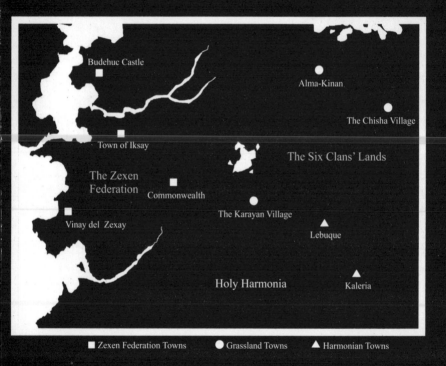

Budehuc Castle

Alma-Kinan

The Chisha Village

Town of Iksay

The Six Clans' Lands

The Zexen
Federation

Commonwealth

The Karayan Village

Vinay del Zexay

Lebuque

Holy Harmonia

Kaleria

■ Zexen Federation Towns   ● Grassland Towns   ▲ Harmonian Towns

-The World of Suikoden III-

This is the fourth volume. I'm truly sorry to have kept you waiting! These days, I have to get myself back on top of my super-full schedule. I've been falling behind; I've really just been caged-in at home.

Well, I really haven't prepared an epilogue, so why don't I give you some insight into the story for a change? This time, a lot of preparation went into making the comic a bit more individual. For one thing, we have the whole "fate" discussion. This was added as a sort of religious term to strengthen the idea that the Alma-Kinan are very religious. Perhaps if you consider the actions of all 108 stars, what you get in the end is this sense of "fate."

Another thing special to the manga was the composition of the Harmonian army. Since the composition of the army is deeply related to the doctrine of that country (how it feels about war), I just created it all as I saw fit. Well, I guess this is a manga, after all, not the game...

There are three soldiers in a small division of mantor trainers, triple that in a middle one, and triple that in a large one. I had to decide how many there were; I thought, "I guess there were about two large divisions this time?"

And as for how "magic" (which doesn't exist in reality) would be used in battle, well, I'll leave that for the volumes to come, I believe. There are still characters who haven't shown up yet that'll use it...

I wish I could put them all in. Well, goodbye. I really am giving it my best...

I want to draw more to indulge myself because there are still some characters who haven't been part of the plot yet (created when those first plans were drawn up way back when). Like Sgt. Joe (laughs).

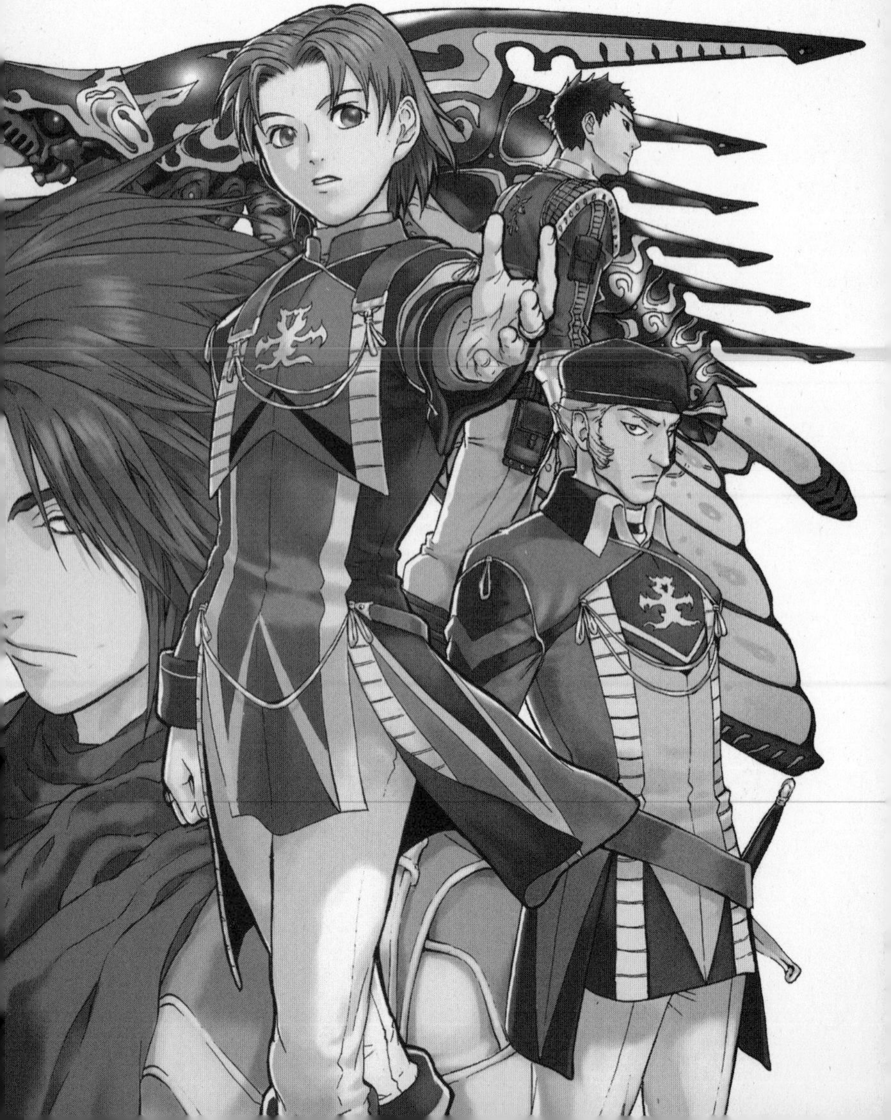

Suikoden III
幻想水滸伝

The battle between Geddoe and Yuber continues...and this time, Yuber won't be surprised by Geddoe's powers! No matter who wins, it seems neither combatant wants Hugo to inherit the True Flame Rune... but what does Hugo want?

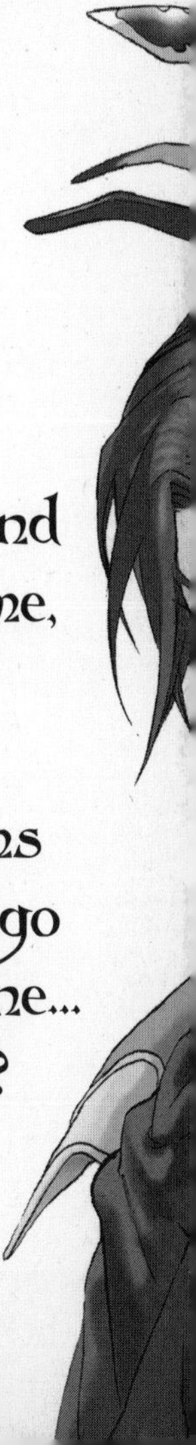

ALSO AVAILABLE FROM  TOKYOPOP®

ALSO AVAILABLE FROM 🎮 TOKYOPOP®

MANGA

.HACK//LEGEND OF THE TWILIGHT
@LARGE
ABENOBASHI: MAGICAL SHOPPING ARCADE
A.I. LOVE YOU
AI YORI AOSHI
ANGELIC LAYER
ARM OF KANNON
BABY BIRTH
BATTLE ROYALE
BATTLE VIXENS
BOYS BE...
BRAIN POWERED
BRIGADOON
B'TX
CANDIDATE FOR GODDESS, THE
CARDCAPTOR SAKURA
CARDCAPTOR SAKURA - MASTER OF THE CLOW
CHOBITS
CHRONICLES OF THE CURSED SWORD
CLAMP SCHOOL DETECTIVES
CLOVER
COMIC PARTY
CONFIDENTIAL CONFESSIONS
CORRECTOR YUI
COWBOY BEBOP
COWBOY BEBOP: SHOOTING STAR
CRAZY LOVE STORY
CRESCENT MOON
CROSS
CULDCEPT
CYBORG 009
D•N•ANGEL
DEMON DIARY
DEMON ORORON, THE
DEUS VITAE
DIABOLO
DIGIMON
DIGIMON TAMERS
DIGIMON ZERO TWO
DOLL
DRAGON HUNTER
DRAGON KNIGHTS
DRAGON VOICE
DREAM SAGA
DUKLYON: CLAMP SCHOOL DEFENDERS
EERIE QUEERIE!
ERICA SAKURAZAWA: COLLECTED WORKS
ET CETERA
ETERNITY
EVIL'S RETURN
FAERIES' LANDING
FAKE
FLCL
FLOWER OF THE DEEP SLEEP, THE
FORBIDDEN DANCE
FRUITS BASKET

G GUNDAM
GATEKEEPERS
GETBACKERS
GIRL GOT GAME
GRAVITATION
GTO
GUNDAM SEED ASTRAY
GUNDAM WING
GUNDAM WING: BATTLEFIELD OF PACIFISTS
GUNDAM WING: ENDLESS WALTZ
GUNDAM WING: THE LAST OUTPOST (G-UNIT)
HANDS OFF!
HAPPY MANIA
HARLEM BEAT
HYPER RUNE
I.N.V.U.
IMMORTAL RAIN
INITIAL D
INSTANT TEEN: JUST ADD NUTS
ISLAND
JING: KING OF BANDITS
JING: KING OF BANDITS - TWILIGHT TALES
JULINE
KARE KANO
KILL ME, KISS ME
KINDAICHI CASE FILES, THE
KING OF HELL
KODOCHA: SANA'S STAGE
LAMENT OF THE LAMB
LEGAL DRUG
LEGEND OF CHUN HYANG, THE
LES BIJOUX
LOVE HINA
LOVE OR MONEY
LUPIN III
LUPIN III: WORLD'S MOST WANTED
MAGIC KNIGHT RAYEARTH I
MAGIC KNIGHT RAYEARTH II
MAHOROMATIC: AUTOMATIC MAIDEN
MAN OF MANY FACES
MARMALADE BOY
MARS
MARS: HORSE WITH NO NAME
MINK
MIRACLE GIRLS
MIYUKI-CHAN IN WONDERLAND
MODEL
MOURYOU KIDEN: LEGEND OF THE NYMPHS
NECK AND NECK
ONE
ONE I LOVE, THE
PARADISE KISS
PARASYTE
PASSION FRUIT
PEACH GIRL
PEACH GIRL: CHANGE OF HEART
PET SHOP OF HORRORS
PITA-TEN

07.15.04T

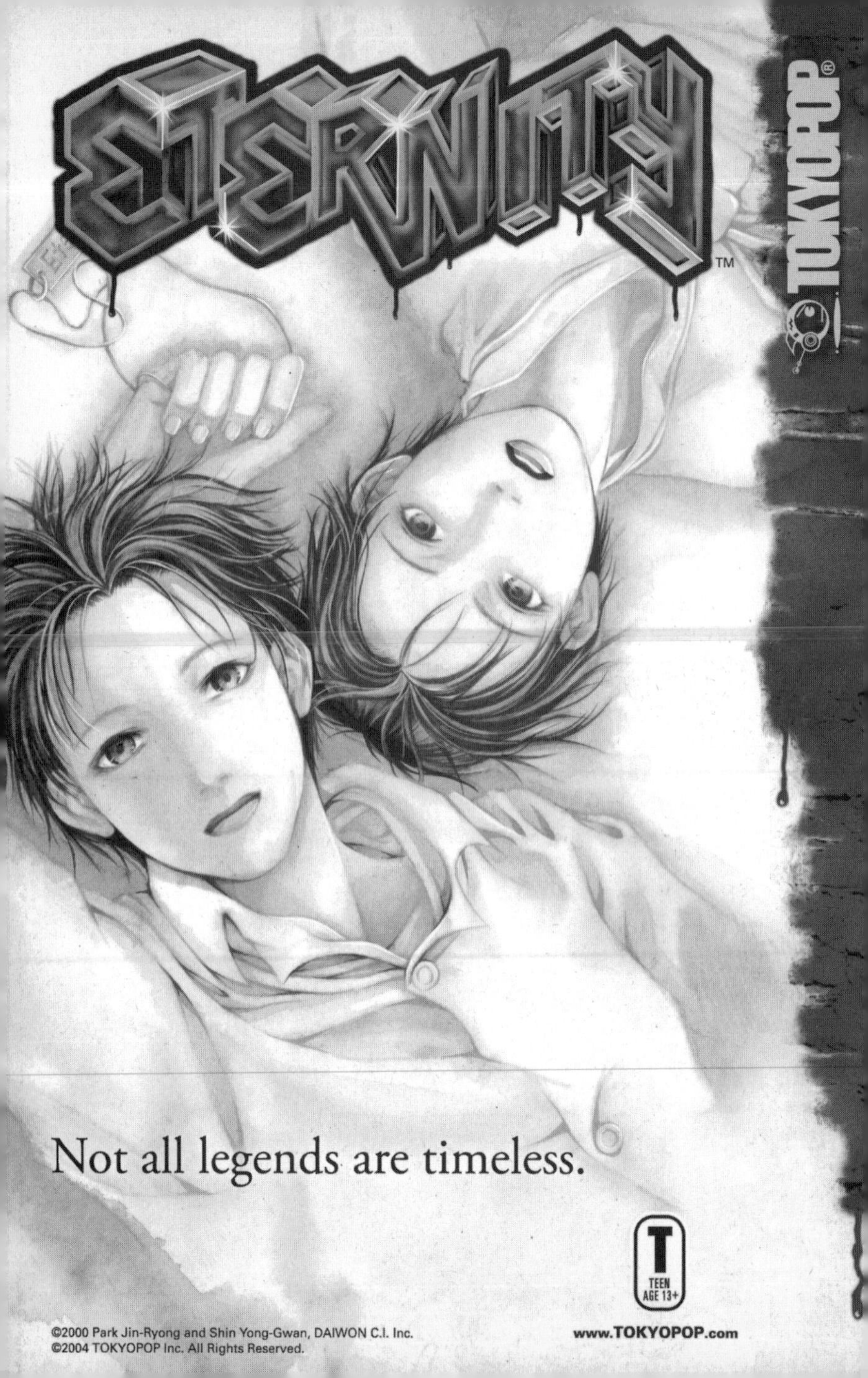
ETERNITY™
TOKYOPOP®
Not all legends are timeless.
T
TEEN
AGE 13+
©2000 Park Jin-Ryong and Shin Yong-Gwan, DAIWON C.I. Inc.
©2004 TOKYOPOP Inc. All Rights Reserved.
www.TOKYOPOP.com

LEGAL DRUG ™

When no ordinary prescription will do...

www.TOKYOPOP.com

STOP!

This is the back of the book.
You wouldn't want to spoil a great ending!

This book is printed "manga-style," in the authentic Japanese right-to-left format. Since none of the artwork has been flipped or altered, readers get to experience the story just as the creator intended. You've been asking for it, so TOKYOPOP® delivered: authentic, hot-off-the-press, and far more fun!

DIRECTIONS

If this is your first time reading manga-style, here's a quick guide to help you understand how it works.

It's easy... just start in the top right panel and follow the numbers. Have fun, and look for more 100% authentic manga from TOKYOPOP®!